Changing Families

Changing Families

Edited by
IRVING E. SIGEL
and
LUIS M. LAOSA

Educational Testing Service
Princeton, New Jersey

Plenum Press • New York and London

Library of Congress Cataloging in Publication Data

Main entry under title:

Changing families.

   Bibliographies: p.
   Includes indexes.
   1. Family social work—Addresses, essays, lectures. 2. Home and school—Addresses, essays, lectures. 3. Socialization—Addresses, essays, lectures. 4. Parenting—Addresses, essays, lectures. I. Sigel, Irving E. II. Laosa, Louis M., 1946–
HV697.C35 1983   362.8′2   83-11192
ISBN 0-306-41288-8

© 1983 Plenum Press, New York
A Division of Plenum Publishing Corporation
233 Spring Street, New York, N.Y. 10013

Printed in the United States of America

Contributors

Phyllis W. Beck, Associate Judge, Superior Court of Pennsylvania, Suite 606, One Montgomery Plaza, Norristown, Pennsylvania

Moncrieff Cochran, Department of Human Development and Family Studies, New York State College of Human Ecology, Cornell University, Ithaca, New York

Paul R. Dokecki, Department of Psychology and Human Development, George Peabody College, Vanderbilt University, Nashville, Tennessee

Paul R. Florin, Department of Psychology, Rhode Island, Kingston, Rhode Island

Kenneth H. Handin, Saint Catherine's Center for Children, Albany, New York

Ruth Hubbell, Research Associate, CSR Inc., 805 15th Street, N.W., Washington, D.C.

Luis M. Laosa, Educational Testing Service, Princeton, New Jersey

Richard R. J. Lewine, Illinois State Psychiatric Institute, 9-West, 1601 West Taylor Street, Chicago, Illinois

James C. Mancuso, Department of Psychology, State University of New York at Albany, 1400 Washington Avenue, Albany, New York

Ivan B. Pless, McGill-Montreal Children's Hospital Research Institute, 2300 Tupper Street, Montreal, Quebec

Douglas R. Powell, Wayne State University, College of Liberal Arts, Department of Family and Consumer Resources, Detroit, Michigan

Irving E. Sigel, Educational Testing Service, Center for Assessment and Research in Human Development, Princeton, New Jersey

Kay Sutherland, Department of Sociology and Anthropology, Southwest Texas State University, San Marcos, Texas

Frank Woolever, Department of Human Development and Family Studies, New York State College of Human Ecology, Cornell University, Ithaca, New York

Preface

In a previous volume, *Families as Learning Environments for Children*, we presented a series of chapters that dealt with research programs on the role of families as learning environments for children. Those studies were based on empirical data and sought answers to basic research questions, with no explicit concern for the application of the results to practical problems. Rather, their purpose was to contribute primarily to conceptualization, research methodology, and psychological theory. Now, in this volume, we turn our attention to intervention—efforts to modify the way a family develops. As in our previous conference, the participants of the working conference on which the present volume is based are research scientists and scholars interested in application. This group is distinct from practitioners, however, whose primary focus is service; participants in this conference have as their primary interest research into the problems of processes of application. Applied professional issues concerning the lives of families come from many varied sources, from some that are distant and impersonal (e.g., the law) to direct face-to-face efforts (educators, therapists). The variety of sources and types of applications are eloquent testimony to the degree to which families are subject to a host of societal forces whose implicit or explicit aim is to modify family functioning. For example, some educators may wish to alter family child-rearing patterns to enhance child development; the clinician seeks to help families come to terms and to cope with a schizophrenic child. The list can be extended. We have been selective, by including representatives from some of the relevant areas. Obviously, professional workers hold to the conviction that the family is a crucial social agent that strives to help socialize the child to the real world—real, often, in parental terms. All applied professional work, whether legal, educational, or clinical, must come to terms with ethical and moral questions. This issue is also addressed in this volume.

Our goal in assembling these scholars in a conference at Educational

Testing Service to discuss the various issues represented here was to provide
an opportunity for researchers directly interested in application to meet
and share their diverse perspectives. Although their papers do not reflect
explicit sharing, each did learn from the other. We believe that those
reading the various chapters that follow will come to appreciate not only
the diversity, but also the basic common purpose represented here—
namely, to help families fulfill themselves, since families in our society do
play a significant role in the socialization of the child.

We wish to acknowledge the support of Winton H. Manning and
Samuel J. Messick, ETS officers, for their financial support. Thanks also to
Jan Flaugher for her help in managing the various conference details; to
Linda Kozelski for her patience in organizing all the manuscripts and for
her editorial assistance in every phase of the production; and to Betty
Clausen for her excellent typing and editorial checking of manuscripts.

IRVING E. SIGEL
LUIS M. LAOSA

Contents

ix

Introduction

IRVING E. SIGEL

Research on various aspects of family organization and processes has a long and honorable history. Professionals from the various social sciences have approached the issues inherent in family functioning with two broad aims: first, to understand the family as a social unit and its concomitant role respective to other social institutions, and second, to identify intrafamilial factors that influence the development of its members, since the family is viewed as a socialization agent for each of its members. In our earlier volume, *Families as Learning Environments for Children*, we described a number of studies that served each of these aims. Those studies, descriptive in nature, contribute to our understanding of the dynamics of the family as a social and psychological learning environment unit. Studies were reported, for example, which dealt with the role of the family in literacy, familial contributions to intellectual development of children, and parental beliefs and perceptions of children. The useful information provided by these studies demonstrates the complex array of factors that in their grand mix serve to influence each member of the family unit.

In this, our second volume, we move to studies of intervention in the lives of families. By intervention we mean direct and indirect efforts aimed at altering the course of the family's anticipated growth, development, and function. Intervention is conceptualized as appropriate not only for families evidencing pathology and forced by circumstances to seek help, but also for families voluntarily seeking intervention to enhance their development. The assumption in this latter case is that a family can enrich itself not only in terms of its individual family members, but also collectively, to improve its quality of life. Thus, the degree to which family members, especially the parent, increase their knowledge regarding principles of individual and group development, to that degree will each member enrich his or her life and that of other family members. Thus there are two types of intervention: (1) a therapeutic-like approach aimed at alleviating family pathology, and (2) an educational approach for enhancement of family functioning. There are also different ways to intervene, whether it be educational or psychotherapeutic. Numerous programs and approaches are available to the public (Harman & Brim, 1981).

This volume includes reports on research addressing different aspects of intervention. Underlying all interventions, however, are fundamental questions: *Why* the intervention, by *whom*, to *what end* and *under* what conditions? This volume will address these questions in the context of diverse viewpoints, procedures, and programs.

In Chapter 1, I argue that irrespective of the why, the who, and the terms of intervention, the intervenor must come to grips with the ethics and values inherent in any program. It matters little whether the intervention is by parent, educator, or medical personnel—the content and the procedures involved reflect values of the programmer. I assert that it is the programmer's responsibility to be aware of ethics and values inherent in intervention activity and to be guided accordingly. I contend that often the professional intervening does not articulate the range of ethical questions. To be sure, professionals do work within codes of ethics established by their professional groups, but I demonstrate that this is only the tip of the iceberg. I provide a decision making model which can be of help in the analysis of the ethical value dimension.

Intervention in the lives of families is not a phenomenon of the 20th century alone. In Chapter 2 Florin and Dokecki provide an historical overview of parent education from ancient times to the present. It is interesting to note that parents have been exhorted by authority figures (priests, community leaders, educators) throughout the years to act in particular ways relative to their child-rearing functions. The belief in the significance of the parents as molders, shapers, and influencers of their offspring is ancient. Parents are responsible for raising healthy, happy, God-fearing children who will take their place in society as responsible citizens. By analyzing the literature produced in the past few hundred years, Florin and Dokecki ably demonstrate the changing perspectives toward child-rearing practices, toward outcomes, and toward values and principles that should guide parents.

Parents are, of course, the focus of most of these papers because parents are viewed as the primary socializing family agents. In spite of the exhortation of Beck in Chapter 3 that parenting is a reciprocal act, wherein children influence parents (and vice versa), most professionals identify the parents as the prime movers in the family setting. Thus, as we shall see in many of the chapters in this volume, the primary emphasis is on the parent's impact on the children.

However significant parents are vis-à-vis control and influence on their children, there are legal constraints and intrusions. Beck, in her chapter, discusses the role of government (at each level) as it intrudes in the lives of families. For example, the state has declared education to be mandatory and has even defined the kinds and lengths of education that are acceptable. Beck describes the laws that pit the authority of the state against the parent, against the child—laws which can interfere with the parent-child relationship. These laws are applied when some form of conflict occurs among family members, for example, truancy, child abuse, or child neglect. Although the role of the legal authority typically does not directly influence the family, the very fact that a body of family laws exists indicates that the state does perceive the welfare of the family and its members as one of its responsibilities.

Legal issues are also dealt with in Hubbell's discussion of foster care in Chapter 9, which follows Beck's legal perspective on the family as a social unit with a corpus of law devoted just to it. The state indirectly influences families through its system of education. This influence is subtle, and not just in terms of the formal courses relevant to parenting. Laosa's research (Chapter 4) is evidence for this assertion.

Although intervention is usually considered an active process, some social institutions serve to intervene only indirectly in family functioning. Laosa identifies the school as a major influence on parent–child interaction, particularly among Chicano families. There is an implicit expectation that without schooling Chicano parents may well continue to interact with their children in ways closer to the expectations and norms of their traditional heritage. Schooling, as we shall see, subtly and indirectly moves these families away from their tradition to general societal norms. Schooling has traditionally been viewed in the United States as the way to reduce ethnic diversity; the educational enterprise has been assigned the task of indoctrination in the language, history, and values of the dominant Anglo-American culture. And the schools do just that, Laosa argues, even though they usually do not perceive their role as to prepare students for marriage and parenthood. The schools do interpret their mission as to prepare students to take their places in society as responsible, economically viable citizens. Nevertheless, the schools, Laosa hypothesizes, do have a wider and more pervasive influence in the lives of their pupils. Although Laosa does not directly address the content of schooling, he does demonstrate that the schooling process *per se* contributes to change both in orientation toward and practice of parenthood. His is a unique study, since social scientists have not identified schooling as a singular experience of such consequence. Usually "school" is embedded in the general social economic index along with "occupation," "income," and "place of residence." Laosa's research shows that schooling is a major contributor to reducing ethnic differences between Chicano and non-Hispanic White child-rearing patterns.

Laosa goes beyond this analysis to inform us of the specific ways parental schooling, family interaction, and children's learning strategies intersect. On the basis of his collection of data, he compares the impact of schooling relative to other demographic factors, such as fathers' occupation and maternal employment.

Laosa uses these and other data to construct a developmental socioculturally relativistic paradigm which he uses to explain the development of cross-situational social competence of young children. The implications for this conceptualization, coupled with the research findings, are discussed relative to their implication for social policy.

Laosa's findings demonstrate that schooling contributes to the child's development, not in terms of direct influence on the child, but as mediated by the educational level of the mothers. Does not this evidence support the contentions of early advocates of free public education, that through schooling some ethnic differences will disappear? Schooling, serving as an acculturation agent, ultimately intervenes in the lives of the family, influencing each member thereof.

A second influence on parent–child interactions is parents' beliefs about their children, in particular the models parents have of parenting. In our previous volume, McGillicuddy-DeLisi reported on parental belief systems as factors influencing parental practice. Chapters 5 and 6 of the present volume address the issue of parental beliefs, each from a different perspective in the context of an intervention program.

In Chapter 5, Sutherland's underlying objective is to identify what knowledge is relevant for parent educators. She identifies seven models which reflect a parent's perspective about parent–child interaction and child development. On the basis of her research with different ethnic groups, she concludes that parent education would be more effective if programs were designed relative to parental belief systems. She demonstrates how she did this; employing the same strategy that Harman and Brim advocate to deal with value conflicts between the clients and the parent educators.

Mancuso and Handlin (Chapter 6) propose a specific model for working with caregivers, basing it on the work of George Kelly: namely, personal construct theory. In contrast to Sutherland, who defines a number of parental models and congruent interventions, Mancuso and Handlin argue for the constructivist perspective derived essentially from the work of Kelly (1958). Their basic point is that scholars who produce intervention programs do so from a conceptual framework, implicitly or explicitly. They present a dichotomous argument that pits a mechanistic perspective against a constructivist one; they explain their predilection for a constructivist orientation. Their argument is well articulated, offering a constructivist alternative to establish a basis for parent-training programs.

Within a constructivist paradigm, Mancuso and Handlin proceed to argue for a discrepancy model to facilitate change in behavior of parent and/or child. For them, "the most explosive force of discrepancy is *reprimand*," which "applies to those events which have been discussed at those points at which people have used such terms as discipline practices, socialization processes, persuasion, and superego building." They proceed to develop this concept.

Mancuso and Handlin built their intervention program on a psychological model with emphasis on the individual's construction of reality, but Powell (Chapter 7) and Cochran and Woolever (Chapter 8) work from a socio-ecological perspective. Powell, studying a group of parents who were in a parent–child support program, seeks to identify the specific socio-ecological variables that influence the parents' participation in such a program. Thus, in contrast to many program evaluation studies which assess the *outcomes* of parent intervention studies, Powell examines the *antecedents* of parent functioning in the program. His proposition is that to understand the dynamics of parent support programs, it is necessary to examine the extra-program life events (e.g., parents' social networks) to enhance our understanding of parent participation. In effect, Powell is adding extra program variables to his evaluation of the program. This unique approach adds an important dimension to an evaluation strategy, taking into account the interaction between parental characteristics and program attributes.

Cochran and Woolever's study derives from Bronfenbrenner's concept of family intervention. Since Bronfenbrenner sees today's family as threatened, to help families survive it is necessary to work from a socio-ecological perspective—that is, to extend the conceptualization of the family from the traditional individual family approach, beyond didactic sets of variables (e.g., self, family dynamics, or neighboring networks), and, as Cochran and Woolever put it, "to look constantly for ways in which those systems interact to make life easier or more difficult for certain kinds of families or individuals." Their second point is the assumption that families have the potential strength to cope with the threats to their existence. From these two basic concepts, the Family Matters program was developed, with the fundamental purpose of helping to empower parents to take a more active role in influencing the growth of their children by using the resources in their socio-ecological life space.

Cochran and Woolever describe the processes of intervention in some detail. The overall aim of these engagements is to establish trust, enlarge the scope of the families' knowledge regarding child development, and to inform them how to use social networks. All these activities are aimed at getting parents to view themselves as active and competent. The Family Matters program is an example of total family and community involvement. Ironically, although this approach has a long tradition in the social work profession, it is one of the few developmental psychology projects that has attempted such a focused program with targeted objectives.

The Mancuso and Handlin, Powell, and Cochran and Woolever studies are extensions and modifications of the parent educational model. These programs work with the nuclear family with its biologically related members living together. But there are times when the nuclear family and its biological members can no longer function as a viable unit. Then it becomes necessary to break up the unit and find appropriate environments for the care of family members. The child welfare system intervenes to provide care, at least for children, when poverty, mental or physical illness, or other factors, prevent parents from caring for their offspring. Foster home placement is often the solution of choice for such situations. In Chapter 9, Hubbell addresses a number of complex issues in foster care policy by her examination of the impact of such care through a "family impact" analysis. This approach involves studying the effects of foster care through policy analysis. Hubbell identifies a host of issues—for example, value assumptions about the preeminence of the nuclear-biological family, the continuity of relationships among family members, relationships between the state and the family, and civil rights of families inherent in day care. Hubbell addresses these problems in the context of a study of a state's policies and practices in foster care. These data yield important insights into the deficiencies of the current situation not only in that state, but nationally, since she integrates the case study with national policies. Hubbell provides suggestions for needed reform. What is of particular value in the Hubbell report is the opportunity to face the complexity of correlating and generating legislation and implementation of policy.

Hubbell's chapter, as well as those that precede it, demonstrate that to provide constructive solutions to the comples issues inherent in these family intervention matters we may well need to restructure our thinking about the family in a broad socio-ecological context.

The early chapters of this volume attend to direct intervention in the lives of families, with the parents as the central target—focusing, for example, on the parents' legal rights and the parents as "students who are to be empowered or supported in the care of their children. If, however, the parents are inept or unable to care for their children, foster care is employed as the treatment of choice.

In all of these intervention approaches, the assumption is that the parents are in need of help. Sometimes the professional, working from his or her own perspective, believes that the parents' role in the lives of their children can be enhanced. In the foster care situation, however, it is usually obvious that the parents cannot cope.

Another area where the parents are defined as culprits, as causes of their offsprings' difficulties, is in the mental health field. Over the years psychological research has addressed questions of a possible relationship between mothering and mental illness. According to Lewine (Chapter 10), in spite of variable findings the myth still persists that mental illnesses such as schizophrenia and depression are rooted in pathological family relationships. The family, in Lewine's terms, becomes the mental health professional's scapegoat. Lewine, although primarily concerned with schizophrenic patients, addresses the issue of blaming the parent—usually the mother—for virtually every type of deviant development: epilepsy, colitis, ulcers, drug addiction, schizophrenia, *et al.* He sets out to demythologize the myth that parents are schizophrenogic. His review of the literature demonstrates that the research addressing the role of parents as causal agents is so seriously flawed that it precludes acceptance of the belief that parents are indeed the primary causal agents of their offsprings' psychotic conditions.

Lewine turns his attention to the parents, not as causal agents, but as evaluators of the mental health worker's attitudes and behavior. What his survey of parents shows is the considerable disaffection parents have regarding mental health professionals and their intervention services. Parents of mentally ill children find that mental health professionals' lack of knowledge and sympathy produce guilt without understanding and do not meet their needs for support and for constructive suggestions for ways to cope with their children. Lewine's results have two important implications, one for the mental health worker, the other for the intervention process. The mental health worker, in order to be effective, has to reorient his thinking and his behavior in order to come to terms with the realities existing among the families. And the credibility of intervention agents becomes important, since most program developers, irrespective of their disavowal of superior knowledge, adjustment, and competence, represent themselves as experts, but prove to be experts who are not sufficiently informed or aware of the conditions they are working with. Perhaps the case that Lewine describes is quite extreme. It may well be that the mental health workers construe themselves in the medical model—of the physician who is an expert and who believes he or she has the answers.

Cochran and Woolever, on the other hand, eschew the medical deficit model and speak to *empowerment*, implying building on existing competence rather than correcting for competence. (Nevertheless, the issue of the *construction* by the expert as a critical variable influencing intervention programs and their success is not attended to.) Lewine does provide a constructive solution to the increasing disenchantment of parents with mental health professions. A review of his suggestion will reveal that the underlying issues he addresses are appropriate for professionals involved in any intervention process.

All the foregoing discussions of intervention focus on the complexities of the intervention process. Pless, writing in Chapter 11 from the point of view of the practicing pediatrician, shows how physicians do not integrate into their regular medical practice—or even see the relevance of—social and/or behavioral science knowledge of patients' families. Apparently this situation often exists, for practical and economic reasons. On the practical level, Pless reports that for the most part, physicians do not need family data to carry out their medical routines or treatments. Since the information is not construed as relevant, physicians do not bother to collect it. Pless also shows how such information gathering increases the amount of time needed for a patient, and how this places an economic bind on both the physician and the patient: Somebody has to pay for the time. For these reasons, practicing physicians tend to ignore family variables which in theory are relevant to the treatment of their patients. In spite of the acknowledged interest in such variables as family status, relationships, and so forth, these characteristics are not perceived as directly relevant to most physicians' day-to-day activity. Pless discusses this issue in detail, supporting his conclusions by data from interviews with practicing physicians.

These chapters represent a sampling of efforts to investigate different types of intervention research. Intervention in the lives of families is a complex area, filled with a broad array of ethical, value-laden issues. In addition, the differing conceptualizations of the family and of the modes of intervening add further complexity to an already complex area of research and practice. To contend that solutions to any of the problems raised in this volume are readily available would be the height of naive optimism. More realistically we will continue to plod our way through difficulties of concept, method, and interpretation, believing that we will eventually come to understand not only how families manage but what they need and how professionals can be of help.

We are believers, still, in the family as a key social unit. To that end our efforts are admittedly value-laden—oriented to understanding and strengthening families so that all of them can more effectively cope with the threats to their existence from within and without.

CHAPTER 1

The Ethics of Intervention

IRVING E. SIGEL

Introduction

In recent years, there have been extensive efforts at educational, economic, and social intervention in the lives of families in the United States. Many intervention programs have been established to break the cycle of poverty (e.g., Head Start), to reduce or eliminate drug abuse, and to remediate an untold array of individual and social problems.

Since many of the programmatic efforts have been supported by the Federal government, evaluation components have been mandated to ascertain the "effects" of these social programs. Much attention and writing have documented the psychological, social, and economic consequences of these programmatic interventions. Thus, Head Start programs were evaluated in terms of gains in intellectual and social growth of the children involved, and work study programs were evaluated in terms of employment records of the participants. Although all these evaluation concerns are important and necessary, I believe that other issues— fundamental ethics–values–morality questions—must be considered in evaluating intervention programs. Although lip service was paid to such notions as culture conflict, the more basic ethics–values issues have been expressed in words more often than in deeds. For example, the Head Start program was organized "to interrupt the cycle of poverty, the nearly inevitable sequence of poor parenting which leads to children with social and intellectual deficits, which in turn leads to poor school performance, joblessness, and poverty, leading again to high risk births" (Cooke, 1979, p. xxiii). The solution that was advocated can be summed up as follows: "Existing evidence suggested that comprehensive intervention for

IRVING E. SIGEL • Educational Testing Service, Center for Assessment and Research in Human Development, Princeton, New Jersey, 08541.

young children had to include, besides cognitive approaches, parent involvement, medical attention, and nutritional enrichment. Experience with a successful outcome for the child had to be provided to ensure adequate motivation" (Cooke, 1979, pp. xxiv–xxv).

Note in this statement the implicit cause–effect model regarding all the social problems listed: the victim is the parent. There is an obvious ethics–values issue here, particularly when no valid research studies have explicitly demonstrated that "correcting" parenting would result in job security, and so forth. After all, thousands of children who grew up in such families did break out of the poverty cycle.

Reading such pronouncements as those by Cooke as rationales for intervention programs raises critical questions regarding the ethics of the types of intervention promulgated, the promises implied, and the ethical use of research evidence to support these claims.

As I reflected about the meaning of intervention and the implications of such activities, it occurred to me that not only Head Start, but indeed all such intervention programs raise issues of ethics and values. Each type of intervention is intended to create individual or group change: the Head Start intervention program set out to change child-rearing practices (often of low-income black parents); clinical psychologists try to change the attitudes and feelings and behavior of their clients; planned parenthood education programs try to change birth control practices of their clients, and so forth. Thus, change is the name of the game. When one enters the arena of creating change in the behavior of others, an implicit and explicit ethical issue is raised that must, in my view, be addressed. Why? The answer is found in my belief that members of a democratic society should have some control over their destiny and that there should be (according to my ethical bias) a reciprocal relationship of shared responsibility. In the course of this chapter, I will develop my argument regarding ethics while I present an analysis of the intervention paradigm.

Individuals involved in intervention studies use at least two sources of information as bases for their program efforts; and experiential base and a research data base. Often strands of knowledge from these two sources are integrated and interpreted in a way that results in a manifestly coherent program. For example, the construction of cognitively based programs for early childhood intervention was based on such theories as Piaget (1950) and Hunt (1961), among others, but none of these theories spelled out how the intervention should proceed. Also, various psychotherapeutic techniques that are used with children may have no good research base— only past clinical experience and extrapolation from studies. Thus, another ethical issue comes to the fore, and that is the use of research data in the service of program advocacy. This issue will be discussed in the context devised by Messick (1980, 1981) for the evaluation of tests, since testing programs are also used in intervention.

All intervention programs are constructed by professionals who do not necessarily agree on the interpretation of the research they read. I believe all professionals evolve a world view—a conceptual system that guides the quality and kind of professional experience they have, the type of research data they read and use, and the way they integrate their knowledge systems. Thus, intervention activities express inevitable individual bias. It is possible, however, to articulate the assumptions and values that guide one in conducting intervention. In this way, the ethics–values question is made explicit.

The chapter has three sections. The first will deal with the role of belief systems and world views in the concept of intervention. This is followed by an analysis of the intervention concept, which I believe derives from psychological reality showing the ethical dilemmas inherent in intervention. Finally, I present Messick's decision-tree model (Messick, 1980) adapted from evaluation of the ethics of assessment to evaluation of the ethics of the uses of research in intervention programs.

Behavior Sciences and World View

The concept of intervention is based on the assumption that human behavior is modifiable through appropriate actions on the part of experts. It assumes further that modifiability is possible because behavioral patterns, values, and feelings are products of experience. Thus, the black child who is a poor reader, the emotionally disturbed teenager, even the adult unable to maintain adequate marital relationships are all functioning inadequately because of prior negative and damaging experience. It follows that amelioration of these negative outcomes is possible because new experiences conceptualized as therapeutic or compensatory can alter the expected consequences of the negative early experience. The intervention concept also reflects the belief that early experiences influence later behavior, and so appropriate training for parents and teachers can prevent negative outcomes. The early-experience perspective should be added to the modifiability-through-experience concept.

Although many intervention programmers agree that particular experiences can ameliorate and modify the course of poor cognitive and/or social development, they hold a variety of presuppositions as to which are the "best," the "correct" experiences. Thus, we find a plethora of early childhood programs, all sharing the same types of outcome objectives, but varying considerably as to how they intend to achieve these goals. For example, Montessori programs are highly structured by the Directress, while programs based on Piaget are open-ended and child-centered. Why these differences?

These differences exist because the program developers derive their program objectives and educational strategies from their views of what children should learn and what the necessary conditions for learning are. The differences are usually attributed to the different theories held among the program's developers. My contention is that the differences are manifestations of unexpressed latent world views. The particular theory chosen as the basis for a program derives not from empirical data alone, but from a concept of how the social and psychological reality are to be studied. Pepper (1942) has referred to these organizational perspectives as *world hypotheses*. World hypotheses for him form the root metaphors which guide the theory building, methodologies, and interpretation of so-called facts that we all engage in.

> For we all have and use world hypotheses just as we have animal bodies, have perception, and move within geometrical relations. It is just because world hypotheses are so intimate and pervasive that we do not easily look at them from a distance, so to speak, as if we saw them in a mirror. (Pepper, 1942, p. 2)

I will integrate Pepper's world view idea into my constructivist perspective, from which I assert that each of us is an active cognizer, organizing the reality of objects (nonsocial and social) into *schemata* that serve to guide our behavior. The schemata contain not only behavioral elements but judgmental characteristics as well. In Kelly's (1955) terms, "A person's processes are psychologically channelized by the way he anticipates events" (p. 46). Anticipations are essentially predictions of events and the concurrent expectancy that these events will actually happen. However, our world is not always a world of certainty; it is also a world of the unexpected. The occurrence of the unexpected, a violation of what is anticipated, generates a disequilibrium in the schemata organization. Such an encounter with unanticipated events requires a readjustment of held anticipations. Readjustments can induce alterations in an existing schema and produce new organizations of reality. The awareness of a violation of an anticipation is not, however, a given. Individuals may not be sensitized to violations because in the course of dealing with complex social events, discrepant elements may be overlooked. At times such nonawareness may be unintentional; for example, a lover may not be aware of the unloving actions of the beloved, a trusting individual may be unaware that trust has been violated by a trusted friend, or a hostile person may not recognize the friendly overtures of someone heretofore an enemy. Thus, in social encounters, either affirmation or disaffirmation of anticipations may occur.

Schemata contain evaluations of the behavior of others as well as of social events. These evaluations are considered here to lie both in the domain of ethics, of moral prespectives, and of cognitive properties of anticipation of the consequences of behavior. Judgments of good or bad, positive or negative, for example, are integral to constructs in the individual's schemata. Actions resulting from the network of constructs are therefore expressive in terms of value and appropriateness of behavior. Parents expecting moral behavior from a child may feel so strongly about the seriousness of a child's action that they may react with striking immediacy. Other parents, who may agree as to the immorality of the act, may react otherwise because of the complexity of the situation. In other words, although agreement exists as to the deviance of the act, valuation of the situation will influence the quality of the parents' response.

Each of us—whether behavior scientist, legislator, lawyer, physician, or whoever—has a construction of reality and an evaluation network that predisposes him to what he will act upon, when, and how.

Narrowing this broad statement for the purview of the social scientist, I would translate "personal construct system" to the "theory of behavior," since actions are instrumental behaviors that are reflected in our professional activities. Even more concretely, the behavior scientist works from a theory of behavior that serves as a framework within which various professional decisions are made. Although it may be the case that each professional is aware of the fact that he is working from a conceptual framework, it is not always true that the same professional acknowledges the construct system as just a construction; he may, rather, confuse it with reality itself. This confusion, if it in fact exists—and is not just my personal construction of the professional reality—may lead the professional to believe that his construct system is a reality and hence true. According to the constructivist perspective, knowledge is constructed (and by the way, this is one reason that there cannot be total agreement among individuals' construct systems). There is also understanding and acceptance of individual differences within the systems. Of importance is the awareness that these systems seek to approximate the truth, that the truth is not the content of the construct. For example, we may all agree that the construction "Psychology" as the science of behavior is acceptable, but the method of how to study behavior, or what else should be included under the rubric "psychology," may vary. My point is that psychological science has many schools, each of which purports to study the same phenomena.

Why do I raise this constructivistic argument here? Because the scientist, as he deals not only with his own brand of science but also with social events, makes decisions about what events are relevant for him. Dreams are relevant data for the psychoanalyst, but not in the same way that they might be for the behavior modifier; chronic illness is not the same phenomenon for the organically oriented physician that it is for the psychosomatically oriented physician.

I shall take this approach, which unfortunately must be schematically presented, as we consider the ethics, politics, and practice of intervention with children and families.

Analysis of the Intervention Paradigm

Obviously, on the basis of the previous discussion of world views, my analysis of the intervention paradigm is a product of my own construction of the activities of intervention programmers. In this section, I present an analysis of the intervention paradigm which may be convergent or divergent from the reader's. My approach is based on the following assumption: all intervention involves a power play between the strong and the weak, the knowledgeable and the uninformed.

Further, all intervention programs intrinsically and inevitably involve questions of ethics and values. Since intervention involves entry into the stream of behavior of targeted individuals or groups, it is really an intrusive act, involving the lives and destinies of others. The very act of intrusion in the life space of another automatically impinges on that person's freedom of action. Therefore, once the decision is made to intervene in any situation, considerations of ethics and values emerge.

Intervention is effected to redirect the behaviors, the beliefs, and the attitudes of the "intervenee." Ethics, values, and morality are all intertwined, since the implicit and explicit conceptions of all participants of what is good and what is right and wrong surface immediately. A law that prevents a teenage girl from getting birth control devices unless a parent gives permission is a good example of an intrusive legal act that intervenes in the life of a youngster. The ethical and moral questions speak to the right of the state to define the girl's behavior in what may be considered a private and personal aspect of her life; the law also presupposes that the teenager needs parental guidance—in effect, the law constricts this person's freedom of choice. Without going into great detail on the complex philosophical and psychological definitions of what is morality, or what are ethics, I will define these concepts simply.

Ethics and morality refer to issues of right and wrong, do's and don'ts, in the context of interpersonal interactions. I begin with the assumption that all individuals have rights, such as the right of privacy, the right of self-determination, freedom of choice, and the like. The debatable issues are the limits in which these rights can be expressed. That we have complete freedom of choice as to the church we attend does not seem a debatable issue in our American society; we are not however free to keep our children from attending school. In some areas, in fact, there is no choice as to which public school one's child can attend. So we have traditionally defined some rights which have options, such as church attendance, and others which have no options, such as public education.

I do not intend to set guidelines for what criteria will be used to determine parameters in general; rather I will focus on one particular issue of rights as far as intervention is concerned. My purpose is to define and to demonstrate why I think all interventions involve ethical and moral issues.

Intervention as an active intrusive process, avowedly, geared to change characteristics of individuals or families, can be subtle or direct, minor or major. The chapters of this volume demonstrate the range of intervention activities, ranging from the removal of a child from its home because of parental difficulties to providing parents with new information regarding child rearing. In my own discussion, I do not intend to focus on the specific type of intervention, because as indicated earlier I believe every intervention by its nature involves ethics and morality.

Two parties form the unit of analysis of the intervention process: the professional expert and the client, the one in the to-be-helped position and the helper. The process may occur in a formal context, with a preprogrammed concept of roles and responsibilities; for example, the formal parent–school relationship, the physician–patient relationship. Or the intervention may be an informal one, as among relatives, friends, or neighbors, in which one party decides to step in to do something about the life and activities of another party. The basic paradigm is always one of influence; one party wants to influence the behavior, insights, or feelings of the other. But in the informal context, we deal with a variety of issues that differ from those in the formal context. I will not go into these issues in this discussion, although as we proceed in our thinking about the intervention issue parallels may emerge (see Cochran & Woolever, Chapter 8; or Powell, Chapter 7). For this discussion, I will focus on the formal intervention question.

What Is Implied by the Concept of Intervention?

Intervention can be defined more precisely as the process whereby individuals or institutions deliberately set out to change the course of ongoing or anticipated behaviors, feelings, and attitudes of others. Such intervention activity always implies the presence of an expert and of a nonexpert; that one of the participants knows what should or could be possible for the other participant. In Project Head Start, the experts ostensibly knew what was good for the parents and for the children. Every intervention program in the educational realm involving parents includes an implicit awareness of what is good. This can mean maintaining the family structure, providing material or psychological support for the parents and the children, providing opportunities for the parents to seek gainful employment, or providing opportunities for the child to get an enriched school experience. I begin with the basic proposition that every intervention program includes an implicit set of values which are embedded in and influence the direction of the program. I would find it difficult to find a program that does not have a built-in value; a value which has moral overtones because not only does it say what is good for the clients, but it also says what the clients should do. For example, I would wager that most intervention programs for parents have as an objective the parents' assumption of responsibility for their own lives; this objective obviously places a value on independence. The objective may not be explicated, but may rather be couched in such terms as helping the parents enhance their personal competence or their confidence in themselves as parents. The failure of the parents to achieve this objective would seem to imply that the program had failed. But one could also argue that the program had not failed, since the parents were quite independent in rejecting the independence value that the intervener anticipated. In this situation the intervention does have a value system—almost a moral system—built into it. We find similar issues involved in every intervention. For example, in medicine, a patient goes to a physician and says, "I've been told I have cancer. I've read about Laetrile treatments and I would like those treatments." The physician replies, "You have no choice. You cannot have those treatments because we know that that treatment is ineffective and fraudulent and its advocates make fraudulent claims. Therefore, I will not allow that type of intervention in your case. However, I do know what you should have, so I will now order chemotherapy for you and after a program of treatments you will have tests to show us the progress that's being made." In this context the patient has two choices: to seek another physician or to comply with the treatment orders. Of course, there is a third choice—to just forget the whole thing—but that is an unlikely decision. We have now seen two examples of intervention. In the first, an educator becomes the active initiator; in the second, a patient seeks help. In each example there is an expert who knows what is best for the client. Also, in each case the client is a supplicant. Consequently, the expert is faced with a number of ethical questions; these will be discussed throughout this chapter.

Intervention Is Authoritative

All intervention, as I have said, has an implicit or explicit authoritative conception of the good, the desirable, and the healthy. The concept of intervention is based on the belief that there is a way to do something to improve the ongoing behavior or situation, to make it more fulfilling, productive, or healthy. As stated elsewhere in this volume, there are lawyers who know what is good for parents and children, there are physicians who know what is good for the patient and the family, and there are clinical psychologists who know what makes children develop into schizophrenics. The concept of the expert, of the authority, is intrinsic to the intervention process. Articulation of the fundamental role of the authority and its concomitant ethical fallout, through dealing with the implications and consequences of that role, is the purpose of this article. The authoritative basis of the intervention rests on the presumption that the expert knows what to do. In spite of all the professional protestations to the contrary, when an expert faces a patient or a client, humility is not his overriding, pervasive posture. The rationale for this is that if the professional presents himself as unknowing or ignorant or doubtful or unsure, the uncertainty communicated to the client may be dysfunctional, destroying the client's confidence in the expert. If the professional presents himself as an expert, the client will be more inclined to accept what is communicated. What does this say about the client? Essentially that they are naive, that they can be cajoled, or that they must be presented only limited or inadequate or incomplete information—that, in effect, they are too incompetent to accept our limitations of what we do not know. How often does one hear a psychologist say to his colleagues, "We don't know much about that." And how often does the same psychologist give speeches to parent–teacher groups, to schoolteachers, or to other clinicians providing strong advocacy positions on certain practices. In intervention studies, when we engage families in research projects we often hold back information, saying we know very little about this problem but we want to bring you together to discuss it. Yet we do have a preplanned program. It is not true that we do not know anything. What is true is that we are trying to find out if what we do know in theory works in the real world. In effect, we should admit we are experimenting and tell why we are experimenting. We dissemble by not telling the clients what the limits of our knowledge are.

Of course, the counter argument is that the client constructs anticipations of the expert, that the client by definition attributes expertise to the professional. Otherwise, why should individuals seek help? My point is that although the relationship between professional and client is one between a knowledgeable person (the professional) and a less knowledgeable one (the client), the professional has to be aware of and communicate to the client just what the limits of his knowledge are. As important, perhaps, is the issue of outcomes or side effects of intervention. Are these ever discussed? For example, what happens to a low-income black family's social network when it shifts its child-rearing strategies as a consequence of a parent education program? Do these changes create new adjustment problems for the family? What are the side effects for children involved in intervention programs? Since intervention refers to alterations in developmental trends, if it is successful there should be changes which may well create disequilibrium in the child. The question is, do the intervention agents discuss such issues with the clients? Is the failure of intervention programmers to do this a failure to act in an ethical manner? What is the intervention agent's responsibility? These issues are ethical issues, and they must be dealt with constantly.

Let us now examine some of the assumptions that underlie parent education programs, using them as prototypes. We will follow that discussion with an examination of intervention programs that deal in education and therapy, beginning with some of the ethical considerations.

Schlossman (1978) distinguishes between intervention and facilitation (facilitation is directed at parents, while intervention is essentially educational), but I would venture to say that parent education as practiced in the poverty programs is basically interventionist because there is a direct intrusion into the organization of families. Their values, their languages, and their practices in child rearing and household management are attacked. Moreover, questions are raised about the family organization. The psychological literature on low-income families, particularly black families, is essentially decontextualized; little reference is made to the socio-historical backgrounds of these families. There is also a serious omission of the fact that poverty is a racial or caste issue. Consequently, the socio-historical context—that is, both the history of black families in this country and the current social scene—is generally overlooked. Yet, there is a belief that if these black parents were to follow through on those child-rearing practices which have been identified through research with middle-income white families as benefiting children, the black children would be adequately prepared for education and would consequently get out of the poverty cycle. This belief, it will be recalled, was what Cooke stated as the assumptive basis of Heat Start. When one stops to reflect on what we are doing with these parents, frequently mandated by Federal policy or by the do-gooders who intervene, we come face-to-face with a value question. Essentially, the low-income black families are judged to be inadequate, incapable of coping, and incapable of instilling the appropriate (middle class) social norms, and it is the ineptness of these parents that contributes significantly to the failure of their children to cope with the existing school situation. In effect, it is the old story of blaming the victim for his or her inadequacy. The intervention programs make minimal efforts to deal with some fundamental racial and economic issues; they focus instead on parental care, most often that of the mother. We overlook the fact that mere survival at a poverty level is in itself an achievement. We further presume that by having follow-through programs, for example, extending Head Start into the public school system, we are basically changing the educational context for these children. Essentially, then, we try to convert the parents to middle-class behavior, by providing what we think are appropriate treatment methods to enhance the children's adequate functioning in school (Laosa, 1983).

As I have said before, the assumptions are that we do have the knowledge base on which to make these advocacies and that if we can convert the parent to our ideology, the parent will thereby become the socialization agent who would generate the appropriate orientation of the children to succeed in school.

There are two basic arguments which must be brought into this discussion: one argument is that the data obtained in our research are appropriate, which implies a simplistic, causal connection between appropriate mothering and child outcome; the second argument is that the failure of social and intellectual development in these children is attributable to inadequate family functioning.

The Parent Education Model as an Example of Intervention

There is no doubt that the family provides a core of experience which facilitates the child's adjustment to his world, be it the ghetto, the public school, or whatever. Preparing children from diverse backgrounds to cope with the demands of various societal institutions may, however, require additional strategies of which some parents may be unaware. On the other hand, poverty level black mothers have to socialize their children for survival in a hostile environment, both within the ghettos and in a generally racist outside world. One mother in our Early Childhood Education Program at SUNY/Buffalo told me that children have to be reared to be tough, to fight to protect themselves, and to be ever watchful of the police, who will believe them guilty irrespective of their protestations of innocence. Whether the solution to the children's adjustment is changing the family or changing the social institutions as a whole is still an open question.

When a group of psychologists, social workers or psychiatrists takes on the responsibility for entering into the life spaces of others and establishes guides for parents or programs that require parents to participate, then a questions arises. Is this oppression, establishing requirements for parents' participation without consulting them? It is a kind of medical model, in which the expert has the knowledge, the patient or client is ignorant, and dosing the patient appropriately (be it with psychological or medical treatment) solves the problem. The parent is not engaged in evolving a mutually acceptable educational program. The parent is not engaged as a coequal in diagnosing the sources of difficulty. In essence, the intervener and the client are not engaged in a cooperative, noncoercive situation. If one argues that coercion, direct or implied, is involved in intervention programs, and if one argues further that coercion of any type raises ethical questions, then it follows that intervention programmers are faced with ethical issues which need to be dealt with. Remember, this is not a situation in which the parent has come for help. The experts have indicated that the reason these people are poor and the reason the children do not learn in school is their inadequate parenting, most often that of the mother. Thus, the advocacy in the parent–child development centers is often that mothers stay home and rear their children—a demand, by the way, not usually made with middle-class children, even those who have trouble in school. There is, moreover, an implicit sexism here: Mothers should stay home and rear their children. This is a cardinal requirement. There are some center-based programs to which parents come with their children; there are home-based programs in which the mother stays home awaiting the entrance of the expert, even though he or she is a paraprofessional. In each instance, the mother is told that her presence is a *sine qua non* for her child's development. The causal connection is made quite explicit. I wonder how much guilt, sense of inadequacy, and deprecation of the mother is implied by these programs. It is important that we face this issue squarely. In construction of the poverty situation, the mother is the guilty party, and she is by definition inadequate and alienated. The victim is guilty because she is creating the situation for her own failure.

I do not see frequent demands made for economic and social justice, for adequate housing, for adequate employment, for adequate support services for these people. From my bias, these social conditions are just as significant for generating and maintaining social problems as the heavy-handed approach to mothers.

Hess, in a recent paper, has described some of these questions. He argues that the knowledge base from which we work should be more tentative:

> The field of evaluation research is strewn with corpses of programs that look good in experimental stages, but could not survive transplanting into the real world. The helping professions have great resources to offer but the task of helping families is difficult and our success rate will sustain only limited claims. (Hess, 1980)

In this volume, we describe parent–child programs. What we need to know from our colleagues is the rationale for their intervention strategies and the data base for their advocacy. The probability is that the data base will come from laboratory research and large-scale research, which tend to deal with limited classes of variables, minimizing if not ignoring the sociocultural and historical context within which the programs are established, as well as from which these parents come. As long as social scientists continue to use the paradigm of the physical scientists there will be a discrepancy between our findings in these more precise situations and our success in applying them in more complex contexts. We must confront our own personal and professional ethical systems as we proceed to intervene in the lives of others with hidden agendas and exaggerated research claims.

Ethics in the Therapeutic Context

I have addressed the question of ethics in intervention in parent–child education settings. Is it legitimate to raise the same question of ethics when we deal with the therapeutic context? Do not clinical psychologists work from the same deficit model as educators and physicians, since the client comes to us because we know how to help? We set up clinics, treatment programs, and the like in which we work with families or with dyads within families claiming that we have a course of treatment that will help solve the client's problems. Interestingly enough, we do not have a single treatment program for all family problems. The treatment of choice depends on the orientation of the clinician. We have a variety of clinical perspectives: the nondirective approach of Rogers, the family therapy of Menuchen, the systems theory of family therapy of Lewis, and others. We have cognitive therapists, psychoanalytically oriented therapists, and other types too numerous to list. Each of these perspectives is offered as a bona fide, legitimate treatment approach. The determination of the strategy, the course of treatment, is the responsibility of the clinical personnel. And for the most part, clients are uneducated or uniformed about the alternatives and the value of each. The parent with a behavior-problem child going to a mental health clinic or a child guidance clinic does not know that this clinic may have a point of view that may or may not be shared by others. We rarely inform parents that there are alternative treatment possibilities. So the parent is left with the belief that the expert has the appropriate treatment—and the parent is the victim again, blamed for so much wrongdoing. Our research shows that parents are responsible for children's schizophrenia, hyperactivity, autism, acting out behavior, drug addiction, and the like. We therefore operate from the assumption that the root of most interpersonal and intrapersonal difficulties that children express are rooted in the family. It follows, according to this logic, that pathology exists in the family and is expressed through family functions. Thus, the parent becomes the patient, and this patient is guilty of committing behavioral acts that have generated difficulty in the children. For low-income families, it is the disorganization, the lack of stimulation—we can all enumerate the litany of problems for that group—which form a contrast to the problems of the middle-class family, for which a different litany, usually couched in the language of pathology, is proposed. Whether or not there is validity in the belief that the pathology is rooted in the social environment of the family is an interesting and tricky question. If it is truly rooted in the family, then there must be an explanation for the fact that usually other members of the family do not have the problem. There must be something particular about that child in that family environment. How much of what we see as psychological pathology is a function of such undefined etiology as biological bases, nutritional bases, the role of sibs, or whatever? These etiological factors are frequently overlooked because we do not have, except in some clear-cut cases, any subtantive, trustworthy information. On the other hand, since we tend to be environmentally oriented, we look for the sources of pathology in the family environment. It is trite to argue that clinicians opt for the illness model instead of focussing on the strengths and coping skills of families.

Do we not have an ethical responsibility to take a critical view of our constructions of behavior pathology? Do we professionals not have an ethical responsibility to go through consciousness-raising experiences to bring to the fore our biases? Should our clients not be informed of treatment limitations and possibilities? Essentially, we have to recognize the empirical bias of much of our practical work and recognize without apology the role of experience. It is perhaps even more important for the social worker, the psychiatrist, or the psychologist to expand his or her conceptual perspectives to include such social factors as culture, value systems, and so forth. It is highly possible that parents, having grown up with particular value systems that they hold to be important and necessary, will run into conflict with what are considered social norms, and that the professional will say to the parent, "You've got to comply with what the real world wants." If the parent refuses to do this, the professional argues that the parent is guilty of resisting. So we say the parent is guilty of not adjusting to the norm. On the other hand, we are frequently heard to argue that conformity to social norms in principle is not the most desirable state, and in our own decision making, we opt for a certain amount of autonomy.

The clinician faces some of the same ethical issues as those faced by professionals involved in parent education. In both instances we are dealing with intervention, that is, systematic efforts at generating change among the participants. The essential argument, I repeat, is that every intervention involves ethical problems.

Role of Evidence in Intervention Programs

The ethical issues I have addressed so far concern the use of one's professional experience and of conceptualization of behavioral growth and development as guides to intervention efforts. Part of our professional orientation, however, is our knowledge of the results of research which relates to various stages of the intervention program. For example, research studies in early childhood education showed that children growing up in orphanages had lower IQ scores than children growing up in families (Skeels, 1966); studies of this type were used to support such environmentalist intervention programs as Head Start. Later reports by Jensen (1969) proposed that heritability was an important influence in the development of intelligence. Although the issue is not yet clearly resolved, advocates do take firm positions on both the environmentalist and the genetic side.

My point is that although the evidence is equivocal, there are those who would reject the equivocal nature of the data and opt for favoring one position over the other. Indeed, very few unequivocal studies are available in the behavioral sciences on which to develop any intervention program. Yet program advocates tend to use research selectively to justify their advocacy. I would venture to say that this state of affairs exists in education, psychotherapy, developmental psychology—in any of the behavioral sciences. This is not to fault a particular study, rather it is to fault those who advocate and justify intervention programs on the basis of research alone. But perhaps a more accurate depiction of the state of affairs would be a pragmatic one, namely, that research provides information which is integrated into one's world view (interpretation and extrapolation), and that intervention programs are developed with these criteria in mind. Of course, it can be argued from the social point of view that society cannot wait for research results which would help define intervention strategies. Consequently, programs must be established on the basis of limited knowledge derived from the available research coupled with logic and experience. These programs may change as new findings emerge. In fact, because the knowledge base is limited, systematic evaluation of ongoing programs might be a source of new data which could be used for revision. This can occur only if the decision makers are receptive to new ideas. If they elect (consciously or not) to be dogmatic in their commitment to their world view, then minimal change will occur.

Athough the interventions are deemed socially necessary, does this lack of evidence mean that nothing should be done? Quite the contrary. My argument is that the ethical approach is to recognize that the rationales for intervention programs have to be examined logically and psychologically, with precise articulation of what the confidence levels are by which the programs are defined. In this way, the programs can proceed in spite of limited research bases and still address the ethical issues. Messick (1980, 1981) has addressed these issues in the context of assessment. I have adapted his model for use in analysis of the ethics of research in intervention programs.

Ethical Considerations in the Use of Research Findings: Messick's Ethics of Assessment Model

Transition Use of Data

In a recent paper, Messick (1980) raises some serious questions regarding test validity and the ethics of assessment. The core issue he addresses is construct validity in psychological test usage. His model is appropriate for an examination of the relationship between research and practice (intervention). The analogy I wish to construct is this: construct validity is to test construction as research results are to application to so-called real life social contexts. In the course of his argument regarding construct validity, Messick writes, "Since the evidence in these evidential bases derives from empirical studies evaluating hypotheses about relationships, we must also be concerned about the quality of those studies themselves and about the extent to which the research conclusions are tenable or are threatened by plausible counter hypotheses to explain the results" (1980, p. 1019). Of four classes of variables involved in Messick's analysis, three are relevant for us. These classes are:

> (1) whether the relationship is plausibly causal from one variable to the other, called "internal validity"; (2) what interpretive constructs underlie the relationships, called "construct validity"; (3) the extent to which the interpreted relationship generalizes to and across other population groups, settings, and times, called "external validity." (1980, p. 1019)

Keeping these in mind in relation to intervention research, we can ask questions about the construct validity of intervention programs. What is the construct validity of the treatment program, since construct validation is after all primarily inferential? The constructivist position leads to a question: What assumptions or general constructs underlie the choice of variables involved in the construct validity issue? And finally, by what criteria are the results applicable across populations? Take any preschool educational program as a case in point. Has the program been evaluated to determine its coherence within the constructs that have been created? What about the relationship between input and outcome measures? Are the outcome measures assessing what the program is purportedly about? Finally, is the treatment relevant to other populations, for example, are Head Start programs relevant for American Indians, Eskimos, urban blacks, and rural whites? Do we assume a universality because all are minority groups?

The construct validity issue is not restricted to education, but applies equally to psychotherapy—in fact, to any active intervention.

A key point in Messick's discussion is that in applied decision making, reliance on construct validity or content coverage is not enough, "that the meaning of the measure must also be comprehended in order to appraise potential social consequences sensibly" (Messick, 1980, p. 1013). He also discusses "the value implications of test interpretation *per se*, especially those that bear evaluative and ideological overtones going beyond intended meaning and supporting evidence" (1980, p. 1013). Substitute the term "research findings" for "test," and the same issues arise. Research studies involve constructs, issues of samples and their selection, validity of measurement, appropriateness of data analytic procedures, and, finally, interpretation of findings. Inspection of Figure 1, Messick's model, can provoke an interesting set of questions that can be used as guides to evaluation.

Let us examine parent education in the context of ethics and values. The reason I selected this topic is that parent education is part of a long-standing effort aimed at improving the quality of parenting, according to Harman and Brim (1980). These authors also point out that "questions regarding the ethics of intervention aimed at achieving role function change are being increasingly and hotly debated. Perhaps more than ever, the intrinsic value of indigenous culture and the dangers of intervention have become significant values" (Harman & Brim, 1980, p. 68). They list a number of ethical and value issues: cultural differences in child rearing, changing values, the limited body of relevant research literature, and, finally, what kind of programs should be used. In the case of parent education, two sets of validity come to the fore: one is the validity of the research presented to the parents as bases for recommending action/ practices, and the other is the validity of the type of education employed. In this context, let me make a more thorough examination of parent education, reminding the reader to keep in mind Messick's feedback model.

A Feedback Decision-Making Model for Evaluating Validity of Research for Intervention: A Values–Ethics Issue

Let us work our way through Messick's model. Considering the course ahead, we have to consider two validity domains: the validity of the research

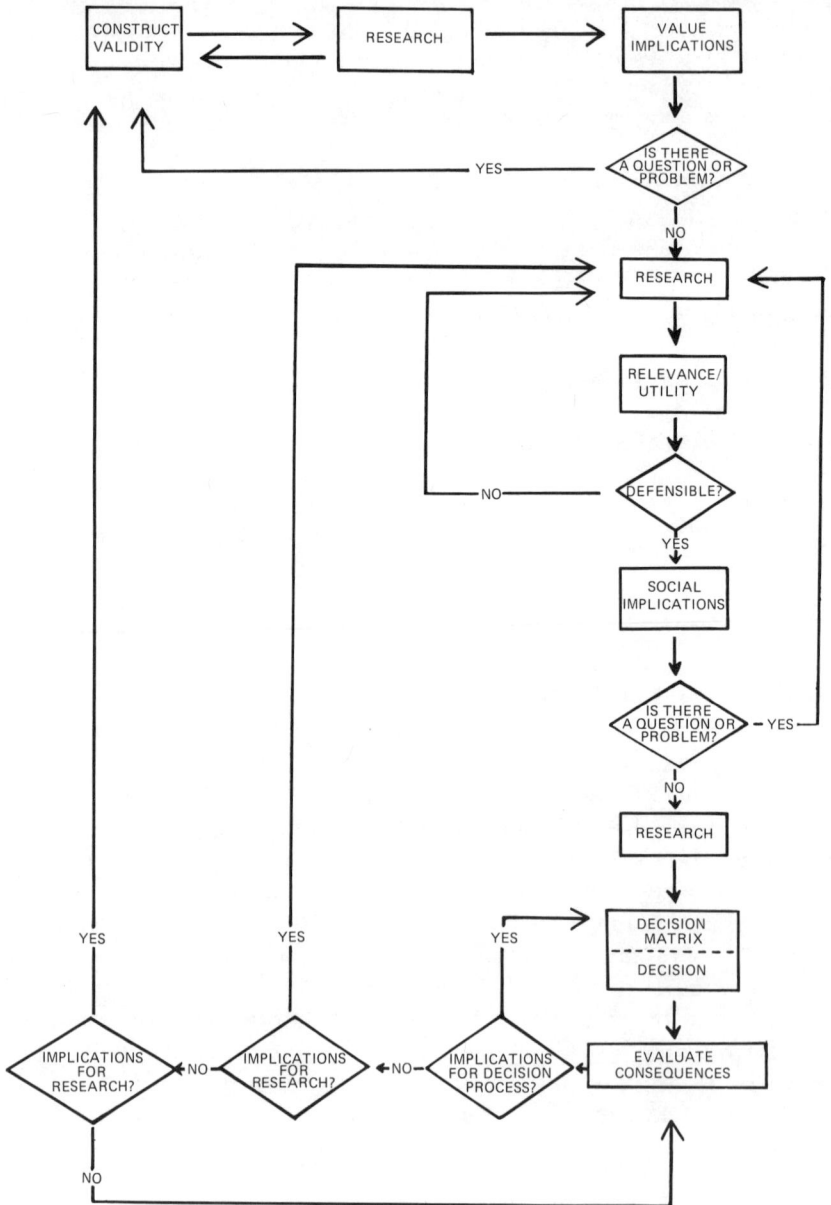

Figure 1. Feedback model for research validity. Adapted from "Test validity and the ethics of assessment" by S. Messick, *American Psychologist*, 1980, *35*, 1012–1027. Copyright 1980 by the American Psychological Association. Adapted by permission of the author.

findings and the valid application of these result to field settings. Messick's model is a type of decision-tree and a feedback model.

The first issue is one of construct validity. In parent education, "the parent educator is confronted with a plethora of material on child development emanating from the various stage theories and is generally encouraged by the tenor of child development professions to make use of them" (Harman & Brim, 1980, p. 139). What constructs are selected from this plethora as bases for organizing programs? Harman and Brim (1980) argue that parent education focused on any single theory—for example, Piaget—may be misleading because the research findings relative to that construct may be poor or nonexistent. Hence to select constructs as organization principles for parent education may be an error. For the sake of this exposition, let us use a case in which the research findings are based on a well designed study (Sigel, McGillicuddy-DeLisi, & Johnson, 1980). The research results are based on legitimate procedures; thus, there is no question about the validity of the findings: Parents who use teaching strategies which involve the child in active problem solving influence the child's subsequent cognitive functioning. The next question requires an evaluation of the value implications.

Two issues arise here: (1) the implicit or explicit value inherent in the research, and (2) the values of the intended audience. In the first instance the research, although seemingly neutral, does make certain assumptions regarding the child as an active learner, while the parent accepts and carries out the role of teacher. The issue in this case may or may not pose a problem to the program builder because it is or is not compatible with his or her orientation. This possible compatibility should not beguile the pro-grammer into believing that the compatibility abjures him from the responsibility of determining the value issues: These values lead to the second problem, the values of the parent group. Let us assume that the group members share the value that the parent's role is to be authoritarian, didactic, and controlling, whereas the research findings being disseminated and the practice advocated are incompatible from such a system—is there not then a value-ethical question? Questions involving value implications are listed on the right side of the diagram. The reader is encouraged to follow this issue through the model. For example, does the proposed use create a problem? If so, is continued advocacy of the child-rearing approach defensible, in view of the incompatibility between the type of behavior defined by the research and the authoritarian value systems of the parents? I realize this is an old question, but it comes to the fore when research findings are to be integrated into practical situations. This is the case with parent education, which is usually a free-choice situation. Yet I can imagine situations which will not be free choice situations; for example, parents of disturbed children or parents of juvenile delinquents can be required to attend parent education classes which use a particular treatment model.

Messick's flow diagram can be a useful guide to at least posing the question and perhaps coming to some resolution.

Ethics Pose a Persistent Problem

I have tended to address the values and ethics questions as virtually a single question. The reason for this conjoining is that in a sense they are, although separate issues, one and the same since I believe that ethics are reflections of a value system. Most professionals, I am sure, would hold to a code of ethics regarding freedom of choice for their clients—including respect for confidentiality, and so forth. But more subtle issues—such as manipulation of the parents' goals, excessive pressure to alter behavior, demands for information the parent deems to be private—all these are integral to one or more of the types of intervention.

What action conclusions does the program developer make consequent to this analysis? It seems to me that one of the critical outcomes of a values–ethics analysis is the raising of the consciousness of the program developers. This is not to say that awareness automatically leads to resolution of ethical or value questions, but it can lead to an articulation and a clarification of what the ethical issues are. To return to the example on parenting: If the teaching strategies conflict with authoritarian child-rearing attitudes, it seems that the parent educator must acknowledge that this difference exists. The educator may then have an open discussion with program participants acknowledging the difference, the apparent value incompatibility, and then let the parents work toward resolution if they elect to. In other words, acknowledgment of differences and acceptance of the fact that differences exist may be a way of dealing with the discrepancy in value.

The major point of this discussion is to raise the ethical issue, reiterating my earlier argument that *all* research and *all* intervention involve value questions. If we accept that argument, the next problem all practitioners face is to acknowledge that the logical sequel to value awareness is that an ethical question is involved whenever one intervenes in the lives of others. On the other hand, my point is not to overwork the parent education model, since it concerns for the most part a population who volunteer for intervention through exposure to education programs, books, magazines, and so forth.

Intervention can also be involuntary, as when families are required to participate in a program. Some courts require family members to have counseling prior to divorce, judges can insist on counseling or psychiatric treatment for certain types of juvenile offenders, and they can remove children from a home for whatever reason. These are other types of intervention.

Involuntary intervention raises even more questions regarding the values–ethics issue. Since society has decided, for example, that one cannot decide to take one's own life, efforts to interfere in suicide attempts are mandated. Then there are interventions with individuals who refuse medical treatment for religious reasons, for example, parents who object to blood transfusions. These represent deliberate intrusions by society into the lives of individuals, based on a basic value in our society—the preservation of life. In Beck's chapter (Chapter 3) other societal values are expressed in laws which circumvent someone's freedom because of value conflicts.

What this discussion has attempted to do is to highlight the ethical issue, since the focus of the remaining chapters is on intervention. Everyone might agree that values–ethics issues are built into the problems of intervention. But I believed that by presenting Messick's feedback model I would provide a formal procedure as a guide.

References

Cooke, R. T. Introduction. In E. Zigler & J. Valentine (Eds.), *Project Head Start: A legacy of the war on poverty*. New York: The Free Press, 1979.

Harman, D., & Brim, O. G., Jr. *Learning to be parents: Principles, programs, and methods*. Beverly Hills, Calif.: Sage Publications, 1980.

Hess, R. Experts and amateurs: Some unintended consequences of parent education. In M. D. Fantini & R. Cardenas (Eds.), *Parenting in a multi-cultural society*. New York: Longman, 1980.

Hunt, J. McV. *Intelligence and experience*. New York: Ronald Press, 1961.

Jensen, A. R. How much can we boost I.Q. and scholastic achievement? *Harvard Educational Review*, 1969, *39*, 1–123.

Kelly, G. A. *The psychology of personal constructs* (2 vols.). New York: Norton, 1955.

Laosa, L. M. Parent education, cultural pluralism, and public policy: The uncertain connection. In R. Haskins (Ed.), *Parent education and public policy*. Norwood, N.J.: Ablex, 1983.

Messick, S. Test validity and the ethics of assessment. *American Psychologist*, 1980, *35*, 1012–1027.

Messick, S. Evidence and ethics in the evaluation of tests. *Educational Researcher*, 1981, *10*, 9–20.

Pepper, S. C. *World hypotheses: A study in evidence*. Berkeley, Calif.: University of California Press, 1942.

Piaget, J. *The psychology of intelligence*. London: Routledge & Kegan Paul, 1950.

Schlossman, S. The parent education game: The politics of child psychology in the 1970's. *Teachers College Record*, 1978, *79*, 788–808.

Sigel, I. E., McGillicuddy-DeLisi, A. V., & Johnson, J. E. *Parental distancing, beliefs and children's representational competence within the family context* (ETS RR 80-21). Princeton, N.J.: Educational Testing Service, 1980.

Skeels, H., Adult status of children with contrasting early life experiences. *Monographs of the Society for Research in Child Development*, 1966, *31*(No. 3).

CHAPTER 2

Changing Families through Parent and Family Education

Review and Analysis

PAUL R. FLORIN and PAUL R. DOKECKI

Concern for the well-being of the American family has been steadily growing over the past several years. The family, the primary social institution of the society, is seen as beset by an increasing variety of stresses and diminishing supports (Lasch, 1977). The argument has been made that all families are experiencing increased demands and could benefit from the availability of resources and supports (Dokecki & Moroney, 1983). Parent education may be one such resource and support approach to strengthening family functioning. But gaining a clear perspective on the potential of parent education is made difficult by the diversity of opinion and comment proffered under this rubric.

For some, parent education holds the promise of an approach to primary prevention (Hobbs, 1975; White, 1980); for others, it is a ruse to avoid acknowledging the failure of compensatory efforts (Schlossman, 1978). For some, it seeks to improve certain families (Bronfenbrenner, 1978); for others, it seeks to improve the institutions with which parents must deal (Gordon, 1977). Although some see parent education as aiding

PAUL R. FLORIN • Department of Psychology, University of Rhode Island, Kingston, Rhode Island 02881. PAUL R. DOKECKI • Department of Psychology and Human Development, George Peabody College of Vanderbilt University, Nashville, Tennessee 37203. This paper was prepared in conjunction with a project funded by the Carnegie Corporation of New York and carried out by the Center for the Study of Families and Children of the Vanderbilt Institute for Public Policy Studies. Portions of this paper appear in the final published report of the project. Portions were also prepared by the first author, under the supervision of the second author, as a major area paper submitted for doctoral candidacy in psychology at George Peabody College of Vanderbilt University. The statements made and the views expressed are solely the responsibility of the authors.

only poor, minority, or special need families, others see it as of potential benefit for all families (Dokecki & Moroney, 1983). Parent education is typically defined as dealing exclusively with child rearing, but some widen its scope to include the family as a system and the needs of everyone, including parents as persons, within that system (Wandersman, 1978). Some construe parent education as a process in which experts impose values on familes (Keniston, 1977), while others see it as parents defining their own needs and using the expert as a resource (Dokecki, 1977).

This listing of diversity could go on. Some of the divergent opinions involve differences in interpretation of the same phenomena; others seem to address different reference points. For parent education is a complex phenomenon. Its history and development have been and continue to be marked by major shifts in purposes, contents, and approaches. Moreover, its history has been intertwined with other childrearing interventions, such as child care and early childhood education. In this chapter we (1) trace the changes that have occurred in the development of parent education, (2) identify the elements that make up an emerging model of parent education, and (3) offer a broad overview of the research literature.

A Framework for Conceptualizing Parent Education

In order to trace the changes that have occurred in the development of parent education, we must have a framework identifying the various factors involved. The framework that follows contains two general categories or levels with four variables at each level:

Broad Societal Context	Intervention Components
1. Goals	1. Knowledge base
2. Societal problems	2. Program goals
3. Values	3. Core approach to intervention
4. Intervention area/strategy	4. Focus of intervention

The *Broad Societal Context* perspective encompasses four variables that have influenced the development of interventions in child rearing. Interventions are developed with (1) particular purposes or *goals* to be served for the society. These goals are based on (2) perceived *societal problems* defined in terms of a discrepancy perceived to exist between "what is" (the present social reality) and (3) societal *values* or ideals about "what should be." The (4) *intervention area/strategy* is the translation of goals into specific activities directed toward a particular social sphere.

Intervention Components consist of (1) the *knowledge base*, the research and theoretical underpinnings that give rise to a particular intervention, which leads to defining (2) *program goals* to be accomplished through a (3) *core approach to intervention*, which has (4) a *focus of intervention* on a particular person or persons.

This framework, of course, greatly simplifies the nature of the forces operating within a society that interact to influence the directions of interventions. Although the variables have been presented in a series of linear sequential steps, the elements of the framework represent a field of forces transacting in complex dynamic ways. Changes in any one of the variables can lead to change throughout the framework. For example, a change in a societal value can lead to different intervention approaches and generate a new knowledge base. Conversely, the knowledge base developed from existing interventions can lead to switches in program focus and goals, which can alter values. As we chart the history and recent developments associated with child-rearing interventions, some of the complex relations possible among elements of the framework should become apparent.

Early Periods of Parent and Child-Rearing Interventions

We have leaned heavily on a recent paper by Greta Fein (1980) to specify the elements of our framework and present a historical overview of parent and child-rearing interventions in the United States. Table 1 (also appearing in Dokecki & Moroney, 1983) outlines the material.

1600–1800

During the 17th and 18th centuries, there was a public outcry for a more moral (religious) citizenry. This concern was translated into a societal goal of obliging individuals, especially the young, to observe moral and religious values. The massive influx of settlers and the resulting social and political turbulence that reigned during this country's birth and early development threatened ideals of social morality. Crime and corruption within society generated a feeling that behavioral standards were needed which would impose order and build cohesion among fragmented and diverse groups of people. The area of intervention seized on was child rearing; the rationale was that since morals are instilled when we are young, the way to produce moral adults is to raise children with moral values. During this period a major approach to intervention was the church sermon, which directed mothers to insure the proper moral development of their children.

Table 1. A Framework for Conceptualizing Parent Education[a]

Intervention variables	1600–1800	1800–1850	1850–1880
Broad societal context			
Goals	Socialize To instill moral values	Socialize	Acculturation (mainstreaming)
Societal problems	Crime and corruption	Immorality and corruption	Waves of rapidly growing cities produce disorder and an underclass not socialized in dominant values
Values	Moral (religious) citizenry	Morally responsible citizens	Stable society
Intervention area/ strategy	Child rearing/ parent education	Child rearing/child centers for lower class Parent education for middle class	Child rearing/ infant schools for immigrants
Intervention components			
Knowledge base	Two emergent philosophies: Calvinistic doctrine of infant depravity Comenius-emphasis on first six years of life. Child held to be innocent and in need of guidance	Two movements based on Comenius: Reform philosophies with regard to poor popular early in the 1800s A belief in the ultimate authority of the individual and legitimacy of self-interest. The assumption that social benefits will be gained when self-interest is exercised	Calvinistic approach dominant Stress on obedience, compliance, and order in children
Program goals	Teach parent to be effective shaper of child's moral development	Change child's behavior	Improve physical condition (health and nutrition) Development and socialization

Core approach to intervention	Religious sermons (occasional religious tracts)	Sunday schools expanded to weekdays Pamphlets, tracts, magazines, and sermons; first maternal association (1820)	Day nurseries run by nurses
Focus of intervention	Mother	Child—lower class Mother—middle class	Child

Intervention variables	1880–1900	1900–1920	1920–1940
Broad societal context			
Goals	Socialize	Massive reform of societal institutions and individuals	Socialize
Societal problems	Corruption (especially political) and immorality in society	Waves of immigrants largely uneducated and unsocialized Uninformed and politically irresponsible citizens Rising divorce rates	An adolescent population unprepared to assume moral responsibility or recognize social norms Parents inept in role
Values	Moral and decent society	Decent, stable society Socially and politically responsible citizens	Morally responsible citizens and stable society
Intervention area/ strategy	Child rearing/ parent education (middle class)	Maternal role (child rearing and awareness) Maternal education middle and lower class)	Child rearing/ parent education (middle class)
Intervention components			
Knowledge base	Philosophical shift with G. Stanley Hall's *Laws of Mental Development* and first	Hall still important but his emphasis shifts to adolescence Dewey's social	Watson, Dewey, Gesell, and Freud Focus on early childhood Personality traits

Continued

Table 1. (*Continued*)

Intervention variables	1880–1900	1900–1920	1920–1940
	empirical studies of child behavior. His laissez-faire policy stressed child's need for freedom to explore and develop Emphasis on early ages First time cognitive and emotional development of children recognized	philosophy and pedagogical theory First mention of executive function of parents Parents have broader responsibilities than child rearing	fixed by age 5 Children should be deferential to authority, socially conformist, and in control of their emotions Emphasis on social and emotional (not cognitive) development
Program goals	Use behavioral science to create a science of pedagogy Effective parents and self-improvement of mothers	Translate professional information to mothers Increase self and political awareness of mothers	Bring child rearing information to mothers Target on child's behavior, habit formation, personality, integration, and social adjustment
Core approach to intervention	Books, pamphlets, and discussion groups	Group discussions Socio-political action groups Home instruction for poor	Nursery schools to give parents lessons in child rearing
Focus of intervention	Mother	Mother	Mother

Intervention variables	1940–Late 1950s	Late 1950s–Late 1960s	Late 1960s–Early 1970s
Broad societal context			
Goals	Help parents fill their role in child care	Redress of inequalities in society through governmental affirmative action	Redress of inequalities in society through governmental affirmative action
Societal problems	Depression and World War II	Disenfranchised urban poor	Disenfranchised urban poor

	lead to industrial mobilization forcing women into labor force making them unable to care for children full time	Institutional racism	Institutional racism
Values	Adequate environment for child development	Equal rights Just society	Equal rights Just society
Intervention area/ strategy	Child care/day care	Anti-poverty interventions Compensatory education	Anti-poverty interventions Compensatory education
Intervention components			
Knowledge base	Watson, Dewey, Gessel, and Freud Focus on early childhood Personality traits fixed by age 5 Children should be deferential to authority, socially conformist, and in control of their emotions Emphasis on social and emotional (not cognitive) development	Developmental research focused on enriching environment and promoting early cognitive development	Research indicating importance of parental influence
Program goals	Day care to allow mothers to be employed outside the home	Equalize educational opportunity Promote school success	Equalize educational opportunity Promote school success
Core approach to inter- vention	Nursery schools (parent participation not encouraged)	Center-based programs run by professionals stressing stimulation of children	Impart knowledge/ skills to parents; mostly didactic
Focus of intervention	Child	Child	Child through parents

[a]Based, in part, on Fein, 1980.

The underlying belief system that this approach to intervention was based on evolved from two earlier distinct philosophies. The first approach was derived from the theories of John Amos Comenius (1592–1670), who has been called "the father of education." Comenius identified the first six years of life as a critical period and viewed the child as an innocent being incapable of distinguishing right from wrong and hence in need of moral guidance. This view demanded an active parent as educator. The opposing view came from the Calvinistic doctrine of infant depravity, in which the child was viewed as coming into the world with an "inborn proclivity to evil" (Fein, 1980). The parental role demanded by this second view was a repressive one, in which the parent was to extinguish negative behaviors rather than instill positive ones. Differences between these philosophies resided less in educational content, or what to teach, than in attitudes toward the child, or how to teach. Both approaches were based on a linear model of growth (Sameroff & Chandler, 1975), which focused on those critical events in childhood that have a direct cause-and-effect relationship to subsequent behavior. This model of human development was to direct the standards for parent–child programs until the 1960s.

1800–1850

Political corruption during this period (especially in the Jackson Administration) caused public alarm and fear of widespread immorality, leading to a renewed demand for proper socialization of the young as a societal goal and a national priority. Child rearing in the lower classes was identified as the most appropriate area for intervention. In the strategy adopted, responsiblity was taken away from the lower-class parents. Early in the 1800s, according to Fein (1980), reformers pushed Sunday schools to expand their services to weekdays and thus insure the proper rearing of the children. So the child was the focus of intervention efforts in the lower classes. Later during this same period, middle-class mothers became the focus of other intervention efforts. In this approach, pamphlets, religious tracts, and magazine articles, as well as sermons on child rearing, were utilized. The philosophical principle that guided this approach was a belief in the "ultimate authority of the individual, the legitimacy of self-interest, and in the idea that social benefits will be gained when self-interest is exercised" (Fein, p. 159).

1850–1880

During this period, waves of immigrants to the rapidly growing cities disrupted the social order and created an underclass unsocialized in the dominant values. The Civil War rent the fabric of society even further and led to a desire for stability. The value of a stable society was to be pursued through interventions seeking the goal of acculturation. The popular intervention approach was child care in day nurseries, operated by churches in accordance with the Calvinist doctrine, stressing obedience, cleanliness, and order (Fein, 1980). The children of the lower immigrant classes were the focus of intervention efforts, and, for the first time, the program goals included physical as well as moral development.

1880–1900

In the 1880s, the writings of G. Stanley Hall and the first normative studies of child behavior provided a new knowledge base for education and the basis for a philosophical shift. This shift represented the end of what Harmon (1971) has referred to as the traditional approach to education. Prior to this time, the question was not so much how children were taught as what they were taught. That is, the content of education had more importance than the process of education. Hall's formulation of the Laws of Mental Development encouraged a laissez-faire policy toward child rearing: Children in the first six years of life were deemed to need freedom to explore and develop. Thus began a concern with the cognitive and emotional development of children and the modern (process over content) approach to education. The societal values remained much the same, but some new importance was attached to society's responsibility to its citizens as well. Again, political corruption (in the Grant Administration) was the visible discrepancy between a moral society and appropriate socialization. Intervention during this period was directed toward the middle-class mother. Behavioral science (derived from Hall's work) was used to create a science of pedagogy. Books, pamphlets, and discussion groups formed the core of educational activities.

1900–1920

During this 20-year period, known as the Progressive Era, in addition to the continuation of goals of individual reform, a new societal goal was introduced: Institutional reform. The dominant societal ideal was a decent society composed of socially and politically responsible and aware citizens. Rising divorce rates, indicating the disruption of the nuclear family, and an influx of immigrants after World War I, creating an unsocialized and uneducated underclass, threatened such an ideal. Within the individual intervention approach, as in the past, the poor received home instruction, which focused on changing and improving the child's behavior, while middle-class programs sought to improve the mother's functioning on a variety of levels. Child-rearing practices derived theoretical support from both Hall (who had shifted his focus to the adolescent) and John Dewey, whose behaviorism stressed the parent's relationship to the broader society as well as to child rearing. Group discussions for middle-class mothers concentrated on the relationship of parents and social institutions, their political responsibilities, and their self-awareness and improvement. Thus the concept was introduced that, in addition to child rearing, parenthood involved family relations with societal institutions. This concept of an "executive function" of parents in mediating the family's transactions with society was to make a reappearance more than half a century later (Berger & Neuhaus, 1977; Keniston, 1977).

The concern of the middle class with social responsibility was channeled into the new institutional intervention approach. This approach attempted to change health, educational, and social institutions to accomodate the economic and demographic transitions that society was rapidly undergoing. The significance of this new intervention approach was that for the first time an intervention, rather than seeking to force individuals to fit existing institutions, sought to reform social conditions and change the institutions.

1920–1940

The 1920s and 1930s saw a return to previous goals of individual reform. The lower class as an object of reform was the domain of the social workers, participating in the settlement house movement. The middle-class adolescent culture was largely viewed as unfit to prepare young adults to assume the responsibilities of the recognized social norms. Parent education was directed toward the middle class. Nursery schools were created to instill good habits in children and to teach middle-class mothers child rearing to practice in the home. Various concepts from the work of Watson, Dewey, Gesell, and Freud (described in detail by Schlossman, 1976), provided a theoretical basis for parent education programs. Emphasis on early childhood as a critical period was supported by a general belief in the formation and irreversiblity of personality traits by age five. To correct the excesses of youth, children were trained to be deferential to authority, socially conformist, and in control of their emotions. Cognitive growth was no longer emphasized in child development, and program goals dealt with habit formation, personality integration, and social adjustment. A new intervention approach that made its appearance during this period was the pre-parenthood education courses in colleges, high schools, and even grade schools. In these courses the basics of child care were to be taught, not after the arrival of a child, but while the future mother was still in school. As we shall see, this approach was to reemerge strongly 50 years later.

1940–Late 1950s

During the next two decades, there were only relatively minor changes in intervention approaches. The major change occurred with respect to the utilization of child care centers. Previously, child care was predominately a child-rearing intervention designed to facilitate acculturation of the children of diverse immigrant groups, or what Gordon (1977) referred to as "mainstreaming." Massive immigration had waned, but a new population had developed that utilized day-care centers. The massive industrial mobilization of World War II saw an enormous number of mothers in the factories; thus the role of mothers as full-time primary caregivers was altered. Women entering the labor market forced the middle class to participate in an institution previously assigned to the poor—day care without a parent education component (Fein, 1980). In fact, as Fein has noted, parents were encouraged not to participate. Similarly, preschools for the affluent became popular; these also made no effort to educate parents.

More Recent Developments

Late 1950s–Late 1960s: Enter Government and the Call for Evaluations

Beginning with the late 1950s, new forces entered the early childhood intervention scene. Prior to this time, the history of interventions and changes in the framework had occurred without large scale government involvement. Complex social forces that crystallized during the late 1950s altered government's laissez-faire attitude and added new dynamics that would create changes in the framework at an ever-increasing rate. (These modern changes are represented by the last three columns of Table 1.) Because this period has been analyzed in depth by so many authors it will be only briefly summarized here.

Rapid technological growth with concomitant industrial mechanization drastically reduced the job market for unskilled and uneducated immigrants and American minority groups. Poor blacks, Chicanos, and

Appalachians were drawn to urban centers in search of work. But economic, social, and political racism, together with widespread unemployment, created a disenfranchised urban poverty class. America was no longer the land of opportunity or the huge melting pot, and this new class demanded civil rights, equal economic opportunity, and affirmative action from the government (Fein, 1980). These demands became institutionalized as political goals (e.g., the war on poverty), and social policies were directed toward the redress of social inequalities. This direction was a prime example of Dokecki and Moroney's (1983) description of most current social policies as "correctives to an economic system that has not achieved a just allocation of goods and services" (p. 21).

Among other antipoverty interventions, compensatory education for the poor became prominent. The basis for this intervention approach was the "culture-of-poverty" theory, which held that an impoverished environment could be, at least in part, compensated for by early educational enrichment programs aimed solely at the child. In this way, the government sought to equalize educational (and thus economic) opportunity. Compensatory programs focused on the preschool years in a child's life, with the major goal being success in school. Programs leaned heavily upon behavioral, developmental, and psychodynamic psychology. Influenced by all these diverse schools of thought, each program, whether synthesis or single model, was based on an interactive orientation (Sameroff & Chandler, 1975) which considers the interaction of individual and environmental attributes. Compensatory education was viewed as the means of providing the necessary environment for the individual child to operate successfully in school. This intervention approach was thus based on a deficit model (Dokecki, Strain, Bernal, Brown, & Robinson, 1975) which sought to alter deficits in the childs's environment in the direction necessary for assimilation into mainstream society.

Dokecki, Hargrove, and Sandler (1983) have described the first generation of compensatory education programming in the late 1950s and early and middle 1960s as consisting of privately sponsored programs (e.g., the Ford Foundations's Great Cities project) and Federal programs such as Project Head Start. This generation of programming was primarily action-oriented, with little emphasis on assessment, evaluation, or systematic experimentation.

As the 1960s progressed, however, evaluations began to appear. The negative ones (e.g., Westinghouse Learning Corporation, 1969), which used primarily cognitive criteria, had several effects. First, there was a call for the end of intervention efforts, as critics used genetic arguments (e.g., Jensen, 1969) to prove that intelligence was inherited and therefore immutable. Second, there was a call for new evaluations to determine whether programs could successfully alter any other behavior or trait—some as yet untested variable, the implication being that program objectives and evaluation were mismatched. There was also a demand for systematic experimentation from academics interested in evaluating specific program curricula and their potential for achieving more lasting effects in the area of intelligence as well as in previously unmeasured areas of child development. In addition, politicians, responding to critics as well as budget constraints, demanded program accountability. Then a group of reviews and secondary analyses emerged. These tried to determine if any programs had succeeded in accomplishing anything and, if they had, for whom. Finally, a second generation of programs concentrating on systematic experimentation was born. Basically these new programs were merely variations on an old theme. They intended to retain the focus on providing stimulating experiences for children within a center where parent involvement was minimal. A number of compensatory education programs during the 1960s did have parent education components, mostly as supplemental to the child development program. Others had dual objectives, intervention with the parent or parents and with the child. What all these programs shared was a common primary goal of cognitive improvement in the child. Evaluations tended to focus on this goal.

Like their predecessors, what these evaluations consistently showed was that IQ could be raised, but that the effects generally did not persist beyond second or third grade (White, 1973). In fact, "the most common outcome of just about any intervention effort was a ten point increase in IQ (even a hastily mounted 8-week summer program)" (Ziegler & Trickett, 1978, p. 791). Other types of outcomes, such as social development, child health, family impact, and community change, were also measured, although much less frequently or rigorously. Since these evaluations focused essentially on antipoverty programs that were developed for political reasons, IQ seemed to be the most acceptable standard for program accountability.

The general result of the series of these early evaluations was confusion rather than certainty. Despite what seemed to be negative results, such programs as Head Start were refunded. Political considerations and active support from participating parents overrode the nature of evaluative data (Mallory, 1979). Researchers began to look at what programs were most successful, why, and for whom. Later on, it would be found that gains in some other areas (e.g., school achievement) persisted longer and were related to both program variables and participation variables. On the basis of these secondary analyses, researchers would conclude that some programs worked well with some children (Lazar, Hubbel, Murray, Rosche, & Royce, 1977). Since, as Powell (1979) has pointed out, "it is easier to produce effects in intervention than it is to identify the specific factors contributing to success" (p. 15), the task became to identify the critical variable.

Late 1960s–Early 1970s: The Emergence of Parents

Of particular importance to this chapter is the fact that reviewers came to the conclusion, albeit a tenuous one, that programs not involving parents do not succeed for very long. Bauch, Vietze, and Morris (1973) stated that conclusion more positively than most reviewers: "Empirically, early education intervention programs that have involved parents have shown long-range effects on the children's academic achievement and performance on tests of psychometric intelligence" (p. 47). Lazar and Chapman (1972) found that parent programs that focused on mothers as primary agents of intervention had a higher frequency of positive immediate cognitive effects on children than those programs that focused primarily on the child. They did caution, however, that the impact of the parent component as separate from the child component was difficult to assess. Fein (1980) noted that the following consensus was reached by reviewers for Head Start programs:

1. The more intensive is parental involvement, the more apparent is the difference in children's performance.
2. When parental self-perception is that of primary educator, the effects on children's intellectual development are stronger than when parents are relegated to a secondary role.
3. Parents' employment as child-care workers seems to have beneficial effects on their children's intellectual development, but there is little knowledge about the effects on the family constellation.

Bronfenbrenner (1974), reviewing the effectiveness of early intervention efforts, stressed the crucial need for intervention with the primary caregivers and their direct involvement in the education of their children. He found IQ gains produced by home-based interventions to hold up "rather well three to four years after intervention has been discontinued" (p. 21). However, he cautioned that the results may have been due to a sampling bias (e.g., motivational differences) rather than the type of intervention.

The results of these and other reviews, which indicated a correlation between high parent involvement and positive outcomes (e.g., Biber, 1970; Mann, Harrell, & Hurt, 1976; MIDCO Educational Associates, 1972; White, 1973), supplied the impetus for parent education to become a formal component of intervention strategies.

The studies of program interventions that indicated the importance of a focus on parents supported those psychologists who claimed that programs of the 1950s and 1960s showed short-lived effects because they failed to involve the family. Several researchers had long viewed the home environment provided by families as the single most important influence on the social and intellectual development of children (Bloom, 1964; Bronfenbrenner, 1974; Hunt, 1961). Developmental psychology was demonstrating, in minor experiments with poverty level children, the important influence of parent–child interaction on intellectual, social, and physical development. The failure of early programs to produce lasting effects was attributed to their inability to change the home environment of the child. These programs were seen as treating the symptom rather than the underlying problem itself, and when the intervention was withdrawn, the symptoms gradually reappeared. Hayes and Grether (1969) believed that over half of the variability in academic achievement could be accounted for by factors outside of the school. Thus, they argued, intervention directed toward the schools—perhaps only the perpetuators and not the creators of the differences—was actually misdirected.

For many (e.g., Ainsworth, 1975), the underlying assumption of parent education programs is that an improvement in environmental conditions through parent education will provide an upgraded environment for children long after program termination. Although some, such as Schlossman (1978), viewed the shift of program focus to parents as a politically motivated evasion of responsibility for compensatory education failures and an instance of blaming the victim, the arguments in favor of such a shift in both applied and basic research appeared formidable. But alternative explanations for the higher success of programs with a parent component were also offered. Palmer (1977) suggested that it was not the involvement of parents per se but rather the individual attention that was responsible for child outcomes. Getting parents involved, he reasoned, simply made the intervention longer and more intense. Also, research specifically designed to address the issue of child-centered versus parent-centered programs proved less than compelling. Home Start compared its approach of regular home visits to Head Start's center-based approach. Love, Nauta, Coelen, Hewett, and Ruopp (1976) found that after 12 months there were no differences between Head Start and Home Start Children on four measures of school readiness. Gilmer, Miller, and Gray (1970) compared an exclusive parent-focus with a combined approach and found that neither parent intervention combined with a preschool program nor an exclusive home intervention with parents produced gains in IQ as high as the exclusively child-focused program. However, the child-focused group showed a greater decrement in those gains over the next two years than did the other two groups. Karnes, Hodgins, Teska, and Kirk (cited in Fein, 1980) compared exclusive child-focused, parent-focused, and omnibus programs and found that when the two focuses were combined in the omnibus programs, effects did not improve. Radin (1972) compared a preschool program with an intensive parent component to one without and found that the children in the former program showed significantly greater increase in IQ than those in the latter group. Researchers who failed to find differences among program models generally accounted for the results in terms of measurement errors, contamination of variables, sampling biases, or other methodological difficulties (Bronfenbrenner, 1974).

The less than unanimous support for parent education programs did little to dampen the enthusiasm for these programs. New programs continued to be developed to meet the demands of the new focus on parents, and previous programs that had a parent focus were reevaluated to determine the specific program types and degree of involvement most effective. In addition, researchers began to give more attention to other intervention effects. The question was no longer about the usefulness of parent education—rather, it was about what it can do and how it can do it best. The quest was simple: to find the most effective vehicle for delivering information and skills to the disadvantaged.

This period saw substantial shifts in the framework we have been utilizing. Shifts in theory produced a new knowledge base, which concentrated on important family influences on the child's development. Intervention approaches consequently shifted to focus on imparting knowledge and skills to parents rather than directly to children. But it should be recognized that other elements remained relatively unchanged. Program goals continued to be measured against child outcomes—usually cognitive outcomes. The entire approach still rested on an antipoverty strategy designed to equalize educational opportunities for the children of the disadvantaged. And the idea persisted that a deficit resided within the groups to be helped. The professional was to impart expert knowledge to parents that would alter the environment of the child.[1]

Program Evaluations of Parent Education

We now present the findings of evaluations of parent education programs that were mostly based on the approaches reflected in the final

[1] We readily acknowledge that during this and earlier periods some critics were calling for more basic changes at all levels of the framework, and that some research and service projects did not follow the basic pattern described above. Our intent, however, is to summarize broadly what appeared to be major trends in the development of parent education approaches.

sections of the framework presented in Table 1. Subsequently we will update and project a framework for the future based, in part, on the results of these evaluations.

The findings that are presented have been gleaned largely from reviews and secondary analyses, although single studies are included when appropriate. We should mention a number of problems that are inherent in reviews and secondary analyses. Two in particular are germane and must be stated as caveats to the reader of program findings. The first limitation is internal to the individual studies. What each study decides to measure is, in a sense, a question asked. The answers produced naturally relate only to those questions, and further questions cannot be asked. Not only are we limited by the questions we ask, but, in fact, those questions create the very reality we experience. The second limitation resides in the reviews and secondary analyses and pertains to the study samples, experimental designs, and measurements used in individual projects. The problems of comparing individual studies with project-developed instruments are obvious. In addition, the diversity of standardized measures (e.g., IQ tests), when they are used, presents similar problems. To compound this latter limitation further, standardized measures of young children typically have poorly established validity and reliability (White, 1973). Moreover, variations in the characteristics of children and parents, in the selection criteria, the procedures for selecting samples, and the methods of assigning subjects to treatment or control groups make cross-study comparisons most difficult. Hurt and Quellet (1975) in their parental skills comparability study attempted to deal with the heterogeneity of the research area by clustering projects on the basis of objectives. They found that objectives concerned with parental skills in support of ongoing programs for children had the highest degree of comparability potential. Even when comparability is high, however, the degree of certainty inherent in the conclusions drawn remains problematic. And although outcomes of objectives are similar, heterogeneity of varibles within programs makes tenuous any attempts to relate categories of program characterisitcs to outcomes. The results presented below should thus be viewed as indicative only of the potentialities of intervention programs, given the broad span of variability.

The studies reviewed were selected primarily on the basis of comprehensiveness and the criteria used in selecting samples. White's (1973) criteria were typical of those employed in other reviews and secondary analyses in his demands that "some good indication exist for attributing the improvement in function to the experimental intervention rather than a host of extraneous variables" (p. 243). The most effective way of ensuring this is to use a control group. Therefore, only studies that had a true or quasi-experimental design were included. Each review generally grouped studies on the basis of either the outcomes objectives they were designed to measure (e.g., child cognitive gains or parent behaviors) or special program characteristics (e.g., were they home based or center based). The question to be asked is what did we learn, if anything, from all these studies of parent education? More specifically, what can parent education do, and under what conditions does parent education do what it can do best?

Effects on Cognitive Development and School Performance

This evaluation section is by far the most extensive, since most programs had specific outcome goals in this area. But before presenting the findings, issues concerning the use of IQ tests should be mentioned. The first issue is the cultural or class bias criticism of standardized IQ tests, which have been heard with increasing frequency. Although these criticisms are certainly relevant to many areas of academic decision making and to bias within the culture at large, they may be somewhat less germane to measurement of parent education outcomes. Since the goal of such programs is the promotion of school success, the use of IQ tests seems justified regardless of any bias inherent in the instrument. Use of gain in IQ scores to measure program success suggests that there has been a gain on a subgoal produced on an instrument that correlates with the further goal of school success. Of course, critics of the schools as presently constituted may quarrel with school success as a valid criterion measure—but that is a separate matter more suited to a discussion of social policy.

Other issues have been raised by Zigler and Trickett (1978) concerning the appropriateness of IQ as a measure for evaluating outcomes. They state that although IQ has high correlations with school performance (.70), nevertheless, these account for only half of the variance in school performance. They propose that there are additional factors beyond IQ that contribute to school success, and that these should also be measured. They contend that what programs really need to measure is social competence, which contributes to school success and of which school success is, moreover, merely a part. Although programs have increasingly focused on other indicators of cognitive abilities, as well as on other outcomes in general, the paucity of standardized measures for these other outcomes is a problem. IQ measures, on the other hand, are more sound psychometrically, and it is precisely those indicators that are most measurable that we tend to select.

Measurement of program effects on IQ has either been built into the initial program design, as with many longitudinal studies, or used in post hoc follow-up studies. The post hoc follow-up studies, unfortunately, tend to suffer from the problem of attrition. It could justifiably be argued that those subjects located differed in some significant way from the unlocated subjects, those who had died, moved, or refused to be reinterviewed.

As a group, parent education programs (like child-centered early education programs) have demonstrated moderate to high immediate IQ gains in program children. Longitudinal evaluations have indicated that the IQ effects of programs focused on parents have persisted into the elementary school years (Goodson & Hess, 1976; Lazar et al., 1977). While these IQ effects gradually decrease over time, their maintenance through the foundation-building grades is important. Relevant to the "fade-out" phenomenon of decrease in IQ effect over time is the following statement by Lazar et al.:

> Of course, changes in I.Q. (or any other index of social competence) involve a
> complex interaction over time between the potential the individual brings to the
> situation at any one point and the environment context. It is not realistic to
> expect that a relatively brief period of intervention would, in and of itself, result
> in *permanent* I.Q. changes, just as a single childhood innoculation does not
> produce life-long immunity to disease. The educational processes that the child
> goes through following early intervention are undoubtedly crucial to the
> maintenance or fading of early gains. (p. 22)

Because school success was a primary intervention goal of most of the evaluated programs, some indirect measures of cognitive abilities such as school performance are actually more direct measures of program goals than IQ tests. In terms of objective indicators of school performance, the following measures have been used: achievement tests, grade retention, and referral for and assignment to special education classes. Although few studies have used all these measures, their uncontestable face-validity and their relationships to social costs and benefits make them highly desirable for evaluating program outcomes.

Data concerning achievement in school measured either by achievement test scores or school grades suggest gain for program children. Results from the Early Training Project (Gray & Klaus, 1970) indicated significant differences between experimental and control children on a standardized achievement test through the second grade. (Differences remained through the fourth grade but were no longer significant.) Both Gray and Klaus and Lazar et al. (1977) point out the important role that the quality of the schooling the children receive after early intervention plays in maintaining results. Palmer (1977) reported that recent results from Levenstein's Mother–Child Home Program (Levenstein, 1970) showed differences in reading and arithmetic achievement test scores between experimental and control children. Achievement test scores from the Learning to Learn Program (Sprigle, 1974) indicated that in third grade, 2 years after program termination, more than 50% of the program children scored at or above their expected level while less than 20% of the control children did so. In addition, 92% of the program children were receiving passing grades, as compared to 60% of the control children.

Recent longer term results are even more encouraging concerning the persistence of achievement effects. Guinagh and Gordon (1976), in a follow-up of participants in the Florida Parent Education Program (Gordon & Guinagh, 1974) six years after program termination, found program children scored significantly higher than the control group on school achievement tests. The Ypsilanti Perry Preschool Project (Weber, Foster, & Weikart, 1978) found significant achievement differences between control and experimental groups at the eighth-grade level, 9 years after the completion of preschool.

Results from studies that measured special education placement and grade retention also indicate benefits from intervention efforts, including those with a parent focus. As Lazar *et al.* (1977) have stated, "The advantage of using these two outcomes as measures of effectiveness of early education programs is that they are concrete and stringent indicators of whether a child has performed acceptably within his or her educational institution" (p. 12). Weber *et al.* (1978) found that 9 years after program termination experimental children from the Ypsilanti Perry Preschool Project had fewer special education placements than control children. Likewise, Guinagh and Gordon (1976) found that six years after the termination of the Florida Parent Education Program significantly fewer experimental than control children were assigned to special education. Similar significant results were also achieved by Levenstein's and Gray's aforementioned projects. Lazar *et al.*, after reviewing these studies, concluded that

> Although the sample size for any individual project is rather small, certainly these data provide clear and strong evidence for the argument that supporting early education programs pays off. The cost of teaching a child in special education classes is substantially more than if he or she could perform acceptably in the normal classroom, to say nothing of the trauma to the child being labeled slow or retarded. (p. 15)

Although the data concerning grade retention are not as dramatic as those concerning special education placement, they do demonstrate reduced rates of failure for children from intervention programs. Lazar *et al.* (1977) reported results indicating that the programs of Gordon, Gray, and Weikart reduced the percentages of students held back in grade in the range of approximately 20% (Gray) to approximately 70% (Weikart). In Sprigle's Learning to Learn project, 2 years after program termination 26% of the program children were at or above their expected grade level compared with 8% of the control group. In addition, only 3% of the program children had fallen more than 1½ years, below grade level, compared with 32% of control children (cited in Goodson & Hess, 1976). Although early results from Levenstein's program indicated that fewer than 5% of the program children were not promoted to the next grade as compared to 16% of the controls, longer term evaluation (Lazar *et al.*, 1977) failed to show any significant differences.

The results from objective measures of school achievement have not been consistent in all areas; however, one can conclude on the basis of a limited sample that parent education programs can improve "children's ability to meet the minimal requirements of schools they enter" (Lazar *et al.*, 1977). Further, the results from the first 12 months of Home Start (Love *et al.*, 1976) suggest support for school readiness efforts. When four school readiness measures were pooled together, they showed a significant difference between Home Start and control children. (It should be noted, however, that these measures did not distinguish between Home Start and Head Start children.)

Less objective measures of school achievement and social-emotional development that have been used in some studies include teachers' ratings and students' self-reports. Guinagh and Gordon (1976), in a six-year follow-up, failed to find any significant differences on teachers' ratings between program and control children for the Florida Parent Education Program. Goodson and Hess (1976) reported the following results for teachers' ratings for children from three programs:

1. Teachers rated children from the Ypsilanti Perry Preschool Program significantly higher than control children through the second grade. Differences remained in the third grade but were no longer significant.
2. Results from Levenstein's Mother–Child Home Program indicated that program children were given consistently higher ratings than control children on their school psychosocial behavior. The program children were also judged by teachers to have significantly fewer academic and behavior problems.
3. In the Learning to Learn Program, 70% of the program children compared with 53% of the control children were rated as having an "appropriate self-concept." Ratings of achievement motivation indicated all program children were above the minimum level necessary for school success, as compared to only 8% of the control children.

Home Start children were also given ratings superior to controls on "test orientation" by teachers (Love *et al.*, 1976). Lazar *et al.* (1977) included a Youth Interview in their longitudinal follow-up studies of 14 preschool intervention programs, asking children to rate their own school performance. The program children, who were by this time in high school, were significantly more likely that the controls to rate themselves better than others in their schoolwork. (These programs combined both child-focused and parent-focused interventions; results were not broken down by type.[2])

Due to the paucity of studies attempting to assess these less objective outcomes as well as to the insufficiently standardized and psychometrically weak measures used, it is difficult to draw unambiguous conclusions. However, because of the role that such subjective measures can play in effecting more objective measures of achievement, they should not be treated casually. The halo effect is a commonly accepted fact of teacher–pupil relations. The relationship between teachers' expectations or categorizations and the classroom performance of children has been demonstrated by several researchers (Dusek & O'Connell, 1973; Mendels & Flanders, 1973; Rist, 1970). In addition, such motivational factors as self-image and expectancy of success are important ingredients of social and academic competence (Zigler & Trickett, 1978). Indeed, Bandura (1977) presented a theoretical framework for explaining behavioral change centered around the core importance of expectations of personal efficacy. Measures relating to these processes should surely be given increased attention. Newbrough, Dokecki, Dunlop, Hogge, and Simpkins (1978) suggest the need for such multi-method evaluation procedures as behavioral observations in the home and school, psychometric assessment of a broad band of child behavior patterns, and parent interviews. Of course, these procedures are expensive, and the cost should be weighed against careful evaluation of the kinds of information needed by decision makers.

Effects on Parental Behavior and Attitudes

Because the primary intervention goal of the parent education programs under review was to produce effects in the child that would lead to school success, most evaluation studies focused on child outcomes. A few, however, did measure intervention effects on the parents and the home environment. Such findings are important for two reasons. First, parent education interventions are supposed to work through the production of changes in the parents' behavior or in the quality of the environment in

---

[2] Two other variables that were part of the Youth Interview, dropout rates and educational aspirations, failed to show significant differences between participants and controls.

which the child is reared. Thus, evidence of changes in parental behavior or home environment indicate that the mediating processes thought to lead to changes for the child are taking place. And the absence of such changes might lead one to the alternative hypothesis—that child outcomes were brought about by program staff (rather than home) influences; thus, they might not be expected to continue once intervention ended. Second, several researchers have found significant correlations between maternal attitudes and children's cognitive and emotional functioning (Lazar & Chapman, 1972). One of the most powerful findings of Shipman, McKee, and Bridgeman (1977) in a six-year longitudinal study was that maternal expectations and aspirations were significantly related to childrens' achievement levels. Thus changes in these important variables could be thought to contribute to what Caldwell (1967) has called "the optimal learning environment" at home, and, therefore, to the child's success in school.

The results briefly summarized here are drawn from the most extensive generalized evaluation of parent education programs to date, that of Goodson and Hess (1976). Although Goodson and Hess examined 28 programs, only a few dealt with the variables under discussion. The number of programs that assessed each variable of interest is indicated in parenthesis.

1. Programs that assessed changes in parent–child interaction found significant program effects in parents' verbal and nonverbal behavior (e.g., teaching style or level of responsiveness):
   a. A significant increase in the use of supportive language was demonstrated (three programs);
   b. Program mothers decreased their use of negative feedback (in two of three programs);
   c. The language of program mothers became more elaborate; the mothers more often expanded on their child's verbalizations and elicited verbal responses from their child (three programs);
   d. Positive changes in mothers' language behavior during child-teaching situations were observed (six programs);
   e. Parents were judged to be more responsive, warmer, more sensitive, or more relaxed with their children (three programs);
   f. Parents were rated as participating more actively than control parents during interaction with their children (two programs).
2. Program families scored higher on measures designed to assess the quality of stimulation available in the home environment (five programs), but effects dropped off after intervention in some cases.
3. Changes were found for program parents in the area of parental attitudes;

    a. Program training significantly increases mothers' sense of personal efficacy (three programs);

    b. Mothers demonstrated positive changes in degree of flexibility in dealing with children and in developmental expectations (three of four programs).

Although these results are encouraging and point to the types of changes expected through parent education interventions, their conclusiveness is limited by the limited samples, difficulties in comparison of nonstandardized instruments across programs, and lack of longitudinal data (Goodson & Hess, 1976).

Finally, if the general response of parents to parent education programs can be considered an effect, then the programs have been an overwhelming success. No studies or reviews examined by us have failed to produce a parental consensus of satisfaction with the effects on their children. Lazar et al. (1977), in posing the question, "Was the program a good thing for your children?" elicited a 100% positive response from participants in home-based programs.

Other Outcomes

Home Start (Love et al., 1976) attempted to measure other outcomes in children, such as medical and dental care, physical development, and nutrition. Measures in the areas of medical and dental care were positive and conclusive after 12 months. However, when these children were compared to Head Start children, no significant differences were reported.

Outcomes in individuals other than the program child have been reported. Gray and Klaus (1970) found some evidence of a vertical diffusion of treatment effects to younger children of program siblings. Gilmer, Miller, and Gray (1970) compared diffusion effects in three types of program interventions with varying degrees of parental involvement. Siblings benefited most when parental involvement was greatest. Such effects can be considered a potential positive side effect of programs involving parents.

Summary of Outcome Effects

To summarize the examined outcome effects of early childhood interventions, including parent education programs:

1. Almost all programs were able to demonstrate an immediate

increase in IQ scores; several programs demonstrated continued effects during the critical years of the primary grades in school;

2. Program children often had higher achievement test scores than control groups in the early grades;

3. Strong long-term benefits in terms of fewer special education placements and grade retentions were demonstrated;

4. Teachers' ratings of program children were positively influenced, and self-evaluations of program children were higher than control children years after program termination;

5. The teaching behavior and attitudes of program parents were influenced in a positive direction;

6. Parents' response to such programs as being of benefit to their children was overwhelmingly positive;

7. Some potentiality for increasing health and dental care was demonstrated;

8. Limited evidence exists for program benefits transferring to younger children in the family.

These results certainly indicate encouraging potentialities for parent-focused early childhood intervention. Taken as a whole, the outcomes available at this time demonstrate a number of positive effects. Any unbridled enthusiasm, however, should be tempered by a number of considerations. In addition to the problems of comparability across studies mentioned in beginning this evaluation, there are other methodological difficulties. Primary among these are questions of potential motivational biases in self-selected program samples (Bronfenbrenner, 1974) and the possiblity that effects may be produced by nontreatment varibles such as social reinforcement dispensed by an enthusiastic and committed staff (Goodson & Hess, 1976). Furthermore, even granting that methodological limitations are negligible and can be taken at face value, there are questions of generalization and replication. The programs and studies generating the data presented here represent highly sophisticated conceptual and functional programs within the parent education field. Can such programs be considered representative of parent education efforts? And if one or several of these demonstration and research programs were to be selected for broad-based service delivery, would the quality demonstrated in the original endure in the replications? (See Dokecki et al., 1983, on issues of replication.)

A final caveat concerns the fact that these programs were mostly designed and implemented for the benefit of low-income families as part of an antipovery strategy. There has been (Amidon & Brim, 1972) and continues to be (Keniston, 1977; S. H. White, 1973) serious questioning of the impact that parent education programs can have on the complex of forces perpetuating poverty in this country. Modesty in the face of immense complexity and satisfaction with limited demonstrated accomplishments might be complementary virtues in such programs.

Influence of Program and Participant Characteristics on Outcomes

Even while the verdict was still out on the question whether or not any intervention was effective, increasing attention was being paid to attempting to identify the effects of different factors on program effectivenes. Some of the primary characteristics examined and the results pertaining to them are presented in the following section.

Program Format and Type of Involvement

The switch in the focus of intervention programs from children to parents was based on research indicating that degree of parental involvement made a difference in child outcomes. But once one has decided to focus on parents, the question becomes in exactly what way to focus. There are differences between merely giving parents information through various channels (e.g., discussion groups, lectures, printed material) and actually training them for the acquisition of specific skills. S. H. White (1973) concluded that the former approach has produced no useful evaluation results and was not successful. Lazar and Chapman (1972) also concluded that programs that had a primary focus on actually training parents were the most effective. Goodson and Hess (1976), in their extensive review, concluded that home visits either alone or in combination with preschool classes for children are associated with higher immediate gains and longer-lived effects than programs using classes for parents, either alone or in combination with the preschool classes. Love *et al.* (1976) also found that both frequency and duration of home visits were related to outcomes in the Home Start program. There has been only one report (Andrews, Blumenthal, Bache, & Wiener, 1975) of a group format being more effective than a home visit format. The weight of the evidence seems to favor the home visit format.

There are several possible factors contributing to these results. Bronfenbrenner (1974) has pointed out that the mother's perception of her role can be the crucial factor in a program. When parents see themselves as the primary agent of intervention and receive recognition for this role, they are more likely to accept responsibility for implementing and insuring the success of program models, both during the program and after the program termination. Karnes, Hodgins, Teska, and Kirk (1969) concluded that when attention, responsibility, or status is shifted away from the parent, the capacity of intervention programs to achieve lasting effects is impaired. The home visit format may support the parent in this primary position better than other formats. The home visit format may also allow for a greater degree of individualization of program content. Luscher (1977) has made a distinction between the societally generated, institutionalized knowledge of socialization (here parent education programs) and parents' personal knowledge of socialization (related to the development of their individual child). He contends that parent education can take place only if a connection is made between the institutionalized knowledge and the parents' knowledge of their own child. Home visits, which promote individualization, may create more opportunities for such connections to take place. Luscher also points to the need for parents to integrate the information into their own everyday existence (see also Dokecki *et al.*, 1983), something perhaps appropriate to the home visit format. But it is possible that exclusive concentration on home visiting misses the opportunity to achieve the benefits of peer interaction accuring to group programs for parents.

Program Content, Degree of Structure, and Detail of Information

A number of investigators have designed studies to validate systematically curriculum models (Karnes, Hodgins, Teska, & Kirk, 1969; Levenstein, 1970; Weikart, 1969). For the most part, particular program content has not seemed to make any difference in program effectiveness. Goodson and Hess (1976) divided the 28 programs they reviewed into three groups with different curricular foci (verbal development, sensory-motor development, and general cognitive development). They found no differences, either immediate or long term, among these three curricular emphases. They concluded:

> On the one hand, it can be cautiously concluded that no one content for parent programs (as described in program materials) consistently produced higher or more stable gains for program children. On the other hand, this statement by itself is incomplete. Certain factors in parent programs other than content seem to make a difference. An example is the validity of the curriculum in the parents' eyes. Further, it seems that the content of a curriculum may be less important in determining program effectiveness than how the curriculum involves parents. (p. 36)

Programs also vary in the degree of structure they contain. Goodson and Hess divided the 28 programs they reviewed into two groups: seven with "high structure" (those with a sequence of predetermined concrete tasks for parents), and the 21 others, which were judged to have medium structure. Degree of structure appeared to be related to the stability of gains, with higher-structured programs having better long-term effectiveness. Goodson and Hess suggested that the concrete activities of high structure may lead to the development of a longer lasting repertoire of new skills. They also pointed to possible benefits of less structure, in that tasks can be individualized for each parent. Stevens (1978) pointed out the necessity for a balance between structure based on clear objectives and personalization of the structure to accomodate differences. Although structure seems to have some role in program effectiveness, the specificity of degree of detail in instruction to parents does not seem to matter. Goodson and Hess found that level of specificity was not related to greater program effectiveness, either immediate or long term. In support of this, Love *et al.* (1976) found that in Home Start the amount of time spent on any particular program component was not related to outcome.

Other Program Characteristics

Since the active participation of parents is so obviously important, any information bearing on increasing or decreasing parental participation in preschool interventions is worth noting. Bauch *et al.* (1973) identified the size of the center as an important factor in parent participation in Head Start programs. Small centers seemed more likely to engage parents in activities. Bronfenbrenner (1974) pointed out that, for some people, going out to group meetings might be less threatening than being taught by a stranger in one's own home. If this is the case, then even though individualized approaches appear more effective, group meetings may have a role in fostering participation (and peer interaction, as noted above). In these cases, as Lazar and Chapman (1972) have pointed out, the skill and sensitivity of the group leader or trainer is crucial in gaining initial attendance and maintaining participation. And concerning program staff, there has been no evidence to suggest that paraprofessionals are any less effective than professional staff persons.

Age of Entry and Duration of Treatment

Palmer (1977) has stated that, in terms of early childhood education programming, whether preschool or parent education, there is not much evidence to indicate that one treatment is better than another as long as age and duration of treatment are held constant. The effects of these variables themselves, however, are of interest. Bronfenbrenner (1974) concluded that parent-centered approaches, unlike compensatory preschool interventions, are more effective in the long run the earlier they are begun, especially if begun during the first three years of life. Lazar *et al.* (1977) concluded from the data from 14 longitudinal studies that "there is now no indication of a 'magic age' at which early intervention is most effective" (p. 28).

There may, however, be a minimal amount of intervention necessary for parent education programs. Stevens (1978) has suggested that programs with durations of 18 to 24 months have been most effective. He concluded: "Long-term consultation that changed in keeping with the increased competence of the parent and the child appeared to be critically important for substantial and sustained changes" (p. 60). One study found further that no treatment at all may be better than too little. Lambie, Bond, and Weikart (1975) actually found negative effects on children's functioning in their minimal treatment group.

Actually, the two variables under discussion have quite often been confounded, since the programs that have lasted longer have also often begun at an earlier age.

Characteristics of Program Participants

Bronfenbrenner (1974) suggested that certain characteristics of program participants could have a greater predictive power for program success than internal program features. Increasing research efforts have been made to identify characteristics of program participants that might influence program outcomes. Murray (1977) conducted a study designed to assess specifically the impact of family characteristics. He examined data from 11 of the studies examined by Lazar *et al.* (1977) and used IQ as a dependent measure. He used measures of mothers' educational level, family socioeconomic status, number of siblings, and birth order and found no effects of these variables on the outcome of intervention, as measured by IQ.

Interestingly, when the focus of family characteristics is broadened to include the kinship system, more instructive results are obtained. Farber, Harvey, and Lewis (1969) found that the particular kinship pattern of a family had more influence on children's performance than program variables. Newbrough *et al.* (1978) provided the following summary:

According to [the Farber research] report of findings, individual kinship organization systems affected children's developing competence by means of socializa-

tion practices that were consistent with their norms. He maintained that the fit
or lack of fit between a particular kinship pattern and the political, economic,
and educational systems of modern American society influenced the functioning
of families, the intellectual competence of their preschool children, and the
ability of the children to profit from educational programs. (p. 51)

Results reported by Kessen and Fein (1975) also support the importance of
examining this broader perspective. They found that, independent of
social class, families with extensive kin relations or extended households—
as compared to those with more restricted relationships—were more
responsive to home-visiting programs.

Summary of Influences on Program Outcomes

A summary of the findings related in the above sections can be briefly
encompassed in groups of variables. Those which seem to have important
impacts on program outcomes are: (a) program format, with a home visit
approach being favored because of one-to-one format, personalization of
program content, and emphasis given to mothers in the role of primary
caregiver; (b) structure of program, with higher structure leading to greater
stability of gains; (c) duration of program, with some evidence that a
minimum length of 18 months is indicated; and (d) type of extended kin
network and its fit with program approach. Those variables that showed
no significant effects on program outcomes were: (a) age of child, (b)
curriculum type, (c) degree of detail in instruction, and (d) paraprofessional staff versus professional staff.

A Return to the Framework: An Emerging Model

Even while the data were being collected on the programs developed
from the parent-focused antipoverty model described earlier and outlined
in the last columns of Table 1, changes in the thinking about and nature of
parent education programs continued. We use the Parent–Child Development Center (PCDC) Project (Dokecki *et al.*, 1983) as an illustration of
several of the changes that took place. The PCDC Project was created to be
the research arm of the Parent–Child Centers (PCCs). It was established in
1969 and charged with the tasks of defining program goals and treatments
and developing appropriate evaluation strategies and instruments. The
PCDCs became experimental research and demonstration programs that
delivered comprehensive social support services to low-income families.
Although the PCDCs are performing important functions in terms of

examining the process of program replication, the major interest here involves the new perspectives that they represent.

First, the PCDC Project was initially established at three different sites with three diverse populations. In Birmingham, the PCDC serves a biracial white and black population; in Houston, it serves bicultural and bilingual Mexican-Americans, and in New Orleans, inner-city black families. What was unique about the PCDC Project was that each site developed its own approach to fit the needs and circumstances of its particular community. This approach was a conscious attempt to recognize and respect the implications of an emerging theoretical perspective in developmental psychology: the ecological approach, which views the child and the family as embedded in a particular context that has important consequences for development. Bronfenbrenner (1974) has identified several levels of variables that can mutually interact in complex ways to affect developmental outcomes. The PCDC projects, in being specifically planned and implemented for each community, have recognized the importance of adapting educational interventions to community characteristics (Harmon, 1971).

Secondly, the PCDC projects, by utilizing an adult pedagogical model for their interventions, gradually moved beyond a deficit orientation and expert professional position. The PCDC adult pedagogy is built on the assumption that parents can express their needs and can accept, reject, or translate educational material by experimenting with it in their life circumstances. This orientation emphasizes the strengths of the low-income family members involved and is based on a "cultural difference model" (Dokecki et al., 1975), which avoids ascribing the causation of problems to deficits within the people experiencing such problems. Furthermore, rather than attempting to train parents in a "one best way" fashion, this orientation seeks to facilitate self-determined behavior that meets self-expressed needs (Weikart, 1977). The parent moves from being a passive recipient of "expert" information, whose need is assessed by and delivered through the professional, to an active collaborator in a process of self-development (Dokecki, Roberts, & Moroney, 1979).

Finally, the PCDC Project broadens the range of services delivered to parents and thus expands the scope of parent education. The traditional focus in parent education was on interventions designed to effect changes in parent knowledge, attitudes, and behavior as focused on the child, usually specifically designed to develop school-related competencies. The PCDC approach not only focused on facilitating the parents' abilities to rear their children and to negotiate successfully transactions with societal institutions (development of the "executive function"), but also promoted objectives and activities that went beyond the parental role and sought to meet the needs of parents as adults.

The PCDC Project results indicate the success of the new perspectives that these programs implemented. Newbrough *et al.* (1978) summarized these results as follows:

> Significant differences or trends between randomly assigned experimental and control groups were found in the development of mothers' attitudes, knowledge, beliefs, and skills both as adult individuals and as parents. Differences were also found in mother–infant interactions on a variety of cognitive and social child outcomes at 36 months of age. Mother and child program effects have persisted beyond program termination to at least 48 months of age. (p. 48)[3]

Not for the Poor Alone

The PCDC Project reflected emerging changes in parent education thinking as applied to low-income and minority groups. One of the major recent changes, however, is the consideration of parent education as of potential support to *all* families. For although parent education programs in isolation from other policy efforts may have less than a controlling role to play in the elimination of poverty in this country, there is another far-reaching problem to which parent education interventions can be applied—the stresses and strains presently experienced by today's families. A major shift in the broad societal context in America during the past decade has been from concern with *problem* families to concern with *all* families.

The suggestion that parent education may be one approach to strengthening and supporting the functioning of all families and not just subgroups emerges from several perspectives. These include:

1. Value analysis, which questions the philosophical underpinnings of social policy in general and which leads to a call for governmental support of all families as a critical means to creation of a "caring and competent society" (Dokecki & Moroney, 1979);
2. Rationales based on a belief that the knowledge ordinarily accumulated by parents has been made obsolete by rapid economic, cultural, and social change and that new knowledge from scientific developments can meet their needs (Luscher, 1977);
3. The idea that becoming a parent is a crucial role transition, which in the modern American family has been made more stressful by the

---

[3] See recent findings by Bridgeman, Hilton, Blumenthal, and Andrews (1980), which present a somewhat less positive picture of PCDC findings, reflecting a variety of political and economic developments since the early evaluation findings were reported.

diminishment of traditional (e.g., extended family) social support networks (Wandersman, 1978);

4. Rationales based on social indicators believed no reflect increased pressures on all families (Minnesota Council on Quality Education, 1979);

5. Self-expressed desire for parent education from large percentages of parents in all spectrums of society (LeMasters, 1957; Yankelovich, Skelly, & White, 1977);

6. Primary prevention arguments in which parent training is seen as developing competence in children and thus preventing mental health problems (Cowen, 1977; Gordon, 1977; Hobbs, 1975; White, 1980);

7. Empirical results indicating that effective parenting styles are not simply related to socioeconomic status (Epstein & Evans, 1979; Shipman *et al.*, 1977).

Strengthening All Families

The combination of these perspectives and rationales has created a shift to an all-families concern. By combining this shift with the changes illustrated in the PCDC Project, we have created a major new model for parent education programs, as presented in Table 2. The major goal at the societal level is the strengthening of all families. The societal problem is the stress presently being experienced by families and social indicators of familial disruption and turbulence. The value sought is strong families as

Table 2. An Emerging Model of Parent Education

Broad societal context	
Goals	Strengthening all families
Societal problem	Familial stress and social indicators of turbulence in response to modern society
Values	Strong families as means to a caring and competent society
Intervention/area strategy	Influences on family functioning and parent and family education
Intervention components	
Knowledge base	Ecology of human and family development
Program goals	Nurture family development through supporting parent roles (direct and executive) and parents' needs as adults
Core approach to intervention	Variety of program needs defined by family, with professional person as resource to family
Focus of intervention	Family as an organized system

to means to a "caring and competent society" (Dokecki & Moroney, 1983). The intervention area of concern is family functioning, and what we now call "parent and family education" is merely one of the strategies. The intervention components consist of a theoretical base of the ecology of human and family development (still in its infancy as an empirical knowledge base), program goals related to the needs of parents for information and skills in both parenting and executive function roles, a core approach of community compatible programs ideally integrated within naturally occurring institution–family contact points, and a focus on the family as a whole.

Service Delivery Issues

Given this perspective, what basic themes have emerged from our review and analysis that might be applied in the future? By way of summary and conclusion: The basic themes that emerged answer four basic questions. These questions are: (a) What is the content of parent education programs? (b) Who are appropriate participants in parent education? (c) What kinds of effects do parent education programs have? (d) How can parent education programs be delivered?

What Is the Content of Parent Education Programs?

We have seen that the content of parent education program has both changed and expanded considerably. Our historical analysis traced the shift to parents as a focus of early childhood interventions. But more importantly, our analysis of the contemporary scene points to an expansion of program content. The traditional approach in parent education stressed information and training directly related to parent–child interaction. Although this approach remains a major component of program services, attention is increasingly being directed to facilitating parents in their role as family managers and supporting their personal needs as adults. Family management functions are exemplified by programs that address family executive functions, acknowledging parents as coordinators of all types of services and experiences for their children and seeking to help parents become more successful in negotiating transactions with societal institutions. Support for parents as adults with their own needs is illustrated by programs that seek to ease the transition into the parenting role or provide services that ease some of the demands of parenthood (e.g., cooperative child care). As the many facets involved in the transition to and performance of the parenting role are identified, we are likely to see more multiple-focus programs. It is as though we are emerging from a simplisitic content orientation to parent education, in which just teaching child development or child-rearing skills was sufficient, and moving toward a process orientation in which the multiple needs of adults as people entering a complex new role must be addressed. Within this chapter, the multiple-demand nature of family roles, including but transcending parent–child relationships, is acknowledged by a shift to the term *parent and family education*.

Who Are the Appropriate Participants in Parent Education Programs?

We have noted several arguments, ranging from value analysis and self-expressed desires to social indicators and research results, that parent and family education may be one approach to strengthening and supporting the functioning of *all* families rather than just low-income families. And, in fact, when the current landscape of parent education programs is examined, the most numerous group served turns out to be middle-class families(Florin, 1980). Clearly, the issue is not whether parent and family education programs should be extended to groups other than the poor—programs for poor families comprise only a small number of these programs. Rather the issue involves developing a rationale for governmental support of parent and family education programs for groups other than the poor (see Dokecki & Moroney, 1983). Another area of expansion in parent and family education programming has been age. Because of both the alarming number of teenage pregnancies and a general concern for parenthood education, there has been a rapid growth of parent and family programs for the youth of our nation. In fact, the largest single parent and family education program we have come across is the "Education for Parenthood" program, now ongoing in more than 2,600 schools across the country.

What Are the Effects of Parent Education Programs?

Here we naturally look to the research evaluations of parent education programs. Doing so, we move from an expansive focus to a very constricted one. It is not that the results of the program evaluations have been unfavorable. We noted several positive outcomes from these programs, especially highlighted by the more longitudinal studies examining school performance. In fact, after examining the same literature, no less a source that the United States General Accounting Office (Duffy, 1979) concluded that parent and family education programs focused on prevention would be a good investment for the nation. Rather, the sense of constriction comes from recognizing the extremely circumscribed nature of the data utilized. Not only were the data drawn from populations limited for the most part to lower socioeconomic groups, but most research questions focused only on a narrow range of child outcomes. This is not to say that these evaluations are useless or were badly designed. The questions asked were those that appeared most appropriate at the time. But we should recognize that, although they make an empirical contribution, they are far from comprehensive in their answer to our question. The newer conceptual developments and programs in the field (Florin, 1980), focusing on the multiple complexities of family functioning, will take equally complex methodologies to measure. We will have to wait for rigorous evaluations of whether the family's executive functions, for example, can be enhanced by programs, or whether parenthood education results in improved decision making regarding child rearing by adolescent parents. Until that time, we must function on intuition, belief, and program experience. Part of the program experience that is encouraging is the fact that the overwhelming majority of parents exposed to parent and family education programs report extremely positive reactions to the programs. This in itself seems a potent argument for the continuing operation and expansion of such programs.

How Can Parent Education Programs Be Delivered?

When we pull back from the close-up view supplied by our empirical research focus, we again encounter a broad and dynamic panorama: There is a large amount of parent and family education activity going on in this nation (Florin, 1980). Our question addresses the nature of service delivery for these activities. Two issues emerge. The first involves the relationship between the service deliverer, usually a professional, and the recipient of these services. This relationship has begun to change from the traditional stance, in which the so-called expert professional delivers services to a passive recipient, to a more collaborative relationship, in which there is a partnership in needs assessment and service delivery. In this latter mode, professionals serve as resources for families who define their own needs and play an active role in a process of self-development. This shift has its foundation in a respect for the competence of adults engaged in self-directed learning, a recognition of the important idiosyncratic knowledge that parents have of their own children and situations, and a responsibility to be accountable to recipients of services. (For a more detailed discussion of this shift, see Dokecki *et al.*, 1979.) The second service delivery issue involves the question of diversity. When we examined the present and emerging parent and family education programs (Florin, 1980), we noted a wide variety of approaches to service delivery. Intercommunity diversity is manifest, in that institutions or organizations most active in promoting parent and family education activities in one community might be totally inactive in other communities. This diversity is evident following an examination of the schools as general service delivery vehicles for parents and family education. As Levine (1978) concluded on the issue of day care, the public schools might be extraordinarily well suited for service delivery in one community while being totally ineffectual in another. Furthermore, diversity can also be manifest *within* given communities. Different cultural, racial, or economic groups might respond differently to the same community institution. These types of diversity present a severe challenge to those seeking to identify the "one best" service delivery vehicle for parent and family education services. The problems posed by this diversity can be addressed by adapting educational intervention to the particular characteristics of individual communities. This "community compatible" programming might be addressed through existing neighborhood or community organizations. Communities would be asked to take responsibility for the support and nurturance of their resident families and thus to attempt to promote human development (see Dokecki & Moroney, 1983 for an extended discussion of this issue). In this way, the existing patterns of ongoing change within communities would be marshalled to meet community-defined needs in ways most adapted to the particular indigenous mechanisms for change (Harmon, 1971). The rapid growth of the mutual help and neighborhood and community development movements (Florin, 1980) promises the availability of vehicles and energies for such enterprises. The challenge to national policy makers interested in promoting parent and family education services is to design and implement large-scale mechanisms while respecting the problems and potentials residing in diversity. Whether this challenge will be successfully met remains to be seen.

References

Ainsworth, M. *Discussion of three models for parent education*. Paper presented at the biannual meeting of the Society for Research in Child Development, Denver, April 1975.

Amidon, A., & Brim, O. G., Jr. *What do children have to gain from parent education?*

Prepared for the Advisory Committee on Child Development. National Research Council, National Academy of Sciences, 1972.

Andrews, S. R., Blumenthal, J. M., Bache, W. L., & Wiener, G. *The New Orleans Model: Parents as early childhood educators.* Paper presented at the biannual meeting of the Society for Research in Child Development, Denver, April 1975.

Bandura, A. Self-efficacy: Towards unifying theory of behavior change. *Psychological Review*, 1977, *89*, 191–215.

Bauch, J. P., Vietze, P. M., & Morris, V. D. What makes the difference in parental participation? *Childhood Education*, 1973, *59*, 47–54.

Berger, P. L., & Neuhaus, R. J. *To empower people. The role of mediating structures in public policy.* Washington, D.C.: American Enterprise Institute for Public Policy Research, 1977.

Biber, B. *Goals and methods in a preschool program for disadvantaged children.* New York: Bank Street College of Education, 1970.

Bloom, B. S. *Stability and change in human characteristics.* New York: John Wiley & Sons, 1964.

Bridgeman, B., Hilton, T. L., Blumenthal, J., & Andrews, S. *Parent-child development centers: Long-term and short-term results.* Paper presented at the annual meeting of the American Psychological Association, Montreal, Canada, September 1980.

Bronfenbrenner, U. *Is early intervention effective? A report on longitudinal evaluations of preschool programs* (Vol. 2). Washington, D.C.: Department of HEW, Office of Child Development, 1974.

Bronfenbrenner, U. Who needs parent education? *Teachers College Record*, 1978, *79*, 767–788.

Caldwell, B. What is the optimal learning environment for the young child? *American Journal of Orthopsychiatry*, 1967, *37*, 8–21.

Cowen, E. L. Baby-steps toward primary prevention. *American Journal of Community Psychology*, 1977, *5*, 1.

Dokecki, P. R. Bureaucratic schools and families: Toward a renegotiation with policy implications. *Peabody Journal of Education*, 1977, *55*, 56–62.

Dokecki, P. R., Hargrove, E. C., & Sandler, H. M. An overview of the Parent Child Development Center social experiment. In R. Haskins (Ed.), *Parent education and public policy.* Norwood, N.J.: Ablex, 1983.

Dokecki, P. R., & Moroney, R. M. *To strengthen families: Value analysis.* Unpublished manuscript, Center for the Study of Families and Children, Vanderbilt Institute for Public Policy Studies, August 1979.

Dokecki, P. R., & Moroney, R. M. To strengthen all families: A human development and community value framework. In R. Haskins (Ed.), *Parent education and public policy.* Norwood, N.J.: Ablex, 1983.

Dokecki, P. R., Roberts, F. B., & Moroney, R. M. *Families and professional psychology: Policy implications for training and service.* Paper presented at the annual meeting of the American Psychological Association, New York, September 1979.

Dokecki, P. R., Strain, B. A., Bernal, J. F., Brown, C. S., & Robinson, M. E. Low-income and minority groups. In N. Hobbs (Ed.), *Issues in the classification of children.* San Francisco: Jossey-Bass, 1975.

Duffy, D. A. *Findings of a national study of early childhood and family development programs prepared for Congress.* Paper presented at the annual meeting of the American Psychological Association, New York, September 1979.

Dusek, J. B., & O'Connell, E. J. Teacher expectancy effects on achievement test performance of elementary school children. *Journal of Educational Psychology*, 1973, *65*, 371–377.

Epstein, A. S., & Evans, J. Parent-child interaction and children's learning. *High/Scope Report.* Number 4. Ypsilanti, Michigan, 1979.

Farber, B., Harvey, D. L., & Lewis, M. *Research and development program on preschool disadvantaged children: Community, kinship and competence: Final report.* Washington, D.C.: U.S. Office of Education, 1969.

Fein, G. G. The informed parent. In S. Kilmer (Ed.), *Advances in early education and day care* (Vol. 1). Greenwich, Conn.: JAI Press, 1980.

Florin, P. R. *Parent education: New models, new modes.* Unpublished manuscript, George Peabody College of Vanderbilt Univeristy, 1980.

Gilmer, B., Miller, J. O., & Gray, S. M. *Intervention with mothers and young children: Study of intra-family effects.* Nashville, Tenn.: Demonstration and Research Center for Early Education, 1970.

Goodson, B. D., & Hess, R. D. *The effects of parent training programs on child performance and parent behavior.* Unpublished Manuscript, Stanford University, 1976.

Gordon, I. J. Parent education and parent involvement: Retrospect and prospect. *Childhood Education*, 1977, 54, 71-79.

Gordon, I. J., & Guinagh, B. J. *A home learning approach to early stimulation: Final report.* Washington, D.C.: National Institute of Mental Health, 1974.

Gray, S. W., & Klaus, R. A. The Early Training Project: A seventh year report. *Child Development*, 1970, 41, 909-924.

Guinagh, B. J., & Gordon, I. J. *School performance as a function of early stimulation. Final report.* Gainesville, Fla.: Institute for Development of Human Resources, 1976.

Harmon, D. *Programming for social change: Theory and method.* Paper submitted to the United Nations Children's Fund, December 1971.

Hayes, D., & Grether, J. *The school year and vacation: When do students learn?* Paper presented at the Eastern Sociological Convention, New York, 1969.

Hobbs, N. *The futures of children.* San Francisco: Jossey-Bass, 1975.

Hunt, J. McV. *Intelligence and experience.* New York: Ronald Press, 1961.

Hurt, M., & Quellet, R. H. *Parenting skills: Comparability study.* Washington, D.C.: George Washington University, Social Research Group, 1975.

Jensen, A. R. How much can we boost I.Q. and scholastic achievement? *Harvard Educational Review*, 1969, 39, 1-123.

Karnes, M. S., Hodgins, A. S., Teska, J. A., & Kirk, S. *A research and development program on preschool disadvantaged children.* Unpublished Manuscript, Urbana, Ill., 1969.

Keniston, K. *All our children. The American family under pressure.* New York: Harcourt Brace Jovanovich, 1977.

Kessen, W., & Fein, G. *Variation in home-based infant education: Language, play and social development. Final report.* Washington, D.C.: U.S. Office of Child Development, 1975.

Lambie, D. Z., Bond, J. T., & Weikart, D. P. Framework for infant education. In B. Z. Friedlander, G. N. Sterritt, & G. E. Kirk (Eds.), *Exceptional infant: Assessment and intervention*, Vol. 3. New York: Brunner/Mazel, 1975.

Lasch, C. *Haven in a heartless world: The family beseiged.* New York: Basic Books, 1977.

Lazar, I., Hubbell, V. R., Murray, H., Rosche, M., & Royce, J. *Summary: The persistence of preschool effects.* Publication No. (OHDS) 78-30129, Washington, D.C.: U.S. Government Printing Office, 1977.

Lazar, J. B., & Chapman, J. E. *A review of the present status and future research needs of programs to develop parenting skills.* Paper prepared for The Interagency Panel on Early Childhood Research and Development, 1972.

LeMasters, E. E. Parenthood as crisis. *Marriage and Family Living*, 1957, 19, 352-355.

Levenstein, P. Cognitive growth in preschoolers through verbal interaction with mothers. *American Journal of Orthopsychiatry*, 1970, 40, 426-432.

Levine, J. A. *Day care and the public schools.* Newton, Mass.: Education Development Center, Inc., 1978.

Love, J. M., Nauta, M. J., Coelen, C. G., Hewett, K., & Ruopp, R. R. *Home Start evaluation study*. Cambridge: Abt Associates, 1976.

Luscher, K. *Knowledge on socialization*. Paper presented at the Cornell University conference on Research Perspectives in the Ecology of Human Development, Ithaca, N.Y., August 1977.

Mallory, B. L. *Project Head Start: The interaction of policy making and program evaluation*. Unpublished manuscript, Center for the Study of Families and Children, Vanderbilt Institute for Public Policy Studies, Nashville, Tenn., May 1979.

Mann, A. J., Harrell, A., & Hurt, M. *A review of Head Start research since 1968*. Washington, D.C.: Office of Child Development, 1976.

Mendels, G. E., & Flanders, J. P. Teacher expectations and pupil performance. *American Educational Research Journal*, 1973, *10*, 203–212.

MIDCO Educational Associates. *Perspectives on parent participation in Head Start: An analysis and critique*. (Prepared under contract No. HEW-05-72-45.) Washington, D.C.: Project Head Start, Office of Child Development, Department of HEW, 1972.

Minnesota Council on Quality Education. *A policy study of issues related to early childhood and family education in Minnesota*. State Department of Education, St. Paul, Minn., January 1979.

Murray, H. W. *Early intervention in the context of family characteristics*. Paper presented at the annual meeting of the American Orthopsychiatric Association, April 1977.

Newbrough, J. R., Dokecki, P. R., Dunlop, K. H., Hogge, J. H., & Simpkins, C. G. *Families and family-institution transactions in child development: An analysis of the family research program of HEW's Administration for Children, Youth and Families*. Center for Community Studies, George Peabody College, Nashville, Tenn. 1978.

Palmer, F. H. *The effects of early childhood intervention*. Paper presented at annual meeting of the American Association for the Advancement of Science, Denver, Colo. 1977.

Powell, D. R. Organizational problems in institutionalizing parent education in the public schools. In *Families and schools: Implementing parent education*. Denver, Colo.: Education Commission of the States, 1979.

Radin, N. Three degrees of maternal involvement in a preschool program: Impact on mothers and children. *Child Development*, 1972, *43*, 1355–1365.

Rist, R. C. Student social class and teacher expectations: The self-fulfilling prophecy in ghetto education. *Harvard Educational Review*, 1970, *40*, 411–451.

Sameroff, A. J., & Chandler, M. J. Reproductive risk and the continuum of caretaking causality. In F. D. Horowitz (Ed.), *Review of child development research* (Vol. 4). Chicago, Ill.: University of Chicago Press, 1975.

Schlossman, S. L. Before Home Start: Notes toward a history of parent education in America, 1897–1929. *Harvard Educational Review*, 1976, *46*, 436–467.

Schlossman, S. The parent education game: The politics of child psychology in the 1970s. *Teachers College Record*. 1978, *79*, 788–808.

Shipman, V. C., McKee, D., & Bridgman, B. *Stability and change in family status, situational and process variables, and their relationship to children*. Princeton, N.J.: Educational Testing Service, 1977.

Sprigle, H. A. *The learning to learn teacher education program*. Jacksonville, Fla.: Learning to Learn School, 1974.

Stevens, J. H., Jr. Parent education programs. What determines effectiveness? *Young Children*, 1978, *33*, 59–65.

Wandersman, L. P. Parenting groups to support the adjustment to parenthood. *Family Perspectives*, 1978, *12*, 117–128.

Weber, C. U., Foster, P. W., & Weikert, D. P. An economic analysis of the Ypsilanti Perry

Preschool Project. *Monographs of the High/Scope Educational Research Foundation*, No. 5, 1978.

Weikart, D. P. *A comparative study of three preschool curricula.* A paper presented at the biannual meeting of the Society for Research in Child Development, Santa Monica, Calif., March 1969.

Weikart, D. P. *Designing parenting education programs.* Paper presented at the Working Conference on Parenting Education, Flint, Michigan, September 1977.

Westinghouse Learning Corporation. *The impact of Head Start: An evaluation of the Head Start experience on children's cognitive and affective development.* Athens, Ohio: Ohio University Press, 1969.

White, B. L. Primary prevention: Beginning at the beginning. *The Personnel and Guidance Journal*, 1980, *58*, 338–344.

White, S. H. *Federal programs for young children: Review and recommendations. Vol. II: Review of evaluation data for Federally sponsored projects for children.* (Contract No. HEW-0S-71-170). Publication No. (0S)74-102. Washington, D.C.: U.S. Government Printing Office, 1973.

Yankelovich, Skelly & White, Inc. *Raising children in a changing society.* Minneapolis, Minn.: General Mills, Inc., 1977.

Zigler, E., & Trickett, P. K. IQ, social competence and evaluation of early childhood intervention programs. *American Psychologist*, 1978, *33*, 789–798.

CHAPTER 3

A Balancing Act

Preserving Family Autonomy and Protecting the Child

PHYLLIS W. BECK

Introduction

Legal policy in the United States relating to the family is based on two deep, firmly-held convictions: one, that the internal life of the family is immune from government interference unless the state can demonstrate a significant reason to intervene (Westin, 1967) and two, that both the family and its individual members have constitutionally guaranteed privacy rights (*Roe* v. *Wade*, 1973).[1] Nevertheless, the government has inter-meddled in family affairs and continues to do so at a sharply escalating rate. Such intrusion is omnipresent (Morris, Giller, Geach, & Szwed, 1980). It occurs each time any branch of the government, and especially the bureaucracy, takes action which affects the family and the individual members in it.

The foundation of the state's authority is predicated on two inherent, vaguely contoured, sources: the police power and the power of the state under the *parens patriae* doctrine (Harvard Law Review, 1980). The police power enables the state to act in order to safeguard the health, morals, and welfare of the community. In contrast, under the doctrine of parens patriae, the state intervenes not for the welfare of the community but of the individual child. Neither power is enumerated in the Constitution, but

---

[1]*Roe* v. *Wade* established privacy rights pursuant to the liberty provision of the Fifth and Fourteenth Amendments to the United States Constitution.

PHYLLIS W. BECK • Associate Judge, Superior Court of Pennsylvania, Suite 606, One Montgomery Plaza, Norristown, Pennsylvania 19401.

derives from the government's inherent authority to act as organizer, protector, and custodian of the community and also of the individual child. The state's power is, however, limited by the Constitution, which is a document restraining governmental authority by providing forceful safeguards to individual freedom and liberty.

Some governmental action is benign—such as laws relating to social benefits for the underclass, compulsory education, and vaccination against disease.

Some governmental action is mischievous—such as laws mandating spousal or parental consent as a precondition of abortion (*Planned Parenthood of Central Missouri* v. *Danforth, 1976; Bellotti* v. *Baird,* 1979) and restrictions on sale and distribution of birth control devices (*Carey* v. *Population Services International,* 1977).

Much governmental action begins as benign but as it progresses becomes counterproductive and even harmful. Examples in this category are juvenile court systems (Katz, 1970; Paulsen, 1966) and foster care placement schemes (Mnookin, 1973).

Governmental regulation relating to the family can be categorized as (1) laws which pit the authority of the government against the authority of the family, (2) action which pits the government against the child, and (3) laws which meddle with the parent–child relationship.

If the world were perfect, families would be parented by knowledgeable, caring, well-meaning, and loving adults. The parents' psychological health and economic resources would be adequate. The government could be persuaded—perhaps—to mind its own business. The state would have no reason to activate its so-called protective function toward the family. Parents would voluntarily and knowingly behave so as to nurture properly their children. However, an idealized world with perfect families is a goal impossible to achieve. The reality is that families at the margin of society are barely able to function on a day-in, day-out basis.

Where the family is inadequate or disintegrating, the government has taken upon itself to exercise its protective function. The extent to which the government can inject itself legally and the extent to which it should inject itself socially is the subject of this chapter.

Laws Which Pit the Authority of the State against the Authority of the Family

Government intervention is not limited to buttressing the marginal family. Its power is also exercised within a moral and educational dimension. The government attenuates the legitimacy of the family when it divests the family of control over certain aspects of its internal life. Some laws establish the states' authority as superior to parents'. Examples of these laws are regulations governing mandatory education for children. In these instances, the states usurp from the parents the authority to decide if their children should be vaccinated or should go to school.

Oregon passed a law mandating not only that all children attend school, but that they attend public schools (*Pierce* v. *Society of Sisters*, 1925). The law denied parents the option to select parochial or private education for their children. In 1925, the United States Supreme Court found the law unconstitutional, since it offended the fundamental liberty of parents, by denying them freedom of choice to make educational decisions for their children. The power of the state to impose reasonable regulations over basic education was made to yield to the right of parents to provide an equivalent education in a privately operated system.

A harder case relating to public education turned on a Wisconsin statute which mandated that children remain in school until they reach the age of 16 (*Wisconsin* v. *Yoder*, 1972). This curtailment of parental freedom to withdraw their children at an earlier age violated the religious beliefs and customs of the state's large Amish community. Amish parents refused to surrender their children after the eighth grade to the public schools. The United States Supreme Court again trumpeted the independence of the family and struck the Wisconsin law as violative of the parents' First Amendment rights, specifically, their freedom to exercise their religious prerogatives.

In other realms, the state interferes not with parents' rights to reasonable superintendence over their children but with the right of the family itself to privacy. The state seeks to establish a moral standard for family members, thereby encroaching on the family's right to determine its own private conduct. A Connecticut law made the sale and use of birth control devices criminal (*Griswold* v. *Connecticut*, 1965). Challengers of the law maintained that it offended family privacy; it invaded the sanctum of the married couple's bedroom. In 1965, the Supreme Court found that the right of family privacy which derived from the "penumbras" of different portions of the Constitution was more pressing than the state's reasons to ban birth control. It struck the Connecticut law.

The line of Supreme Court decisions heralding personal and family privacy reached its climax in 1973 when the Supreme Court denied states the authority to pass laws forbidding early abortion (*Roe* v. *Wade*, 1973).

The states' attempts to erode family autonomy or to invade family privacy have been met with judicial objection. The direction of the law is clear: States cannot interfere unnecessarily or unreasonably in the lives of families which seem to be getting along well enough by themselves. "The history and culture of Western civilization reflect a strong tradition of parental concern for the nurture and upbringing of their children. The primary role of parents in the upbringing of their children is now established beyond debate as an enduring American tradition" (*Wisconsin* v. *Yoder*, 1972). And, the right to family and personal privacy has also advanced to accepted principles in American jurisprudence.

Laws which pit the authority of the government against the authority of the family have generally failed to pass constitutional muster. Respect for the integrity of the family remains paramount, and governmental enactments violating that integrity are difficult to sustain.

Laws Which Pit the Authority of the State against the Child

The second category of state law or state action pits the authority of the state against the child. The states' authority was initially exercised for benign motives. States sought to protect children from the ravages of the adult criminal justice system by establishing juvenile courts early in the 20th century (Katz, 1970; Mack, 1909). The theory behind the juvenile court was that the court would act as the defender rather than the prosecutor of the child. Juvenile courts were viewed as non-adversarial arenas, friendly places which sought to rehabilitate, not punish, the child. The concept of the juvenile court assumed wise, benevolent, and foresighted judges supported by a capable, effective, and knowledgeable social service staff. Constitutional standards of the adult criminal court were unacceptable as overly rigid, confining, and counterproductive to the mission of the juvenile court. By the 1960s, it was clear that the benefits of the system were illusory and the denial of constitutional rights to children undermined their guarantee of a fair trial. Many children were treated more capriciously and harshly than they would have been by the adult system.

Starting in 1967 with *In re Gault*, juvenile justice was made more "just" by granting children such basic rights as counsel, notice, fair hearing, and a verdict reasonably supported by the evidence. The standard of proof in juvenile courts became the same as in adult criminal courts, "beyond a reasonable doubt" (*In re Winship*, 1970). Although juveniles were entitled to many procedural protections, the Supreme Court stopped short of complete identity between juvenile and adult criminal courts. Children in juvenile courts have been denied trial by jury (*McKeever* v. *Pennsylvania*, 1971), a right afforded adult criminal defendants.

In addition, states passed laws making children who engaged in antisocial, non-criminal behavior—status offenders—subject to the jurisdiction of the juvenile court. Underaged runaways, truants, incorrigibles, youngsters in need of medical care, and youngsters who might be in danger of falling into habits of vice may be classed as status offenders (*Matiello* v. *Connecticut*, 1969). Similar behavior on the part of adults would not subject them to the criminal justice system. These errant children are brought before the court by school authorities, the Department of Welfare, or by the parents themselves.

There is a strong movement to erase the concept of status offenders from the law books and to extinguish the court's jurisdiction over them. The court, it is argued, should not be involved in family squabbles and should not act as an instrument of control for schools and public agencies. There appears to be a growing realization that the acts of the juvenile courts have not been salutary to status offenders. No one can authoritatively assert how these status offenders are best handled. But the pendulum has swung to the pre-20th-century position. Legal commentators are encouraging voluntary social service networks under whose guidance parents and children will resolve their intergenerational difficulties without involvement of the courts or interference of the state (Foster & Freed, 1972).

Teenagers are subject to a panoply of civil restrictions in addition to the restrictions imposed by the criminal justice system. The law refers to individuals who have not reached the age of majority as "nonaged" or "infants." If the age of majority is 18 in a particular jurisdiction, all newborns, as well as those who are 17 years and 11 months old, are nonaged or infants, and are treated identically under the civil law. As to adolescents, even the *use* of the terms nonaged or infant is condescending. Gradation of legal rights and duties based on age is limited to such areas as driving, drinking, and working.

A newborn and a 17-year-old lack legal capacity to the same extent to enter into a binding contract, to sue, to consent to medical care, to convey property. In most jurisdictions, a nonaged person's domicile, regardless of his chronological age, is that of his parents. The district in which he can vote, as well as the location in which he can attend school, is determined by the domicile of his parents. Legally, it is irrelevant that he may be independent and live apart from his family.[2]

This legal incapacity of youngsters, especially adolescents, is a vexing problem. The 16-year-old who cannot live under the same roof as his or her parents because he or she cannot accept their discipline or because their generational ideologies clash, moves out or is put out. However, he or she lacks legal capacity either to sign a lease—a contract—in order to house him/herself, or to purchase necessities on credit. Worse yet, unless the teenager has been emancipated by court decree—that is, given the legal status of an adult—the parent may have the option of initiating a

---

[2] For a newer approach to domicile, see *Jolicoeur* v. *Mihaly*, 5 Cal.3d 565, 488 P.2d 1, 96 Cal. Rptr. 697 (1971) (*en banc*).

proceeding in the court to have the adolescent adjudicated a status offender. The parental allegation may be simply that the adolescent is incorrigible; the ultimate court adjudication may find that the youngster is a status offender and transfer the custodianship of the teenager from the parent to the state. The motive of the parents may be punitive. For the law to make provision for parents to take such action is unconscionable. It is unrealistic to think that the child will benefit from the transfer of custodianship from the parents to the state. In most cases, these children should be on their own with legal capacity to take care of themselves.

To provide relief for adolescents, 16 states[3] have passed comprehensive emancipation laws under which courts have authority to grant 16-year-olds adult status in whole or part. This development is positive and a necessary recognition of the accelerated maturity of today's youth.

Laws which pit the authority of the state against that of the child were initiated with high-minded purposes; the state would protect and defend the child. Before the 1960s, many such laws were optimistically viewed as a way of making the government and the child friendly partners. As these laws evolved, the realization developed that many of them had failed. Critical scrutiny has been imposed on the juvenile court system and the concept of status offenders. The trend has been to limit their force while broadening the scope of emancipation, which permits the child freedom from both governmental and parental intrusion.

Laws in Which the State Interferes with the Parent–Child Relationship

The government should not intermeddle in domestic affairs between the parents and the child, but it does. The state's rationale for intervening is the protection of the child. The government asserts that its goal is the best interests of the child and its instrumentality for pursuing that goal is usually its social work bureaucracy. An analysis of this class of laws reveals that they fall into two ill-defined and overlapping categories: laws under which the state is the ally of the parent, and laws under which the state is the ally of the child.

Parents' control over their children is aided by the state in several ways. In regard to adolescents, parents may rely on legislative enactment to limit their youngsters' access to birth control (*Carey* v. *Population Services International*, 1977) and abortion (*Planned Parenthood of Central*

---

[3]The states which have comprehensive emancipation provisions are Alabama, Alaska, Arkansas, Colorado, Florida, Georgia, Kansas, Louisiana, Maine, Michigan, Mississippi, Oklahoma, Oregon, Tennessee, Texas, and West Virginia.

Missouri v. *Danforth,* 1976) and to limit their youngsters' capacity to consent to most medical treatment.[4]

Litigants question some of these statutes as being overly restrictive to adolescents. In a recent case (*Planned Parenthood of Central Missouri* v. *Danforth,* 1976), the United States Supreme Court struck that part of a Missouri statute which required parental consent as a precondition to abortion for a minor. The Court developed the "mature minor" doctrine, enunciating the concept that certain adolescents were capable of making knowledgeable choices. Parental involvement was deemed unnecessary and perhaps even harmful.

It is difficult to determine if legislatures which pass laws restricting adolescent freedom in matters of reproduction are doing so in order to protect the youngster, or whether they are doing so because of their anti-abortion bias.

A similar conflict was exposed in a New York State law controlling the distribution of contraceptives to youngsters under 16. The law made it a crime for non-physicians to distribute nonprescription contraceptives (*Carey* v. *Population Services International,* 1977). The United States Supreme Court found the statute an unreasonable and unconstitutional burden on the youngsters' decision.

The Court continues to make inroads in granting the adolescent autonomy from parental control and autonomy from needless state regulation. Behind its decisions is the obvious recognition that many adolescents are capable of deciding significant personal issues for themselves and that for certain purposes they should be granted legal rights akin to those of adults.

The government also intermeddles in the parent–child relationship in enforcing abuse and neglect statutes (Areen, 1975). In practice, these laws usually relate to younger children. The state clearly allies itself with the child when it places the abused or neglected child under its wing. Charges against parents initiate a process which may climax in termination of parental rights (Wald, 1975, 1976).

Abuse and neglect statutes are difficult to draft. They frequently suffer from the legal infirmity of vagueness because the concept itself is ill-defined. Such laws refer to the faults and habits of a parent (Louisiana Revised Statutes Annotated §13:1569), the immorality and depravity of a parent (Tennessee Code Annotated §37-202), and the absence of moral supervision by parents (*Alsager* v. *District Court,* 1976). Such statutory standards lack adequate definiteness. Standards in law must be precise

---

[4] An exception to this general rule is that minors can validly consent on their own to medical treatment for venereal disease, etc. See Pennsylvania Statutes Annotated title 35, § 10101 (Purdon) (1970).

enough to define the expected or proscribed conduct. What does the law mean and how are parents to evaluate their own actions when the standard in the statute refers to "faults and habits of parents"? Courts have consistently struck abuse and neglect statutes on the ground of vagueness, because the statutes do not—perhaps cannot—adequately define the adult behavior to be controlled.

Abuse and neglect laws must achieve a delicate balance. They must afford adequate protection to youngsters and yet be sufficiently definite to pass constitutional muster. The evil of vagueness is twofold: It not only neglects to provide parents with a clear standard for their behavior, it also increases judges' personal discretion. Without a clear statutory guide, judges can assert and act out of their prejudices as to child-rearing and adult behavior (Katz, 1971).

Additionally, abuse and neglect statutes raise a central policy dilemma, that is, whether abuse and neglect should be limited to proof of physical harm or be broadly construed to include psychological damage (*Singleton* v. *State*, 1973). A compelling argument for limiting the offense to physical harm is the impossibility of identifying emotional abuse. The argument is made that emotional abuse is "too imprecise in terms of definition, cause, treatment and consequences" (Goldstein, Freud, & Solnit, 1973. It is hopeless to try to make a causal connection between parental behavior and the child's psychological condition. Emotional abnormalities can be caused by any number of factors; to link them determinatively to parental treatment is unjustified.

On the other hand, it is claimed that a finding of abuse based on emotional neglect is quite possible. Observable symptoms can be relied on. If the child shows "severe anxiety, depression or withdrawal or untoward behavior," he or she ought to be considered abused or neglected if these symptoms are found in combination with "parents [who] are not willing to provide treatment" (Institute of Judicial Administration and American Bar Association Joint Commission, Juvenile Justice Standard 2.1C, 1980).

The broader concept of abuse and neglect has also come under fire. Critics allege that such laws have been enacted to curb and undermine the poor (Crouch, 1980). They maintain that cultural diversity is sometimes mistakenly interpreted as abuse or neglect. The argument emphasizes that societies outside the Western or middle-class system discipline children in harsher ways. Families may also live in crowded and possibly unsanitary conditions. Judged by Western or middle-class standards, these children may appear abused or neglected. However, no such inference can be drawn if the judgment is made on the basis of the children's original culture. These critics charge that abuse statutes result in such children being unfairly taken from their parents or in forcing the parents into behavior that conforms to Western or middle-class norms. They decry the consequences and predict that vigorous enforcement of such laws will result in a homogenous society divorced from cultural diversity. Others, to the contrary, assert that conformity to broad polymorphous Western or middle-class models allows for cultural differences, and abuse or neglect—especially in its extreme form—is clearly identifiable no matter what the family's cultural background.

Another issue that requires analysis is foster care (Diethorn, 1977). The question of whether the statutory enactments support the child or the parent is a complex one. The answer depends in part on the stage of the state's involvement in the foster care process. Sometimes the system favors the parent; other times it favors the child. When a child is removed from the natural home, the authority of the state is generated to safeguard the child. When a child is returned to his natural home, the authority of the state is sometimes used to vindicate the parents. During the in-between phase—when the child is shuffled from foster home to foster home—the state appears to be promoting its own bureaucracy, and neither the children nor the parents are served.

The foster care system is employed when a child is removed from the natural home involuntarily because the parents are unfit or the environment is unacceptable; or voluntarily when the child is abandoned or when domestic circumstances prevent one or both parents from maintaining the home, as for example, when the parents are ill and hospitalized.

Whether the commitment to foster care is voluntary or involuntary, the social service department, an agency of the state, is charged with rehabilitating and reuniting the original biological family unit. Given this overall charge, social workers tend to discourage the development of close psychological ties between the foster family and foster child. No matter how unrealistic the expectation of the child's returning home may be, social service workers discourage intimacy in the foster home.[5] Adherence to this dogma, however, urgently requires reconsideration. Children who are unlikely to be returned home should be identified as early and quickly as possible. And those children should not be discouraged from forming attachments with the foster families into which they may eventually be adopted or permanently placed.

The traditional approach of vindicating the right of natural parents has been attacked. It has been suggested that the "best-interests-of-the-child" standard should prevail in determining if children will remain in foster care or be returned to their natural parents. The Supreme Court has repeatedly rejected the best interest standard (*Smith* v. *Organization of*

[5] In a *New York Times* editorial dated September 13, 1980, it was noted that "typically a foster child stays rootless for five years; for one in six of the city's 21,000 charges, the wait exceeds ten years."

Foster Families for Equality and Reform, 1977) and has deferred to the rights of the natural parents (*Quilloin* v. *Walcott*, 1978). In a legal contest between natural parents and foster parents, the odds on favorites are the natural parents. The child does not have a legal right to the best possible home; the child's natural parents do, however, have a legal right to their child.

The most popular proponents for the best-interests-of-the-child approach are Goldstein, Freud, and Solnit, whose influential book *Beyond the Best Interests of the Child* (1973) flatly espouses the child's remaining always with his or her "psychological parent."[6] With few exceptions, however, courts are still predisposed to return the child to his or her biological parent (Smith, 1979). The courts will not engage in a comparison between the quality of life in the natural home and in the foster home; they ally themselves with natural parents. It is interesting to note that in the initial removal of the child from the biological parents' home and placement of him or her in foster care, the applicable standard is the best interests of the child. However, the standard applicable to returning the child is not the child's best interests but the natural parents' fitness. Therefore, even if the foster home is superior, the child will be returned to the natural home if his or her parents become capable of providing care.

All persons involved with foster care—no matter which principles they champion—realize that the frequent and continued shifting of children from home to home is undesirable and unhealthy. However, social workers find themselves under a duty to do so. In order to find foster homes in this ongoing shuffling process, social service departments have placed children in homes out of state. Recent litigation has challenged the authority of the state to do this (Bureau of National Affairs, Inc., 1977). The challenge is based on the right of parental access to their children for purposes of visitation.

The entire foster care system is in disarray, and only a few obvious problems have been considered. We are hopeful that ongoing research will both shed light on the system and suggest legislative changes to improve it (Katz, 1978).

In foster care, it appears that the states' concerns are directed toward the child's interests in the initial removal, toward the parent's interests in returning the child to the natural home, and toward neither's interests in shifting the child from home to home.

---

[6] In their later work, *Before the Best Interests of the Child* (1980), the authors urge very strict and narrow standards for removing a child from his or her natural home. Once the threshold for removal has been reached and removal has been accomplished, then the concept of psychological parenting takes effect.

A variation on the theme of best-interests-of-the-child is found in custody disputes between parents. In cases of this class, it is unclear whether the court allies itself with the child or with the parent. Traditionally, it has been thought that the court adjudicated custody matters as the child's ally. However, this has not always been true. In inter-parental disputes, the courts customarily awarded children to their mothers without considering the father as custodian. Courts reached this decision on the basis of the "tender years" presumption: It was presumed that the mother was the better parent, especially for young children. Only proof positive that she was unfit evoked a disposition in favor of the father. A competitive examination of the mother and father and their respective homes was rarely undertaken. The court's alliance with the mother, instead of the child, has weakened in recent years. Passage of Equal Rights Amendments in 16 states,[7] and the expansion of the equal protection doctrines of the Fifth and Fourteenth Amendments, have challenged the mother's superior position. Parents in a custody dispute stand on a more equal footing (*Commonwealth ex rel. Spriggs* v. *Carson*, 1977), although the balance is still in favor of the mother.

In many jurisdictions in which the natural parents are the parties to the dispute, the courts are moving toward the best-interests-of-the-child standard, scrutinizing both the mother and the father, as well as the domestic environment each has to offer. Where courts follow this standard, they champion the interests of the child.

If custody involves the natural parent and a third party, for example a relative, the court staunchly allies itself with the natural parent. In almost all cases, the biological parent is preferred without considering the child's best interests. A child does not have a legal right to a happy home, which may mean a home with a relative or a friend. Parents maintain certain rights to their children akin to property rights even if as a consequence the child will be reared in a less desirable environment.

By and large, the court's preference for natural parents is sound, except where the separation has been prolonged or the circumstances are extreme—that is, where either the parenting or the environment is clearly damaging. The court is ill-equipped to make determinations to exclude natural parents on equivocal psychological data. The judge has only limited training and experience to bring to the role of psychological

[7]The states which have adopted equal rights amendments are Alaska, Colorado, Connecticut, Hawaii, Illinois, Maryland, Massachusetts, Montana, New Hampshire, New Mexico, Pennsylvania, Texas, Utah, Virginia, Washington, and Wyoming. The earliest state constitutional provisions for equal rights for both men and women are found in Utah (1896) and Wyoming (1890). Massachusetts approved the most recent such provision on November 2, 1976.

evaluator, and the sophistication of psychology has not reached the point at which it can reliably evaluate relationships between home environment and the child's psychological health. Of course, when the circumstances are extreme, psychologists as well as judges can ascertain present psychological damage and predict future mental health deterioration.

In summary, the state is directly and substantially involved in the parent-child relationship. As to adolescents: Courts are beginning to restrict parental function where the child's and parents' interests clash. They recognize that the accelerated maturity of adolescents has made it desirable for young people to decide matters for themselves, especially in the area of reproduction.

As to younger children: The government attempts to protect them through abuse and neglect laws and through the use of foster care systems. Despite its many difficulties, the enforcement of abuse and neglect statutes has been effective. The foster care system, on the other hand, has been judged inadequate.

The law of child custody is in flux, and courts are reexamining it. In all these matters, legislatures and courts require guidance from developmental psychology to enact and interpret laws more responsively.

Conclusion

Legal policy in the United States enshrining the independence and integrity of the family free from governmental interference has, of necessity, yielded to reality.

Governmental involvement in family life falls into three categories: (1) laws which pit the authority of the government against the authority of the family; (2) action which pits the government against the child; and (3) laws which meddle with the parent-child relationship.

The family as a subject has given legislators a broad stage on which to act. Laws which impinge on the family relate to health, education, juvenile offenders, status offenders, abuse and neglect of children, foster care placement, and custody, to name just a few matters of concern. It has been the business of the court to examine legislation relating to these matters. The goal of this judicial scrutiny is to uphold laws which safeguard the child and the family without unconstitutionally infringing on their autonomy and integrity.

Neither the legislators nor the courts have given substantial consideration to developmental psychology. But this trend, although still vigorous, does appear to be shifting. A reflection of the shift is the court's development of the concept of the "mature minor."

In the past decade, family law has developed into a significant part of the legislative and court agenda. How the development proceeds and the law is molded depends on the knowledge and insights of lawyers, legislators, and judges. It is important that scientific advances in developmental psychology be woven into the legal fabric.

References

Alsager v. *District Court*, 545 F.2d 1137 (8th Cir. 1976).

Areen, J. Intervention between parent and child: A reappraisal of the state's role in child neglect and abuse cases. *Georgetown Law Journal*, 1975, *63*, 887.

Bellotti v. *Baird*, 443 U.S. 622 (1979).

Bureau of National Affairs, Inc. *Family Law Reporter*, 1977, *3*, 2607.

Carey v. *Population Services International*, 431 U.S. 678 (1977).

Commonwealth ex rel. Spriggs v. *Carson*, 470 Pa. 290, 368 A.2d 635 (1977).

Crouch, R. International convention efforts and the current status of children's rights in the U.S.A. *Family Law Reporter*, 1980, *6*, 4023.

Diethorn, R. *Report of the task force group on foster care system organization.* Harrisburg, Pa.: Commonwealth Child Development Committee, 1977.

Foster, H., & Freed, D. J. A Bill of rights for children. *Family Law Quarterly*, 1972, *6*, 343.

Goldstein, J., Freud, A., & Solnit, A. *Beyond the best interests of the child.* New York: The Free Press, 1973.

Goldstein, J., Freud, A., & Solnit, A. *Before the best interests of the child.* New York: The Free Press, 1980.

Griswold v. *Connecticut*, 381 U.S. 479 (1965).

Harvard Law Review. The constitution and the family. *Harvard Law Review*, 1980, *93*, 1156.

In re Gault, 387 U.S. 1 (1967).

In re Winship, 397 U.S. 358 (1970).

Institute of Judicial Administration and American Bar Association Joint Commission. *Juvenile justice standards.* Cambridge, Mass.: Ballinger Publishing Co., 1980.

Jolicoeur v. *Mihaly*, 5 Cal.3d 565, 488 P.2d 1, 96 Cal. Rptr. 697 (1971) (*en banc*).

Katz, S. Juvenile justice reform: A historical perspective. *Stanford Law Review*, 1970, *22*, 1187.

Katz, S. *When parents fail.* Boston: Beacon Press, 1971.

Katz, S. Freeing children for permanent placement through a model act. *Family Law Quarterly*, 1978, *12*, 203.

Louisiana Revised Statutes Annotated § 13:1569 (West) (1978) (Supp. 1981).

Mack, J. The juvenile court. *Harvard Law Review*, 1909, *23*, 104.

Matiello v. *Connecticut*, 395 U.S. 209 (1969).

McKeever v. *Pennsylvania*, 403 U.S. 528 (1971).

Mnookin, R. Foster care—in whose best interest. *Harvard Educational Review*, 1973, *43*, 599.

Morris, A., Giller, H., Geach, H., & Szwed, E. *Justice for children.* Atlantic Highlands, N.J.: Humanities Press, 1980.

Paulsen, M. G. Juvenile courts, family courts and the poor man. *California Law Review*, 1966, *54*, 694.

Pennsylvania Statutes Annotated title 35, § 10101 (Purdon) (1970).

Pierce v. *Society of Sisters*, 268 U.S. 510 (1925).

Planned Parenthood of Central Missouri v. *Danforth*, 428 U.S. 52 (1976).

Quilloin v. *Walcott*, 434 U.S. 246 (1978).

Roe v. *Wade*, 410 U.S. 113 (1973).

Singleton v. *State*, 200 S.E.2d 507 (Ga. Ct. App. 1973).

Smith, S. Psychological parents v. biological parents: The court's response to new directions in child custody dispute resolution. *Journal of Family Law*, 1979, *17*, 545.

Smith v. *Organization of Foster Families for Equality and Reform*, 431 U.S. 816 (1977).

Tennessee Code Annotated § 37-202 (Supp. 1977).

Wald, M. State intervention on behalf of "neglected" children: A search for realistic standards. *Stanford Law Review*, 1975, *27*, 985.

Wald, M. State intervention on behalf of "neglected" children: Standards for removal of children from their homes, monitoring the status of children in foster care, and termination of parental rights. *Stanford Law Review*, 1976, *28*, 623.

Westin, A. F. *Privacy and freedom*. New York: Atheneum, 1967.

Wisconsin v. *Yoder*, 406 U.S. 205 (1972).

CHAPTER 4

School, Occupation, Culture, and Family

The Impact of Parental Schooling on the Parent-Child Relationship

LUIS M. LAOSA

Some of the most heated controversies regarding the educational enterprise today center on questions about the consequences of schooling. The issues addressed in these controversies are important for both practical and theoretical reasons and for policy considerations. With regard to international concerns, some people view training in basic educational skills as essential to economic development; others, however, question the assumptions that underlie this view (cf. LaBelle & Verhine, 1975; Laosa, 1976; Lockheed, Jamison, & Lau, 1980). At the national level, substantial public expenditures have gone into educational programs that seek to break the "cycle of poverty" by teaching basic educational skills and by promoting literacy.

Reprinted from the *Journal of Educational Psychology*, 1982, *74*, 791–827. Copyright 1982 American Psychological Association.

LUIS M. LAOSA ● Educational Testing Service, Princeton, New Jersey 08541. Portions of this article were written while the author was the recipient of a research grant (90-C-1257) from the United States Administration for Children, Youth, and Families. Field research during 1974–1975 on parental behavior was supported in part by a faculty research grant to the author from the Spencer Foundation through the Graduate School of Education, University of California, Los Angeles. The statistical analysis of the data was supported in part by a grant (RR05729-02) from the Biomedical Research Support Grant Program, National Institutes of Health, through Educational Testing Service. Collection and analysis of the data on language use in Chicano families in Austin during 1973–1974 was supported in part by a grant (OEG-0-73-6646) from the U. S. Office of Education through the University of Texas at Austin.

As the fiscal outlays for education either increase or decrease, there is an increase in concerns about the effectiveness of educational programs and requests for evaluations of their impact (Laosa, 1982b). At the same time, and partly as a result of these concerns, some social scientists are focusing their theoretical and empirical research on questions about the effects of schooling on cognitive development. For example, in one line of research, a great deal of effort is devoted to attempts at disentangling the effects of schooling from the effects of mere maturation on cognitive development (Rogoff, 1981; Sharp, Cole, & Lave, 1979; Stevenson, Parker, Wilkinson, Bonnevaux, & Gonzalez, 1978).

Most of the concerns about and research on the consequences of schooling focus on the impact of schooling on *individuals*. For example, the widely publicized research by Coleman, Jencks, and their associates (Coleman, Campbell, Hobson, McPartland, Mood, Weinfeld, & York, 1966; Jencks, Smith, Acland, Bane, Cohen, Gintis, Heyns, & Michelson, 1972) and the more recent investigations by Heyns (1978) and by Rutter and his co-workers (Rutter, Maughan, Mortimer, & Ouston, 1979) reflected concerns about the effects of schools on the academic achievement of children. Similarly, the study by Hyman, Wright, and Reed (1975) was motivated by questions about the enduring effects of schooling on the acquisition of knowledge and the receptivity to further knowledge during adulthood.

In sharp contrast to the amount of attention and research devoted to the impact of schooling on *individuals*, relatively little research or even attention has been directed to answering questions about the possible effects of schooling on *family interaction patterns*. This is unfortunate, because research on the impact of schooling on the parent–child relationship is probably a key to many future discoveries that would shed light on current questions and concerns about education and human development. Indeed, the available evidence leads me to proffer a two-fold general hypothesis: (a) Among the enduring effects of schooling on the individual are certain behavioral dispositions that determine how he or she will behave as a parent, for example, how the person will interact with his or her children. (b) In turn, parental behavior will have important consequences for the child's development of specific cognitive skills, learning strategies, and personality characteristics. This hypothesis is an elaboration, integration, and extension of the usual conceptual approaches. The usual approaches focus *either* (a) on the consequences that schooling (the individual's or his or her parents') may have for the individual's cognitive development *or* (b) on the consequences that environmental processes in the home, particularly the parent–child relationship, may have on the child's cognitive and/or personality development. My two-fold hypothesis differs from the usual approaches

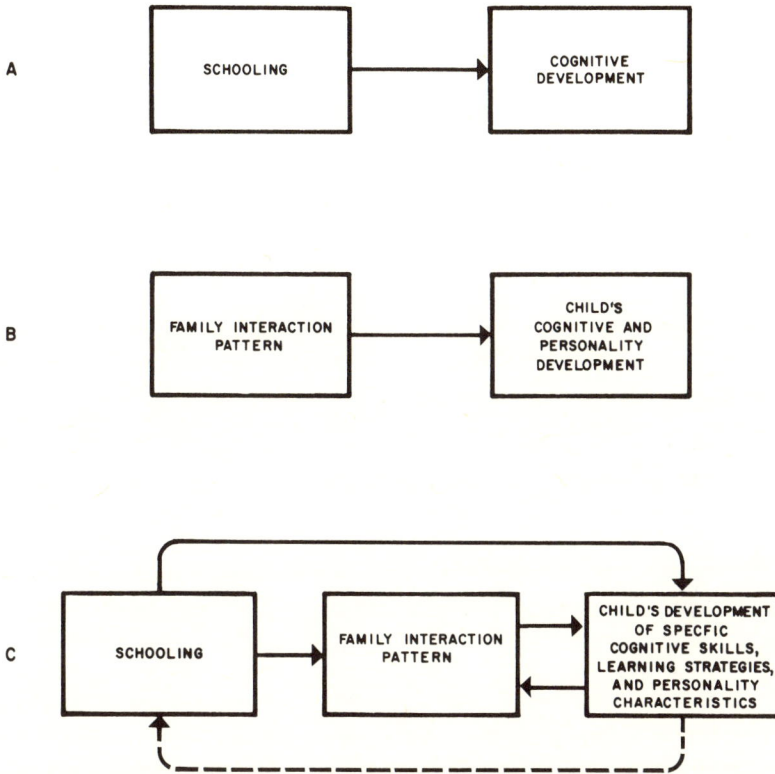

Figure 1. Three conceptual models. Models A and B depict the usual conceptual approaches. They focus either (A) on the consequences that schooling (the individual's or his or her parents') may have for the individual's cognitive development or (B) on the consequences that environmental processes in the home, particularly the interactions in the family, may have on the child's development. Model C is an integration, elaboration, and extension of the usual approaches. It introduces family interaction as a mediating variable between parental schooling and the child's development of specific cognitive skills, personality characteristics, and learning strategies. It therefore calls for an analysis of the impact that schooling may have on the nature of the parent–child relationship.

primarily by introducing family interaction as a mediating variable between the length of parental schooling and the child's development (Figure 1). Therefore, it seems that a logical point of departure for my inquiry, and hence my primary focus in this chapter, would be an examination of the impact of schooling on families—more specifically, on the impact of parental schooling on the parent–child relationship, since the parent–child relationship is a paramount aspect of the family environment of children. In the course of this inquiry, I shall attempt to determine whether parental schooling, parental occupational status, and maternal employment each have a distinct pattern of influences on educationally related aspects of the parent–child relationship.

I shall conduct this inquiry in the context of issues regarding ethnic diversity, individual variability within ethnic groups, and educational and occupational equity, giving particular attention to Chicano families. As we shall see, the findings regarding the impact of parental schooling on the parent–child relationship suggest plausible explanations of the frequent scholastic failure observed among the members of certain ethnic minorities in the United States. Therefore, as a secondary focus, I shall sketch in broad outline a theoretical model that causally links parental schooling, family interaction processes, and children's scholastic performance.

Schooling is seldom thought of as having an impact on the family. However, I will present evidence suggesting that schooling exerts a powerful, pervasive, and enduring influence on the family, perhaps more so than any other experience. At the outset I should remind the reader that practical, ethical, and legal considerations make it virtually impossible to conduct studies of schooling that incorporate controlled experimentation in their research designs. For example, it is impossible to randomly assign persons to receive varied amounts of schooling, although a few investigators (e.g., Irwin, Engle, Yarbrough, Klein, & Townsend, 1978; Stevenson *et al.*, 1978) have created approximations to this type of design. As a result of these constraints, almost all of the research conducted to date, including that which I shall report here, usually precludes definitive conclusions regarding cause-and-effect relationships. Therefore, although I shall speak of the "impact," the "effect," or the "consequences" of schooling, it should be understood that there may be plausible alternative hypotheses regarding, for example, explanations of the direction of effects or explanations based on the possible confounding of variables as a result of unexamined covariation. Nevertheless, the data I will present here are, I believe, useful and illuminating insofar as they begin to provide at least tentative answers to questions about the impact of schooling on the parent–child relationship.

Schooling and Social Class

Traditionally, schooling attainment level is included within such global constructs as social class and socioeconomic status, and a great deal of research has focused on social-class and socioeconomic influences on the parent–child relationship (for reviews see Deutsch, 1973; Hess, 1970; Laosa, 1981). However, schooling attainment level is seldom examined separately as a specific variable. Indeed, the usual research approach has prevented an examination of the effects of schooling as a separate variable. In the usual approach, such sociodemographic variables as schooling attainment level and occupational status are subsumed aggregately under a general "index of social class." Perhaps the most popular of these composite indices is Hollingshead's (1957) *Two-Factor Index of Social Position*, a combination of occupation and schooling. A plethora of other composite indices of social class and socioeconomic status exists, most of which are only minor variants of each other (Laosa, 1981). Their use has prevented an examination of the effects of schooling as a separate variable.

For the purpose of my analysis, it seems more useful to view social class *not* as a unitary composite index, but as a conglomerate of specific variables that must be examined separately. The need for a separate examination of each variable becomes more evident in light of recent research suggesting that such sociodemographic variables as occupational status and prestige may have different meanings across cultural groups (Laosa, 1978; Light & Smith, 1969; Shipman, McKee, & Bridgeman, 1976; Stricker, 1976). This was indeed the approach followed in a study that I recently completed (Laosa, 1978). Let us turn now to a review of that study, which assessed the impact of women's schooling and occupational status on their maternal behavior.

Maternal Schooling and Maternal Teaching Behavior

In a recent study (Laosa, 1978), I examined the effects of women's schooling and occupational status on the teaching strategies that they, as mothers, use with their own young children. The research plan called for selecting a population in which adults vary widely with regard to schooling attainment level, in order to insure a sufficiently wide distribution for statistical analysis. Therefore, Chicano[1] families were selected as study participants because of the wide diversity in schooling attainment level among Chicano adults.[2]

The mothers were observed in their homes teaching cognitive-

[1] The term *Chicano* or *Mexican-American* refers to persons who trace their lineage to Hispanic or Indo-Hispanic forebears who resided within Spanish or Mexican territory that is now part of the southwestern United States. It also refers to persons who were born in Mexico and now hold United States citizenship or otherwise live in the United States or whose parents or more remote ancestors immigrated to the United States from Mexico.

[2] Since the research plan called for analyzing both maternal and paternal variables, an effort was made to select only intact families; therefore, all but one of the Chicano families were intact. The same selection criterion was applied to the non-Hispanic White participants in the studies to be described in other sections of this chapter; all but three of the families in the non-Hispanic White sample were intact. All the couples were endogamous with regard to these ethnic categories.

Table 1. Spearman Rank Correlations of Maternal Teaching Strategies with Parental
Schooling and Occupational Status in Chicano Families, by Mother–Son
and Mother–Daughter Dyads

Teaching strategy and dyad structure	Mother's schooling	Father's schooling	Mother's occupation	Father's occupation
Modeling				
Mother–son	$-.68^{c}$	$-.78^{c}$	.02	$-.26$
Mother–daughter	$-.31$	$-.18$	.14	.15
Visual cue				
Mother–son	$-.03$	$-.09$	$-.11$	$-.04$
Mother–daughter	$-.30$	$-.19$	$-.49^{b}$	$-.11$
Directive				
Mother–son	.02	.16	.15	$-.11$
Mother–daughter	$-.02$	$-.18$	$-.24$	$-.20$
Praise				
Mother–son	$.67^{c}$	$.68^{c}$	.06	.22
Mother–daughter	$.72^{c}$	$.66^{c}$	.04	.09
Negative verbal feedback or disapproval				
Mother–son	.11	.21	.10	$-.02$
Mother–daughter	$-.03$	$-.16$	$-.24$	$-.30$
Inquiry				
Mother–son	$.65^{c}$	$.56^{b}$	.07	$.40^{a}$
Mother–daughter	$.54^{b}$	$.50^{b}$	.08	.23
Negative physical control				
Mother–son	$-.44^{a}$	$-.16$	.03	$-.22$
Mother–daughter	.10	.03	$-.32$	.03
Positive physical control				
Mother–son	.08	$-.22$	.33	$-.27$
Mother–daughter	$-.12$	$-.23$	$-.25$	$-.03$
Physical affection				
Mother–son	*	*	*	*
Mother–daughter	.20	.30	$-.14$	$-.25$

Note: The coefficients are based on 20 mother–son dyads and 23 mother–daughter dyads. Asterisks indicate where coefficients were not computed because of very low frequency. Data from Laosa, 1978.
[a] $p < .05$, one-tailed test.
[b] $p < .01$, one-tailed test.
[c] $p < .001$, one-tailed test.

perceptual tasks to their five-year-old children. Using the Maternal
Teaching Observation Technique (Laosa, 1980c), trained observers
recorded the frequency of occurrence of nine categories of maternal
behavior. Reliability and short-term stability analyses indicated that these
measures represent adequately reliable and moderately stable attributes of
maternal behavior (Laosa, 1980c). The analyses and results described below

are based on rates of occurrence per minute, obtained by dividing frequencies by duration of observation.

Table 1 shows the results of the correlations between maternal teaching behaviors and the mothers' and their husbands' schooling levels and occupational statuses.[3] These data lead us immediately to the general conclusion that the schooling level attained by a Chicano woman is a very strong predictor of the strategy that she, as a mother, will use to teach her own children. In contrast, the measured occupational status, either the woman's or her husband's, is generally unrelated to the woman's choice of maternal teaching strategies.[4]

Specifically, what impact does schooling seem to have on the mother's choice of teaching strategies? The most significant results, all of which involve parental schooling level, are as follows. *Modeling,* the frequency of the mother's doing part of the work for the child's observation and imitation, is inversely correlated with the mother's and her husband's schooling. *Praise,* the frequency of the mother's praise or verbal approval for the child's activity or product, is directly correlated with the mother's and her husband's schooling. *Inquiry,* the frequency with which the mother asks the child a question, is also directly correlated with the mother's and her husband's schooling. There is also, but for boys only, an inverse relationship between the mother's schooling level and *negative physical control,* the frequency with which the mother directed toward the child the kinds of behavior that generally would be considered as physical punishment. These correlations are generally strong.

For a closer examination of the relationships uncovered by the statistical analyses, Figure 2 displays how frequently Chicano mothers of different schooling levels used modeling, inquiry, and praise as teaching strategies. The frequencies of these three maternal teaching strategies vary markedly as a function of maternal schooling level. This graph also shows

---

[3] Schooling level was measured as the number of completed years of formal schooling. The usual occupational status of the fathers was measured using the following scale, adapted from that used by the U.S. Bureau of the Census: 1 = private household workers; 2 = service workers except in private households; 3 = laborers and farmers; 4 = equipment operators; 5 = craftsmen, foremen, and kindred persons; 6 = sales, clerical, and kindred workers; 7 = small business owners, managers, or administrators; 8 = professional and technical; 9 = large business owners or managers. The same scale with an additional point (0 = housewife, does not work outside the home) was used to measure mother's usual occupational status. If a person usually held more than one occupation, the highest one was selected for analysis. The means, standard deviations, and ranges for these variables are shown in Table 25.

[4] I do not mean to imply that such choices are under the conscious control of the individual or that the individual is consciously aware of the pedagogical principles or psychological processes underlying her behavior.

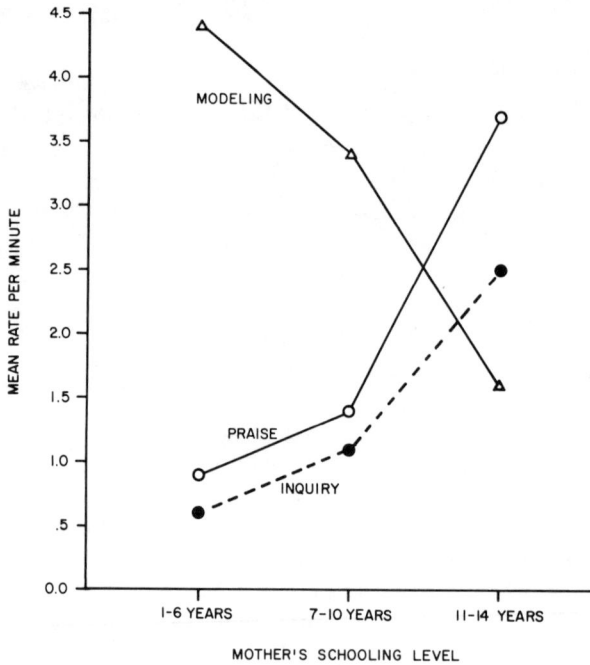

Figure 2. Three maternal teaching strategies as a function of maternal schooling level in Chicano families. (n = 15 for 1–6 years, 13 for 7–10 years, and 15 for 11–14 years.) Data from Laosa, 1978.

evidence of a threshold level (10 years) after which the effect of additional schooling on these maternal teaching strategies becomes even more pronounced.

In discussing these results, LeVine (1980) has called attention to the striking similarity between the approach to teaching employed by the more highly educated Chicano mothers and the academic style of many school classrooms. The more highly schooled Chicano mothers taught using a more conversational style (*inquiry*) rather than motoric demonstration (*modeling*), and they especially included verbal reinforcement (*praise*). One might say they "imitated" the academic style of the school classrooms in which they had spent so much of their lives.

Returning to the data at hand, it can be seen that the father's schooling was almost as good a predictor of maternal teaching behavior as the mother's own schooling. This is not surprising, given the moderately high correlation between mother's and father's schooling (Spearman rank correlation = .66, Pearson product–moment correlation = .64, n = 42, $p < .001$). This correlation is probably the result of assortative mating and indicates that in Chicano families both marriage partners tend to have relatively similar levels of formal education.

In marked contrast to the strong correlations between maternal behavior and length of schooling, there was hardly any relationship between maternal behavior and occupational status. These contrasting results reveal an important distinction, namely, the distinction of the effects of schooling from the effects of occupational status on maternal teaching behavior. This distinction never would have come to light had the study followed the usual measurement approaches that either aggregate occupational status and schooling level into a global "index of social class" or rely exclusively on occupational status to measure "social class" or "socioeconomic status." Later I shall return to this distinction. I shall examine it in the context of certain unresolved issues involved in the measurement of occupational status, issues that should have a direct bearing on how we interpret the observed lack of correlation between maternal behavior and occupational status. In addition, (and of broader social significance because of its policy implications for questions regarding equality of occupational opportunity) I will examine the link between length of schooling and occupational attainment; I will attempt to determine whether this link is weaker for Chicanos than it generally is for non-Hispanic Whites. Before turning to these issues, let us continue our examination of the impact of schooling on maternal behavior.

The absence of a relationship between variables is often as illuminating as are the correlations that reach statistical significance. In this regard it is worth noting that length of schooling did not make a difference on all the categories of teaching behavior that I observed. Specifically, neither the mother's nor her husband's schooling attainment level correlated significantly with the mother's choice of the following teaching strategies: *visual cue*, the frequency with which the mother attempts to attract the child's attention toward a given aspect of the task by sliding, pushing, or lifting a part or portion of the model being assembled, but short of fastening or unfastening any parts; *directive*, the frequency with which the mother verbally commands the child to pursue a given course of action; *negative verbal feedback or disapproval*, the frequency with which the mother verbally indicates to the child that a given course of action taken by the child is incorrect or that she is displeased with the child or with the child's activity or product; *positive physical control*, the frequency with which the mother manually controls the child's motor behavior to facilitate the child's performance on the task; and *physical affection*, the frequency with which the mother makes physical contact with the child to express a favorable feeling toward the child. The absence of significant correlations between these categories of behavior and the mothers' schooling level indicates that these maternal teaching strategies occurred with approximately equal frequency among Chicano mothers of relatively high, medium, and low schooling attainment levels. The fact that not all the behavior categories were affected by schooling should alert us to the risks involved in overgeneralizing the effects of schooling to all aspects of maternal teaching behavior.

The results of this study suggest that, at least among Chicano women, schooling has a marked impact on certain behavioral dispositions that determine the manner in which women, once they become mothers, interact with their children. Such findings raise provocative questions about the role that schooling plays in influencing the evolution of *culture*, and specifically in influencing the evolution of cultural patterns of family interaction. Some of these questions were posed in a subsequent study, to which we now turn.

Culture, Maternal Schooling, and Maternal Teaching Behavior

The research results just reviewed led me to hypothesize that schooling is a powerful force in the evolution of cultural patterns of family interaction. This was indeed the hypothesis that prompted a subsequent study, which I recently completed (Laosa, 1980b). I adopted a research design and analysis plan that would permit, first, an assessment of differences in the teaching strategies of mothers in two distinct ethnic populations—specifically, two ethnic populations whose adult members would differ, on the average, with respect to both length of schooling and occupational attainment. Next, the plan would permit the determination of whether ethnic-group differences in maternal teaching strategies remain or disappear after removing the influence that schooling and occupational inequalities might have in sustaining or creating them.

Specifically, the study involved two major steps. First, I compared the teaching behavior of mothers toward their own children in two distinct ethnic groups—Chicano and non-Hispanic White.[5] I chose these two ethnic groups because Chicanos on the average complete fewer years of schooling and attain lower-status occupations than do non-Hispanic Whites. I found ethnic-group differences in the teaching behavior of mothers. Second, I posed the following question. Will the observed ethnic-

---

[5] The term *non-Hispanic White* refers to all white, English-speaking persons who were born in the United States and are not Chicano or members of other Spanish-origin groups. The terms *Anglo-American* and *Anglo*, which I have used in other writings following the general usage of these terms in the southwestern United States, refer to the same population to which I refer in this article as non-Hispanic White.

group differences in maternal teaching behavior disappear in future generations when women in the two ethnic groups become exposed to equal amounts of schooling and/or to equal occupational experiences as a result of increased equality of educational and occupational opportunity?

To answer these questions, the analyses were performed as follows. First, analyses of variance were performed to compare the two ethnic groups on each category of maternal teaching behavior. Next, a series of four analyses of covariance was performed on each category of maternal teaching behavior, making the ethnic group comparisons while statistically holding constant, respectively, mothers' and fathers' schooling levels and occupational statuses. To improve normality of distribution, to improve linearity of regression, and to stabilize approximately the variances, the rates-per-minute for each behavior category were transformed to $\sqrt{x} + \sqrt{x+1}$ (Freeman & Tukey, 1950) for use in these parametric analyses. To test the assumption of homogeneous slopes, F ratios were calculated to assess the interactions between the covariates and the independent variables; with very few exceptions, this assumption was met for these analyses (Laosa, 1980b, 1981).

The analyses revealed significant differences in the teaching strategies of Chicano and non-Hispanic White mothers. Specifically, the Chicano mothers used *modeling, visual cue, directive*, and *negative physical control* as teaching strategies more frequently than did the non-Hispanic White mothers. On the other hand, the non-Hispanic White mothers used *inquiry* and *praise* as teaching strategies more frequently than did the Chicano mothers. The mothers in the two ethnic groups did not differ in their use of *negative verbal feedback or disapproval, positive physical control*, and *physical affection*. These were the results obtained before statistically holding constant schooling level or occupational status. When the ethnic-group comparisons were made while holding constant the mothers' and their husbands' occupational statuses, the ethnic-group differences in maternal teaching strategies generally remained significant. However, when the ethnic-group comparisons were made while statistically holding constant the mothers' schooling attainment level, all the ethnic-group differences in maternal teaching strategies became nonsignificant.

For a closer examination of these results, Figure 3 depicts the (untransformed) frequency rates at which Chicano and non-Hispanic White mothers used each of the nine teaching strategies. The brackets represent the mean differences (M_D) in rates between the two ethnic groups. The asterisks indicate where the F ratios of the ethnic-group differences in rates transformed to $\sqrt{x} + \sqrt{x+1}$ were significant. The bar graph in the upper half of the figure presents the unadjusted rates. On the average, Chicano and non-Hispanic White mothers differed significantly in their use of *modeling* (M_D = 2.14), *visual cue* (M_D = .75), *directive*

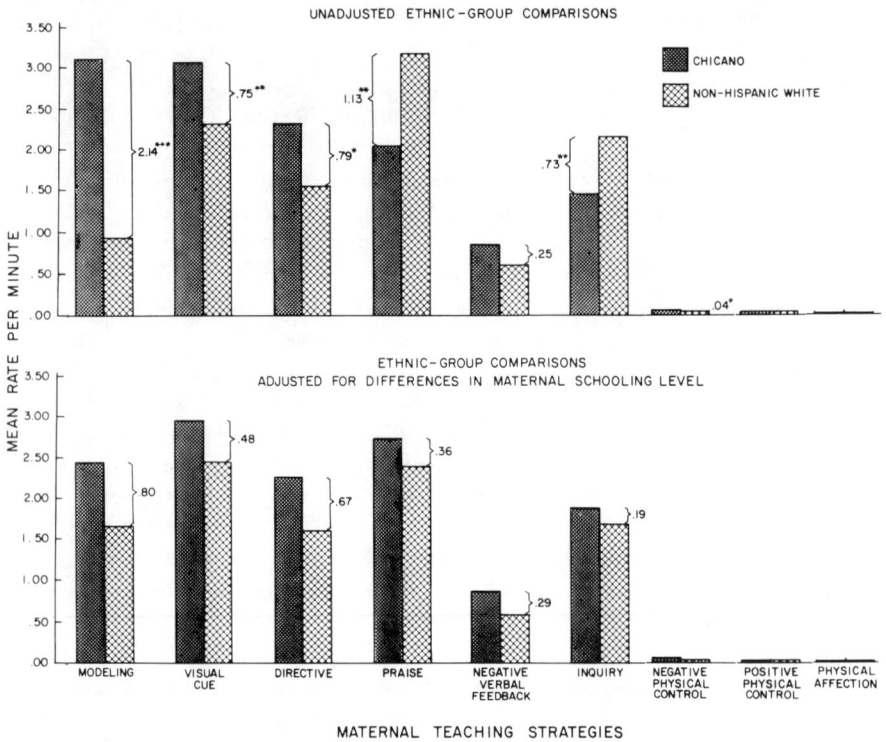

Figure 3. Ethnic-group comparisons of maternal teaching strategies: Unadjusted comparisons and comparisons adjusted for differences in maternal schooling level. (Asterisks indicate where the F ratios of the ethnic-group differences were significant: $*p < .05$, $**p < .01$, $***p < .001$; $df = 1, 78$.) Data from Laosa, 1980b.

($M_D = .79$), *praise* ($M_D = 1.13$), *inquiry* ($M_D = .73$), and *negative physical control* ($M_D = .04$). In contrast, the bar graph in the lower half of Figure 3 shows the rates adjusted for differences in maternal schooling level. When the rates are thus adjusted for differences in maternal schooling level, the ethnic-group differences in maternal teaching strategies are reduced and all become statistically nonsignificant. For example, after the adjustment was made for the differential in mothers' schooling level, the ethnic-group difference in the mothers' use of modeling was reduced by 63%—from 2.14 to only .80—and became nonsignificant. Similar although less dramatic reductions in the magnitude of the ethnic-group difference occurred for almost all the other teaching strategies.

In sum, by taking into account the influence of schooling on maternal teaching behavior, the observed ethnic-group differences in maternal teaching strategies were reduced and became statistically nonsignificant.

Thus, the ethnic-group differences in maternal teaching strategies are explained (statistically) by the ethnic-group differential in length of maternal schooling.

These results add confirmatory evidence to the hypothesis that schooling is a powerful force in the evolution of culturally determined patterns of family interaction. They also suggest that when educational equity finally becomes a reality and Chicano and non-Hispanic White women attain similar levels of schooling, at least some of the present-day differences in child-rearing practices that we observe today between these two cultural groups will diminish considerably and perhaps even tend to disappear.

In the next section I shall review research suggesting that the mother's choice of teaching strategies can influence her child's development of characteristic *approaches to learning*. I also shall discuss the relevance of this research to our understanding of classroom interactions and its implications for interpreting the frequent scholastic failure among Chicanos and other educationally disadvantaged populations. Based on these and other considerations, I shall propose an explanatory model of the high incidence of scholastic failure in these populations. In subsequent sections I shall present further evidence bearing on the empirical validity of the model in my examination of the links between parental schooling and other aspects of the parent–child relationship.

Parental Schooling, Family Interaction, and Children's Learning Strategies: An Explanatory Model of Scholastic Performance

One wonders about the effects that the parent's habitual choice of teaching strategies might have on the child's development of characteristic *learning strategies*. By *learning strategies* I mean one's preferred and/or most proficient way of approaching a learning or problem-solving task. For example, it seems reasonable to hypothesize that children of parents who habitually teach through modeling will develop a learning strategy characterized by "observational learning" or by "learning through looking"; by contrast, children of parents who typically teach through inquiry might develop a learning strategy or information-processing approach characterized by "going beyond the information given" or by "verbal symbol manipulation." The results of a recent study (Laosa, 1980a) provide indirect confirmatory evidence for the general hypothesis that the parent's choice of teaching strategies can influence the child's development of characteristic learning strategies.

In that study (Laosa, 1980a), I examined the relationships between the mothers' teaching strategies and their children's development of *cognitive styles*. Now, where do individual differences in learning strategies figure in relation to cognitive styles? Cognitive styles are conceptualized as characteristic ways of organizing and processing information—as stable preferences that determine a person's typical mode of perceiving, remembering, thinking, and problem-solving (Messick, 1976). Whereas a cognitive style is regarded as a self-consistent way of processing information, that is, as a stable trait or a pervasive disposition in the individual, a learning strategy is the process that takes place as the person attempts to learn a task or solve a problem. In short, the process that is activated in the individual toward attainment or solution of a learning or problem-solving task is, at least in theory, sometimes determined by his or her cognitive style (Laosa, 1977a).

Correlations between the mothers' teaching strategies and measures of their children's cognitive styles revealed trends suggesting that the teaching strategies to which the young child is exposed in the home may influence which cognitive style the child develops (Laosa, 1980a). It is, of course, always difficult to ascribe directionality with correlation data; however, both the pattern and the direction of the relationships conformed to the stated hypotheses derived from theory. Hence, the observed links between maternal teaching strategies and the children's cognitive styles provide indirect support for the general hypothesis that the mother's choice of teaching strategies will have an effect on her child's development of characteristic learning strategies.

These results, together with those reviewed earlier suggesting a resemblance between the teaching strategies of the more highly schooled mothers and the instructional strategies of academic classrooms, lead me to propose a hypothetical model to explain the high frequency of scholastic failure among Chicanos and other populations in which the parents, on the average, have completed relatively few years of schooling. The general hypothetical model can be summarized as follows: The children of the more highly-schooled parents learn to master in their homes the form and dynamics of teaching and learning processes that "take after" those of the school classroom. Because of this relative similarity, the interactional processes that these children learn to master at home will have *adaptive* value in the classroom. Therefore, insofar as the children of the more highly schooled parents learn to master classroom-like interactional processes in their homes, they will have a decided advantage over the children of the lower-schooling parents since the latter, by contrast, learn to master in their homes the form and dynamics of teaching and learning processes that have comparatively little adaptive value in the classroom. A graphic schematization of this hypothesis, or explanatory model of scholastic performance, is shown in Figure 4.

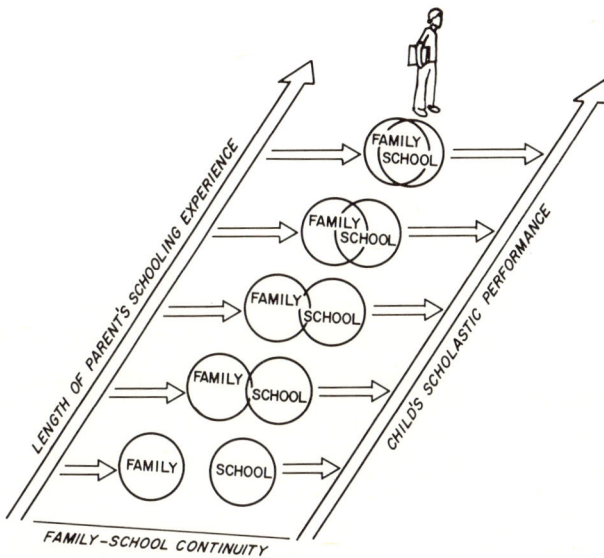

Figure 4. Symbolic depiction of the hypothesis linking schooling, family interaction patterns, and scholastic performance.

According to this general hypothesis, each family and its children evolve a system of relations to make sense of each other. Thus, the family and its children develop a characteristic way of dealing with each other in teaching and learning situations (and other situations as well). To the extent that the relational systems of family and school differ, the child and the school teachers will be unable to draw on a shared process of teaching and learning (Laosa, 1974, 1977b, c, 1979; McDermott, 1977). As a result of this *discontinuity* between the family and the school, the child and the teachers will spend a great portion of their time simply attempting to make sense out of one another's behavior. Hence, school failure for many probably occurs because student and teachers are unable to make sense of each other's relational system. The model further posits—and the present data suggest—that the extent to which the family and the school will share in common a relational system for teaching and learning depends, at least in part, on the length of the parents' schooling experience.

This hypothetical model emanates in part from the socioculturally relativistic paradigm that I proposed recently to explain children's cross-situational development of social competence. Briefly, according to the *developmental, socioculturally relativistic paradigm* (Laosa, 1979), social competence involves functional adaptations to specific environments. Insofar as different environments may have their own specific demand characteristics for functional adaptation, for a child being successful in two different environments (e.g., home and school) may depend on the degree of overlap in the demand characteristics of the two environments.[6]

The scope of the model extends beyond its applicability to instructional interactions. For example, the model can be applied to the interactional processes involved in the assessment of academic progress, for example, testing. As an illustration, consider the results showing that inquiry, or question-asking, was relatively infrequent among the lower-schooling families. Based on this finding, it seems reasonable to hypothesize that the children of the lower-schooling parents are less likely than are those of the more highly-schooled parents to have experience and familiarity with the interactional conventions of test procedures. As a result of their relative lack of experience and familiarity with the form and dynamics of question-asking as an interactional mode, in a testing situation the children of the lower-schooling parents are likely to be at a disadvantage vis à vis the children of the more highly schooled parents since the latter have learned to master this interactional mode in their homes. Rather than being able to focus their attention freely on the content of the test, the children of the lower-schooling parents will "waste" precious time and mental energy trying to make sense of the relatively unfamiliar mode of communication entailed on the conventions of the test procedures.

Thus far we have examined data on the relationship between parental schooling and teaching strategies, and the results indicate that schooling may have an impact on the strategies that mothers use to teach their own children. A teaching strategy is a *process* that takes place as a person attempts to teach a task to someone. As such, a particular teaching strategy may be used to teach a variety of different tasks, each of which may have a different *content*. We now turn to an analysis of the impact that schooling may have on parent–child interactions that center on a specific content, namely, reading.

Parental Schooling and Reading to the Child

Does schooling have an impact on the content of the parent–child interaction? The analyses reported in this section were conducted to

---

[6] The general idea that minority children experience discontinuities between home and school and that such discontinuities can lead to dysfunctional adaptive responses is of course not an original one. Such discontinuities have been suggested by other writers (see, for example, Cárdenas & Cárdenas, 1973; Cole & Bruner, 1971; Ramírez & Castañeda, 1974; more recent writings include, for example, Cárdenas & Zamora, 1980; Henderson, 1980; Lightfoot, 1978; Ogbu, 1981; see also McNeil & Laosa, 1975; for examples of dysfunctional discontinuities between the home and extrafamilial institutions other than the school see Laosa, Burstein, & Martin, 1975).

examine the influence that schooling may have on how frequently men and women, once they become parents, read to their children. Certainly, parent–child interactions can center on many different types of content, of which reading is only one. Reading was selected for study because previous research has shown that the amount of time that parents spend reading to their children may have important consequences for the child's intellectual development (see Hess & Holloway, 1979, for a review).

The data for this study were obtained from the same families that participated in the two studies of maternal behavior reviewed earlier in this chapter. Each mother was administered a home interview that included questions about how frequently each parent read to his or her kindergarten child. The questions were as follows: First, the mother was asked whether she had ever read to the child. Next, if the answer was affirmative, she was asked to indicate how often she read to the child, using the following scale: 0 = never, 1 = about once a month or less, 2 = about twice a month, 3 = about once a week, 4 = more than once a week. The same procedure was used to obtain information about how frequently the father read to the child.

Table 2 presents the Pearson product–moment correlations between the frequency of parental reading to the child and the parents' schooling attainment levels and occupational statuses, separately for Chicano and non-Hispanic White families. All the significant correlations involved schooling. The more highly schooled mothers and fathers read to their children more frequently than did those with less schooling. In contrast, neither parent's occupational status was related to how frequently he or she read to the children. A similar pattern of correlations was obtained in both ethnic groups.

For a closer examination of the relationships uncovered by the

Table 2. Correlations between How Frequently Parents Read to Their Children and the Parents' Schooling Level and Occupational Status, by Ethnic Group and Sex of Parent

Ethnic group and sex of parent	Mother's schooling	Father's schooling	Mother's occupation	Father's occupation
Chicano families				
Mother reads to child	$.33^a$	.14	−.02	.17
Father reads to child	.13	.24	−.06	.10
Non-Hispanic White families				
Mother reads to child	$.37^b$	$.40^b$	−.19	.10
Father reads to child	$.27^a$	.16	−.14	.15

Note: Chicano families: n = 42–43. Non-Hispanic White families: n = 40.
[a] $p < .05$, one-tailed test.
[b] $p < .01$, one-tailed test.

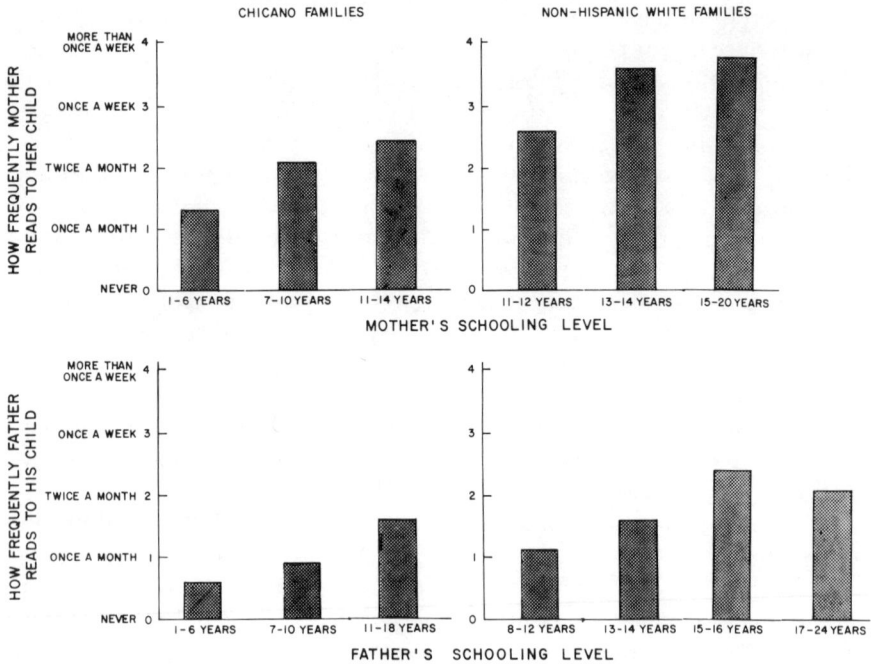

Figure 5. How frequently Chicano and non-Hispanic White parents of varied schooling levels read to their young children. (Chicano mothers: n = 15 for 1–6 years, 13 for 7–10 years, and 15 for 11–14 years. Chicano fathers: n = 18 for 2–6 years, 10 for 7–10 years, and 14 for 11–18 years. Non-Hispanic White mothers: n = 22 for 11–12 years, 10 for 13–14 years, and 8 for 15–20 years. Non-Hispanic White fathers: n = 10 for 8–12 years, 10 for 13–14 years, 11 for 15–16 years, and 9 for 17–24 years.)

correlational analyses, Figure 5 displays the means of the reading scale as a function of parental schooling level, separately by sex of parent and ethnic group. In general, the frequency of parental reading to the child increases continuously as a function of parental schooling level. There appears to be, however—at least for non-Hispanic White fathers—a threshold level (16 years) beyond which additional years of schooling do not result in an increase in the frequency of paternal reading to the child.

The next set of analyses was performed, first, to compare the two ethnic groups with regard to how frequently parents read to their children and, second, to determine whether any observed ethnic-group differences could be explained (statistically) on the basis of the ethnic differential in parental schooling level and occupational status. The analyses are based on a two-by-two factorial design, using ethnic group and child's sex as independent variables and the frequency with which mothers and fathers read to their children as dependent variables. As before, the analyses were performed in five different ways. First, an analysis of variance with fixed effects, classical model, was performed on each dependent variable. Next, four analyses of covariance were performed on each dependent variable, using mothers' and fathers' schooling levels and occupational statuses, respectively, as covariates. Table 3 shows the unadjusted means and standard deviations of how frequently the Chicano and non-Hispanic White parents read to their children, and Table 4 presents the F ratios of the analyses of variance and covariance. Table 5 shows the F ratios of the interactions between the covariates and the independent variables; for only one of the 16 analyses was this interaction significant, indicating that in general the assumption of homogeneous slopes was met for these analyses.

Comparisons of how frequently Chicano and non-Hispanic White parents read to their children revealed significant ethnic-group differences. The non-Hispanic White mothers read to their children more frequently than did the Chicano mothers. Similarly, the non-Hispanic White fathers read to their children more frequently than did the Chicano fathers. When the two ethnic groups were compared while statistically holding constant the parents' occupational status, the same ethnic-group differences emerged. However, when the two ethnic groups were compared while statistically holding constant the parents' schooling level, the significant ethnic-group differences vanished.

These results suggest that the intellectual disadvantage observed among many ethnic minority children can be explained by the fact that

Table 3. Means and Standard Deviations of How Frequently Parents Read to Their Children in Chicano and Non-Hispanic White Families, by Sex of Parent and Sex of Child

Dyad structure	Chicano	Non-Hispanic White
Mother reads to son		
Mean	1.60	3.37
S.D.	1.46	1.13
Mother reads to daughter		
Mean	2.17	2.86
S.D.	1.46	1.28
Father reads to son		
Mean	1.00	2.10
S.D.	1.45	1.65
Father reads to daughter		
Mean	1.00	1.57
S.D.	1.28	1.43

Note: The number of cases is as follows: Chicanos: 20 mother–son and 23 mother–daughter dyads. Non-Hispanic Whites: 19 mother–son and 21 mother–daughter dyads.

Table 4. *F* **Ratios of Analyses of Variance and Covariance for Measures of How Frequently Chicano and Non-Hispanic White Parents Read to Their Children**

Dependent variables, degrees of freedom, and covariates	Main effects		
	Ethnic group	Sex of child	Interaction
Mother reads to child			
F (1, 77)	14.32^c	.05	3.44+
F (1,76), mother's occupation covaried	15.04^c	.02	3.82^a
F (1, 76), father's occupation covaried	8.62^b	.20	2.93+
F (1, 76), mother's schooling covaried	1.15	.05	1.57
F (1, 75), father's schooling covaried*	2.45	.36	2.62
Father reads to child			
F (1, 77)	5.48^a	.42	.89
F (1,76), mother's occupation covaried	6.15^a	.59	1.13
F (1, 76), father's occupation covaried	2.81+	.20	.66
F (1, 76), mother's schooling covaried	.81	.43	.40
F (1, 75), father's schooling covaried*	.73	.16	.54

*Information on the father's schooling level was unavailable for one family.
+$p < .10$.
^{a}$p < .05$.
^{b}$p < .01$.
^{c}$p < .001$.

Table 5. Tests of the Assumption of Homogeneous Slopes: *F* Ratios of the Interactions between Covariates and Independent Variables

Dependent variables, degrees of freedom, and covariates	Interactions	
	Covariate × Ethnicity	Covariate × Sex
Mother reads to child		
F (1, 79), mother's occupation	.33	.47
F (1, 79), father's occupation	.36	2.25
F (1, 79), mother's schooling	.54	.42
F (1, 78), father's schooling*	1.45	3.35
Father reads to child		
F (1,79), mother's occupation	.10	5.91^a
F (1, 79), father's occupation	.02	1.89
F (1, 79), mother's schooling	1.45	.00
F (1, 78), father's schooling*	.00	1.22

*Information on the father's schooling level was unavailable for one family.
^{a}$p < .05$.

ethnic minority parents on the average have attained fewer years of schooling than nonminority parents. These results also suggest that when educational equity finally becomes a reality and Chicanos and non-Hispanic Whites attain similar levels of schooling, at least part of the present-day intellectual disadvantage of many ethnic minority children will disappear as both minority and nonminority children will experience similar amounts of literacy-related stimulation in the home.

These data thus provide additional confirmatory evidence for the first part of the hypothetical model linking school, family, and scholastic performance. Specifically, the data suggest that the length of parental schooling determines the degree to which there will be continuity between school and family with regard to one domain of the teaching and learning process—namely, reading.

It is interesting to note, parenthetically, that in the analyses of variance there were significant ethnic-group by sex-of-child interactions, which became nonsignificant when parental schooling was held constant. These interactions that emerged prior to holding schooling constant indicate that, in Chicano families, mothers read more frequently to their daughters than to their sons. The reverse occurred in non-Hispanic White families, where mothers read more frequently to their sons than to their daughters. Also interesting is the fact that, in both ethnic groups, mothers read to their children more frequently than did fathers, a finding that may have implications for the development of sex-role stereotypes about intellectual behavior.

In the next section I attempt to determine whether parental schooling and parental reading to the child seem to have an influence on the child's early acquisition of literacy skills.

Parental Schooling, Reading to the Child, and Early Development of Literacy

Having already established various links between the length of the parent's schooling and the parent's behavior, and also between the parent's behavior and the child's development of characteristic learning strategies, can we now adduce evidence regarding the part of the model that postulates an effect on the child's development of specific cognitive skills? (Figure 1.) Specifically, can we establish a set of empirically concatenated links between parental schooling, family interaction patterns, *and* children's development of specific cognitive skills? The analyses that follow were performed to test the hypothesis that, in contrast to the lower-schooling Chicano families, the more highly schooled Chicano families are more

**Table 6. Parental Correlates of Literacy Skills
among Chicano Preschoolers**

Parental variables	Correlation with preschool literacy
Mother's schooling	.28[a]
Father's schooling	.11
Mother's occupation	.24
Father's occupation	.00
Mother reads to child	.32[a]
Father reads to child	.12

Note: The coefficients are point-biserial correlations between the parental variables and whether the child acquired any literacy skills before kindergarten; the latter was scored dichotomously: 1 = no (74%), 2 = yes (26%). n = 42-43.
[a]$p < .05$, one-tailed test.

effective in developing their children's readiness skills for the quintessential task of the school, namely, the development of literacy.

The analyses were performed to test the hypothesis that parental schooling and parental reading to the child are positively related to the child's acquisition of literacy skills before entry into kindergarten. The data were derived from the home interviews with the mothers, conducted when the children were in kindergarten. The results, shown in Table 6 and in Figure 6, support the hypothesis. The children of the more highly

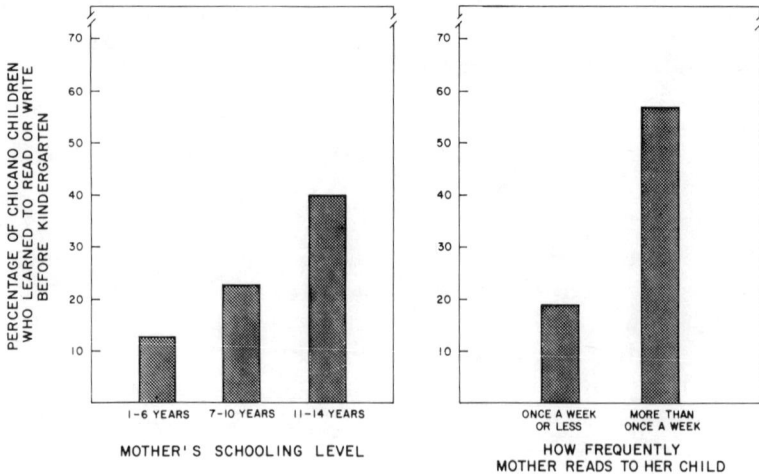

Figure 6. Percentage of Chicano children who acquired literacy skills before kindergarten—as a function of (a) their mothers' years of schooling and (b) the frequency with which their mothers read to them. (n = 43.)

schooled Chicano mothers (i.e., generally the Chicano mothers who read more frequently to their children) were more likely to have acquired some measure of literacy before starting kindergarten than were the children of the lower-schooling Chicano mothers (i.e., generally the Chicano mothers who read less frequently to their children). These results provide confirmatory evidence for the general hypothesis that the children of the more highly schooled Chicano mothers will be better prepared for school and hence will experience a greater degree of family–school continuity than will the children of the lower-schooling Chicano mothers.

It is interesting to note that, whereas *maternal* schooling and maternal reading to the child correlated significantly with the child's acquisition of preschool literacy, *paternal* schooling and paternal reading to the child did not correlate significantly with the child's acquisition of preschool literacy. This contrast is particularly intriguing because these families were intact. Indeed, the contrast suggests that the mother in Chicano families tends to have a stronger influence on the child's early acquisition of literacy than does the father.

Two other aspects of the parent–child relationship that I will consider in this chapter are the parents' aspirations for their childrens' education and the family's choice of language for use in the home. Let us turn now to an examination of the relationship between parental schooling and parental aspirations for the child.

Parental Schooling and Educational Aspirations for the Child

Does parental schooling have an impact on the family's aspirations for the education of the child? The analyses reported in this section were conducted to examine the influence that parental schooling and occupational status may have on the family's expectations, or aspirations, regarding the young child's future scholastic achievements. Educational aspirations were chosen for study because of their potentially influential role in the child's academic development (see Marjoribanks, 1979, for a review).

The data were obtained from the Chicano and non-Hispanic White families with a kindergarten child described elsewhere in this chapter. As part of the home interview, each mother was asked the following questions regarding her aspirations for the formal education of her kindergarten child: "*Realistically*, how much education do you think your child will receive?" "*Ideally*, how much education would you like your child to receive?" "What is the minimum amount of education you think your child should receive?" The mothers answered each question using the following scale: 1 = complete elementary school, 2 = complete junior high school, 3 = graduate from high school, 4 = attend technical or vocational school, 5 = attend some college, 6 = graduate from college, 7 = obtain a master's degree, 8 = obtain a professional degree (e.g., M.D., Ph.D., LL.D.).

Table 7 presents the Pearson product–moment correlations between the mother's educational aspirations for her child and the mother's and her husband's schooling attainment levels and occupational statuses, separately by ethnic group. For a closer examination of these relationships, Figure 7 graphically presents the means of the educational aspiration scales as a function of maternal schooling level, again separately by ethnic group. In both ethnic groups there is a positive, generally significant relationship between the mother's educational aspirations for her child and the mother's and her husband's schooling attainment levels. The mothers in the more highly schooled families held higher educational aspirations for their children than did the mothers in the lower-schooling families.

The two ethnic groups differ, however, with regard to the relationship between educational aspirations and *occupational status*. In the Chicano families, there is no relationship between maternal aspirations for the child's education and either parent's occupational status. In contrast, in the non-Hispanic White families the father's occupational status is a significant predictor of maternal aspirations for the child's education.

Do the Chicano and non-Hispanic White families differ in the level of aspirations they hold for their children's education? If they differ, can the ethnic-group difference in educational aspirations be explained

Table 7. Correlations of Maternal Aspirations for the Child's Education with Parental Schooling and Occupational Status, by Ethnic Group

Ethnic group and aspiration variable	Mother's schooling	Father's schooling	Mother's occupation	Father's occupation
Chicano families				
"Realistic" aspirations	.26[a]	.37[b]	−.11	−.02
"Ideal" aspirations	.16	.34[b]	−.18	.20
Minimum education	.29[a]	.32[a]	.00	−.01
Non-Hispanic White families				
"Realistic" aspirations	.45[b]	.45[b]	−.03	.40[b]
"Ideal" aspirations	.33[a]	.37[b]	−.03	.39[b]
Minimum education	.51[c]	.61[c]	−.22	.53[c]

Note: n = 40–43 for Chicanos and 39–40 for non-Hispanic Whites.
[a] $p < .05$, one-tailed test.
[b] $p < .01$, one-tailed test.
[c] $p < .001$, one-tailed test.

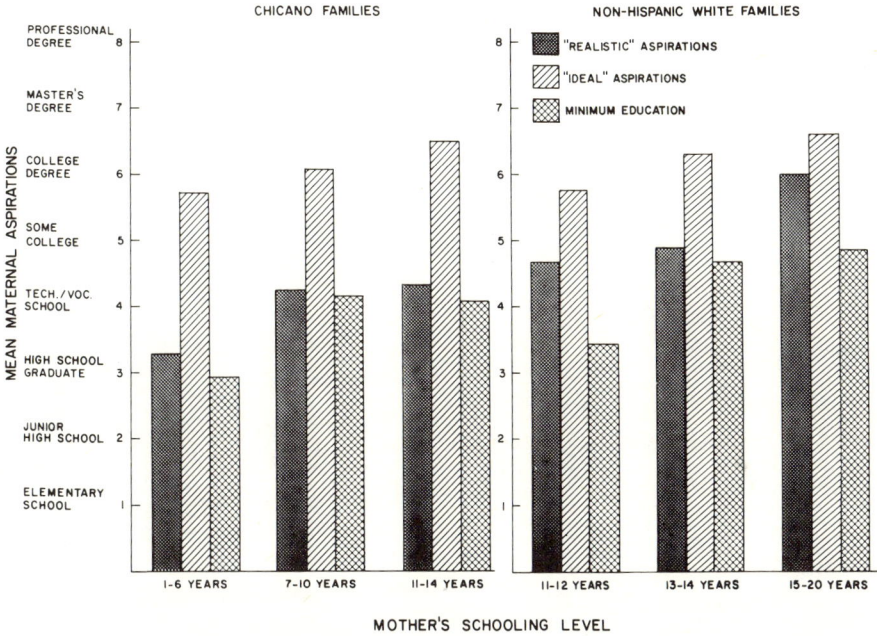

Figure 7. Maternal aspirations for the child's education as a function of maternal schooling level in Chicago and non-Hispanic White families.

statistically by the ethnic differential in parental schooling level and occupational status? To answer these questions, a series of fixed effects, classical model analyses of variance and covariance were performed using the three measures of educational aspirations as dependent variables. As before, the independent variables were ethnic group and sex of child and the covariates, the parents' schooling levels and occupational statuses. Table 8 shows the unadjusted means and standard deviations for the measures of educational aspirations. Table 9 presents the F ratios of the analyses of variance and covariance. The assumption of homogeneous slopes was met for the analyses of covariance, as evidenced by nonsignificant $(p > .05)$ F ratios for the interactions between the covariates and the independent variables.

The analyses of variance revealed no significant Ethnic Group or Sex main effects or interactions, either for the mother's "ideal" educational aspirations for her child or for the minimum amount of education she thought her child should receive. In contrast, both main effects were significant for the mother's "realistic" educational aspirations for her child.

Table 8. Means and Standard Deviations of Maternal Aspirations for the Child's Education in Chicano and Non-Hispanic White Families, by Sex of Child

	Chicano		Non-Hispanic White	
Aspiration variables	Boys	Girls	Boys	Girls
"Realistic" aspirations				
Mean	4.10	3.81	5.58	4.48
S.D.	1.48	1.83	1.07	1.29
"Ideal" aspirations				
Mean	6.00	6.17	6.44	5.76
S.D.	1.69	1.70	1.25	1.09
Minimum education				
Mean	3.55	3.83	4.21	3.86
S.D.	1.57	1.40	1.36	1.15

Note: The number of cases is as follows: Chicano: 20 boys and 21–23 girls. Non-Hispanic White: 18–19 boys and 21 girls.

The non-Hispanic White mothers, as a group, had higher "realistic" aspirations for their children's education than did the Chicano mothers. This was the result obtained before holding constant the mothers' or the fathers' schooling level or occupational status. When the two ethnic groups were compared while statistically holding constant the parents' occupational status, the same ethnic-group difference emerged. However,

Table 9. F Ratios of Analyses of Variance and Covariance for Measures of Maternal Aspirations for the Child's Education in Chicano and Non-Hispanic White Families

	Main effects		
Dependent variables, degrees of freedom, and covariates	Ethnic group	Sex of child	Interaction
"Realistic" aspirations			
$F(1, 77)$	10.70^b	4.57^a	1.58
$F(1, 76)$, mother's occupation covaried	11.27^c	4.92^a	1.81
$F(1, 76)$, father's occupation covaried	5.99^a	3.53	1.22
$F(1, 76)$, mother's schooling covaried	.64	5.01^a	.44
$F(1, 75)$, father's schooling covaried*	.17	2.14	1.18
"Ideal" aspirations			
$F(1, 77)$	.00	.51	1.74
Minimum education			
$F(1, 77)$	1.13	.00	.77

*Information on the father's schooling level was not available for one family.
[a] $p < .05$.
[b] $p < .01$.
[c] $p < .001$.

when the two ethnic groups were compared while statistically holding constant either parents' schooling level, the significant ethnic-group difference in educational aspirations vanished.

In sum, these results indicate that in both ethnic groups, maternal aspirations for the child's education increase as a function of parental schooling. The results further indicate that Chicano mothers, as a group, hold lower aspirations for their children's education than do non-Hispanic White mothers. Additional results provide confirmatory evidence for the hypothesis that the ethnic-group difference in aspirations for the child's education is the result of the ethnic differential in parental schooling. These results suggest that when educational equity finally becomes a reality and adults in both ethnic groups attain similar levels of schooling, the observed ethnic-group difference in parental aspirations for the child's education will disappear, as Chicano and non-Hispanic White parents will come to hold similar aspirations for their children's education.

It is worth noting, parenthetically, that in both ethnic groups there was a sex difference in educational aspirations. In both the Chicano and non-Hispanic White families, mothers held lower educational aspirations for their daughters than they did for their sons.

Perhaps the most salient characteristic of many Chicano families is their use of a language other than English in the home—namely, Spanish. Let us turn now to an examination of the relationship between parental schooling and choice of language for parent–child interaction.

Parental Schooling and Home Language

Culture and language are closely intertwined. Earlier I examined evidence suggesting that schooling is a powerful force in the evolution of culturally determined patterns of family interaction. Does the influence that schooling seems to exert on the family extend as well to the use of language in the home? The analyses reported in this section were performed to examine the relationships of parental schooling and occupational status with the family's choice of home language. The first set of data I will use for this purpose are based on the sample of 43 Chicano families in Los Angeles described earlier. The data were obtained through home interviews with the mothers when the children were in kindergarten. Each mother was asked to indicate whether English, Spanish, both languages with equal frequency (not mixing the two languages within individual sentences), or a "mixture" of both languages was used as the most frequent means of oral communication between each parent and his

Table 10. Languages Used in Parent–Child Interactions in Chicano Families, by Sex of Parent and Directionality of Interaction: Los Angeles Sample

Sex of parent and directionality of interaction	Language category			
	English	Spanish	Both	Mixture
Mother to child	30%	56%	5%	9%
Child to mother	44	54	0	2
Father to child	33	56	7	9
Child to father	44	49	2	5

Note: Each figure is the percentage of homes where a given language category was used as the most frequent means of oral communication. n = 43 households.

or her five-year-old child.[7] The interviews were conducted by bilingual (English–Spanish) Chicano women.[8]

Table 10 presents the percentage of Chicano households where each language or language combination was used as the single most frequent means of oral communication between parent and child, separately by sex of parent and directionality of interaction. Approximately 50% of the families used Spanish as the most frequent means of communication between parent and child. About one-third of the families used English, and relatively few families used either both languages with equal frequency (as separate codes) or an intermixed variety of both.

Table 11 presents the point-biserial correlations of language use—whether English was used (1 = no, 2 = yes) and whether Spanish was used (1 = no, 2 = yes) as the most frequent language—with parental schooling and occupational status, separately by sex of parent and directionality of the interaction. It is clear from these results that there is a strong association between parental schooling and home language use. It is also evident that schooling is a much better predictor of home language use than is

[7] The term *mixture* as used here refers to the use of grammatical, lexical, and phonological aspects of both English and Spanish within single sentences; it includes more than occasional borrowing, loan translations, or loan blends (for detailed examples see Cornejo, 1973). Evidence from linguistic research (e.g.,Cornejo, 1973)suggests that there is a high degree of "grammaticalness" in such intermixed varieties of English and Spanish.

[8] The use of reports as a method of collecting language use data may be subject to response bias resulting from normative attitudes that may affect informants' judgments. In the studies reported here great care was taken, however, to eliminate as much as possible this potential source of bias by employing and carefully training only interviewers who were indigenous to the ethnic, language, and geographic communities from which they obtained data. Moreover, the distinctions involved in the range of possible responses were explained to each informant in detail and with examples in order to define consistently for the participants such terms as "most often," "equal frequency," and "mixture" (Laosa, 1975).

Table 11. Correlations between the Languages Used in Parent–Child Interactions in
Chicano Families and the Parents' Schooling Level and Occupational Status,
by Sex of Parent and Directionality of Interaction: Los Angeles Sample

Language, sex of parent, and directionality of interaction	Mother's schooling	Father's schooling	Mother's occupation	Father's occupation
English				
Mother to child	.58[c]	.51[c]	−.03	.08
Child to mother	.73[c]	.61[c]	.31[a]	.28[a]
Father to child	.65[c]	.60[c]	−.03	.30[a]
Child to father	.73[c]	.61[c]	.31[a]	.28[a]
Spanish				
Mother to child	−.77[c]	−.65[c]	−.18	−.35[b]
Child to mother	−.77[c]	−.67[c]	−.28[a]	−.30[a]
Father to child	−.49[c]	−.74[c]	.07	−.21
Child to father	−.62[c]	−.63[c]	−.22	−.14

Note: $n = 12$–13.
[a] $p < .05$, one-tailed test.
[b] $p < .01$, one-tailed test.
[c] $p < .001$, one-tailed test.

occupational status. Parent–child interactions in the homes of the more
highly schooled Chicano parents tended to take place more frequently in
English than in Spanish. Conversely, parent–child interactions in the
homes of lower-schooling Chicano parents tended to take place more
frequently in Spanish than in English. These relationships are very strong.

For a closer examination of the relationships uncovered by the
correlational analyses, Figure 8 displays the percentage of Chicano homes
in which English was used as the most frequent language of parent–child
interaction, separately by parental schooling level, sex of parent, and
directionality of the interaction. The use of English as the single most
frequent means of oral communication between parent and child increases
dramatically with increasing length of parental schooling.

Unpublished data from an earlier study (Laosa, 1975) provided a
welcome opportunity to test the generalizability of these findings. In
contrast to the data presented above, which are based on a sample of
Chicano households in Los Angeles, California, the data to which we now
turn are based on a sample of 100 Chicano households in Austin, Texas.
The two data sets also differ with regard to the age of the focal children and
the specificity of the measures. These differences between the two data sets
are relevant, as we shall see, to the interpretation of the results; therefore, I
shall describe them here in some detail. Whereas the focal children in the
Los Angeles sample were in kindergarten, those in the Austin sample were
distributed in equal proportions in the first, second, and third grades.

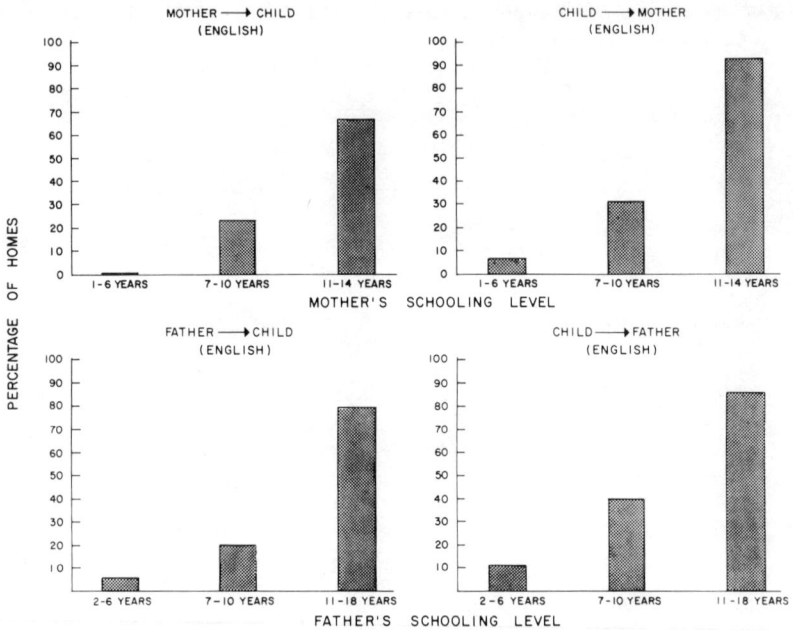

Figure 8. Percentage of Chicano homes where English was used as the most frequent language for parent-child interaction, by parental schooling level, sex of parent, and directionality of the interaction. (Los Angeles families, $n = 43$.)

Although the same item format was used for obtaining the home language data in both studies, the Los Angeles study focused on the languages used for specific dyadic interactions, whereas the Austin study focused more broadly on the languages used by the focal child and by the adult members of the household, respectively, when interacting with all the other members of the household. Like the Los Angeles sample, the Austin sample was selected to be as representative as possible of Chicano families with young children with regard to the distribution of socioeconomic status.

Table 12 reproduces the percentage of Chicano families in Austin where each language or language combination was used by the focal child and by the adults in the household as the single most frequent means of oral communication in the home. A comparison of these data with those obtained in Los Angeles (Table 10) reveals differences as well as similarities. The two Chicano samples differ perhaps most markedly with regard to the use of English–Spanish "mixture." The Austin families used "mixture" more frequently than did the Los Angeles families. By contrast, the Los Angeles families used Spanish more frequently than did the Austin families. Regional differences such as these are not surprising; indeed, they

Table 12. Languages Used by Children and Adults in Chicano Households: Austin Sample

| Age group | Language category | | | |
	English	Spanish	Both	Mixture
Adults	26%	23%	11%	40%
Children	45	2	23	30

Note: n = 100 households. Data from Laosa, 1975.

can be observed readily by the trained observer traveling across different Chicano communities throughout the southwestern United States.

The two samples are, however, markedly similar with regard to the use of English. Adults used English as the most frequent home language in one-fourth to one-third of the households. Children used English as the most frequent home language in about one-half of the households. This generational difference in both samples indicates an increase in the use of English by children over parents. I shall discuss this intergenerational language shift in greater detail later when I examine the influence of the parents' home language on the child's choice of home language.

To continue our examination of the relationship between schooling and home language, Table 13 presents the point-biserial correlations

Table 13. Correlations between the Languages Used
in Chicano Homes and the Mothers' Schooling Level,
by Generational Group: Austin Sample

Language and generational group	Correlation with mother's schooling
English	
Adults	.30[b]
Child	.18
Spanish	
Adults	−.31[b]
Child*	—
Both	
Adults	.15
Child	−.05
Mixture	
Adults	−.24[a]
Child	−.03

Note: n = 82 households.
*A coefficient was not computed because of an extreme dichotomous cut.
[a] p < .05, one-tailed test.
[b] p < .01, one-tailed test.

between home language use and maternal schooling for the Austin households. (Two characteristics of this data set preclude analyses involving paternal schooling and parental occupational status: an absence of data on maternal occupation and an unidentified proportion of father-absent households.) For purposes of these analyses, again each language category was a dichotomous variable (1 = no, 2 = yes).

These correlations, particularly those involving the children, are much lower for the Austin sample than they are for the Los Angeles sample (Tables 11 and 13). To understand this contrast, consider first the afore-mentioned age and schooling differential between the children in the two samples: the Los Angeles children were in kindergarten; the Austin children were older, in elementary school. Therefore, the observed drop in the correlation between maternal and child variables as the children progress from kindergarten to elementary school is not surprising, given the expected increase in extrafamilial influences with age and schooling. Indeed, these results appear to reflect the emerging influence of the child's school experiences on his or her use of language at home and a resultant lessening of the influence exerted by the family. Second, consider the difference in measurement specificity. As we saw earlier, the language variables in the Los Angeles data measure specifically the interactions between the child and each parent. In contrast, the language variables in the Austin data measure interactions in a much more general and inclusive manner. As measurement specificity decreases, so should one expect an increase in the variety of sources of variance affecting the measurements in the variables and, therefore, an ancillary decrease in the precision with which the variables can be predicted. Some as yet unspecified combination of these reasons probably explains the lower magnitude of the correlations in the Austin data.

Notwithstanding the difference in the magnitude of the correlations, the results obtained with the Austin sample partially replicate those obtained with the Los Angeles sample. The Austin data thus provide additional confirmatory evidence for the hypothesis that there is a significant association between maternal schooling and home language use. Children in the homes of the more highly schooled Chicano mothers tended to be exposed to adult language more frequently in English than in either Spanish or a "mixture." Conversely, children in the homes of the lower-schooling Chicano mothers tended to be exposed to adult language more frequently in Spanish and in "mixture" than in English.

It is difficult to decide which of two alternative hypotheses seems to explain better the obtained correlations between schooling and language use. On one hand, it is quite plausible that the longer a bilingual or limited-English speaking person stays in school, the greater is the likelihood that he or she will learn and/or adopt English as the dominant language. After all, bilingual education in the public schools of the United States is a relatively recent phenomenon. Most adult Chicanos today have attended schools in the United States and therefore their schooling has been in English. On the other hand, it also is plausible that Chicanos who came from predominantly Spanish-speaking backgrounds encountered greater difficulty in schools, and hence discontinued their schooling earlier than did predominantly English-speaking Chicanos—as a result of linguistic problems (e.g., difficulties in understanding the subject matter taught in English), paralinguistic problems (e.g., difficulties in coordinating speech with implicit meanings of gesture), and/or affective problems (e.g., language attitude and value conflicts). These plausible explanatory hypotheses are not mutually exclusive, however. Indeed, evidence that I will discuss later, together with the results of an earlier study (Laosa, 1977b) indicating that teachers behave less favorably toward Spanish-dominant Chicano students than toward English-dominant Chicano students, suggest that the observed correlations between length of schooling and language use can be explained, at least in part, by the joint influence of the processes embodied in both hypotheses. It is, however, exceedingly difficult to identify all the contributing processes and, as we shall see below, practically impossible to identify the separate influences of each.

Nativity

The link between nativity and schooling among Chicanos results in a tangled nexus of covariation that defies isolation of their unique influences on parental behavior. Table 14 presents the point-biserial correlations of parental nativity to parental schooling and occupational status for the

Table 14. Correlations of Nativity with Schooling Level and Occupational Status in Chicano Families

Variables	Mother's nativity	Father's nativity
Mother's schooling	.66[c]	.45[c]
Father's schooling	.54[c]	.43[b]
Mother's occupation	.22	−.06
Father's occupation	.31[a]	.34[b]

Note: n = 12–13.
[a] $p < .05$, one-tailed test.
[b] $p < .01$, one-tailed test.
[c] $p < .001$, one-tailed test.

sample of Chicano families in Los Angeles. Nativity is a dichotomous
variable: 1 = born in Mexico, 2 = born in the United States. In these
families, 51% of the mothers, 46% of the fathers, and 81% of the children were
born in the United States; the others were born in Mexico.

The Chicano parents born in Mexico completed, as a group, fewer
years of schooling than those born in the United States. These results
replicate those obtained in previous studies, including national surveys
(Baral, 1979; Brown, Rosen, Hill, & Olivas, 1980; Featherman & Hauser,
1978; Grebler, Moore, & Guzman, 1970). The difference in the schooling
level of the Chicanos born in Mexico and those born in the United States
probably manifests the lower average schooling of the national population
of Mexico; however, it is difficult to interpret the difference without
additional data, including, for example, the age and the schooling level at
the time of immigration.

Table 15 shows the relationship of nativity to home language use for
the sample of Chicano families in Los Angeles. It is not surprising that
Chicanos born in the United States were more likely to use English as the
principal home language—and conversely less likely to use Spanish—than
were those born in Mexico. These results, too, replicate those obtained in
national samples (e.g., Macías, 1979; National Center for Education
Statistics, 1978). The important point to note, however, is that in both
pattern and size, these correlations between home language and nativity are
strikingly similar to the correlations between home language and
schooling, which we examined earlier (Table 11).

Table 15. Relationship between Nativity and Home Language Use in Chicano Families

Language, sex of parent, and directionality of interaction	Mother's nativity	Father's nativity	Child's nativity
English			
Mother to child	.54[c]	.50[c]	.32[a]
Child to mother	.87[c]	.58[c]	.42[b]
Father to child	.68[c]	.65[c]	.33[a]
Child to father	.87[c]	.58[c]	.42[b]
Spanish			
Mother to child	−.78[c]	−.58[c]	−.42[b]
Child to mother	−.82[c]	−.53[c]	−.45[c]
Father to child	−.50[c]	−.48[c]	−.30[a]
Child to father	−.72[c]	−.54[c]	−.37[b]

Note: The measures of relationship are phi coefficients. n = 13.
[a] $p < 0.5$, one-tailed test.
[b] $p < .01$, one-tailed test.
[c] $p < .001$, one-tailed test.

The father's nativity was almost as good a predictor of the mother's characteristics as was the mother's own nativity; obversely, the mother's nativity was almost as good a predictor of the father's characteristics as was the father's own nativity. This is not surprising, given the moderately high association between mother's and father's nativity (phi coefficient = .63, $p < .001$, $n = 43$). This suggests that Chicano marriages tend to be endogamous with regard to country of birth.

Table 16 presents the correlations between maternal nativity and maternal teaching strategies, and Table 17 the correlations between parental nativity and the remaining categories of parental behavior. Here, too, the correlations between maternal behavior and nativity are markedly similar to the correlations between maternal behavior and schooling, which we examined earlier (Tables 1, 2, and 7).

Can we distinguish the effects of nativity from the effects of schooling? Because of the apparent colinearity, the resulting problem of "bouncing" betas, and the size of the sample, it is practically impossible to isolate with precision by means of multivariate analysis the separate effects of schooling and nativity. Only with a highly stratified and very large sample, and a great deal of information on each participant, might one be able to estimate with acceptable precision the unique contributions of these variables. At present, I can indicate only that these variables are intricately interwoven and thus illustrate the highly complex nature of the phenomenon under study.

The same conclusion can be reached on the basis of a factor-analytic

Table 16. Correlations between Maternal Nativity and
Maternal Teaching Strategies in
Chicano Families

Teaching strategy	Correlation with nativity
Modeling	−.44[b]
Visual cue	−.18
Directive	−.07
Praise	.49[c]
Negative verbal feedback or disapproval	−.05
Inquiry	.44[b]
Negative physical control	−.10
Positive physical control	−.33[a]
Physical affection	.15

Note: The correlations are point-biserial coefficients. The maternal teaching strategies were expressed as rates-per-minute transformed to $\sqrt{x} + \sqrt{x + 1}$. $n = 43$.
[a] $p < .05$, one-tailed test.
[b] $p < .01$, one-tailed test.
[c] $p < .001$, one-tailed test.

Table 17. Correlation of Nativity with Frequency of Parental Reading
to the Child and Maternal Aspirations for the Child's
Education in Chicano Families

Reading and aspiration variables	Mother's nativity	Father's nativity
Parental reading variables		
Mother reads to child	.38[b]	.15
Father reads to child	.24	.10
Maternal aspiration variables		
"Realistic" aspirations	−.03	.00
"Ideal" aspirations	.06	.17
Minimum education	.28[a]	.13

Note: The correlations are point-biserial coefficients. $n = 11$–13.
[a] $p < .05$, one-tailed test.
[b] $p < .01$, one-tailed test.

study of Chicano families recently reported by Valencia, Henderson, and
Rankin (1981). These investigators also obtained sizable correlations
between parental schooling, nativity, and home language use. Moreover,
when they entered these three and other variables into a factor analysis,
these three then formed a single, clearly defined factor.

The available evidence, then, including that which I will present later,
suggests the hypothetical causal model shown schematically in Figure 9.
Welcome would be research designed to test this and alternative theoretical
models using recent advances in causal inference methodology (e.g., Laosa,
1982a) applied to samples of sufficiently large size to permit reasonably
stable parameter estimates. Welcome, too, would be research to test the
relative fit of models to different populations. Whereas the model shown in
Figure 9 might fit the data for Chicanos, parts of it might yield different
parameters and a different fit for other Hispanic populations in the United
States. For example, it can be hypothesized that the parameters for nativity
will differ for Chicano and Cuban-American families as a result of differences underlying the decision to immigrate to the United States.
Similarly, this model might not fit the data for certain ethnic and religious
groups for which institutions other than the school (e.g., religious
traditions) provide the primary impetus for the fostering of literacy and
scholarship. Let us turn now to an examination of the relationship
between parental and child language.

Parental Language and Child Language

What impact will the language pattern that adults use in the home
have on the language pattern that the child adopts for use in the home?

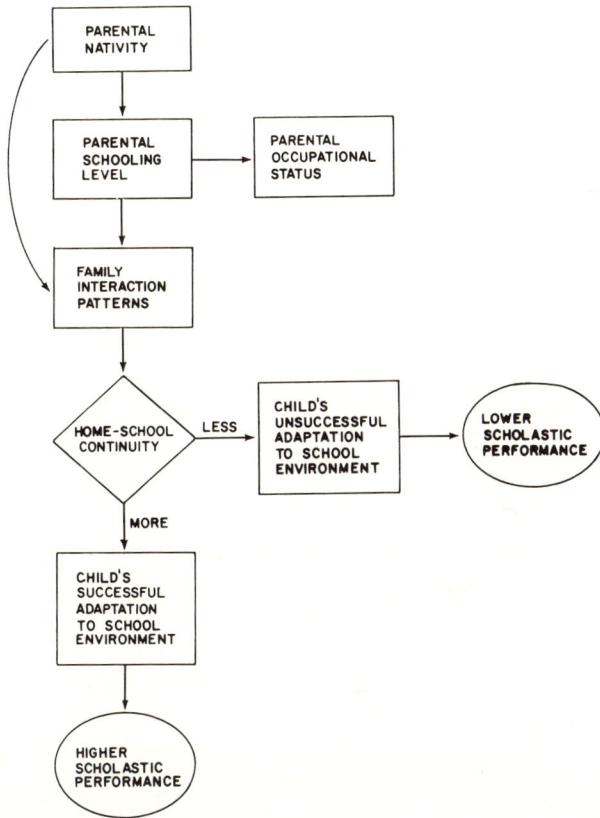

Figure 9. Hypothetical causal model of family influences on Chicano children's scholastic performance.

When the data are analyzed at the level of individual differences within families, as in Tables 18 and 19, the following associations can be observed between the parent's use and their children's use of language. Chicano parents who used English as the most frequent home language tended to have children who spoke mainly English at home. Chicano parents who used Spanish as the most frequent home language tended to have children who spoke mainly either Spanish or an intermixed variety of Spanish and English at home. Chicano parents who used both Spanish and English (as separate codes) with approximately equal frequency as the most frequent language pattern in the home tended to have children who used mainly the same pattern of separate languages at home. Finally, parents who spoke an intermixed variety of Spanish and English as the most frequent language pattern at home tended to have children who spoke primarily the same

Table 18. Relationship between Parental and Child Language Use in Chicano Homes:
Los Angeles Sample

	Mother to child		Father to child	
Dyad structure and language	English	Spanish	English	Spanish
Child to mother				
English	.64	−.91	.78	−.53
Spanish	−.60	.86	−.74	.58
Child to father				
English	.64	−.91	.78	−.53
Spanish	−.54	.78	−.68	.68

Note: The measures of relationship are phi coefficients. For all coefficients $p < .001$, one-tailed tests; $n = 43$.

intermixed variety of Spanish and English at home. Thus, these Chicano children tended to adopt for home use a language pattern similar to that which their parents used.

There was, however, a general increase in the use of English and a concomitant decrease in the use of Spanish among children over parents. A similar increase in the use of English with age can be observed in national survey data (Macías, 1979). This trend can be observed most clearly when the data are considered at the level of generational and age differences. Indeed, the intergenerational *language shift* is particularly evident in the sample of elementary school children (Table 12), but much less marked in the sample of children who had not yet entered the first grade (Table 10). As we saw earlier, this difference between the samples conforms to the hypothesis that causally links the school experience to the increased adoption of English as the familial language of Chicanos. Specifically, it conforms to the hypothesis that, in the United States, increased length of

Table 19. Relationship between Adult and Child Language Use in Chicano Homes:
Austin Sample

	Adult language			
Child language	English	Spanish	Both	Mixture
English	.48[c]	−.15	−.08	−.10
Spanish	.00	.26[b]	−.07	.05
Both	−.16	−.08	.43[c]	−.01
Mixture	−.25[b]	.31[b]	−.21[a]	.21[a]

Note: The measures of relationship are phi coefficients. $n = 99$ households. Data from Laosa, 1975.
[a] $p < .05$, one-tailed test.
[b] $p < .01$, one-tailed test.
[c] $p < .001$, one-tailed test.

schooling augments the likelihood that the bilingual or limited-English-speaking individual will adopt English as the dominant language of the home.

The theoretical relevance of the language use data to the conceptual model linking parental schooling, family interaction, and the child's scholastic performance—specifically, their relevance to what the model predicts concerning the child's scholastic performance—can be seen more clearly when regarded in light of two sets of previous findings. One set concerns the relationship between language use and language proficiency among bilingual speakers. Whereas language *use* measures indicate what an individual typically does, language *proficiency* refers to what an individual can do, for example, how well the individual can understand and speak the language, usually its standard form. The findings of at least two studies suggest a positive relationship between language use and language proficiency (Cooper & Greenfield, 1969; Edelman, 1969). Bilingual speakers appear to be generally more proficient in the language they use more frequently. The other set of findings concerns teachers attitudes and behavior toward language-minority students. Teachers appear to communicate, sometimes explicitly and often in a subtle and perhaps unconscious manner, certain attitudes with respect to the language and/or culture of the student (Cohen & Laosa, 1976; Laosa, 1977b). More specifically, the results of several studies show that teachers behave unfavorably toward, and hold negative attitudes and low expectations of, students whose speech style differs from standard English (Bailey & Galván, 1977; Choy & Dodd, 1976; Laosa, 1977b; Ramirez, 1981; Ramírez, Arce-Torres, & Politzer, 1976; Williams, Whitehead, & Miller, 1972). Based on all these considerations, it seems reasonable to hypothesize the following sequence of connected processes and outcomes as part of the general explanatory model of Chicano children's scholastic performance: The Chicano child who speaks mainly Spanish and little English at home will have relatively high proficiency in Spanish, but relatively low proficiency in English. This child will experience, therefore, linguistic problems in the English-language classroom. These problems will be compounded by affective conflicts and motivational blocks resulting from feelings and perceptions that the language of the home is ignored and devalued in the formal learning environment. Together, these difficulties will put the child at a disadvantage in the academic environment and depress his or her scholastic performance. Both the incidence and the magnitude of this sequence of processes and outcomes among Chicano children will be inversely related to parental schooling level.

Interpersonal communication involves much more than language, however. It is difficult, perhaps even impossible, to separate language from subjective culture. In addition to the proficient use of language, effective communication involves many different kinds of knowledge that individuals bring to bear in control of their interactions with others. Communication involves an implicit pattern of expectations and understandings regarding the meaning of paralinguistic cues—and of the coordination of these cues with speech—that are shared by the members of a cultural-linguistic group. Several years ago (Laosa, 1977b) I reviewed evidence suggesting that when teachers and students do not understand and share such implicit patterns of expectations and meanings of behavior, many opportunities that could elicit expressions of willingness to cooperate, expressions of affection, sympathy, etc., result only in frustration and increased misunderstandings. Ethnographic research (e.g., Byers & Byers, 1972; Philips, 1974) provides strong support for this hypothesis, suggesting that cultural-linguistic "rules" that help define the roles played among interlocutors can affect the success of teacher-student communications perhaps as much as language proficiency itself.

Let us return now to questions regarding the impact of occupational careers on parental behavior.

Occupational Careers and Parental Behavior

The analyses described in the preceding sections revealed that, in these Chicano families, neither the mothers' nor their husbands' *occupational status* had much of an impact on most of the examined parental behaviors. In contrast to the generally strong effects of parental schooling on parent–child interactions, the associations between parental occupational status and parent–child interactions were either weak or absent. The following examples illustrate the nature of these findings. The mothers who were employed as service workers and laborers used teaching strategies that were similar to those used by the mothers employed in sales and clerical occupations. Mothers and fathers employed as laborers and those in technical and professional occupations read to their children with approximately equal frequency. Similarly, occupational status exerted relatively little influence on the mother's aspirations for the child's education or on the language pattern used in parent–child interactions in the home.

Any interpretation of these results should be tempered by a recognition of the unresolved issues involved in the measurement of occupational status. The scales used to measure occupational status in this study are of the type typically used for this purpose in psychological and educational research (footnote 3). However, different criteria can be used to group and to rank-order occupations, and we are not at all certain that one manner of grouping and rank-ordering occupations is more appropriate than another. Indeed, occupations can vary along many different dimensions. These include, for example, the prestige, power, economic, authority, and job complexity dimensions. Each dimension presents a potentially distinct source of criteria for grouping and rank-ordering occupations. Alas, at the most fundamental level, conclusive empirical evidence does not exist to tell us which dimensions are the most important for measuring social stratification, although this topic has been for many years the subject of intense *sociological* research.

I propose that, in *psychological* and *educational* research, the single most relevant criterion for judging the importance of social stratification measures should be their explanatory or predictive value for the dependent variables under investigation. Thus consider again, but now in the context of this proposal, the following results: In Chicano families, the scales used to measure maternal and paternal occupational status were found to be weak and often ineffectual predictors of the dependent variables under investigation, namely, specified parental behaviors; in contrast, maternal and paternal schooling levels were found to be strong predictors of these parental behaviors.

Clearly, much more work must be done before definitive answers can be given to questions regarding the effects of occupations on parental behavior. Perhaps a general paradigm can serve as a reference point for future research on the impact of occupational careers on parental behavior. The guiding framework can be expressed in four broad questions derived from Hess' (1970) review and synthesis of earlier work on this topic: (a) What are the conditions of the external occupational world in which the parent spends his or her working hours? (b) What are the adaptive consequences that parents acquire in interaction with their occupational world? (c) In what specific forms do these adaptive orientations appear in the parents' interactions with their children? (d) What are the behavioral outcomes of these experiences in children? Underlying these questions is a hypothetical model that postulates a linkage between society, its institutions and conditions of life, and the behavior of adults who then act as socializing and teaching agents for their children. Valuable would be studies that elaborate and empirically test hypothetical models of this type. Also valuable would be research that analyzes the psychological and educational dimensions underlying given occupational roles and that then attempts to examine the impact of specific occupational experiences on the parents' choices of strategies for teaching their own children (cf. Kohn, 1963, 1977). Welcome, too, would be studies that examine the relationships between parental behavior and different measures of social stratification. Finally, there is also a need for research on the generalizability of measures across different populations. For example, the perceived status and prestige of occupational roles may differ across

sociocultural groups and may even vary over time within a given socio-
culture as a result of changes in the labor market and in the sex and ethnic
ratios of occupations.

A somewhat different and much broader set of questions centers on the
effects of maternal *employment*, that is, whether the mother does or does
not work outside the home. The following section examines the effects of
maternal employment on the behavior of Chicano parents toward their
young children.

Maternal Employment and Parent–Child
Interaction in Chicano Families

Questions about the impact of maternal employment on patterns of
family interaction take on added significance when they are considered in
the context of recent secular trends toward families more typically having
two wage earners. Despite the increase in employment rates for mothers,
which is indeed greatest for families with children (U. S. Department of
Labor, 1978), little is known about whether mothers who are wage earners
have styles of interacting with their children that are different from those
observed in mothers who are not in the labor force.

The analyses presented in this section were conducted to examine the
relationship between maternal employment and parental behavior in intact
Chicano families. The analyses are based on the aforementioned sample of
Chicano families with a kindergarten child. Maternal employment—that
is, whether the mother was employed outside the home at the time of the
interview, conducted when the focal child was in kindergarten—was a
dichotomous variable: 1 = employed, 2 = not employed outside the home.
In 33% of the families the mother was employed. In all but two of the
families the mother's employment status at the time of the interview
corresponded to their usual employment status.

The results revealed that maternal employment in these intact
Chicano families had no significant effect on any of the parental behaviors
examined in these analyses ($p > .05$, two-tailed tests). Specifically, whether
the mother was or was not employed bore no relationship to the strategies
that she used in teaching her young child (Table 20). Similarly, maternal
employment was unrelated both to the frequency of parental reading to the
child and to the maternal aspirations for the child's education (Table 21).
Finally, maternal employment bore no relationship to the languages that
the parents used in interacting with their children (Table 22).

It is worth noting, however, that although maternal employment was
unrelated to the languages that the *parents* used in interacting with their
children, there was a trend suggesting that maternal employment *was*

Table 20. Correlations between Maternal Employment and
Maternal Teaching Strategies in Chicano Families

Teaching strategy	Correlation with employment
Modeling	−.19
Visual cue	.24
Directive	.08
Praise	−.01
Negative verbal feedback or disapproval	.06
Inquiry	−.18
Negative physical control	.22
Positive physical control	.03
Physical affection	.11

Note: The correlations are point-biserial coefficients. The maternal teaching strategies were expressed as rates-per-minute transformed to $\sqrt{x} + \sqrt{x + 1}$. None of the coefficients is significant, $p > .05$, two-tailed tests; $n = 43$.

related to the languages that the *children* used in interacting with their parents (Table 22). Considering that maternal employment is frequently associated with the placement of the child in some form of day-care facility, this finding suggests the hypothesis that, among Chicanos, maternal employment exerts an indirect influence on the child's language use—an influence that is perhaps mediated by the day-care environment.

In conclusion, the results suggest that maternal employment in intact Chicano families does not have much of an impact on the categories of parental behavior examined in this study. This finding is harmonious with Zinn's (1980) contention that although the wife's employment in Chicano families may result in a shift away from traditional conjugal roles, it is not

Table 21. Correlations of Maternal Employment with
Frequency of Parental Reading to the Child
and Maternal Aspirations for the Child's
Education in Chicano Families

Parental reading and aspiration variables	Correlation with maternal employment
Parental reading	
Mother reads to child	.16
Father reads to child	.18
Maternal aspirations	
"Realistic" aspirations	.10
"Ideal" aspirations	.28
Minimum education	.06

Note: The correlations are point-biserial coefficients. None of the coefficients is significant, $p > .05$, two-tailed tests; $n = 41–43$.

Table 22. Relationship of Maternal Employment
to the Languages Used in Parent–Child
Interactions in Chicano Homes

Language, sex of parent, and directionality of interaction	ϕ with maternal employment
English	
Mother to child	.02
Child to mother	−.28
Father to child	−.05
Child to father	−.28
Spanish	
Mother to child	.18
Child to mother	.25
Father to child	−.02
Child to father	.18

Note: The measures of relationship are phi (ϕ) coefficients. None of the coefficients is significant, $p > .05$, two-tailed tests; $n = 13$.

necessarily associated with changes in other culturally determined aspects of family life. Additional research is needed, however, to determine whether maternal employment has an impact on other categories of parental behavior and on other aspects of the parent–child relationship. Also needed are studies that examine the effects of different conditions and circumstances associated with maternal employment. The circumstances under which maternal employment occurs are likely to moderate the impact that maternal employment *per se* can have on the parent–child relationship (e.g., LeCorgne & Laosa, 1976).

As these results would suggest, in these Chicano families there was no significant relationship between maternal employment and maternal schooling level, although there was a trend suggesting that employment is more frequent among the more highly schooled Chicano mothers than among the less schooled Chicano mothers (point-biserial $r = -.21$). Interestingly, neither was there a significant relationship between maternal employment and husband's schooling or occupational status. There was also no significant relationship between maternal employment and nativity (Table 23).[9] It thus appears that factors other than the mother's schooling attainment level, her husband's schooling and occupational status, and either person's nativity determine whether Chicano mothers of

[9] The correlations of mother's employment with her schooling level and her husband's schooling level and occupational status were nonsignificant also for the non-Hispanic White sample (point-biserial $r = -.07$, .18, and .07, respectively).

**Table 23. Relationship of Maternal Employment
to Paternal Occupational Status,
Parental Schooling, and Nativity
in Chicano Families**

Variables	Correlation with mother's employment
Mother's schooling[a]	−.21
Father's schooling[a]	−.11
Father's occupation[a]	.01
Mother's nativity[b]	−.18
Father's nativity[b]	.05

Note: None of the coefficients is significant, $p > .05$, one-tailed tests; $n = 42-43$.
[a]Point-biserial coefficient.
[b]Phi coefficient.

young children in intact families become employed. In the next section I shall examine the influence of schooling on occupational careers.

Schooling and Occupational Attainment

To illuminate additional facets of the research results reviewed in the preceding sections, let us examine the association between schooling attainment and occupational status, specifically for Chicanos. Knowledge about the strength of this link is likely to accomplish two objectives. First, it may increase our understanding of the observed contrast between, on the one hand, the sizable correlations between parental behaviors and parental schooling and, on the other, the lack of correlations between the same behaviors and occupational status. Second, and of broader social significance, it may help answer a critical question regarding equality of occupational opportunity: Is schooling attainment level a good predictor of occupational status among Chicanos as it generally is among nonminorities?

To accomplish these objectives, correlations were computed between schooling attainment and occupational status, separately by ethnic group, for the Chicano and non-Hispanic White families that participated in the studies reported in the preceding sections. These families resided in Los Angeles; they had a child in kindergarten and almost all were intact. The ages of the parents were similar across ethnic groups (Chicano fathers: $M = 35.4$, $SD = 6.2$; non-Hispanic White fathers: $M = 34.4$, $SD = 5.9$; Chicano mothers: $M = 33.8$, $SD = 6.5$; non-Hispanic White mothers: $M = 30.6$, $SD = 4.6$). As indicated earlier, the Chicano and non-Hispanic

Table 24. Comparison of Sample Characteristics With National Statistics

Sociodemographic characteristic	Chicano		Non-Hispanic	
	Study sample	National sample	Study sample	National sample
Employed adult males				
In white collar occupations	12%	18%	48%	43%
In blue collar occupations	76	63	48	45
In service occupations	12	12	5	9
In farm occupations	0	7	0	4
Years of schooling completed:				
By adult males	8.9[a]	9.4[b]	14.7[a]	12.5[b]
By adult females	8.8[a]	9.4[b]	13.2[a]	12.4[b]

Note: The national statistics on occupational status are from the U.S. Bureau of the Census, Current population reports, Series P-20, No. 339. The correspondence between the occupational categories used in this source and the occupational scale described in footnote 3 and used in the analyses reported in this chapter is as follows: white collar = scale values 6–9, blue collar = 3–5, service = 1–2, farm = 3. The national statistics on schooling are from the U.S. Bureau of the Census, Current population reports, Series P-20, No. 290 and No. 314.
[a] Mean.
[b] Median.

White families were selected to be as representative as possible of their respective ethnic populations with regard to the distributions of paternal occupational status and parental schooling level. A comparison of these samples with those drawn by the U. S. Bureau of Census revealed assuring similarities, increasing our confidence that the samples indeed are generally representative of their respective populations with regard to the distributions of these sociodemographic variables (Table 24).

Two types of correlation coefficients were computed: Pearson product–moment correlations and Kendall's tau correlations corrected for ties. Whereas the Pearson product–moment correlation provides a measure of the linear relationship, Kendall's tau is a nonparametric statistic and thus requires no assumptions about the distributions of cases on the variables. The two types of analyses yielded similar results. The correlations are shown in Table 25, separately by sex of parent and ethnic group.

The correlations between schooling attainment and occupational status are lower for Chicanos than they are for non-Hispanic Whites, particularly so for men. These results would seem to suggest that, for Chicanos, staying longer in school generally does not result in a higher status occupation. Put differently, the results suggest an ethnic-group difference in the net occupational returns to schooling. The occupational benefits of a unit of increment in schooling appear to be fewer for Chicanos than for non-Hispanic Whites. This, indeed, is the interpretation that in

Table 25. Means, Standard Deviations, and Correlations between Schooling Attainment Level and Occupational Status of Chicano and Non-Hispanic White Mothers and Fathers of Five-Year-Old Children

Variable	Correlations				Chicano			Non-Hispanic White		
	Mother's schooling	Father's schooling	Mother's occupation	Father's occupation	Mean	S.D.	Range	Mean	S.D.	Range
Mother's schooling		.64[b]	.18	.32[a]	8.8	3.4	1–14	13.2	2.0	11–20
		.51[b]	.15	.25[a]						
Father's schooling	.79[b]		.10	.33[a]	8.9	3.9	2–18	14.7	3.1	8–24
	.68[b]		.09	.23[a]						
Mother's occupation	.25	−.03		−.10	1.7	2.6	0–8	2.5	3.3	0–8
	.20	.01		−.04						
Father's occupation	.60[b]	.55[b]	.13		4.4	1.3	2–8	5.7	1.7	2–8
	.57[b]	.49[b]	.10							

Note: Of each top-bottom pair of coefficients, the one on top is a Pearson product-moment correlation and the one at the bottom is a Kendall's tau correlation. Coefficients above the main diagonal correspond to the Chicano sample ($n = 42$–43). Coefficients below the main diagonal correspond to the non-Hispanic White sample ($n = 40$). The scales used to measure the variables are described in text footnote 3.
[a] $p < .05$, one-tailed test.
[b] $p < .001$, one-tailed test.

previous papers I (Laosa, 1978, 1981), and others as well, have given to such ethnic-group differences in the size of the correlation between schooling attainment and occupational status. More recently, however, I have come to question this "differential returns" interpretation specifically with regard to the correlation between schooling and occupational status for Chicanos.

My skepticism stems from a reexamination of assumptions and further analysis of the data. The "differential returns" interpretation of the ethnic-group difference in the size of the correlation can be seen to rest almost entirely upon the assumption that a continuous linear relationship exists between schooling attainment and occupational status for the entire possible range of both variables. Consider, however, a rival assumption that seems equally plausible, namely that the relationship between schooling attainment and occupational status is discontinuous—that is, that the individual's place on the occupational scale is predicted best by such a dichotomy as whether the individual did or did not graduate from high school (or did or did not attend college for two years, etc.). The relative validity of these rival assumptions cannot be tested adequately, since the Chicano and non-Hispanic White distributions overlap only partially and hence any comparisons must be restricted to the overlapping segments of the respective bivariate distributions. Note in Table 25 that the means for the two ethnic samples are different with regard to both schooling attainment and occupational status; even the ranges in schooling attainment are very different for the two ethnic samples. These differences are indeed as they should be, since the samples were selected to be as representative as possible of their respective ethnic populations with regard to the distributions of these variables. In the absence of large samples with oversampling of Chicanos at the upper ends of the (schooling and occupational) distributions and, conversely, oversampling of non-Hispanic Whites at the lower ends, these rival assumptions cannot be tested. Therefore, the observed ethnic-group difference in the size of the correlation between schooling attainment and occupational status remains difficult to interpret.

Indeed, one can hypothesize that, had the Chicano and non-Hispanic White samples been matched on schooling level, the size of the correlations would be similar across ethnic groups. As a partial test of this hypothesis, I performed the analysis shown in Table 26. The analysis was designed to determine whether Chicanos and non-Hispanic White males derive equal gains in occupational status from a given unit of increment in schooling. The focus of analysis is on the unit of increment from between 8 and 11 years to between 12 and 15 years of schooling. The focus on this dichotomy is forced by the ethnic-group differences in the respective distributions of schooling attainment and occupational status, and by the relatively small

Table 26. Mean Occupational Status of Chicano and Non-Hispanic White Fathers
for Two Levels of Schooling

Ethnic group	Years of schooling		Mean difference
	8–11	12–15	
Chicano	4.1	4.6	.5
	(n = 10)	(n = 10)	
Non-Hispanic White	4.5	5.0	.5
	(n = 6)	(n = 17)	

Note: The mean ages of the fathers in the four cells were, clockwise from upper left, 35.2, 35.5, 33.1, and 33.8.

size of the samples. In order to emphasize the practical meaning of this analysis, let us treat the mean difference in occupational status within each ethnic group as the gain in occupational status associated with this unit of increment in length of schooling. The results clearly indicate that the mean gain in occupational status attainment associated with staying longer in school in order to complete high school and several years of college is identical for both ethnic groups (.5). The results further lead to the conclusion that, at least for this unit of increment in schooling, the absolute effects of schooling on occupational status attainment are the same for Chicano and non-Hispanic White males. Additional research is needed to determine the generalizability of this finding to other units of increment in schooling. Future studies are also needed to examine the generalizability of this finding to other states and geographic regions, since interstate and regional differences may exist with regard to both the presence and the degree of enforcement of fair employment practices. Nevertheless, at present this finding provides sufficient grounds for skepticism regarding the interpretation of the observed ethnic-group difference in the size of the correlation between schooling and occupational attainment as an index of ethnic inequality in occupational returns to schooling. In sum, these results suggest that the occupational returns to schooling are similar for Chicano and non-Hispanic White fathers of young children.

None of the above should draw attention away from the fact that Chicanos, like some other ethnic groups, are overrepresented at the lower ends of both the schooling and occupational attainment distributions, and that, in this sense, there are ethnic-group inequalities in our society. With regard to the schooling inequality, consider, for example, the results of a large-scale study conducted by the U. S. Commission on Civil Rights (1971). In harmony with the data I have reported here, the results of that study revealed that fully 40% of the Chicano students in the southwestern United States never completed high school; in contrast, only 14% of all non-

Hispanic White children in the region failed to complete high school. Sadly, the gap in educational achievement between Chicanos and non-Hispanic Whites appears to have increased within the past few years (M-L Group for Policy Studies in Education, 1978). With regard to the occupational inequality, consider again the results shown in Table 26. Within a given level of schooling attainment, occupational status attainment is lower for Chicanos than it is for non-Hispanic Whites. Definite ethnic-group inequalities exist in both schooling and occupational attainment.

The results of this study suggest that the process by which Chicanos as a group come to hold occupations of inferior status is best explained by a "queuing" hypothesis of worker allocation (Briggs, Fogel, & Schmidt, 1977; Grebler *et al.*, 1970). In this queuing process, the prospective worker gets in line (figuratively) for the highest-status occupation that he or she has a reasonable chance of acquiring. Employers move down the queue selecting those applicants they think will perform best. Workers not chosen for the most desirable jobs must then get in line for the lower-status ones until they are selected for employment. To increase efficiency in the processing of applicants, employers exclude from hiring consideration all workers in the queue who lack the specified amount of schooling. In general, Chicanos are at the disadvantage in the queuing process because their schooling is low. The result of this disadvantage, together with the queuing process, is the allocation of this group, in numbers out of proportion to their population, to the lower-status occupations.[10]

All in all, however, the data I have presented here give cause for optimism. Having ascertained that Chicanos on the average complete fewer years of schooling and attain lower-status occupations than do non-Hispanic Whites, and taking note of the finding that both ethnic groups apparently have equal rates of occupational returns to schooling, one can be optimistic, indeed, about the impact of social policies that seek to extend and improve educational opportunities for ethnic minorities as a means of alleviating the longstanding disparities in occupational attainment.[11]

---

[10] Having been reminded of this process, one can ask whether the exclusion of persons with low schooling from manual (and some nonmanual) jobs is an unacceptable form of discrimination. One can argue that if there is no difference in job performance or if the more highly schooled group has only a slight advantage, screening on the basis of schooling attainment, in the absence of evidence demonstrating superior performance by the more highly schooled, is discriminatory (Fogel, 1968).

[11] I should hasten to caution the reader, however, that even with occupational equality there might still exist possible *earning* differences resulting from lower pay received by Chicanos when they are employed in the same job classification (but not in the same firm) as non-Hispanic Whites (Briggs, Fogel, & Schmidt, 1977). Possible earning differences might be the result of discrimination by some employers on the basis of race, ethnicity, English language familiarity, or speech accentedness.

Some Conclusions

The studies reviewed and the data presented in this chapter indicate clearly that there is a strong connection between the amount of schooling that individuals receive and how they, as parents, interact with their children. Because of the practical, ethical, and legal considerations that make it virtually impossible to use random-assignment experiments to research the impact of schooling attainment, it is sometimes difficult and usually impossible to draw definitive conclusions about causal relationships from these data and from virtually all of the other data thus far available on the topic. Indeed, given the nature of the subject at hand, it may be impossible to do so, ever. Nevertheless, the present data provide, I believe, useful and illuminating information about the relationship of schooling to parental behavior. In many instances, simply to know whether a relationship exists is in itself a valuable datum, for both practical and theoretical reasons.

Although the samples used in the studies reviewed and reported here are relatively small, comparisons of these samples with data reported routinely for national samples by the U. S. Bureau of the Census and by the National Center for Education Statistics revealed marked similarities, both in the distributions of key sociodemographic variables and in the interrelationships among these variables. This cross-sample convergence increases our confidence in the results reviewed and reported in this chapter.

I was able to show that there are ethnic-group differences in parental teaching behavior and in other educationally relevant aspects of the parent–child relationship. Moreover, I was able to demonstrate that these ethnic-group differences in parental behavior are probably the result of the difference between minority and nonminority parents in average schooling attainment level—as a group, Chicano parents have completed fewer years of schooling than have non-Hispanic White parents. I also demonstrated that the present-day ethnic-group differences in parental behavior may disappear when our society finally achieves equality of educational opportunity and individuals in the two ethnic groups attain similar levels of schooling.

From the results that I have presented, one can hypothesize that for the average Chicano child there is quite an abrupt discontinuity between the home environment and the school environment. Compared with the parent–child interactions in the average Chicano family, the parent–child interactions in the average non-Hispanic White family resemble much more closely the types of interactions that one expects to find in a school classroom. This hypothesis is akin to the more general continuity-discontinuity hypothesis that I discussed several years ago (Laosa, 1977c,

1979) as a plausible explanation of the extremely high school drop-out rate and academic underachievement among Chicanos. It also seems reasonable to hypothesize—based on the results presented here—that, regardless of ethnicity, the home-school discontinuity will be particularly abrupt for children of parents with relatively low schooling. That is, the parent–child interactions in the homes of the more highly schooled parents will resemble much more closely the types of interactions that the child can expect of a teacher in the classroom. Additional research is needed to test more directly these hypotheses. Of particular value would be longitudinal research that compares family–child and teacher–child interactions and that assesses the effects of various forms and degrees of family–school continuity-discontinuity (match-mismatch) on scholastic performance, using sufficiently large samples to permit generalizations beyond the single case.

As yet we have no adequate data about the processes in schooling that might lead to the observed differences in the behavior of parents with varied levels of schooling. A plausible explanatory hypothesis is that the school encourages the adoption of specialized modes of communication. Valuable would be research that seeks to illuminate the specific processes involved. In general, the increased participation of a group in formal schooling seems to be part of a process of cultural change toward what is called "modernization" (Inkeles & Smith, 1974). At the present time, non-Hispanic Whites, as a group, have participated more fully in this process and hence have been affected by it to a greater extent than Chicanos. For Chicanos to share more fully than heretofore in the process of "modernization" may have the effect of eliminating cultural differences between the two groups and of moving toward the creation of a society where present-day differences between the two ethnic groups in patterns of family interaction eventually disappear.

The findings reported here have important implications for policy. They suggest that the academic disadvantage of many minority children may be the result of the lower level of schooling among minority parents. Specifically, the relatively low schooling of minority parents may result in such family–school discontinuity that it may, in turn, have a deleterious effect on the minority child's academic achievement. When we observe children of the more highly educated parents excelling in school, might the reason for this be that the teaching, learning, and assessment processes in school are like those they have learned to master at home? And conversely, when we observe the children of the lower-schooling parents—and this includes the average Chicano and Black child—failing in school, might the reason for this be that the form and content of the teaching, learning, and assessment processes in school are different from those they have learned to master at home? If we can answer these questions in the affirmative, then it would appear that to improve the academic achievement of minority children we must increase family–school continuity. It seems that one way to do this is to improve our educational system so as to reduce the extremely high dropout rate of minorities, thereby eventually increasing the schooling level of minority parents. However, it seems that to reduce this school dropout rate we must achieve family–school continuity. Is this a dilemma that points to an impasse? Not necessarily. It would appear that effective change must be a two-way dialectical process that involves both schools and parent–child interactions (Laosa, 1979, in press). The data I have presented here indicate some aspects in which schools can become more like the home (e.g., teaching strategies, bilingualism). Conversely, these data also indicate some ways that parents can better prepare children for school (e.g., reading, teaching strategies, bilingualism). Finally, the findings on occupational returns to schooling, albeit tentative because of the relatively small sample size, provide grounds for optimism about the beneficial impact of social policies that seek to alleviate ethnic disparities in occupational attainment by extending educational opportunities to ethnic minorities.

References

Bailey, K. M., & Galván, J. L. Accentedness in the classroom. *Aztlán International Journal of Chicano Studies Research*, 1977, *8*, 83–97.

Baral, D. P. Academic achievement of recent immigrants from Mexico. *NABE Journal: The Journal of the National Association for Bilingual Education*, Spring 1979, *3*, 1–13.

Briggs, V. M., Jr., Fogel, W., & Schmidt, F. H. *The Chicano worker*. Austin, Texas: University of Texas Press, 1977.

Brown, G. H., Rosen, N. L., Hill, S. T., & Olivas, M. A. *The condition of education for Hispanic Americans*. Washington, D.C.: U.S. Government Printing Office, 1980.

Byers, P., & Byers, H. Non-verbal communication in the education of children. In C. Cazden, V. John, & D. Hymes (Eds.), *Functions of language in the classroom*. New York: Teachers College Press, 1972.

Cárdenas, B., & Cárdenas, J. A. Chicano, bright-eyed, bilingual, brown, and beautiful. *Today's Education*, 1973, *62*, 49–51.

Cárdenas, J. A., & Zamora, G. The early education of minority children. In M. D. Fantini & R. Cárdenas (Eds.), *Parenting in a multicultural society*. New York: Longman, 1980.

Choy, S. J., & Dodd, D. H. Standard-English-speaking and nonstandard Hawaiian-English-speaking children: Comprehension of both dialects and teacher's evaluations. *Journal of Educational Psychology*, 1976, *68*, 184–193.

Cohen, A., & Laosa, L. M. Second language instruction: Some research considerations. *Curriculum Studies*, 1976, *8*, 149–165.

Cole, M., & Bruner, J. S. Cultural differences and inferences about psychological processes. *American Psychologist*, 1971, *26*, 867–876.

Coleman, J. S., Campbell, E. Q., Hobson, C. J., McPartland, J., Mood, A. M., Weinfeld, F. D.,

& York, R. L. *Equality of educational opportunity*. Washington, D.C.: U.S. Government Printing Office, 1966.

Cooper, R. L., & Greenfield, L. Language use in a bilingual community. *Modern Language Journal*, 1969, *53*, 166–172.

Cornejo, R. J. The acquisition of lexicon in the speech of bilingual children. In P. Turner (Ed.), *Bilingualism in the Southwest*. Tucson: University of Arizona Press, 1973.

Deutsch, C. P. Social class and child development. In B. M. Caldwell & H. N. Ricciuti (Eds.), *Review of child development research* (Vol. 3). Chicago: University of Chicago Press, 1973.

Edelman, M. The contextualization of school children's bilingualism. *Modern Language Journal*, 1969, *53*, 179–182.

Featherman, D. L., & Hauser, R. M. *Opportunity and change*. New York: Academic Press, 1978.

Fogel, W. The effects of low educational attainment and discrimination on the occupational status of minorities. In *The education and training of racial minorities* (Conference Proceedings of the Center for Studies in Vocational and Technical Education). Madison: University of Wisconsin, 1968.

Freeman, M. F., & Tukey, J. W. Transformations related to the angular and the square root. *Annals of Mathematical Statistics*, 1950, *21*, 607–611.

Grebler, L., Moore, J. W., & Guzman, R. C. *The Mexican-American people: The nation's second largest minority*. New York: The Free Press, 1970.

Henderson, R. W. Social and emotional needs of culturally diverse children. *Exceptional Children*, 1980, *46*, 598–605.

Hess, R. D. Social class and ethnic influences on socialization. In P. H. Mussen (Ed.), *Carmichael's manual of child psychology* (Vol. 2). New York: Wiley, 1970.

Hess, R. D., & Holloway, S. *The intergenerational transmission of literacy*. Report prepared for the Department of Health, Education, and Welfare, National Institute of Education. Stanford University, June 1979.

Heyns, B. *Summer learning and the effects of schooling*. New York: Academic Press, 1978.

Hollingshead, A. B. *Two factor index of social position*. Unpublished paper, New Haven, 1957.

Hyman, H. H., Wright, C. R., & Reed, J. S. *The enduring effects of education*. Chicago: University of Chicago Press, 1975.

Inkeles, A., & Smith, D. H. *Becoming modern: Individual change in six developing countries*. Cambridge, Mass.: Harvard University Press, 1974.

Irwin, M., Engle, P. L., Yarbrough, C., Klein, R. E., & Townsend, J. The relationship of prior ability and family characteristics to school attendance and school achievement in rural Guatemala. *Child Development*, 1978, *49*, 415–427.

Jencks, C., Smith, M., Acland, H., Bane, M. J., Cohen, D., Gintis, H., Heyns, B., & Michelson, S. *Inequality: A reassessment of the effect of family and schooling in America*. New York: Harper and Row, 1972.

Kohn, M. L. Social class and parent-child relationships: An interpretation. *American Journal of Sociology*, 1963, *68*, 471–480.

Kohn, M. L. *Class and conformity: A study of values*. Second edition. Chicago: University of Chicago Press, 1977.

LaBelle, T. J., & Verhine, R. E. Education, social change, and social stratification. In T. J. LaBelle (Ed.), *Educational alternatives in Latin America: Social change and social stratification*. Los Angeles: UCLA Latin American Center Publications, 1975.

Laosa, L. M. Child care and the culturally different child. *Child Care Quarterly*, 1974, *3*, 214–224.

Laosa, L. M. Bilingualism in three United States Hispanic groups: Contextual use of language by children and adults in their families. *Journal of Educational Psychology*, 1975, *67*, 617–627.

Laosa, L. M. Developing arithmetic skills among rural villagers in Ecuador through nonformal education: A field experiment. *Journal of Educational Psychology*, 1976, *68*, 670–679.

Laosa, L. M. Cognitive styles and learning strategies research: Some of the areas in which psychology can contribute to personalized instruction in multicultural education. *Journal of Teacher Education*, 1977, *28*, 26–30. (a).

Laosa, L. M. Inequality in the classroom: Observational research on teacher-student interactions. *Aztlán International Journal of Chicano Studies Research*, 1977, *8*, 51–67. (b)

Laosa, L. M. Socialization, education, and continuity: The importance of the sociocultural context. *Young Children*, 1977, *32*, 21–27. (c)

Laosa, L. M. Maternal teaching strategies in Chicano families of varied educational and socioeconomic levels. *Child Development*, 1978, *49*, 1129–1135.

Laosa, L. M. Social competence in childhood: Toward a developmental, socioculturally relativistic paradigm. In M. W. Kent & J. E. Rolf (Eds.), *Primary prevention of psychopathology (Vol. 3): Social competence in children.* Hanover, New Hampshire: University Press of New England, 1979.

Laosa, L. M. Maternal teaching strategies and cognitive styles in Chicano familes. *Journal of Educational Psychology*, 1980, *72*, 45–54. See also Correction, ibid., 1980, *72*, 444.(a)

Laosa, L. M. Maternal teaching strategies in Chicano and Anglo-American families: The influence of culture and education on maternal behavior. *Child Development*, 1980, *51*, 759–765. (b)

Laosa, L. M. Measures for the study of maternal teaching strategies. *Applied Psychological Measurement*, 1980, *4*, 355–366. (c)

Laosa, L. M. Maternal behavior: Sociocultural diversity in modes of family interaction. In R. W. Henderson (Ed.), *Parent-child interaction: Theory, research, and prospects.* New York: Academic Press, 1981.

Laosa, L. M. Families as facilitators of children's intellectual development at three years of age: A causal analysis. In L. M. Laosa & I. E. Sigel (Eds.), *Families as learning environments for children.* New York: Plenum Press, 1982. (a)

Laosa, L. M. The sociocultural context of evaluation. In B. Spodek (Ed.), *Handbook of research in early childhood education.* New York: The Free Press, 1982. (b)

Laosa, L. M. Parent education, cultural pluralism, and public policy: The uncertain connection. In R. Haskins (Ed.), *Parent education and public policy.* Norwood, N.J.: Ablex, in press.

Laosa, L. M., Burstein, A. G., & Martin, H. W. Mental health consultation in a rural Chicano community: Crystal City. *Aztlán International Journal of Chicano Studies Research*, 1975, *6*, 433–453.

LeCorgne, L. L., & Laosa, L. M. Father absence in low-income Mexican-American families: Children's social adjustment and conceptual differentiation of sex role attributes. *Developmental Psychology*, 1976, *12*, 470–471.

LeVine, R. A. Influence of women's schooling on maternal behavior in the third world. *Comparative Education Review*, 1980, *24*, (No. 2, Part 2), S78–S105.

Light, R. M., & Smith, P. V. Social allocation models of intelligence: A methodological inquiry. *Harvard Educational Review*, 1969, *39*, 484–510.

Lightfoot, S. L. *Worlds apart: Relationships between families and schools.* New York: Basic Books, 1978.

Lockheed, M. E., Jamison, D. T., & Lau, L. J. Farmer education and farm efficiency: A survey. *Economic Development and Cultural Change*, 1980, *29*, 37–76.

M-L Group for Policy Studies in Education. *Minority education 1960–1978: Grounds, gains, and gaps* (Vol. 1). Chicago: CEMREL Inc., 1978.

Macías, R. F. *Mexicano/Chicano sociolinguistic behavior and language policy in the United States.* Unpublished doctoral dissertation. Georgetown University, 1979.

Marjoribanks, K. *Families and their learning environments: An empirical analysis.* London: Routledge & Kegan Paul, 1979.

McDermott, R. P. Social relations as contexts for learning in school. *Harvard Educational Review,* 1977, *47,* 198–211.

McNeil, J. D., & Laosa, L. M. Needs assessment and cultural pluralism in schools. *Educational Technology,* 1975, *15* (12), 25–28.

Messick, S. Personality consistencies in cognition and creativity. In S. Messick (Ed.), *Individuality in learning.* San Francisco: Jossey-Bass, 1976.

National Center for Education Statistics. Place of birth and language characteristics of persons of Hispanic origin in the United States, Spring, 1976. *Bulletin.* Washington, D.C.: U. S. Department of HEW, Education Division, October 20, 1978.

Ogbu, J. U. Origins of human competence: A cultural-ecological perspective. *Child Development,* 1981, *52,* 413–429.

Patella, V., & Kuvlesky, W. P. Situational variation in language patterns of Mexican American boys and girls. *Social Science Quarterly,* 1973, *53,* 855–864.

Philips, S. U. *The invisible culture: Communication in classroom and community on the Warm Springs Reservation.* Unpublished doctoral dissertation. University of Pennsylvania, 1974.

Ramírez, A. G. Language attitudes and the speech of Spanish-English bilingual pupils. In R. P. Duran (Ed.), *Latino language and communicative behavior.* Norwood, N.J.: Ablex, 1981.

Ramírez, A. G., Arce-Torres, E., & Politzer, R. L. *Language attitudes and the achievement of bilingual pupils.* Research and Development Memorandum No. 146. Stanford, Calif.: Stanford Center for Research and Development in Teaching, School of Education, Stanford University, 1976.

Ramírez, M., III, & Castañeda, A. *Cultural democracy, bicognitive development, and education.* New York: Academic Press, 1974.

Rogoff, B. Schooling and the development of cognitive skills. In H. C. Triandis & A. Heron (Eds.), *Handbook of cross-cultural psychology* (Vol. 4). Boston: Allyn and Bacon, 1981.

Rutter, M., Maughan, B., Mortimer, P., & Ouston, J. *Fifteen thousand hours.* London: Open Books, 1979.

Sharp, D., Cole, M., & Lave, C. Education and cognitive development: The evidence from experimental research. *Monographs of the Society for Research in Child Development,* 1979, *44* (1–2, Serial No. 178).

Shipman, V. C., McKee, J. D., & Bridgeman, B. *Disadvantaged children and their first school experiences: Stability and change in family status, situational, and process variables and their relationship to children's cognitive performance.* Princeton, N.J.: Educational Testing Service, 1976.

Stevenson, H. W., Parker, T., Wilkinson, A., Bonnevaux, B., & Gonzalez, M. Schooling, environment, and cognitive development: A cross-cultural study. *Monographs of the Society for Research in Child Development,* 1978, *43* (3, Serial No. 175).

Stricker, L. *Dimensions of social stratification for whites and blacks: The Toledo Study.* Princeton, N.J.: Educational Testing Service, 1976.

U. S. Bureau of the Census. Persons of Spanish origin in the United States: March 1975. *Current population reports* (Series P-20, No. 290). Washington, D.C.: U. S. Government Printing Office, 1976.

U. S. Bureau of the Census. Educational attainment in the United States: March 1977 and 1976. *Current population reports* (Series P-20, No. 314). Washington, D.C.: U. S. Government Printing Office, 1977.

U. S. Bureau of the Census. Persons of Spanish origin in the United States: March 1978. *Current population reports* (Series P-20, No. 339). Washington, D.C.: U. S. Government Printing Office, 1979.

U. S. Commission on Civil Rights. *The unfinished education: Report II of the Mexican American educational series.* Washington, D.C.: U. S. Government Printing Office, 1971.

U. S. Department of Labor, Bureau of Labor Statistics. *Workers of Spanish origin: A chartbook.* Washington, D.C.: U. S. Government Printing Office, 1978.

Valencia, R. R., Henderson, R. W., & Rankin, R. J. Relationship of family constellation and schooling to intellectual performance of Mexican American children. *Journal of Educational Psychology,* 1981, *73,* 524–532.

Williams, F., Whitehead, J. L., & Miller, L. Relations between language attitudes and teacher expectancy. *American Educational Research Journal,* 1972, *9,* 263–277.

Zinn, M. B. Employment and education of Mexican-American women: The interplay of modernity and ethnicity in eight families. *Harvard Educational Review,* 1980, *50,* 47–62.

CHAPTER 5

Parents' Beliefs about Child Socialization

A Study of Parenting Models

KAY SUTHERLAND

Introduction

It is one of the tenets of anthropology that societies vary in their cultural beliefs about the nature of the world in which they live. Human groups differ in their beliefs about the way rain is created, how diseases spread, and what is the best way to teach a child. These differences extend to the most basic beliefs we have about the nature of the physical world: about human nature, about the supernatural, and about how human beings learn and relate to each other. A recent article in the *Annual Review of Anthropology* devoted dozens of pages to the different ways in which anthropologists (among others) have tried to define "family" and the different beliefs various cultures have about the best way to live together and to raise children (Yanagisako, 1979). Accepting cultural variation in beliefs and values concerning the family and parenthood is too seldom acknowledged when the subject matter is closer to home. Experts in many fields tend to ignore the cultural diversity of child-rearing beliefs and values in the United States, often to the detriment of families, children, and programs—indeed, to the richness of everyday life. The finding that most startled the 1980 White House Conferences on Families was the lack of agreement concerning definitions of family life, parenthood, and socialization (Sutherland & Meditch, 1980). It should not have been such a surprise.

The lack of agreement was not limited to differences between rich and

KAY SUTHERLAND • Department of Sociology and Anthropology, Southwest Texas State University, San Marcos, Texas 78666.

poor, native and non-native, or between different ethnic groups, although these were important and pronounced. There were also very important differences between those who considered themselves to be experts and those who introduced themselves as, for instance, "just housewives." Perhaps the results were surprising to the Conference because differences between expert and "folk" beliefs concerning the family are seldom acknowledged, although they have been with us for a long time. This leads us to ask the following questions: Are there "folk models" of the socialization process, as well as expert ones? If so, what is the range of cultural beliefs about the family and child rearing in the United States? Do these beliefs vary from one ethnic group to another, within ethnic groups, and from one generation to the next?

This chapter will provide some preliminary answers to these questions. In the course of a study of low-income parents in the southwestern United States (black, Anglo, and Mexican-American), it was discovered that parents seem to have core beliefs, fundamental premises about the nature of things that underlie their child-rearing values and behavior. These beliefs and values in turn form a philosophical framework, a set of premises which serve to guide parents' behaviors with their children (McGillicudy-DeLisi, 1979; Sigel, McGillicudy-DeLisi, & Johnson, 1980; Sutherland, 1980a). Contrary to the popular view that parents do not have systematic, logical beliefs about the child's development, parents' models of child socialization do exist and can be elicited.

From interviews with parents about their child-rearing beliefs, data emerged on seven parenting models (logically related concepts about child rearing held by the parents); these "folk models" (as opposed to the researchers' or experts' models of child rearing) challenged the widely held belief that parents are deficient in having a model of child rearing before they come to a workshop, that parents present a tabula rasa with regard to theories of child rearing. The data also revealed ethnic differences in beliefs and practices about child rearing which challenged the view that parenting materials would be appropriate for any ethnic group. The data found tentative correlations between two types of parenting models and abuse of the parent as a child, suggesting a relationship between beliefs and past child abuse which has implications for child abuse programs. This chapter will focus on one of the findings—the emergence of the seven parenting models.

The research, based on a study of parent education workshops on discipline techniques, had as its original purpose an evaluation of its impact on the participants. The government, responding to an increased demand for parenting materials, had funded a regional laboratory to develop multimedia materials for parent education workshops.[1] These materials were called "multimedia training packages"; the one that was evaluated was entitled "Way to Discipline Children." It consisted of four sessions, each session lasting 1½ hours, covering four discipline techniques: listening, setting limits, praising, and rewarding. The format included a group leader and a group of 6–12 parents; films, tape cassettes, flip charts, games, brochures, and handouts were used. These materials had been evaluated by short questionnaires which had not, however, captured the range of attitudinal effects the participants and leaders were informally reporting: What was needed was a qualitative evaluation using an anthropological perspective. The data gathered addressed some of the controversial issues surrounding parent education.

This chapter is divided into four major sections. The first section presents the logic of the anthropological perspective. The implication of this section is that the anthropological perspective is not simply an approach which states that we need to obtain another person's viewpoint, but is actually a theory concerning the knowledge that is relevant to attainment of an understanding of an event. A further implication of the anthropological perspective is that it demonstrates a logical relationship between explicit assumptions about the nature of knowledge and the methodological implications of these assumptions.

The second section of this chapter discusses one aspect of the socialization process—parental beliefs about child rearing. The approach here is that the parental socialization of a child is fundamentally a learning process, which involves the parent's theory of learning, that is, how the parent thinks the child learns. This parental theory of learning is what I have called a parenting model, the most essential ingredient of which is the parent's view of the nature of the child, of the equipment, so to speak, that the child brings into the world. I found seven parenting models that cut across three ethnic groups. I will discuss these in some detail.

The third section of the chapter discusses some ethnic differences revealed in interviews of the parents. Although these ethnic differences were not as fully explored as the parental beliefs, they suggest that we might find even more ethnic differences in parental beliefs about child development, and that these ethnic differences should be taken into account by intervention programs.

The fourth section discusses the implications for intervention pro-

[1] The research was conducted from September 1978–December 1979 at the Southwest Educational Development Laboratory within the Division of Community and Family Education. It was funded by the National Institute of Education (Sutherland, 1980a, b).

grams of the findings on parenting models. It suggests that intervention programs might take into account parental beliefs about child development prior to their participation in the program, and it suggests a methodological framework for programs to work with. There is no quick way to ascertain parenting models, although the findings suggest some important questions to ask parents which may help us begin to expose their belief systems.

Perhaps the most important point of this chapter is that we should ask ourselves two questions: What knowledge is relevant in both research and intervention programs? And, more specifically, whose knowledge? Berger and Luckman (1967) argue that society depends on a social stock of knowledge, but that this knowledge is distributed unevenly and, furthermore, is relevant to social status. Thus knowledge can be associated with social power and authority. Some argue for accepting the status quo, the argument that since some of us know more, we should use this knowledge. They ask, "Why do they intervene if they don't know more?" Others argue that it is not so much a question of who has more knowledge but rather of what knowledge is valued by society. Obviously those in power will assume that the knowledge they have is more relevant. This assumption feeds into a deficit model of learning: "We know, you don't know, and what we know is important; therefore you need to learn what we know." Many intervention programs make this assumption. What is being argued here is that deciding what knowledge is relevant (for example, what research variables to choose, or what information is needed to an intervention program) is an arbitrary process and necessarily incomplete. In order to work with as complete information as possible, one needs to have a framework, a concept of knowledge that is as complete as possible. I have suggested here such a framework, one which takes into account different constructions of reality, and a method for discovering the different constructions of reality. Through research on parent education programs, I illustrate how this approach helped me to discover some sophisticated ideas about parenting that intervention programs may not be aware of. It is not that parents' beliefs about child development did not exist as folk knowledge, but rather they were not considered important. Clearly, the approach advocated here is not elitist, nor does it condone a hierarchal distinction between "expert" knowledge and "folk" knowledge.

The Logic of the Anthropological Perspective and the Methodological Implications

The decision to use a qualitative approach resulted in conceptual and methodological implications which help explain why an evaluation of a parent education workshop developed into a study of parents' beliefs about child rearing. It should be useful, then, to outline this anthropological perspective used in this research. This perspective involves a set of logically interrelated assumptions which differ from a quantitative approach and which influenced the methods and conceptual framework used in the study (Table 1).

The first assumption is that the reality of one's data is a series of social constructs as viewed by the participants in the interaction. The social construction of reality in this case refers to the data resulting from the interaction between the investigator and the informant (Berger & Luckman, 1967). The methodological implication of this view of reality is that in this method the investigator must try to understand the informant's point of view and the influence (or "role") of the investigator in constructing this reality. As Ray Rist puts it (Rist, 1977):

> Reality is more than the observable deed or expressed words. Qualitative methodologies assume there is value to an analysis of both the inner and outer perspective of human behavior. This inner perspective or "understanding" assumes that a complete and truthful analysis can only be achieved by actively participating in the life of the observed . . . , to take the role of the other, . . . through understanding the definition of the situation from the view of the participants. (p. 44)

This means the process of knowing is (Rist, 1977)

> essentially one of inductive analysis. Theory begins with an extrapolation from "grounded events." One begins not with models, hypotheses or theorems, but rather with the understandings of frequently minute episodes or interactions that are examined for broader patterns and processes (Glaser & Stauss, 1967). It is from an interpretation of the world through the perspective of the subjects that reality, meaning, and behavior are analysed. (p. 44)

The goal is to discover the definitions and conceptions and perceptions of others—in this case, the parents' perceptions of the impact of the parent education workshop. (See Lewine's discussion of the "empathetic model" in Chapter 10 below.)

The specific methods that we used in the study to arrive at our goal—the parents' definitions and perception of impact and discipline techniques—were (1) the use in the pre- and post-interviews of open-ended questions which did not impose the investigator's definitions of discipline or impact; (2) the use of two participant observers during the workshop sessions to provide a check on the data collected; and (3) a pilot test to eliminate language and conceptual biases. For example: during the pilot test, one of the questions which was eliminated was "What are the ways you discipline your child?" This question resulted in a response which elicited only negative, castigative discipline techniques. The concept "discipline" was defined differently by the parents than by the materials in the workshop.

Table 1. The Logic of the Anthropological Perspective

Anthropological assumptions	Conceptual implications	Ethnographic techniques
Reality is a social construct which involves the viewpoints of others (the participants of the culture). Wilson (1977) states that individuals have "meaning structures."	The goal of research is to discover the definitions concepts of others—	Through participation, through observation, through open-ended interviews using descriptive questions and probes.
It follows that if reality is the social construction of meaning, then reality is multi-dimensional, involving a diversity of viewpoints meanings.	The ethnographer expects to find intra-cultural diversity, rather than cultural uniformity. Wilson (1977) calls this "multi-modal research."	Techniques require a means for checking out multiple views through triangulation and structured and contract questions.
	Data analysis must occur simultaneously with data collection in order to understand the multiple dimensions of reality so that regularities and patterns will emerge.	Techniques require a method for data collection and data analysis, such as multiple methods of record-keeping, data summary sheets, and data coding sheets.
Since reality is subjective, with multiple views, the investigator is also part of that subjective reality; that is, the observer is not separate from the observed.	The role of the ethnographer is one of involvement, not detachment.	This involves knowledge of your own biases, awareness of the role you are playing and of others' perception of you, the importance of establishing trust and rapport, participation, and observation.
Reality involves "inner and outer" perceptions (Rist, 1977).	Informants' theories and explanations (folk theories) carry as much weight as ethnographer's theories.	This involves (1) questions that seek causation, (2) repeated contact with persons to discover their explanations, (3) ethical considerations, such as trust through participation and observation in as many diverse settings as possible.
Social reality including beliefs and behavior is interrelated and overlapping; there are patterns of common understanding in all cultures along	The holistic approach seeks to understand interrelationships of diversity. The context is important. There is no	Through triangulation or checking the data through three independent sources.

Table 1. (*Continued*)

Anthropological assumptions	Conceptual implications	Ethnographic techniques
with diversity of viewpoints. If reality is the social construction of multiple perceptions, it follows that the common patterns of understanding which emerge from all meanings must come from causation that is holistic and not singular.	single cause of behavior; therefore, the ethnographer expects to look for unknown variables, to look for negative evidence (Glaser & Strauss, 1967).	

If reality is the individual's construction of meaning, then reality is multidimensional, involving a diversity of viewpoints. The investigator expects to find, rather than cultural uniformity of meaning, intra-cultural diversity—what Stephen Wilson calls (1977) a "multinational" research approach. For the anthropologist, the in-depth participation to find the participants' views, the questions carefully phrased to incorporate the participants' terms, and the triangulation of data through triple checking of the participants' views are more the methods of validity than a focus on consistency in instrument items would be. Multidimensional meaning also implies that analysis of the data occurs simultaneously with data collection—not only to have an "inner" and thorough understanding of the different perceptions, but also to find patterns and cultural themes. The analysis is essentially inductive, with cultural regularities *emerging* during the data collection process rather than being confirmed *after* the data have been collected. The "proofs" are necessarily incomplete; some of the perceptions that emerge early in the study are more thoroughly checked than perceptions that emerge later in the study, but always there is the methodological imperative to return to the participants for confirmation of meanings.

The anthropologist is a part of the data collection process; the observer is not separate from the observed. In this phenomenological approach to understanding one's data, the anthropologist becomes a part of the understanding process (Sutherland & Perry, 1981). When two people are involved in an interview, both have equal access to the interview experience. This interview interaction provides the way to eliminate the barrier to the interviewee's experience. Through it, the anthropologist can participate in the world view of the interviewee in much the same way other participants have access to each other's experiences. However, direct access to someone's mind or thought is neither possible nor required. What is required is the ability to experience another's point of view and, together with that other, to delimit the essence of what is being talked about, which surfaces in and is created through the interview. As long as the social scientist views the mind of the parent as a hidden world which is only dimly reflected in behavior and which must not be contaminated by the investigator's participation in the parents' experience, there is no way of discovering the culture presumed to reside in that hidden world. It is true, of course, that one can never know a mind as it knows itself, but one can know the mind of a person in another culture as well as minds within that culture can know each other. The investigator, in principle, has a much access to the mind of the informant as another person in the informant's culture. A phenomenological approach, which foregoes objectively in favor of involvement, provides meaningful access to the mind of the other and resolves the dilemma of finding access to knowledge other than one's own (Sutherland & Perry, 1981).

The method chosen is one of involvement rather than detachment—thus the emphasis on participation and observation. Since the meaning of one's data is derived from the meaning the participants give it, it follows that (Rist, 1977)

> qualitative researchers will seek validity through personalized, intimate understandings of the social phenomenon, stressing close in observations to achieve factual, reliable, and confirmable data. (p. 46)

Since we were looking for the causal explanations proposed by the parent, explanations which we call *folk theories*, we assumed that these folk theories had the same validity as the investigator's theories. This assumption became crucial in the development of parenting models.

There is another assumption in qualitative research that plays an important part in methodology, and this is the causal relations are holistic, in the sense that the context is related to beliefs and behavior. The holistic approach does not look for a single cause of behavior; rather, the investigator seeks a diversity of causal explanations. The patterns of meaning emerge from the multiple perceptions of the participants in a diversity of settings. For those involved in the parent education workshop impact study, this necessitated participating with the parents in the workshop, interviewing the parents in their homes, and recognizing the context of the parents' prior experiences as a factor in the impact of the workshop.

To summarize the anthropological assumptions and their conceptual and methical implications as they applied to the impact study:

1. *Assumption:* Reality is a social construct—the result of an interactional process—which involves the viewpoint of others.
   Conceptual Implications: The goal of the investigation is to discover the definition of "impact" from the participant's view.

Methodological Implications: The meanings as the parents perceive them are discovered through participation in the parent education workshops and through the use of open-ended questions using probes and the incorporation of the parents' responses into the probes.

2. *Assumption*: If reality is the social construction of meaning, then it follows that there will be a multiplicity of meanings.[2]

Conceptual Implications: We defined *impact* as "a range of effects," expecting to find a multiplicity of meanings of the major concepts used in the study, such as *impact, discipline, values, control.*

Methodological Implications: An expected multiplicity of meanings requires a method of sorting out patterns of meanings from idiosyncratic meanings; thus, data analysis must be built into data collection. This was achieved through the use of data summary sheets initiated after each interview with a parent and the incorporation of analytical data into the next interview probes. Triangulation of data that had been collected resulted in the progressive refinement of the parents' concepts during the data collection process.

3. *Assumption*: If reality is the social construction of multiple perceptions the parents hold, it follows that the interviewer's perceptions are also a subjective part of that reality.

4. *Assumption*: The interviewer (and her models of causation) are the same kind of subjective phenomena as the parent (and her models of causation). Both are perceptions of reality.

Conceptual Implication: If reality is subjective, it follows that the causal explanations of the parents have the same validity as the causal explanations of the interviewer.

Methodological Implications: Now only were the parents asked to give descriptions of their behaviors with their children and their beliefs about child rearing, they were also asked to give explanations for connections among these beliefs and behaviors. These explanations and causal relationships were the avenue through which the *parenting models* emerged.

5. *Assumption*: If reality is the social construction of multiple perceptions, it follows that the common patterns of understanding which emerge from the multiple meanings must come from a

---

[2] See Chapter 8 of this volume for a similar view; that cultural differences are valid, that "beliefs are biases" (i.e., subjective), and that there is a similarity between the holistic approach in anthropology and the ecological model.

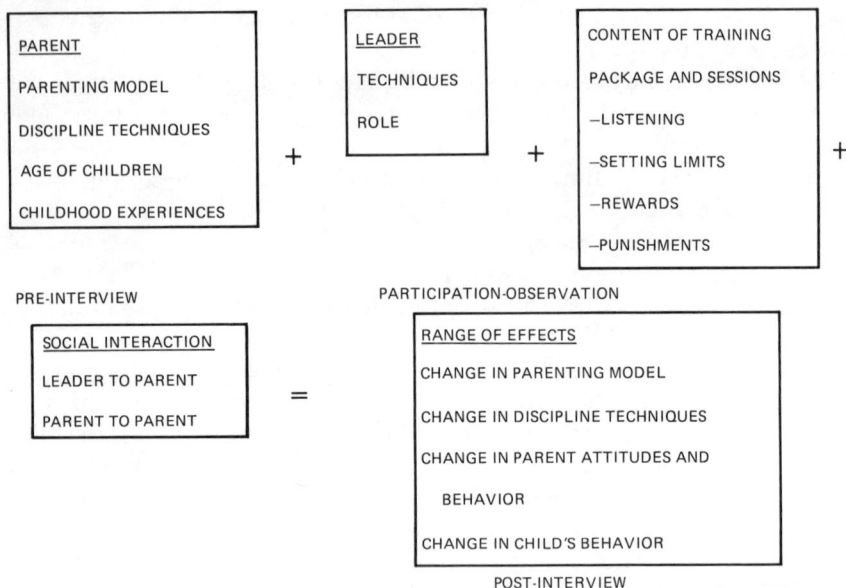

```
┌──────────────────────────┐      ┌──────────────────┐      ┌──────────────────────────┐
│ PARENT                   │      │ LEADER           │      │ CONTENT OF TRAINING      │
│                          │      │                  │      │                          │
│ PARENTING MODEL          │      │ TECHNIQUES       │      │ PACKAGE AND SESSIONS     │
│                          │      │                  │      │                          │
│ DISCIPLINE TECHNIQUES    │  +   │ ROLE             │  +   │ ─LISTENING               │  +
│                          │      │                  │      │                          │
│ AGE OF CHILDREN          │      └──────────────────┘      │ ─SETTING LIMITS          │
│                          │                                │                          │
│ CHILDHOOD EXPERIENCES    │                                │ ─REWARDS                 │
│                          │                                │                          │
└──────────────────────────┘                                │ ─PUNISHMENTS             │
                                                            └──────────────────────────┘
PRE-INTERVIEW                            PARTICIPATION-OBSERVATION
```

Figure 1. Heuristic model of how participant training outcomes may occur.

framework which does not see causation as singular but rather as interrelated and holistic.

Conceptual Implications: A holistic framework seeks multiple variables, seeks the contextual setting of perceptions, seeks unknown variables, and seeks negative evidence.

Methodological Implications: The study built contextual holism into the interview questions by seeking prior beliefs about discipline techniques that the parents brought to the session; this was accomplished by exploring other beliefs and behaviors that encompassed and influenced discipline techniques.

The concepts of *impact* and *discipline* were defined by the participants; the concepts are embedded in the larger socio-ideological context. The context of impact was the social interaction of the training sessions themselves and belief constructs related to impact; and the context of discipline techniques was the child-rearing beliefs, childhood influences, and parental experiences of participants.

The model of learning that we[3] developed (Figure 1) assumed that prior experiences, such as the parents' beliefs, childhood experiences, and

---

[3] I would like to acknowledge discussions with Susan Heck in developing the heuristic model.

techniques of discipline, were necessary to understand the changes parents would experience. Also influencing the potential impact were the leadership role and techniques, the content of the package and its relevance, and the social interaction between the participants and the leader. The measures and explanations of impact came from a comparison of the data collected from interviews before and after the training sessions and from the observation of what went on during the training sessions.

The data collected with the use of two methods: (1) interview schedules based on self-report, and (2) participatant observation of the training sessions. A pre-interview was conducted before the training sessions and a post-interview was conducted four weeks after the training sessions. Each interview lasted approximately one hour. Interviews were taped and transcribed. The transcript totaled approximately 30 pages per interview. At least two interviewers participated, observed, and tape-recorded the sessions at each training session.

Data Analysis

There were several sources of data for analysis: (1) information was gathered from the participants about their parenting models and techniques of discipline during the interviewing and from social interaction during the training sessions; (2) information was gathered from the training sessions about the leadership skills, the social interaction among the participants, and reactions to the content of the package; (3) information was gathered in a post-interview from the leader and at least one of the parents about their assessment of the impact of the sessions on each of the participants.

There were 10 coding categories developed to measure impact: five coding categories related to change in parents' discipline techniques; four coding categories related to other changes in parents, and one coding category related to change in child behavior. The coding categories were based on self-report by the parent and not on home observation. Each coding category had either an attitudinal or behavioral component. Reinforcement of prior experience was not coded as a change, nor were negative effects about the session (did not learn anything, was bored, etc.). The coding categories were:

Change in Parent: Discipline Techniques
1. Listening (attitudinal, behavioral)
2. Setting Limits (attitudinal, behavioral)
3. Rewards (attitudinal, behavioral)
4. Punishment (attitudinal, behavioral)

5. Other discipline techniques (diminuation of screaming, yelling, threatening, increase in patience, increase in ignoring bad behavior) (attitudinal, behavioral change)

Change in Parent: Other

6. Increase in self-confidence
7. Increase in role as disciplinarian
8. Other changes (less "protective," more cognizant of the child's feelings, more conscious of the importance of the parenting role)
9. Parenting model change (change in control variable, change in self-development variable, change in the environment variable)

Change in Child

10. Change in the child's behavior

The unit of coding was a statement or paragraph by the parent. Each parent was given an "impact score." The best possible score was 10, which indicated that the parent reported change in every one of the 10 coding categories.

Data analysis was divided into two phases (Table 2). The first data analysis phase occurred at the time the data were being collected; hypotheses occurred after all the data had been collected. Independent checks to validate the data consisted of (1) the use of at least two independent coders during both phases of data analysis; (2) interviews of the leader and one parent after the training session; and (3) the use of briefing sessions with the independent coders to check discrepancies in interpretation. The primary methods used to analyze data were (1) summary coding sheets from the transcribed interview tape during both phases, and (2) the development of computer coding sheets to identify data sources for the variables.

Validation of the data occurred in various phases of the project:

1. *Data Collection*: The presence of at least two interviewers in any given workshop allowed for triangulation of data on workshop sessions.
2. *Preliminary Data Analysis During Data Collection*: After the pre- and post-interviews with each parent, the interviewer compiled expanded notes from her verbatim notes; she was then required to fill out a data summary sheet which summarized her initial analysis of the interview data. The summary sheets were read from transcribed tapes by the author and another research assistant. These data were then triangulated; a verbal discussion of inconsistencies followed.
3. *Final Data Analysis Phase*: During the final analysis stage, summary coding sheets represented the conceptual emergence of the parenting model, now more clearly formulated. These sum-

Table 2. Process of Data Collection and Data Analysis: Impact Study

Prototype parent	Data collection	Data analysis: Phase I during data collection	Data analysis: Phase II
Pre-interview	Interviewer collects 1. Pre-interview 2. parent information sheet 3. questionnaire	1. Interviewer writes up field notes. 2. Summary sheet by interviewer. Tape is transcribed. 3. Summary sheet by intern. 4. Summary sheet by Sutherland. 5. Discussion between research associate and interviewer.	1. Computer coding sheet for pre-interview questionnaire and parent information sheet by work study student. 2. Summary coding sheet by research associate. 3. Discussion of differences in interpretation with research associate and work study student.
MM sessions	One interviewer takes "script" of parent. One interviewer notes nonverbal actions, seating arrangement, etc.	1. Debriefing session with research associate and interviewers immediately after session. 2. Interviewers turn in field notes based on observation schedule.	Research associate analyze tapes not transcribed.

Table 2. (*Continued*)

Prototype parent	Data collection	Data analysis: Phase I during data collection	Data analysis: Phase II
Post interview	Interviewer collects 1. post-interview 2. questionnaire	1. Interviewer writes up field notes within one week. 2. Interviewer turns in summary sheet. 3. Tape is transcribed. 4. Intern underlines transcribed tape and fills out summary sheet. 5. Research associate underlines transcribed tape and fills out summary sheet. 6. Discussion of tape between research associate and interviewer.	1. Computer coding sheet prepared for transcribed interview and questionnaire by work study student. 3. Summary coding sheet prepared by research associate. 4. Discussion of differences, interpretations, and revisions between research associate and work study student.

maries were triangulated, and inconsistencies and incomplete data were discussed.

The Sample

The potential participants for the sample were initially contacted by the parent education program directors at each of four sites. The staff attended an orientation session at each site to describe the study to the parents. Afterwards, the parents were asked to volunteer to participate. A total of 30 low-income mothers from four different sites participated in the study (Table 3).

The attrition rate for the study was high—40% of all participants came to at least one session—but not unusual for this type of parent training session. Seven fathers who initially began the workshop all dropped out, a problem many parent education programs encounter. The fathers who dropped out were contacted, and they stated that they did not feel comfortable with so many women. So if parent education programs are to reach fathers, the high attrition rate suggests that a special effort must be made.

Evaluation of the parent training package took place at four sites in Austin, Texas. Two sites were Title XX day-care centers, one site was a program in child development for CETA day-care workers, and the fourth site was a parent education program in an after-school program for elementary children.

The parents were asked three primary questions concerning their beliefs about child rearing: How does the child learn? What is the parent's role in the learning process? What is the relationship between the parent and the environment (including both significant others and the physical setting)? A number of beliefs about child rearing that had not been originally investigated had emerged during the research. The original variables were then found to be limiting, they had already begun to change during the course of data collection. However, for the purpose of this chapter, we will discuss the original three variables that comprise the parenting model as an integrated static whole, with the understanding that they have already undergone a refinement and elaboration.

The parenting model consisted of three variables:

1. Does the child learn through (+) others or without (−)others?[4]

---

[4] Note that the distinction made here focuses on self-development vs. other-development. Self-development (− others) is a belief in an innate potential in the child. Other-development (+ others) is a belief in the need for significant others (excluding the parent) in the child's learning.

Table 3. Characteristics of the Participants in the Impact Study

Characteristics	Total number	Characteristics	Total number
Ethnicity		Household composition	
Anglo	10	Single parent	10
Black	9	Nuclear	12
Chicana	12	Male/female friend	2
Income		Extended family	4
Under 3000	7	Separated	3
3000-5000	7	Number of children	
5000-7000	11	1	6
7000-9000	4	2	15
10,000 +	1	3	6
NA	1	4 or more	4
Occupation		Average number of children	2.32
Managerial	1	Ages of children	
Services	3	1 year or less	9
Clerical	7	2-4 years	17
Operatives	1	5-6 years	20
Crafts	3	8 years	11
Student	3	9 or over	15
Aid Dependent Children	1	Total	72
CETA Program	12		
Education			
Below 12th	9		
12 or GED	6		
Above 12	16		

Table 4. Breakdown of Table 3 by Each Variable

	Number and percentage of parents by ethnicity					
	Anglo parents ($n = 10$)		Chicana parents ($n = 12$)		Black parents ($n = 9$)	
Variables in parenting model	Number	Percentage	Number	Percentage	Number	Percentage
+ Control	6	60.0	7	58.4	7	77.7
− Control	4	40.0	5	41.6	2	22.2
− Other	8	80.0	6	50.0	5	55.5
+ Other	2	20.0	6	50.0	4	44.4
+ Environment	7	70.0	9	75.0	5	55.5
− Environment	3	30.0	3	25.0	4	44.4

+ Others   The child learns through the help of significant others.

The child is not capable of learning alone.

− Others   The child learns by him/herself through self-development.

2. Is mediation or control of the environment by the parent important for learning to take place?[5]

+ Environment   Parental control of the environment is important to the child's learning and needs to be mediated.

− Environment   Control of the environment is not important for learning because the child makes his/her own interpretations.

3. Does the parent direct and control learning?[6]

+ Control   The parent directs learning through instilling information or conditioning.

− Control   The parent does not direct learning or exhibit control.

The first variable concerns the innate potential of the child—does the child learn essentially from this innate potential and thus through some self-developmental process, or is the child a tabula rasa, requiring external intervention for learning to take place? This variable forces a dichotomy that is not completely true to the parent's expressions of the variable. It was found, however, that this is an important variable for the parent, and that it forms the basis of the parent's expression of her role with the child. Ongoing research will refine the subtleties of this variable. The second variable emerged during the course of data collection, during a session in which ethnic differences between Chicanas and blacks came into sharp focus. A heated discussion followed the playing of a taped vignette about two children—a 5-year-old and a 6-year-old—playing with matches and causing a fire in a wastepaper basket. The discussion centered around whether it was the mother's "fault" for leaving the matches there, or the children's, since they "should have known better" than to play with matches. At first, the discussion seemed to involve differences in opinion about (1) the responsibilities of a child at that age and (2) the role of the mother,

---

[5] The environment is defined as the social and physical environment. This variable was added during the data collection phase.

[6] Note that two of the variables (control, environment) refer to parental control. Control in the parenting model variables was emphasized partially because the parenting models were being developed for a package that emphasized control and discipline. Current research on the parenting models deemphasizes the control variable.

Table 5. The Parenting Models

Parenting models	Control	Other	Environment
1. Maslow model[a]	−	−	−
2. Gesell	−	−	+
3. Obedience and self-reliance model	+	−	−
4. Authoritative-transitional model	+	−	+
5. Adlerian model	+	+	−
6. Behaviorist model	+	+	+
7. Calvinist model	+	+	+

[a] Of the possible combinations, two were not found (− control, + others, − environment; − control, + others, + environment). These two models, which assume that neither the parent nor child is responsible for learning, would possibly occur in communal type societies.

but as the discussion continued, it became clearer that it involved the *relationship* between either the child and the environment or the parent and the environment, and this was related to the mother's concept of the environment as either hostile or nonhostile. It was not a question of the mother's mediating role in relationship to the environment for the child's socialization. The black mothers' view was that the world is hostile and parents cannot really do much to change it—so when the dangers arise, the mother must do something about them by protecting the child through control of the child's environment. The completed data revealed that the majority of parents of all three ethnic groups had an overall belief about controlling the environment, but that the black mothers were less controlling than mothers in the other two ethnic groups (see Table 7).

The third variable was chosen primarily because the impact study was about discipline techniques. It was reasoned that beliefs about control would give an understanding about discipline techniques. Again, the dichotomy forced the data. Futher, this variable proved to be the least satisfactory, since it least reflected the actual data collected. Part of this problem lay in the concept of parental control.

Out of all the possible parenting models based on a combination of the three variables, the parents fell into seven, some of which overlapped contemporary child-rearing models (Mead, 1976) (see Table 5).

Since the parenting models proved invaluable in understanding the effect of the training session on the participants, a short description of each parenting model follows. The models were derived from the data, and the names given fit some of the experts' models; but, it should be noted, the source of the description of the models was the parents, not the experts.

1. *The Maslow Model* (-control, -others, -environment).
   There is little or no parental control. The parent should abandon the right to use power. The child learns through non-directed

experiencing. The child needs to be left alone to actualize him/ herself, and out of the child's experiences will come a positive self-concept. The positive self-concept will then create good relations with parents and others. The value orientation is towards self-exploration. Historical influence of the model comes from Rousseau's idea that a child, in its natural state, has all the internal potential for self-development. The environment, then, is not dangerous or hostile, but rather there to be explored. It is up to the child to learn. The parent's role is as a friend who provides "guidance"; who says when asked, "You don't tell a child what to do, you ask him." The child's view is equal to the parent's.

2. *The Gesell Model* (- control, - others, + environment).

   The child develops on his own through well-defined "stages of growth." There is little or no parental control. The child tends toward self-regulation and self-exploration. The parent's role is to create the right conditions within the environment. The child is free to develop the kind of relationship with the parent that the child desires. Parents with this model tend to allow "choices" within the environment, and tend to view themselves as "protective," with an emphasis on what the parent "should do" and not what the child should do. Historically, this model gained popularity in the 1930s and continues to be popular today.

3. *Obedience and Self-Reliance Model* (+ control, - others, - environment).

   The parent has the ultimate authority and prerogative with the child, but the child develops and learns on his/her own. There is an emphasis on self-discipline, self-exploration, and self-reliance. Each person, including the child, bears individual responsibility for socialization. A parent should be obeyed because that is the parent's role. The parent cannot control the outside environment and can in no real sense protect the child from the world; it is the child's responsibility to figure out how to "get along." The parent desires both obedience and self-reliance on the part of the child.

4. *Authoritative-Transitional Model* (+ control, - others, + environment).

   The parent's role as authority is given; further, the parent believes in controlling the environment for the child. The child has the internal potential to develop on his/her own, but generally there is conflict with the parent. The most salient feature of this model is that the parent is in a state of transition. The parent is questioning the importance of asserting authority since he/she believes in the child's self-development. There is conflict between a belief in controlling the child and the environment and a belief in letting the child self-develop. (Note that all parents in this model were abused as children.)

5. *The Adlerian Model* (+ control, + others, + environment).

This model focuses on the parent–child–others relationship and there is little focus on the parent's control of the environment. (The "environment" is group interest.) The child is born with a goal-setting desire to develop from a position of powerlessness to a position of social power; the child is also born with an innate desire to work toward group and social interest, which Adler (1937) called "altruism." The role of the parent is to teach the child the "proper" behavior to work toward group interest. Power and authority are given and the parent recognizes that authority and power. The parent's role is to use it with respect and to demonstrate, through example, how to develop social interests. The parent is a necessary presence for the child to learn "right from wrong."

6. *Behaviorist Model* (- control, + other, + environment).

Social control of the individual is inevitable, and all learning experiences of the child are due to external stimuli (operant conditioning). Reinforcement is necessary for learning or change to take place. The role of the parent is to control the external stimuli in a positive way—to provide the necessary reinforcement for the child to learn. The emphasis is on the parent–environment relationship mediating the learning of the child. Historically, the model has its roots in John Locke and the passive view that man grows to be what he is made to be by his enviornment.

7. *The Calvinist Model* (+ control, + other, + environment).

The child is born with undesirable passions which are "sinful." The parent's duties are to teach proper behavior, set a good example, and internalize the norms in the child through punishing and instilling guilt. The child tends toward evil and the parent views the environment as dangerous and hostile, so both must be controlled equally by the parent. The child is basically irrational and thus needs reinforcement from authority, that is, the parent. There is an internal conflict between the individual's "sinful/animal" desires and the needs of society. Socialization requires learning through the "proper" external control. Like the behaviorist model, it is a stimulus–response model of socialization. Historically, the Calvinist view was prevalent in Anglo-Saxon countries and is close to Freud's assumptions about the nature of the individual.

The parents, when they expressed their role in the child's socialization process, did not often describe it simply as one of "control," but described it rather in many more complex ways, such as role modeling, instilling values, the importance or non-importance of verbal instruction, and instilling "proper" behavior. The bottom line, as Piaget pointed out, is that the parents are "in control" in the sense that they have greater knowledge, experience, and responsibility. But the degree to which parents either adhered to this belief or questioned it was the basis on which the dichotomy was made. The controlling parents would say, "I am the mother and they have to do what I say." The non-controlling parents would not say that. However, there is a problem with the variable of "control" that was used in the impact study. The control variable in child development research is so widespread that it has been the dominant variable for the last 30 years of child development research, under the guise of the "authoritarian-permissive" distinction. Even Diane Baumrind's excellent research, which modified the variable and pointed out that the two extremes result in problems in child rearing for parents, accepted the variable as a legitimate reflection of the dominant theme in the socialization process. Part of the problem lies in the presumably unequal relationship between parent and child. Even Piaget accepted what he assumed was the basic inequality in the parent–child relationship: an inequality in power. This assumption simplifies the complexity of the socialization process. I would contend that the parent's relationship to the child as a belief is derived from the parent's belief about the nature of learning and knowledge, and that as a derivative belief, the description of the role of the parent emanates from the parent's beliefs about learning, and not from beliefs specifically about "control." The present study did not "prove" this contention, but it is worth future research activity. The focus on control, for instance, has resulted in a lack of distinction between beliefs about control and negative discipline techniques, so that controlling attitudes are automatically assumed to result in negative discipline techniques—a situation found not to be true in this study. No evidence was found for the hypothesis that the more controlling the parenting model, the greater the use of negative discipline techniques. Another danger in focusing on the power relationship between parent and child is that such a focus does not allow a researcher to explore the diversities of the parent–child relationship.

In our later research we eliminated the concept of parental control and replaced it with the reciprocal data categories of "the role of the child" and "the role of the parent." This encourages a two-way dynamic view of the socialization process rather than a one-way, hierarchical view of the socialization process.

Parenting Models and Discipline Techniques

As we have discussed, each of the seven parenting models consists of a possible relationship among three belief constructs about child socializa-

er, *control*, and *environment*. Is there any association between any ̣ree belief constructs and any of the six discipline techniques?
̣e cross-tabulated each of the belief constructs with each of the six ̣line techniques (listening, praising, rewarding, settling limits, withholding privileges, and spanking) with two statistical measures (one using χ^2 as a measure of the strength of association, the other using the multivariate canonical correlation). The χ^2 gives a one-to-one direct association, whereas the canonical correlation gives a profile of a parent's beliefs and discipline techniques. We found with the χ^2 tabulations that the parents' belief in control was positively associated with setting limits and negatively associated with listening, and that the parents' belief in the child's self-development was positively related with listening and negatively related with setting limits. Perhaps even more significant than these findings were first, the lack of association between the two belief constructs, and second, the use of reward or punishment as we might have expected from the importance placed on their use in research.

The canonical correlation supported the χ^2 results. We found that the belief constructs about the innate potential of the child (*other* variable) and the role of the parent (*control* variable) were associated with the discipline techniques of listening and setting limits.

Ethnic Differences

The impact study found ethnic differences in parenting models, value orientations, and discipline techniques, but did not find ethnic differences in impact. The ethnic differences in parenting models and discipline techniques give insights that might be useful for parenting workshops.

There appear to be ethnic clusterings with respect to some of the parenting models, although it is clear that overall the parenting models cut across the ethnic group (Table 6). The Anglo parents clustered around the non-controlling, self-developmental parenting models (Models A, B, C). The Chicana parents clustered around two extremes, the Gesell parenting model (B) or the Calvinist model (G). The black parents cut across a number of parenting models, but were more heavily represented (44%) in the Behaviorist model. Some of the parenting models were represented exclusively by one ethnic group, such as the Authoritative-Transitional parenting model by Anglo parents and the Calvinist model by Chicana parents. Overall, the Anglo parents, more than the black and Chicana parents, viewed the child as being born with an innate potential for self-development. The black parents, more than the Anglo or Chicana parents, viewed the role of the parent as a controlling one. The black parents were

Table 6. Parenting Models by Ethnicity

| | Ethnic groups | | | | | |
| | Anglo parents | | Chicana parents | | Black parents | |
Parenting Models	Number	Percentage	Number	Percentage	Number	Percentage
1 (− − −)[a]	1	10.0	1	11.1	1	11.1
2 *− 0 +)	3	30.0	4	33.3	1	11.1
Subtotal	4	40.0	5	41.6	2	22.2
3 (+ − −)	1	10.0	1		3	
4 (+ − +)	3	30.0	0		0	
Subtotal	4	40.0	1	8.3	3	33.3
5 (+ + −)						
Subtotal	1	10.0	1	8.3	0	0.0
6 (+ + +)						
Subtotal	1	10.0	2	16.6	4	44.4
7 (+ + +)						
Subtotal	0	0.0	3	25.0	0	0.0
Total	10	100.0	12	100.0	9	100.0

[a] (− − −) + − Control. − Other. − Environment.

the least concerned with the parent exercising a controlling role with respect to the child's environment.

Ethnic Differences and Discipline Techniques

The majority of parents in all ethnic groups tended to rely on positive discipline techniques more than negative discipline techniques both before and after attending the parent education workshop (Tables 7, 8, and 9). The group who relied almost exclusively on negative discipline techniques consisted only of 25% of the Chicana parents. A review of the discipline used before the workshop and those reported in use after the workshop showed all three ethnic groups responded best to "listening more." The majority of the parents did not spank their child nor did they reward their child. The majority listened to their child and praised their child. The majority took away privileges as a discipline technique after the workshop.

We found that:

1. If a parent does not believe in control, the same parent also tends to

Table 7. Canonical Correlations of Belief Constructs with Discipline Techniques

Belief constructs		Discipline techniques	
Other	.57657	Listening	.58815
Control	.54508	Praise	.22722
		Reward	.16862
		Set limits	.66567
		Withhold privilege	.18040
		Spank	.10290

believe in the self-development abilities of the child, and tends to listen to the child but not to set limits.

2. If a parent does believe in control, that same parent also believes that a child needs others for development to take place, and that same parent tends to set limits but does not tend to actively listen to the child.

It is clear that the two belief constructs, which focus (1) on the innate potential of the child and how the child learns and (2) on the degree of control a parent believes she should exercise, have strong predictive

Table 8. Parenting Models and Discipline Techniques by Ethnicity: Pre-interview

		Parenting Model	Reliance on positive techniques		Reliance on negative techniques	
controlling / other development	7			C		CC
	6	B[a]				
		BB	A[a]	B C	C	
	5	A C				
	4	A	A		A	
non-controlling / self-development	3	BB A C	B			
	2	AA CC				
		CC	A B			
	1	A	B C			
	Total	17	7	2	2	
		Listen	Listen	Don't listen	Don't listen	Don't listen
		Praise	Praise	Praise	Praise	Don't praise
		Don't spank	Spank	Don't spank	Spank	Spank

[a] A = Anglo, B = Black, C = Chicana.

Note. The Calvinist Model has a built-in assumption of use of negative discipline techniques.

Table 9. Parenting Models and Discipline Techniques by Ethnicity: Post-interview

Parenting Model	Reliance on positive techniques			Reliance on negative techniques		
7		C C[a]		C		
6	A[a] C C B B B B					
5	A C					
4	A		A	A		
3	B B A B		B			
2	A A A C C C C		B			
1	A		B C			
Total	22	2	5	2		
	Listen Praise Don't spank	Listen Don't praise Don't spank	Listen Praise Spank	Don't listen Praise Don't spank	Don't listen Praise Spank	Don't listen Don't praise Spank

[a] A = Anglo, B = Black, C = Chicana.

potential for two specific parental behavioral patterns, namely, listening and setting limits. It is equally clear that the two belief constructs do not have strong predictive potential for whether a parent rewards or punishes her child. The policy implications for these findings will be discussed in the concluding section.

Ethnic Differences in Values

There were a number of differences among the ethnic groups in the values[7] the parents expressed. These were noted but were not incorporated into the parenting model or discipline techniques.

The black parents reported a relationship with their children which I have called the "law of balanced reciprocity"; the Anglo and Chicana parents did not report this relationship. The black parents expressed this view to their child as follows: "If you want me to do something for you, you

[7] Values refer to a sense of obligation or "ought"; beliefs and distinct from values in that they have no moral connotation and are unprovable givens or assumptions about the nature of things.

have to do something for me." A mother illustrated this principle with a story about teaching her daughter to vacuum the house. When the daughter did not complete the task, the mother said nothing. When Saturday came and the daughter wanted to go to the movies, the mother said, "You didn't vacuum the house. I asked you every day for three days. Now you want me to do something for you. You want money for the movies. When you do something for me, I will do something for you." This teaching of a strictly accountable mutual obligation was not expressed by any of the Anglo and Chicana parents.

It should be emphasized that this balanced reciprocity is different from unbalanced reciprocity. Balanced reciprocity is characteristic of barter and market relationships. A parent who emphasizes balanced reciprocity instills in the child the value that, as one parent put it, "You don't get something for nothing." Thus, the child becomes accustomed to establishing and expecting relationships which are held accountable in terms of investment and return.

It may seem paradoxical that the black parents, who expressed the most control in their parent–child relationships, establish a set of dynamics which allows the relationship to evolve into a more equalitarian partnership. The black parents themselves do not see this as contradictory, but rather as complementary. The child does not separate from his family in adulthood; the obligation to mutually help was built into the parent–child relationship at an early period. This mutual obligation aids the parent in survival during old age and ensures a long-lasting relationship with the child.

This balanced reciprocity partially explains why the black parents tended to rely more consistently on rewarding as a discipline technique, both before and after the parent education workshops. The black parents, more than those in the other ethnic groups, responded positively to the technique of rewarding, regardless of the parenting model they held. The black mothers' tendency toward the Behaviorist Model is clearly associated with their attraction to rewarding or external stimulation as a discipline technique and the principle of balanced reciprocity. The reciprocity principle emphasizes an immediate, accountable return for an emotional investment, as does the Behaviorist Model; both emphasize a stimulus–response interaction.

Balanced reciprocity as a value tends to rely less on internalized guilt as a mechanism for reciprocation, and the black parents did not speak as much about internalized guilt as did the Anglo and Chicana parents. The use of guilt to enforce behavior was most extreme with the Chicana parents employing the punishment model. Their idea was that the child was born with original sin and should automatically feel guilty, an idea that cuts across both Roman Catholic and Protestant beliefs.

However, there are differences between Anglos and Chicanas in the view of the self. For Chicanas, each child is born with a unique "self" a *don* (a gift from God). The parent's role is to discover that gift or talent and to cultivate it. The Anglo parent, like the Chicana parent, feels that a child is born with potentials, but that these are not well-defined. An Anglo child is not viewed as having a propensity from the very beginning, so the role of the Anglo parent is to provide the needed external stimulus or opportunities for the child.

As Chicano children develop, they are taught to view their self as a constant, a core part, while Anglo children are taught less sense of core self; their definition of "self" includes a sense of changeability and malleability. For example, the Chicano grows up with the view that he will not change that much. A Chicana once told me that, on being quizzed in her orals for her P.hD, she was asked, "What do you expect to be doing five years from now?" She felt that this was an inappropriate question; her immediate reaction was, "I expect to be doing what I am doing now." The question was strange to her, not because she did not have career ambitions, but because the implication of the question was that she might be a different person, a different self. Anglos, on the other hand, assume that one can change one's self, as through self-improvement or therapy.

The view of the child as having a "self" from birth rather than developing a self or personality is evident in the distinction between "You are what you are" and "You are what you do." Anglo parents will ask a child who is arriving home from school such questions as "What did you do in school today?" Chicano parents will ask less specific and individual-istic questions, such as "¿Que pasó" ("What's been happening?"). Through the questions asked by Anglo parents the Anglo child learns that he or she should be "doing something"; action becomes important in self-identity. The identity of self through "doing" is a more fragile process, because "doing" can change, and the implication is that the "self" is changed by this changeable "doing."

The parenting models did not capture these ethnic differences in values. Such differences can be analyzed only through more research into and refinement of the belief constructs of parents, through which value differences in different ethnic groups can be integrated with belief constructs.

Policy Implications

The evident increase in parenting classes, parent education workshops, and parenting specialists in public schools is a response to the general public attitude that in an increasingly complex society parents need expert advice in order to raise their children well. The need for such advice has been much debated, as have the benefits derived from it (Ehrenreich & English, 1979; Grubb, 1980). The argument of these authors is that in order to understand the effects of parent education and other family intervention programs, we must account for the degree to which the experts' models of child rearing are compatible with the parents' models of child rearing. According to this critical view, parenting classes often incorporate deficit models of education or behavior modification models of child rearing which either demean the parents' abilities or impose a view of child rearing that is alien to the parents, especially to those who belong to ethnic minorities. Our most important research finding involved the discovery of logically interrelated belief constructs held by the parents (we called them "parenting models"), and the implications of this discovery for understanding parental behavior, the socialization process, former influences, and the impact of family intervention programs.

A major conclusion of our study is that the changes parents experience can best be explained by an understanding of the parents' beliefs about child rearing. The parenting models helped explain why parents experience specific changes in beliefs and behavior. (McGillicuddy-DeLisi, 1980; Sigel, McGillicudy-DeLisi, & Johnson, 1980).

Formulation of the belief constructs that comprise the parenting models was an important step. First, conceptualization of the parenting models allowed data to be gathered at a beliefs level which is distinct from attitudes and behaviors. Second, the data thus gathered have shown a relationship *betweeen* belief constructs. And third, these data have shown a relationship between belief constructs and discipline techniques. The close relationship between beliefs about the innate potential of the child and the controlling role of the parent should be investigated further. The parenting models have served as a heuristic framework for formulating the parameters of logically related belief constructs. Further research should try to clarify some of the problems in the definitions of control, authority, and the parental distinctions about the nature of the child. Even during the course of the data collection, it became clear that the belief constructs were more complex than the two-way distinctions being made, that the belief constructs needed to be clarified, and that the belief constructs needed to incorporate ethnic differences in values.

The association of the "other" and "control" variables with the discipline techniques of listening and setting limits has a number of implications for family intervention programs. First, this association suggests that a family intervention program can ascertain the parents' parenting models by asking them about their techniques of listening and setting limits. It also suggests that behavior modification programs which focus on rewards and punishment are not tapping some parents' belief constructs. And it suggests that programs which emphasize active listening, such as Thomas Gordon's PET program, are responsive to the relationship between parents' belief constructs and their discipline techniques. (However, parent education programs which focus *solely* on listening as a technique are missing the connection between belief constructs and another discipline technique—namely, setting limits.) Finally, the association suggests that family intervention programs should look at the following relationships when constructing their curricula.

Belief constructs
   1. How the child learns and the basic nature of the child;
   2. The extent to which the parent "controls" the child's learning through:

Discipline techniques
   1. Listening to the child;
   2. Setting limits for the child.

How the parent mediates the environment, whether the parent rewards the child, whether the parent spanks the child, and whether the parent withholds privileges—these do not seem to be crucial beliefs or discipline techniques.

In conclusion, the following recommendations for parent education programs are offered:

   1. Parent education programs will have a greater likelihood of effecting change if they are sensitive to—and design activities which are built around—the basic assumptions and beliefs the parents hold about child rearing.
   2. The concept of active listening, which the impact study found parents were particularly receptive to, should be incorporated into parent education workshops, along with material on setting limits.
   3. Given the ethnic differences found in the parenting models of the participants in the impact study, it is recommended that training workshops be sensitive to ethnic differences regarding parenting beliefs and behavior.

Future research should make finer distinctions about the nature of the child and the nature of learning. For instance, ethnic differences suggest that the degree of changeability of the "self" or of one's "nature" should be researched. The data on black parents suggests that the definition of balance and imbalance in parent–child reciprocation should be further refined. Clearly, the environmental variable also needs to be further clarified, into (1) the role of the significant other and (2) the nature of the physical environment, whether it is basically hostile or nonhostile. Finally, future research should focus on exploring ethnic differences in folk models of child socialization.

References

Adler, A. *Practice and theory of individual psychology*. New York: Harcourt Brace, 1924.

Berger, P. & Luckman, T. *Social construction of reality*. New York: Doubleday, 1967.

Ehrenreich, B. & English, D. *For her own good: 150 years of the experts' advice to women*. New York: Anchor/Doubleday, 1979.

Glaser, B. & Strauss, A. *Discovery of grounded theory*. Chicago: Aldine, 1967.

Grubb, N., & Lazerson, M. *Broken promises: The state, children, and families*, New York: Basic Books, 1982.

Mead, E. *Six approaches to child rearing*. Provo, Utah: Brigham Young University Press, 1978.

McGillicuddy-DeLisi, A. *The relation between family configuration and parental beliefs about child development*. Paper presented at the Family as a Learning Environment Conference, Educational Testing Center, Princeton, New Jersey, November 1979.

Rist, R. On the relations among educational research paradigms: From disdain to detente. *Anthropology and Education Quarterly*, 1977, *8*, 2.

Sigel, I., McGillicudy-DeLisi, A., & Johnson, J. *The effects of spacing and birth order on problem-solving: Competence of preschool children. Final Report*, Office of Population Research, National Institute of Education, January 1980.

Sutherland, K. *Qualitative evaluation of parent education workshops and the use of parenting models*. Paper presented at the American Educational Research Association, Boston, Massachusetts, April, 1980. (a)

Sutherland, K. *Executive summary of an evaluation of parent training packages*. Project PRIMO, Division of Community and Family Education, Southwest Educational Development Laboratory, Austin, Texas, 1980. (b)

Sutherland, K. & Meditch, A. The traditional family; the right solution? *Texas Observer*, April 26, 1980.

Sutherland, K. & Perry, N. Dancing with the natives: A phenomenological approach to folk models of socialization. *Contemporary Philosophy*, 1980, *8*(7), 2-5.

Wilson, S. The use of ethnographic techniques in educational research. *Review of Educational Research*, Winter 1977, *47*(1), 245-265.

Yanagisako, S. Family and Household. *Annual Review of Anthropology*, 1979, 161-208.

CHAPTER 6

Prompting Parents toward Constructivist Caregiving Practices

JAMES C. MANCUSO and KENNETH H. HANDIN

Opening

Christopher now resides in a residential child care facility. He is quartered with and shares the daily activity of a group of four other 3- and 4-year old children. He proceeds through his days under the direction of various young, female child care workers, most of whom have had several years of college work. A not-uncommon interaction between Christopher and one of these child care workers will proceed as follows:

> *Setting:* The worker is helping the young children in their attempt to scale a jungle gym network. The children are clamoring for a turn and for the worker's help. She has managed to develop the rudiments of a working line up, so that the children will each have her help in the project. Christopher intrudes into the first position in the line. The original holder of that position objects. Christopher resolves his problem by pushing the objector out of his position.
>
> *Worker:* Christopher, we're taking turns. Please go to the back of the line.
>
> *Christopher:* NO!
>
> *Worker:* All right, no more climbs till Christopher goes to the back of the line.
>
> *Setting:* There are many signs that the waiting children are aroused. Christopher does not move.
>
> *Worker:* We're waiting, Christopher.
>
> *Setting:* Christopher, staring at worker, does not move. The worker takes a physical stance to indicate that she will not be moved. Christopher continues to stare. After a short pause, the worker moves toward Christopher. She reaches to

JAMES C. MANCUSO • Department of Psychology, State University of New York at Albany, Albany, New York 12222. KENNETH H. HANDIN • Saint Catherine's Center for Children, Albany, New York 12208.

take his arm. He flops to the ground. The worker bends to pick him up. He
vigorously kicks her shoulder.

Worker (using a vocal delivery in the 80–90 decibel range): Christopher, you're
going to spend the next 15 minutes in the "time-out room."

Setting: Christopher remains lying on the ground. The worker tries to move
him toward the building containing the room. He refuses to locomote. He
does kick and struggle to escape.

Christopher (shouting repeatedly): Get off me, fuckhead.

Setting: Another worker comes to share in helping Christopher to a dose of
"time-out."

Christopher was placed in the residential program after the police had
responded to a report, made by a neighbor, that the boy was being beaten by
his mother. When they investigated they found that the boy was a mass of
unbelievable bruises, covering his backside from the lumbar region to the
knees. Our society has developed mechanisms by which authorities may
intervene when parenting practices are deemed to be grossly inappropriate;
under child protection laws the boy could be placed under the care of child
protective services.

The Scholar's Role Relative to Parenting Practices

As scholars we are called upon to provide a conceptual framework to
guide the understanding of the processes by which Christopher developed
his behaviors. Believing as we do in our culture that some of the parents'
behaviors are implicated in the development of the boy's behaviors, we will
also seek to explain the parents' behaviors. After having made the moral
judgment that we shall be doing *good* by altering the unwanted portions of
these people's behaviors, we might undertake to develop intervention
programs.

As scholars we will proceed to develop intervention programs on the
basis of our beliefs about—our knowledge networks relative to—behavior
and its development. The belief system set forth in this chapter develops
from a central focus on the tenet that people's interpersonal interactions
reflect their implicit personality theories, their knowledge networks
relative to human interaction (see Damon, 1978). Christopher, at age 4½,
has a system of beliefs about control and the exercise of control in
interpersonal situations. His mother has a system of beliefs that guide her
efforts to regulate Christopher's behaviors. And the child care worker has a
network of cognitions about social behavior relative to the development
and progress of behavior. The mother and the worker, like the scholar (who
should use an explicitly formulated theory of persons), have evolved a
personality theory which guides their intervention strategies.

Some Guesses about the Beliefs of the Worker and the Parent

The task of extracting the implicit personality theory that guides a person's interpersonal behavior, expecially those that guide his influencing and reprimanding strategies, is, prima facie, a ponderous task. If we observe the child care worker and the mother in our example, we can nevertheless make some strong assumptions about their behavior-regulating beliefs. In the first place, they obviously believe that their immediate and direct interventions can alter a child's behavior. Secondly, they believe that some kind of pain–pleasure principle is implicated in behavior change. The worker might have heard that cessation of pleasure is more effective in altering a response than is administration of pain. Thus, she might explain that the time-out room deprives the child of a pleasurable input—attention, which is assumed to be pleasurable. Deprivation of social contact fits the formula applicable to punishment, in that it can produce "a reduction of the future probability of a specific response [for example, resisting instruction] as a result of immediate delivery of a stimulus for that response" (Azrin & Holz, 1966). Child care workers are not likely to endorse strongly a retributive reprimand, preferring restitutive reprimands; but they do perceive reprimand effectiveness in terms of a kind of pain–pleasure construct and believe that leniency–severity is a main variable in reprimand sequences (Handin & Mancuso, 1980; Mancuso & Handin, 1980a).

Our guess about Christopher's mother's belief is less ascertained. Having observed Christopher's skill at resistance to regulation, we can believe that he was subjected to his mother's violence when his mother escalated the severity of the punishment, believing that pain alters behavior. And we would guess that she also believed that "more is better." This belief, after all, may be an unhedged version of one of Johnston's (1972) "methodological rules for maximizing the effectiveness of punishment procedures," stated as follows: "The initial intensity of the punishing stimulus should be as great as possible and continued intensities should also be at the highest reasonable levels" (p. 1034). This guess about the mother's beliefs corresponds to Wasserman's (1967) findings that child-abusing parents not only regard punishment as a suitable reprimand technique, but also defend their right to use physical coercion.

The knowledge network which we believe to underlie the worker's and the mother's behavior change conduct can be seen as emanating from a mechanistic world view. (The term *mechanist* and the term *contextualist*, which will appear at various points in this chapter, are taken from Pepper's [1942] root metaphor analysis of metaphysical positions. The place of mechanistic and contextualist paradigms in behavior sciences is discussed explicitly in Mancuso [1977], Sarbin [1977], and Sarbin and Mancuso [1980].) In short, the worker and the mother see behavior change in terms of force and counterforce: the application of energies and the removal of energies to strengthen the bond of stimulus to response. The machine is the root metaphor for a person, and from this base the worker and the mother elaborate their implicit personality theories.

The child care worker differs from the mother in that her implicit theory was buttressed by selected concepts which were made available to her as she worked her way through some college psychology courses. There she learned about positive reinforcement schedules, stimulus–response bonds, and removal from the positive reinforcement of social contact. The child-abusing mother accumulated her mechanistic belief system by soaking up the mechanism purveyed by parents in social groupings, by talk show moderators, and by parents' magazines. From these she learned that "children will listen if they know that you mean what you say." Both the worker and the mother might have read available lower level texts on parenting which would say something like: "Behavior that is reinforced is likely to recur" (Fine, 1979, p. 78); or (Norton, 1977)

> If a parent wants punishment to be as effective as possible, the parent would severely punish the child each time the child misbehaved. Using less severe punishment is not likely to be as effective in changing the child's behavior, and the child is more likely to repeat the behavior in the future. (p. 61)

Such popularized professional expositions of mechanistic principles offer a system of belief that validates the conventional wisdom. In fact, the system fits well with the industrial capitalistic views of man which have prevailed since Adam Smith presented the iron law of wages. These views are the conventional wisdom of our society. It is no surprise, then, that the surge of parent training program planning and research in the last decade has been guided by mechanistic principles.

Mechanistic Principles in Parent Training Practices

At some point the child care worker and the mother described above will surely receive advice to enroll in a parent skill development program. If one were to believe that the available publications reflect the availability of particular kinds of programs, one would bet that the worker and mother would be instructed in using behavior modification techniques. Mechanistically oriented programs are described in dozens of publications (for example, Creer, Renne, & Christian, 1978; Forehand, Sturgis, McMahon, Aguar, Green, Wells, & Breiner, 1979; Goocher, 1975, and Simpson, 1980). Many of these reports describe the success of techniques that teach workers and parents to identify target behavior, to fix schedules of reinforcement, to shape and maintain behavior, and to determine appropriate means of removing the sustaining reinforcements of unwanted behavior (see Atkeson & Forehand, 1978; Berkowitz & Graziano, 1972, for a review of processes and outcomes).

Selected Concerns about Mechanistic Parent Training Programs

Some publications have raised questions about the shortcomings of these mechanistic programs. For example, to what extent do parents apply their new-learned techniques to promote or to diminish behaviors other than those which were the target behaviors during the planned parent training exercises? If a parent learns to apply mechanistic techniques to teach the child to eat broccoli, will he use the same techniques to teach her to go to bed at a scheduled time? Forehand and Atkeson (1977), after reviewing studies which address the question of the generality of treatment effects, concluded as follows:

> Few clear-cut conclusions regarding generality of treatment associated with parent training can be drawn . . . some studies suggest that generality occurs, whereas others fail to find generality. Unfortunately, the more rigorous the method of assessment, the less positive are the results. For example, all studies using parent verbal reports or only one or two brief observations reported temporal generality; however, Patterson's (1974) systematic follow-up revealed less positive temporal generality in that "booster shots" were often needed. If one chose to disregard the method of data collection and the number of generality measures (which is probably an unwise decision), a number of studies have presented support for temporal generality and setting generality from clinic to home. Generality from home to school and behavioral generality are the two areas in which the least compelling evidence is available. (pp. 589–590)

Such are the observations which are offered by adherents of the mechanistic paradigm as they discuss generality. One expects that in time, considering the positivistic epistemology of the mechanistic orientation, investigators will report ways by which one can train child caregivers to transfer their acquired techniques across settings and behavior.

A Contextualist View of Generality

From outside the paradigm—that is, from the contextualist position which guided our earlier discussion of the implicit child development theories of the caregivers—we would offer a different perspective on critical issues relative to the use of mechanism in discussions of the learning and application of child rearing practices.

We would begin by trying to understand why mechanism is used to frame much of the thought relative to parent training, whereas developmental psychology in general has taken a clear turn toward using a contextualist paradigm. Somehow the bulk of the literature on parent training has been impervious to this paradigm revolution; we would invite speculation on this state of events. We will note, however, one possible basis for the preservation of this bastion of mechanism.

Consider first that any article on training of caregivers inevitably will make an early reference to children's "behavior problems" or "deviant behavior." These unwanted behaviors become the target behaviors in behavior modification training programs. The mechanistic parent trainer has responded to the front-line applied psychologist who works with desperate caregivers; that is, those judged to have failed in their parenting roles. The mechanists offer a technique that will work immediately to remove signs of failure. Noncompliance, out-of-seat behavior, aggressive acts, enuresis, fearful behavior, and overeating are the behaviors that caregivers are most commonly trained to remove by mechanistic techniques. Such behaviors, reported and observed outside the context of the stream of ongoing parent–child interactions, are readily cast into the *effect* position in a cause–effect sequence. Mechanist psychology provides the frame for such sequences.

Effects can be removed by training caregivers to eliminate causes, to supply countercauses, or to establish different cause–effect sequences. More or less cause can produce more or less effect! More reward produces more compliance! Less attention produces less out-of-seat behavior! Caregivers are instructed to make finer discriminations along a restrictive-permissive continuum! The reports of the successes of parent training programs are, of course, reports about the success of efforts to manipulate those specific cause–effect sequences.

Our view of the child-rearing process leads us to conclude that these very successes reflect a major failing of mechanistic parent training programs. Earlier in this chapter we proposed that caregivers seem to respond to children in terms of their belief systems regarding child development processes. We will go on to propose that a successful, growth-producing caregiver must adequately take into account the child's knowledge networks. From this position we conclude that mechanistic parent training programs fail, in that they inform parents that they need only cognize the cause–effect relationships, and that they need not take into account the child's cognitions.

Generality and Meaning

Consider again the critical questions about generality of behavior modification interventions, which have come from within the mechanist paradigm. When a parent has been trained to reinforce a child to comply with that parent's commands, will the parent also reinforce compliance with the requests of the child's sister? If compliance with the mother has been achieved, will the child also comply with the father, the aunt, and the teacher? A behavior-explaining paradigm that focuses intently on cause-effect linkages does not adequately explain generalization, even though the term might be used blithely to cover a concept embedded in a theory.

We cannot escape the premise that generality immediately refers to meaning. A genus is generated by a person. If we can learn anything from the study of thousands of years of thought about epistemology, we can learn that categories are constructed by persons. One cannot naively believe that a child automatically looks out and "sees" categories. A huge psychological development underlies the invention and instantiating of categories. Thus, if the mechanist tries to look at generalization of the effects of his prescribed parenting techniques, he must confront the hypotheses that the child's psychological status—the child's system of meanings—will determine generalization. The child's categories determine the similarities between the stimuli that are assumed to be causes in the cause-effect link. Likewise, his or her categories determine the similarities between behaviors—the effect in the cause-effect linkage. If the child's compliance does generalize after having been reinforced to comply with the mother's request, we would want to consider the place of the child's categories in that generalization.

An analysis of the growth of contextualism in the study of psychological development shows that the movement was powered primarily by efforts to incorporate an understanding of meaning into our studies. The master of the science, Piaget, provided six decades worth of evidence that the same stimulus means many things to many children, depending on a particular child's state of cognitive development. Furthermore, the development of these meanings is epigenetic. Meaning develops epicentrally in the context that includes the child's knowledge structures as well as the input deriving from the outside world. In short, the child's "response" (the structure the child imposes on input) is as much a "cause" of the "stimulus" as is the event which generated the input. Developmental psychology has been forced to take into account the epigenetic evolution of meaning. Constructivism is now a clearly established perspective in developmental psychology (see, for example, Bornstein & Kessen, 1979; Ornstein, 1978; Uzgiris & Weizman, 1977). Specifically, investigators have supplied a broad base of concepts that can be used in considering the meanings that a child can bring to the social interactions in which his behavior is being regulated (see, for example, Damon, 1978; Eimer, Mancuso, & Lehrer, 1980).

The Basis of a Constructivist Parent Training Program

Rychlak (1981) has offered a careful analysis of the parallels in the constructivist theories of G. Kelly (1955) and J. Piaget (1974). In a similar analysis Sigel (1978) has spelled out the constructivist/contextualist foundations of Kelly and Piaget's work. He caps his commentary with the statement that "The [underlying] paradigm can be called *dialectical constructivism*. The individual is in dynamic relationship in reality— immersed—not of it, but in it" (p. 337). Handin and Mancuso (1980) have described the ways in which constructivist psychological theories may provide the foundations of a parent training program. The following pages contain a review of some propositions developed by Kelly and Piaget. These propositions are taken to be the essential assumptions used to develop a constructivist parent training program.

The Motivational Principle

Kelly (1955) offers the following as his Fundamental Postulate: "A person's processes are psychologically channelized by the ways in which he anticipates events" (p. 46). With this proposition Kelly specified the contextualist conditions by which behavior change is instigated. In another language one could say, "People try to maintain their capacity to predict," or, "People try to avoid failure in information processing."

Piaget's concept of equilibration places similar emphasis on antici-pation. A published extended discussion between Piaget and Bringuier (1980) contains the following interchange:

> BRINGUIER: What about equilibration?
> PIAGET: It refers to assimilation and accomodation in relation with each other; it may be stable. In an intelligent act there is an equilibrium because the other two do not hurt each other but rather support each other.
> BRINGUIER: Why "equilibriation" and not simply "equilibrium"?
> PIAGET: Because its a process, not a balance of forces.
> BRINGUIER: Equilibriation is dynamic?
> PIAGET: Yes, it's the self regulation. An equilibriated system is a system in which all the errors have been corrected. It isn't a static equilibrium like an immobile balance scale; it's the regulating of behavior.
> BRINGUIER: It's always a question of reacting.
> PIAGET: Exactly. The process leads toward equilibrium but since equilibrium is never attained—thank heavens!—because the whole world would have had to be assimilated. (p. 44)

Powers (1973), speaking of behavior as the control of perception, specifies a similar constructivist motivational principle: "The purpose of any given behavior is to prevent controlled perceptions from changing away from the reference condition" (p. 50)—the reference condition being the anticipatory schema. Grossberg (1980) provides a systematic description of a neurological model that would underlie a person's activity at those points at which there is initiated a "downstream" neural model that cannot adequately incorporate the "upstream" model generated by input.

Each of these constructivist behavior scientists has worked with a similar concept to explain the instigation of and alteration in the flow of a person's behavior. A person's anticipations; his schemata or "reference signals" are totally implicated in the channelization of his processes. All input into the continuously active psychological system is processed. Each input pattern becomes integrated to a person's knowledge system as schemata, drawn from long term memory organizations, are constructed to transmute that input. When a reference signal cannot be adequately set— when there is an inability to assimilate input—the system is disequilibrated and the person is activated to achieve assimilation by accommodating existing schemata. One can learn. One may "metaphorize," which is to say, other available constructions may be processed to provide an input-to-schema match. Under other circumstances one may diminish the input (by withdrawal or by aggression) or one may "artificially" lower (by use of drugs) the physiological arousal that accompanies these disequilibrated states.

One could diverge from the purpose of this discussion of a constructivist motivational principle and become involved in offering evidence of the utility and validity of a statement like Kelly's fundamental postulate. Such a repetition of what can be found elsewhere (Deci, 1975; Mancuso, 1977; Mancuso & Adams-Webber, 1982) would not, at this point, help to explain further a constructivist approach to parent training.

The Parent's Role in Promoting Psychological Growth

Kelly's (1955) exposition of personal construct theory included a statement, called the "sociality corollary," which broadly describes the process of social influence. "To the extent that one person construes the construction processes of another, he may play a role in a social process involving the other person" (p. 95). Mancuso (1977) tied Kelly's sociality corollary to the constructivist motivational principle and proposed that the successful parent is a successful novelty moderator. The gist of this proposition is found in a compatible quotation from Sigel (1978): "First and foremost the educational environment must create discrepancies and subsequent conflicts and uncertainties" (p. 337). The point is: A successful child caregiver can play a role with a child only if he is able to construe the child's construct system, so that he can present the kind of moderate discrepancies which will lead the child to successful metaphor making.

To construe a child's construct system successfully, one may think about cognitive development from a position built on the kinds of stage theories that have evolved from Piaget's work. A caregiver may consider a child's construction system in terms of childhood understandings of numbers, space, social interactions, and classification; the caregiver may consider these processes in the terms used by investigators who have followed Piaget.

Additionally, a parent may understand a child's construction systems by attempting to develop, for his own use, principles about how construction systems function. The parent might, in the first place, think about individual, developing construction systems as they are implicated in different children's behavior. The parent might consider what happens when there is failure to assimilate or anticipate. The limited applicability of the child's category systems, and the limits which those systems place on accommodative processes, might be considered, as might the ways in which the cultural milieu promotes the development and use of different constructs.

For example, the caregiver might consider how to shape a child's construction of broccoli under the following circumstances: Steamed broccoli, served with butter and lemon, appears on the table. Taste, texture, and odor would provide novel input. "I'd like you to eat some broccoli," says the parent. If the television advertisers have been the social source of constructs about food, the child will readily construe the novelty-produced arousal under the construct dislike–like. If the parent does not think in terms of construction, novelty, arousal, and reconstruction, he might readily interpret the child's reaction from a mixed formist/mechanist view. The child, holding a formist view, would believe that he is a form who, by nature, abhors broccoli. The parent might add a mechanistic motivational assumption, whereupon he will say, "I don't care whether or not you like broccoli. You're going to eat it, or you'll just march right up to your bedroom."

Alternatively, he could be a parent who would consider the child's behavior from a constructivist perspective. The broccoli eating would not be an isolated problem in the child's life. "I'd like you to eat some broccoli," he might say. "You haven't learned to eat that yet, but when you try it you'll find that it is something like cabbage. You might find it strange, like when you tried the pasta with *pesto genovese.*" The dislike–like construct is not used. The child is primed to anticipate the novelty and arousal, and the connections with the child's already-developed meanings are called forth. In short, if the parent wishes to promote the development of a person who exposes him or herself to growth, the parent's distancing strategies (Sigel, 1970; Sigel, McGillicuddy-DeLisi, & Johnson, 1980) should follow from a thorough construing of the child's construction processes. That is, by successfully construing the child's construction system the parent can "create psychological distance between the individual and the environment," thereby making "demands on the person (individual of any age) to infer from the observable present" (Sigel, McGillicuddy-DeLisi, & Johnson, 1980, p. 10). Through meeting these demands, we assume, the child is prompted to achieve construct system growth and reorganization.

Emotion and Anticipation

There can be no diminution of the salience of the arousal that is implicated in a person's failure to anticipate. Berlyne (1978), after exploring and analyzing the positive relationships between level of subjective uncertainty and general arousal, declares:

> As Lindsley (1957) has put it, rises in arousal have repercussions on efferent processes, and central processes. In other words, they tend to mean increases in the vigor, speed, and efficiency of bodily movements (the amount of effort invested in them—Kahneman, 1973), in the sensitivity and information-gathering capacities of the sense organs, and in the ability of the brain to discriminate, analyze, and base decisions on incoming and stored information. There are plenty of indications that all these functions are at their peak when arousal is moderately high but decline when arousal approaches its upper extreme, thus conforming to the inverted-U-shaped curves that have been much discussed in the relevant literature. (p. 152)

In short, massive physiological processes are activated in the child who enters a phase of unsuccessful assimilation. And at this point in the history of psychology we have learned that arousal-associated physiological processes alter the body in ways that produce distinctive changes at sensory endings throughout the body. The stomach contractions that are associated with arousal alter the state of the pressure-sensitive neurons embedded in muscle tissue. Vasodilation and constriction similarly produce sensory input. Such arousal-associated sensation must be integrated, as must all input. Sharing the cultural constructions that are available, we can communicate with one another by applying the label emotion to interpretations of these special input patterns.

As constructivists we think of people's attributions to these internal arousal-produced input patterns in the same terms that we think of one's use of knowledge networks to assimilate any other input. People build theories about their selves through the same processes they use in building theories about any event that is associated with input (see Mancuso & Ceely, 1980; Mancuso & Sarbin, 1983, for discussion of self theories). A significant part of the theory of self that applies to emotions frames one's understanding of how to maintain equilibration, thereby maintaining a tolerable arousal state. Early in life one may learn, for example, that adults are useful consultants in times of disequilibration (see White, Kaban, Shapiro, & Attanucci, 1977, for an elaboration of the relationship between children's competence and the use of "adult consultants" in problem situations). Conversely, a child can learn that adults impose disequilibrating conditions, and that the adults contribute further to already initiated disequilibriation.

These formulations lead us to believe that caregivers who fail to manage discrepancy successfully will fail to deal successfully with a child's arousal (read: emotions). The ineffective caregiver will not recognize that each discrepant situation has the potential of putting the child into an intolerable state of arousal. Such a caregiver will fail to help the child to build a useful theory of emotion by which to interpret its own arousal. And, most disastrously, the caregiver will create situations in which the child can learn to use extremely unacceptable behaviors to create environmental conditions that diminish the input of stimuli that cannot be integrated.

Reprimand and the Novelty Moderator

Novelty and arousal figure prominently in the theory of reprimand which fits to the overall theory that guides our constructivist approach to parent training. Reprimand represents the single potentially most explosive source of discrepancy. Every reprimand situation, in that reprimands introduce arousal producing discrepancies, can become an unfortunate event in which the parent tries to keep the child in a heightened state of arousal while the child explores every possible means of avoiding discrepancy.

What Is Signified by the Term Reprimand?

Our term *reprimand situation* applies to those events which have been discussed at those points at which people have used such terms as *discipline practices, socialization processes, persuasion,* or *superego building.* Following the mechanistic approach that had been prevalent in developmental psychology, those who discussed these processes (Bandura &

Walters, 1959; Glueck & Glueck, 1950; Sears, Maccoby, & Levin, 1957; Whiting & Child, 1953) wrote about punishment, reward, impulses, delay of gratification, and other forces assumed to be casually implicated in rule following. Later commentators (Hoffman, 1976; Kohlberg, 1969; Parke, 1974) have needed to respond to guiding mechanistic conceptions about reprimand. Mechanistic conceptions gave little place to considerations about construction systems and their place in transgression. And with their emphasis on force concepts like punishment and reinforcement, theories of behavior regulation frequently gave a force-like perspective to parent practices. To build the model on dynamic mechanistic lines, the parent-provided force was taken to be a counterforce to an energic parameter in the child's psychological system. The parenting practice, from this point of view, was directed toward producing control of impulses: anger, sexual impulses, need for attention, and so forth.

In a theoretical world that is dominated by these concepts, it has been difficult to choose a term to label those actions in which a parenting-person attempts to promote a child's reconstruction. Our choice of the term *reprimand* is based on our satisfaction that this term is not overridden by force conceptions. Etymologically the word does come from a gerundive form of the Latin verb *premere*, to press. Thus, it relates to the concept of pressing back. We know that the term has come to have a negative connotation; and that, too, influenced our choice. All input that disconfirms an anticipatory schema will create arousal, and people ordinarily do not seek out the attentional diversions that follow disconfirmation. Other terms could have served—rebuke, reproach, reprove, reformulate, and so on—but each alternative has a major shortcoming. We decided that the term reprimand best labels our conception: the effort to prompt the transgressor to re-schematize the transgressive event.

Some Parameters of a Constructivist Theory of Reprimand

A constructivist theory of reprimand builds on an initial assumption that the child's unwanted behavior reflects actions which are congruent with his or her overall construction scheme. Similarly, the reprimand follows from the reprimander's construction of the event. The reprimander's conduct follows from his observation that the transgressor has acted in a way that implies a contradiction of the reprimander's view of the rule-governed situation. A rule, described in similar terms, is a socially approved way of constructing an event. To say that the child has "broken a rule" is to say that the child has applied a construction which is discrepant from that which has social approval. Thereupon, one might paraphrase Kelly's "choice" corollary, and propose the following: A person will accept a reprimand (another person's construction of an event) if he or she anticipates that doing so provides possibilities for extending and defining his construct system.

This propositional framework prompts a search for data corresponding to a series of questions internal to the theory. How does one calculate optimum levels of discrepancy in the shaping of reprimands? Does a person's conception of reprimand's functions and effectiveness relate to the ways in which he or she personally responds to reprimand? What are the relationships between one's conceptions of reprimand and the ways in which one shapes reprimands? Does one's conception of reprimand relate to one's effectiveness as a reprimander? Are there developmental progressions in the development of conceptions about reprimand? And, on the broadest theory-based levels, does a person who uses a constructivist view of reprimand end up with a child who is more skillful in responding to rules?

A series of publications contain reports of data that help to define some of the parameters in this theory and to provide provisional answers to some of these questions. These studies follow a straightforward research strategy. Subjects are shown various transgression–reprimand sequences; they are asked, in different ways, to report their perceptions of the situation. Mancuso and Allen (1976) have shown that kindergartners, third graders, and sixth graders differ in their perceptions of transgressors who have been exposed to retributive and explanatory reprimands. To sixth graders, a child exposed to either reprimand is "better" than one exposed to no reprimand, suggesting that they see reprimand as casual. Kindergartners seem to take reprimand as a labelling process. If an adult has reprimanded, the transgressor is "badder" than is the non-reprimanded transgressor. Third graders seem to take the labelling view of coercive reprimand and the ameliorating view of explanation.

In a pair of reports, Mancuso and Handin (1980a; Handin & Mancuso, 1980) describe findings of studies of child care workers' perceptions of reprimand. They found that the severity–leniency construct appears to be used as a first order judgment dimension in most people's evaluation of a reprimand. Contrary to expectation, the severity–leniency construct appears to plot into a socially disapproved-socially approved construct more readily than into an ineffective-effective construct. People are concerned about severity being judged as socially bad, and this judgment can override the evaluation of effectiveness. Restitutive reprimand is judged to be most desirable by 75% of all participating caregivers, while 75% percieve retributive reprimand as being least proper. Explanatory reprimand received a mixed review: 30% of the participants see explanatory reprimand as least proper, while 30% see it as most proper. Some findings relating peer-judged worker effectiveness to choice of reprimand are as follows: Having located a group of participants who would judge explanation to be the desirable reprimand, the researchers found that 50% of the group were rated as highly effective by their worker peers as only a small percentage (15%) of the lower peer-rated workers advocated explanatory reprimand.

Another study (Aldrich & Mancuso, 1976) has focused on the views of reprimanded transgressors who, in turn, respond differently to reprimand. Among other things, all the kindergartners indicated that they expect continued transgression from all reprimanded transgressors—except one who openly accepted the mother's explanatory reprimands. Sixth graders varied their judgments to reflect the variations in the transgressor's response to reprimand.

Other related works explore such subjects as children's perceptions of transgressors as a function of intentional and accidental transgression (see Mancuso, Morrison, & Aldrich, 1978), and School of Education students' views of reprimand. Eimer, Mancuso, and Lehrer (1980) have brought together the results of a major effort to apply a stage development framework to children's perceptions of reprimand processes. This work suggests that kindergarten children view reprimand as a matter of direct, overt control. By sixth grade the children consider the psychological qualities of both parent and child. Conceptions at the lowest stage represent a simple, nonreflective association of bad acts with bad consequences, and there are no signs that reprimand is perceived as a cause of behavior change. At slightly more advanced stages, the purpose of reprimand is seen to be the force-laden suppression of disapproved behavior. The effectiveness of reprimand is thus seen to be a direct positive function of severity. At the most advanced stages in the sequence, which appear in children at the sixth grade level, reprimand conceptions reflect a well differentiated and integrated psychological systems view of the relations between the belief systems of both the reprimander and the transgressor. An effective reprimand is seen as a reprimand which takes into account a transgressor's age, level of development, and motives for transgressing. In short, these sixth graders show that they can take into account constructivist principles.

The studies of these investigators lead toward the final goal of exploring the relationship between perception of reprimand and the use of and responsivity to reprimand. Certainly, it is logical to believe that one's perception of reprimand will guide one's use of reprimand techniques. Thus, no matter what the experts will finally say about reprimand effectiveness, the use of various forms of reprimand depends on the implicit personality theory of the user. The other side of the coin is harder to inspect.

How does the transgressor's perception of reprimand affect his response? How does the transgressor's perception of reprimand alter the relationship between the use of a particular reprimand and the outcome of that use?

These investigations also relate closely to our constructivist parent training program. We hope to affirm the efficacy of these views of reprimand as we try to instruct parents in ways to direct children's growth.

Description of a Constructivist Parent Training Program

In the foregoing text we explore some of the assumptions that underlie a constructivist interpretation of parent–child interaction. Those assumptions provide the base of the parent training program that has been initiated and advanced at Saint Catherine's Center for Children, Albany, New York.

This constructivist program has been designed to alter the ways in which parents construe child development and their role in the developmental process. The program is of course aimed at prompting parents to use a constructivist approach.

A Contextualist's Parent Training Program

The instruction strategies used in a constructivist parent training program would be directed toward facilitating the parents' development of the conception that people engage in behaviors in an attempt to develop and maintain structured, internally consistent explanatory schemata from which to define the meaning of self and to explain the interactions with events and others. Further, parents should be trained to develop an understanding that although adults and children are involved similarly in the process of applying implicit theory, the content and structure of individual theories differs. Having participated in the program, a parent should be able to cognize the differences between adult and childhood construings. Coincidentally, a parent should come to construe the child's construings, so that these construings and not only overt behavior, become a focus of interaction.

A contextualist parent training program directly faces another major challenge. An implicit personality theory frames events in ways that may lead one to adopt a naive realist epistemology. To deal with the realist challenge, the training program to be described begins with exercises designed to make parents more aware of their own constructive activities. The program involves three separate, but inter-coordinated strategies, as follows: (1) The parent study group, (2) individual parent–child sessions, and (3) counseling and home training sessions. (A program manual, prepared by the staff, is available for inspection.)

The Parent Study Groups

Parents are invited to participate in a group instructional program with six to eight other participants. Sessions are conducted weekly. The instructional package is comprised of 19 sessions organized into seven topic areas. Instruction is aided by the use of films, videotapes, filmstrips, workshop exercises, and discussions. The group is co-led by two professional workers with extensive knowledge of the contextual child rearing perspective.

Topic 1: Why Learn about Parenting?

To provide parents with the motivation for staying with the program, the first topic directs itself toward exploring bases for taking a constructivist approach to the study of parenting. Such activities allow participants the opportunity to resolve some of the disequilibriation that is often experienced by participating parents, who are being encouraged to develop concepts to cover events for which they already have an extensive knowledge system.

Topic 2: Developing an Awareness of Personal Beliefs and Their Effect on Behavior

The three sessions dealing with this topic are designed to introduce the process of implicit theory building and utilization. Parents are involved in activities which attempt to make more explicit the construction process and the relationships between a person's constructions and a person's behavior. Parents are led to construe their own constructive processes. Parents are directed to observe the relationship between their construing activities and their behavior. The final session on this topic is designed to help parents explore their constructions specific to the business of raising children. Parents explore such questions as "What do I believe about parenting?" and "What do I believe about how children develop psychologically?"

Topic 3: Children Have Beliefs, Too!

Building on the notions already introduced, exercises related to this topic facilitate the parents' development of the notion that children, too, are involved in implicit theorizing. The four sessions demonstrate how the logical and social/moral reasoning of children develops with age. Emphasis is placed on the differences that children and adults utilize in constructions of reality. Films and discussions help parents explore the reasoning (theorizing) performed by typical children of various ages.

Topic 4: Why Children Do What They Do

The next series of sessions helps parents conceptualize the relationship between the child's implicit theory and his or her behavior. Several activities are used to attempt to help parents understand that the child's behavior is a function of his or her construction of events. Children choose to behave in ways that are consistent with their views about themselves and others. To elucidate further the notion that children behave in ways that support their constructions, parents are asked to conceptualize specific constructions that a child might maintain that are related to certain behaviors. For example, parents are asked what the differing perspectives of two children might be regarding grown-ups; they are given two children, one who typically utilizes grown-ups as consultants, and one who seldom orients to adults. The parents would be led to consider the former child's conception as "Grown-ups are helpful; they can help me out of a jam," in contrast to the latter child's construction, "Grown-ups just want to boss me; they never let me do things my way."

Discussions of the bases of children's emotional responses conclude the activities of this topic area. The disequilibriation notion is utilized to explain the emotional functioning of the child. Parents are asked to perceive emotional upset as occurring when the child experiences input that is discrepant from his world view and is unable to resolve the discrepancy. Feelings of happiness and pride are explained in terms of the child's successful attempts at integrating discrepant input. Workshop exercises which direct parents to "try to think of what the child believed was going to happen, that did not happen" are utilized to facilitate the parent's understanding of the place of the child's construction system in the child's emotional responses.

Topic 5: Building Relationships with Children: A Process of Sharing

The experiences designed for this topic area represent an attempt to convey to the parents the full implications of Kelly's (1955) sociality corollary. Exercises are assumed to help parents conceptualize the unproductive interactions they experience with their children in terms of the differences of perspectives or implicit theoretical assumptions applied by the child and the parent in the particular context. Parents are instructed in using methods of parent–child interactions that will enable the child to express his perspective. They also are informed about distancing strategies (Sigel, 1970). Parents also are guided toward using tactics that facilitate their child's development of perspective taking skills. Activities exemplify the sequence of developmental stages through which researchers (Selman, 1980) have observed children progress. All of this, of course, involves the parents' attempts to understand the child's construing system.

Topic 6: Teaching the Child Appropriate Beliefs

Parents are encouraged to adopt the notion that day-to-day parent–child interactions do influence the types of constructions the children develop about parents, other grown-ups (that is, teachers, babysitters, etc.), and themselves. Instructional activities are aimed at helping the parent understand that such constructions underlie the social responsiveness, positive or negative, of the child. Parents are led to consider the specific kinds of experiences which help a child to develop such implicit constructions as "It's okay for others to regulate my behavior" or "Grown-ups are helpers, they help me to resolve disequilibriation."

Reprimands, which are treated as exemplars of discrepancy introduction, are discussed in terms of interactions that guide the child's theory-building efforts. Reprimand is discussed in terms of having the child reconstrue the event in a way which will more readily enable the child to assimilate the reprimander's view relative to the behavior being discussed. The role of the parent as regulator of input is stressed. Parents can learn that their reprimand has less chance of bringing about restructuring if the child is kept in an extended state of disequilibrium. The child will not profit from a confrontation in which he is required to invalidate one important part of his self system by accepting the parent's construction of the rule related event. Parents are encouraged to create certain family routines, aimed at giving the child easy-to-construe repetitions of events. If the parent has grasped some of the principles of the constructivist approach he or she will recognize that routine setting forestalls the arousal that accompanies unexpected intercession into a child's ongoing activity. And, of course, with less occasion to disrupt the child, there are fewer opportunities for the child to resist, and less potential for the child's development of confrontational response. Parents are also taught techniques which should forestall arousal when it is necessary to disrupt the child. Any parent who has grasped the foregoing basic ideas about arousal can learn effective distraction techniques. The parent can learn to intercede in the child's activity by producing a slightly novel, attention-getting input. Parents are shown that it is easy to entice a trouble-bound toddler into another game-like activity. By using this technique the parent can lead the toddler to construe himself as a willing participant in pleasant, ongoing activity, rather than as the victim of coercive regulation.

In short, when White *et al.* (1977) speak of creating a child proof environment, the parent can think metaphorically of a psychological environment in which the child can safely construe. In such an environment there will be less occasion to take recourse to coercive measures which say to the child, in effect, "If you don't construe this event as I wish you to construe it, you will be disequilibriated by an even more discrepant stimulus input."

Topic 7: Problem-Solving Skills for Parents

The final sessions of the instructional section of the program prepare the parent to implement the contextual principles that have been introduced in the earlier sessions. A problem-solving and evaluation method is presented to the parents for their use in developing and evaluating their ongoing interactions with their children. When applying this method to determine how to solve a problem they are experiencing with their child, parents are reminded to consider the child's construction of particular events. The method consists of six short steps.

The parent begins by identifying and defining the problem situation (Step 1). Next the parent considers the child's construction of the particular event in question; that is, the parent attempts to define specific constructions related to the behavior (Step 2). Step 3 requires the parent to identify his or her own constructions of the event, to attempt to define specific beliefs related to the issue at hand. Steps 4 and 5 ask the parent to think of alternative solutions to the problem and to evaluate them. Solutions are evaluated in terms of the specific possible effects that the experience, defined by the solution, would have on the constructions subsequently developed by the child relative to himself and the parent. If the considered solution will lead the child to reconstruct the event in a way thought to be productive, the solution is adopted. If not, other solutions are developed.

Since the problem-solving method requires the use of all of the concepts taught in prior sessions, the use of the method represents a way of helping parents to integrate further these new and perhaps strange contextual ideas. This method also facilitates the parents' utilization of interactions which promote productive conceptualizations by the child, since it helps parents consider the possible unwanted residual effects of using coercive or power assertive reprimands. The method leads parents to engage in evaluation of a solution which extends beyond "It works, doesn't it."

Individual Parent–Child Sessions

Parents and their children also participate in weekly, individual, one hour play sessions supervised by a professional worker. These sessions provide the medium within which the program's guiding concepts can be individualized. In these sessions parents are led to see the place of the concepts in their direct familial contexts.

During the first half-hour of the individual session, the parent plays with the child while being observed and videotaped through one-way mirrors. During a second half-hour, the worker and parent review the videotape. The worker guides a discussion which aids the parent in identifying the implicit theoretical assumptions used during the interaction by both the parent and the child. The professional focuses on the relationship between the child's constructions and the parent's constructions and behavior. The worker attempts to have parents view disruptions of the parent–child interaction in terms of divergent implicit perspectives. Throughout the review of the tape, parental attempts at input moderation are discussed. Moments at which parental regulation of the child's input became necessary or occurred are discussed. These discussions help the parent relate the concepts being examined to the everyday parent–child experience.

In alternate sessions, the worker and parent exchange roles. The worker interacts with the child and the parent observes. As with the parent–child interaction, the child–worker interaction is videotaped. The worker and parent review the tape in much the same way as was done with the parent–child interaction.

Observing the worker interact with the child gives the parent an opportunity to observe interactions conducted according to the program's principles. The parent has the opportunity to view the ways the child behaves when presented with solvable disequilibriating experiences.

During discussions the worker helps the parent devise home-living routines (such as bedtime or mealtime routines) that do not expose the child to unnecessary, prolonged disequilibration. The parent learns to help the child adapt to behavioral expectations by considering the child's level of theorizing when developing routines and by facilitating the child's development of those new constructions that led to successful performance of the expected behavior.

Counseling and Home Training Sessions

Occasionally parents who are referred to the training program at Saint Catherine's Center are not encouraged to participate in the activities described. Staff has determined that these people are not likely to profit from these services. Partly as a result of environmental factors such as economic hardship, and partly because these persons have developed constructions of social reality that seriously impede their relating to others, these parents are consistently in a state of high psychological discomfort. In an attempt to ready these parents for the training curriculum, clinical counseling services are offered. These services attempt to facilitate the resolution of personal psychological difficulties so that these people can concentrate specifically on an exploration of issues related to being an effective parent.

Home training services are offered to parents who are isolated from the community and are hesitant to engage in a formal study of parenting. In these cases, a trained worker visits the home on a regular basis to attempt to establish a relationship with the parent. Worker and parent try to explore the difficulties the parent is experiencing with the children.

Attempts are made to create trust in the parents so they will agree to participate in the instructional programs described earlier. When parents cannot be persuaded to join a formal group, the worker visits the home and utilizes the interactions occurring between parent and child during the visit as a basis for the parent's exploration of the issues central to the training program.

Measuring Parent Role Constructions

It may be that the most serious impediment to the development of constructivist approaches to parent education has been the problem of measurement. Since a constructivist hedges at taking isolated measures of events, his work will not fit the neat cause–effect sequence that psychology has taken as the paragon of scientific utterances. A contextualist would, for example, believe that a tally of a particular type of response, by a parent or by a child, would not successfully reflect the achievement of training goals. Behaviors have meaning only in the context in which they occur. A highly aggressive threat delivered in one context does not have the same meaning that it would have in another context. Given these reservations, the constructivist cannot produce the modish outcome studies that find ready publication outlet.

Assessment is further complicated in that meanings and contexts are the focus of constructivist thought. Standard measures of meaning often take the form of simple "attitude" scales. One who works with help-seeking parents knows that attitude measures will be compromised by matters of the social desirability of responses and the actual comprehension of measurement statements.

Considering these matters, an investigator who would take a contextualist approach to the parenting process would be drawn to the multivariate approaches that psychological statisticians have generously produced. When Sigel, McGillicuddy-DeLisi, and Johnson (1980) study parenting and familial variables they demonstrate a systems approach to causality; to formalize their approach they use a path analysis model. Similarly, we have been trying to apply multivariable approaches to assessing outcomes of our program.

Basically, Kelly's (1955) approach to role repertory analysis, as elaborated by Rosenberg (1977; Gara & Rosenberg, 1979), has provided the model for developing a Parent Role Repertory Analysis. The initial development of the Parent Role Repertory (ParRep) analysis was reported elsewhere (Mancuso & Handin, 1980b). In current practice the data collection process involves obtaining data to fill in a 16 by 14 matrix. The rows in the matrix are, essentially, statements about child rearing. The columns in the matrix are descriptions of parent roles. (See Appendix for 16 statements and 14 parent roles.) In the process of completing the matrix a parent is given one of the parent role descriptions printed on a card. He is then asked to think about child rearing as the person described in the role would. The role descriptions, where possible, are assigned a proper name. The parent is reminded repeatedly, through questions such as "How would Bob Wilson, who has tried to raise his children to do things the first time they are asked to do them, respond to this statement?" The parent is asked to indicate how hard it would be to get the person in the role description to believe a statement. The choices are: (1) Very hard, (2) May be possible to get him to believe this, (3) Very easy.

The 14 roles are presented to the participating parents, who are asked to assume the roles and to tell about the described parent's views on each of the 16 statements. In this way the participating parent makes 244 separate judgments.

Analysis and Rationale

Each matrix can be processed through multidimensional scaling, cluster analysis, and two-way permuted clustering designed by Rosenberg and his research group. The details of this methodology are reported by Rosenberg (1977). Additionally, the data can be analysed for the supersets and subsets of roles and statements that are implied in each matrix. The method used for this analysis is described in Gara and Rosenberg (1979).

The problems with this overall approach remain those that one must face when using multidimensional methods. How does one make inter- and intra-individual comparisons? In the first efforts (Mancuso & Handin, 1980b) to use the ParRep, we simply looked at analyses of the 16 matrices, 9 of which had been produced by parents who had participated in the first run-through of the program. Seven of the 16 matrices were produced by parents of hard-to-regulate children. These parents would have been suitable candidates for the program. By inspecting the output of the analyses, each of the authors ranked the 16 matrices in terms of theory-guided, subjective estimates of goodness. The authors agreed closely on their rank ordering of the matrices. Four of the 9 program-involved parents produced the four matrices that were judged to be most ideal. Three of the 9 program-involved parents produced the least ideal matrices. All seven of the preprogram parents produced matrices that were identified as being antithetical to an ideal that would fit the judges' subjective standards.

Creating the Ideal Parent

This approach to the data is far from satisfactory. Our group has been exploring other approaches. Using an updated set of parent role-types and parenting statements, we have developed the following comparison matrix: Each of the authors produced a data matrix, responding "as if he were the ideal parent—the perfect constructivist." The authors' two data matrices were then put through the analytic procedures.

Using the procedures described in Rosenberg (1977) allows one to extract a distance measure, d, to describe the degree of relationship between each row and all the other rows. Distance measures for columns are also obtained. Thus, for example: As part of the data analysis, one obtains a d-measure to describe the relationship that the respondent imputes, through his ways of judging how different parents respond to child-rearing statements, to exist between each row; that is, each child-rearing statement. Similarly, the analysis yields a d-measure to describe the relationship imputed to parent roles. From an analysis of our 16×14 data matrix one extracts a symmetrical matrix of 120 d-measures for rows and 91 d-measures for columns (relationships between parent roles).

After each author's "ideal parent" data matrix had been analyzed, the two separate rows' d-matrices (distances for child-rearing statements) were strung into a vector and product–moment correlation was performed to assess the relationship between the 120 pairs of d-measures. This process was repeated for the columns' (parent roles) d-measures. The correlation coefficient for the rows' d-measures was .679. The correlation coefficient of the columns' d-measures was .816. In that these coefficients are very unlikely to have been chance occurrences, we were led to believe that we had frequently agreed about how an ideal parent would think about the beliefs of the parent role types described, although we had obviously disagreed at several points.

We then reviewed the points of disagreement. We decided that our major disagreements had come from having imposed different interpretations on several of the roles and statements. We revised the troublesome items, convinced that if we had interpreted the stimulus material differently, there would be variations in parent responses that would be attributable to unclear language. Thereupon, each of us reconsidered our responses, and we completed new matrices. These were again analyzed, and the resulting d-matrices were again correlated. This process produced the following correlations: Correlation coefficient from rows' d-measures = .747; from columns' distance measures r = .878. We had come yet closer to production of the response pattern of the "Ideal Parent." Then we made a direct comparison of our separate matrices. For each point at which we disagreed, we settled on an agreeable response. The final matrix is now in our computer file, where it is called Ideal Parent.

Subset and Prototype Analysis

This matrix may be subjected to a variety of multidimensional analyses. It is particularly informative to inspect cluster analyses of an individual ParRep matrix. As an example, Figure 1 displays a two-way permutation of a cluster analysis of the data matrix produced by the low socioeconomic status mother of a child who has been judged to be quite competent by the personnel of the child's school. From the display one can easily develop a narration—like that composed by the authors to accompany Figure 1—to represent verbally the belief system that is assumed to have guided the production of the matrix. One may think of this narrative as the "macrostructure" which guides the parent's production of "stories" or "scripts" to describe the parent–child interactions in which the parent will engage (see Mandler & Johnson, 1977; Thorndyke, 1977, for a discussion of the idea of macrostructure in stories). Thereupon one may make a subjective estimate of the correspondence of the macrostructure underlying the matrix of Ideal Parent and the macrostructure underlying any other parent's matrix.

Another, less subjective comparison of parents' matrices has been derived from Gara and Rosenberg (1979). The logic of their work is derived from some of the current literature on categorization, prototypes, and subsets (see Rosch, 1978; Tversky, 1977), as these ideas apply to person perception. In Gara and Rosenberg's study a prototype is an event (a person) which (who) is judged to share many features with other events, and is in this way classed as similar to those events. Additionally, a prototypic event retains a small set of its own distinctive features. In a person-categorizing task, for example, "Mother" could be a prototype (or

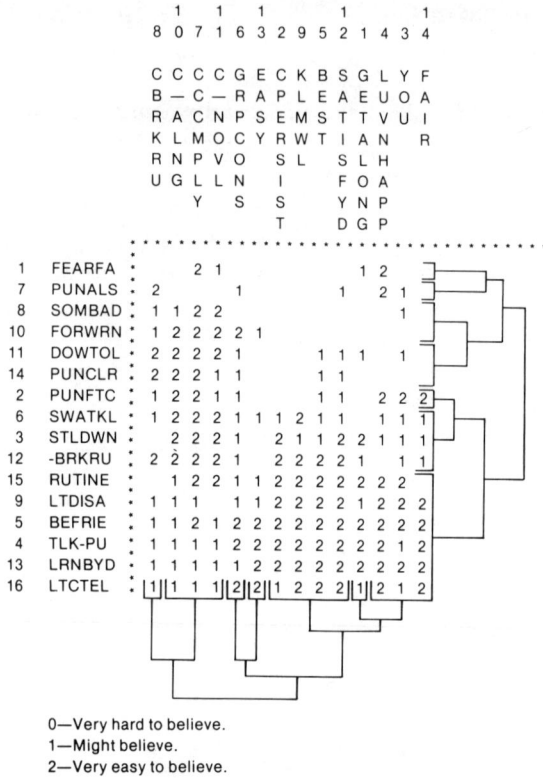

Figure 1. Plot of two-way permuted cluster analysis of ParRep matrix. (This matrix was completed by the mother of an elementary school child judged to be competent by the personnel of the child's school.) Narrative: "Good parents (right center of matrix) take into account their children's views (statements at bottom of matrix) more than do poor parents (left of matrix). Good parents clearly reject strong coercion. Good parents do see some sense in endorsing some 'tough' approaches (Statements 11 down to 12). Poor parents, on the other hand, are very tough, and pay less attention to child's perspective. I'm not quite a 'best' parent; I, like the parent who loves and is concerned about the happiness of the child, can get tough."

superset) for Mary, Helen, and Michael. The three named persons would be ascribed many shared features, which are also shared with Mother, who, in turn, is ascribed her own distinguishing features. Those relationships are quantified through use of an implicative phi statistic, as proposed by Francis (1961).

In analyzing the ParRep matrices one may use Gara and Rosenberg's methods to consider, for example, the following questions: Does a parent's view of parenting practices reflect his underlying belief that such practices may be put into meaningful categories? May these sets of statements then be characterized by a prototypical representative of a category? To apply the Gara and Rosenberg techniques, the questions would be transliterated as follows: Does a parent produce a matrix in which certain parenting statements emerge clearly as prototypes which are associated with other parenting statements that are distinct subsets of the prototypic statements? In more concrete terms, does this parent believe, for example, that letting a child explain his position implies (positively or negatively) that one should punish a child who has failed to do what he is told to do?

The way a respondent judges that an item is valued (positively or negatively) by varied parent types determines that item's inclusion in one or another category. For example, two items are similar and belong to the same category if a set of parent types is judged to accept both, whereas another set of parent types is judged to reject the two items in the contrast pair. A statement about child rearing emerges from the analysis as a prototype of a subset of statements if a series of conditions is met, as follows: (1) the statement is successively contrasted to other statements, in terms of which parent types are judged to believe (or reject) that statement; (2) a respondent judges that most members of a subset of parent types simultaneously believe both statements of the contrast pair, and; (3) The prototype item maintains this kind of relationship with several other items. Additionally, (4) the prototype item is very likely to have a reverse relationship to other items in the set of 16 parent statements. And finally, another feature of a prototypic statement deserves note, although this feature is not crucial in defining a prototype: (5) Prototypic items also show a minor positive superordination of some other set of items.

As an example of the process, consider Parenting Statement 2: The child who has done something really bad deserves a really hard punishment, and the child who has done something that is not so bad deserves an easier punishment (PUNFTC). In Ideal Parent's matrix this statement is a prototype item. It superordinates the following subset of items: 6.SWATKL; 7.PUNALS; 11.DOWTOL; and 14.PUNCLR (see Appendix for text of items). Ideal Parent believes that, as a rule, anyone who accepts the above statement on expiative punishment (Statement 2.PUNFTC) would also accept the other statements in the above subset of statements. Anyone who rejects this statement would reject the other statements.

The analysis also shows that in Ideal Parent's matrix there is a subset of items regularly related to the items which are a subset of this Statement 2 (which advocates an "eye-for-an-eye" approach to reprimand). The negatively superordinate items are those which advocate allowing a child to work out its own construction of encountered events. (See items 9, 10, 13, 15, and 16 in Appendix, Child-Rearing Statements.)

Ideal Parent's matrix contains several clear prototype items. The most clearly prototypical statements are those which subsume parent behavior statements that would be endorsed by the parent types that Ideal Parent would judge to be *bad*. On the other hand, items that would be endorsed by "good" parents stand in clear negative contrast to the items which are subsumed by the prototypical statements.

Comparing the Prototype Structures of Parents

These measures are ultimately, useful in assessing outcomes of our parent-training program. To obtain some assurance of the validity of our measures we have explored ways to answer the following question: Do successful parents think of child-rearing practices from the perspective of the knowledge network which is similar to that created for Ideal Parent?

To conduct further evaluation of our measures we have selected a sample of parents of children who have been judged by their school's personnel to function rather competently. A contrast sample has also been selected. This latter sample is composed of parents of children who, owing to their high propensity to engage in unwanted behaviors, have been referred for special day-care services. Some of these parents are candidates for our parent-training program. The school sample contains eight mothers. The school sample families occupy social positions commensurate with their residence in inner city neighborhoods.

Each of the mothers was assisted in completing the ParRep matrix. The prototype analysis of parenting statements was one of the procedures used to analyze each matrix. An inspection of the results of the 15 separate analyses shows that the mothers in the two samples are clearly distinguishable. Six of the seven mothers of the competent school children produced matrices which contain clear prototype and subset relationships. Only one of the eight mothers of day-care children produced something that could be taken as a reasonable prototype–subset pattern.

The mothers of the school children show that their beliefs about child-rearing statements are integrated into patterned relationships. This is not the case with the mothers of the day-care sample. In their belief system they fail to regard any one statement as a logical complement or as a logical contradiction of any other statement or set of statements. Thus, as they see it, any parent type could accept any one of the statements without contradiction of other beliefs or without showing that he or she would endorse another statement.

Interestingly, little consistency is seen across school sample mothers on inspecting the statements that are given prototype status. In one matrix we find that Statement 4 (Talking works better than punishing) emerges as a prototype; whereas in another matrix Statement 3 (A child should settle down when told to settle down) is a prototype. This finding points to the direction in which we will attempt further analyses. After several efforts to compare the matrices of these low socioeconomic status mothers to the matrix of Ideal Parent, we will not expect to find correspondence in the belief system content. Henceforth we will look for correspondence in patterns inherent in the belief system. In short, our efforts to develop a suitable assessment of our program has led us to the conclusion that, at minimum, *children who operate reasonably successfully in social situations have been in the care of parents who hold a reasonably integrated system of beliefs about child-rearing practices.*

The ParRep and Program Evaluation

As we proceed in our efforts to develop our constructivist parent-training program we must consider the possibility that parents of some kinds of children may produce matrices that reflect specific content relations, in addition to expected minimum patterns. Perhaps specific content differences distinguish the parents of different samples of children. We do believe that we have a valuable multivariate methodology, and that the logic of cluster analysis (see Sattath & Tversky, 1977) is totally compatible with our overall view of the psychological processes involved in parenting behavior. Our measurement problems, however, remind us of the complexity of applying contextualist approaches to the study of behavior.

First, the data collection process has been arduous. The parents who are referred for improvement of parenting skills do not usually show high levels of verbal skills. The language of an assessment device must be direct. The task must be simple. The investigator must work hard to build and to maintain the parent's involvement in the task. Second, partly owing to the difficulty of the data collection process, it is not easy to make rapid changes in the instrument. If one spots a snag, such as a poorly phrased role description, it is not easy to make a change, because one cannot readily return to gather data from participants from whom inappropriate data has already been collected. The progress of developing this technology, then, has been slow; even if we could convince other scholars of the merits of this approach we cannot offer hope that there will be a rapid, happy outcome. Aside from these basic problems, there remains an already apparent, third problem: What techniques can be used to show that meaningful changes in construing systems have developed through the training program? The kinds of statistical tests of differences which have been developed to assess the mechanistic concepts of change processes are not applicable to the multidimensional approaches. Eyeball tests of matrices will not meet journal editor approval.

Reasserting the Promise of Constructivism

Beyond the current impediments to conducting convincing investigations of constructivist approaches to parent training one can see the general promise of contextualism in the study of child development. Contextualist-constructivist approaches now dominate the research and theoretical literature of developmental psychology. Constructivist pedagogic practices have been widely advocated and instituted in educational settings. The widespread use of constructivist paradigms, as a single factor, should encourage behavior scientists to reconstrue the parenting process in constructivist terms.

The social realities that surround this advocacy cannot, however, be ignored. Mechanist ideologies dominate our psychological thought. Aristotle's contempt for the relativistic sophists is comfortably echoed in industrial societies. In our world it is useful to have a view of man which includes the use of external controls to teach acceptance of the "realities" which are "discovered" by scientists who are supported, as was Aristotle, by territorial and psychological imperialists. In these mechanistically guided societies those children who fail to respond to regulation are euphemistically called "emotionally disturbed" or "hyperactive." Thus they become targets for control prescriptions—drugs and "reinforcements." Would we do less well in creating cooperative, growing members of the society if we accepted that each of us builds his or her own reality? From this acceptance it would follow that our parenting practices should be aimed at promoting the development of people who are aware of their own construing processes and of the relationship of those processes to the construing processes of others.

Such, we believe, are the ideological conditions which surround our psychological work. As scientists our major obligation remains our commitment to developing strong, valid conceptions to explain behavior. As a formal scientific enterprise, we have undertaken to frame parent practices in constructivist terms. Nowhere have we become more aware of the reactivity and reflexivity of our scientific work. When we take the constructivist approach we clearly assert that the very acceptance of this belief system will alter behavior by altering one's beliefs about oneself; that is, by altering one's self-cognizing system. If one—parent or child—construes his or her self as an active construer of both "out there" events and those events (sometimes called emotions) enveloped by his skin, one behaves differently from the person who views his or her self as the heir to his or her reinforcement history or as the victim of his or her passions.

In this presentation we have tried to provide the support for the assumptive structure that underlies a constructivist approach to child-rearing practices. We have also tried to show that the approach may be used to design and evaluate parent-training programs. We must, unfortunately, hedge our presentation, by frequent references to our exploratory practice and evaluation methods. We are optimistic, however, about the outcomes that will result from the growing, serious consideration that is being given to constructivist approaches to child care.

As we assert the scientific promise of constructivist approaches to parent training, we ask that others join us in an effort to become fully conversant with the reactive and reflexive aspects of our discipline. More specifically, we are asking for valid conceptualizations—for example, of how one mother prompts her child to construe rolled oats as pleasing, while another, convinced of her child's basic nature, serves the Sugar Frosted Corn Crunchies that her child's taste demands.

ACKNOWLEDGMENTS

We would like to acknowledge gratefully the collaboration of the Parent Training Program staff at Saint Catherine's Child Care Center. The staff—Dorothy McDonald, Gail McCabe, Jane Trumpy, Navralean Chavers, Maria Riccio, and Sharon Handin—working with the second author, have been assiduous assistants since the initiation of the Program.

Appendix

Parent Roles and Child-Rearing Statements Used in the Parent Role Repertory Matrix

Parent Roles

1. Frank Gable gets along beautifully with his children. Frank and his children can work out anything that might trouble them. What would Frank say about this? (GETALONG)
2. Picture Sally Smith. Sally has raised a child who really sticks to what needs to be done. If Sally's child starts to put together a puzzle, or to learn something . . . she sticks right to it. (CPERSIST)
3. How hard would it be for you to believe this statement? (YOU)
4. Helen Bruno really loves her child. She wants her child to be a happy child. (LUVNHAPP)
5. Mary Jones is the *best* mother there could be. (BEST)

6. Three or four couples are at a little gathering, they are talking about their young children, talking about how to raise the children. How hard would it be for these couples to believe this statement? (GRPCONS)
7. Bob Wilson has really tried to raise his children so that they do things the first time they are asked to do them. (CCOMPLY)
8. Jim Klinger has a fifth grade child that can't seem to do the right thing. Jim's child fights the rules more than anybody in fifth grade. When Jim was raising his child, how hard would it have been for him to believe this statement? (CBRAKRU)
9. Ruth Kramer is a mother who knows the best thing to do when children get upset. (KLMWLL)
10. Faye Dunn has raised a child who doesn't get along with other people outside of the family. Faye's child just has trouble getting along with other people. (C-ALNG)
11. Barbara Moore has a child who can't stand being in new situations. Barbara just hasn't helped her child to put up with anything new—new food, new places, new people. Barbara's child really fusses whenever the family tries something different or new. (C-NOVL)
12. Sue Doyle really feels satisfied with herself as a parent. Sue feels that she does a good job. She's very happy being a mother. (SATISFYD)
13. Joe Hooker is the kind of parent who doesn't always try hard to get his children to do what they are told to do. He's kind of easy on them. (EASY)
14. John Powers is a man who is known to be very fair with his children. John's friends, and all the other kids always say, "John Powers is fair in whatever he asks his children to do." (FAIR)

Child-Rearing Statements

1. A child who learns to do what his father says to do will grow up to be a person who won't get into trouble. (FEARFA)
2. The child who has done something really bad deserves a really hard punishment, and the child who has done something that is not so bad deserves an easier punishment. (PUNFTC)
3. A child should settle down whenever he's told to settle down. (SETLDWN)
4. When a child has done something that a parent doesn't like, talking to the child works better than punishing the child. (TALK-PU)

5. Even though parents must teach their child to follow rules, the child can be a friend to his parents. (BFRIEN)
6. When a child is having temper tantrums, it helps to give it a good swat on the rear. (SWATKL)
7. A ten year old and a four year old are no different when it comes to punishment. If the four year old breaks something he gets the same punishment as the ten year old who breaks something. (PUNALS)
8. There are a lot of children who end up causing trouble, even though the parents are really good parents. (SOMBAD)
9. It doesn't hurt to let a child disagree when a parent tries to explain something the child did wrong. (LTDISA)
10. Always try to tell a kid what is going to happen before it happens. (FORWRN)
11. Punish a child whenever he does not do what he is told to do. (DOWATOL)
12. Once a parent makes a rule, a child should never be allowed to break the rule . . . no matter what. (-BRKRU)
13. If you are trying to teach a child something, like how to put on his shoes, let him work it out his own way. (LRNBYD)
14. A parent makes it clear to his children that they will be punished whenever they do something stupid. (PUNCLR)
15. When it's time to put a child to bed do things in the same order each night—like, a bath first, then a snack, then a story—the same order each night. (RUTINE)
16. Let a child tell what he thinks when his parents ask him to do something. (LTCTEL)

References

Adams-Webber, J. An analysis of the discriminant validity of several repertory grid indices. *British Journal of Psychology*, 1970, *61*, 83–90.

Aldrich, C. C., & Mancuso, J. C. Judgments of a child involved in accidental damage and responding differentially to adult reprimand. *Perceptual and Motor Skills*, 1976, *43*, 1071–1082.

Atkeson, B., & Forehand, R. Parent behavioral training programs for problem children: An examination of studies using multiple outcome measures. *Journal of Abnormal Child Psychology*, 1978, *6*, 449–460.

Azrin, N. H., & Holz, W. C. Punishment. In W. K. Honnig (Ed.), *Operant behavior*. New York: Appleton-Century-Crofts, 1966.

Bandura, A., & Walters, R. H. *Social learning and personality development*. New York: Holt, Rinehart & Winston, 1963.

Berkowitz, B. P., & Graziano, A. M. Training parents as behavior therapists: A review. *Behavior Research and Therapy*, 1972, *10*, 197–317.

Berlyne, D. A. Curiosity and learning. *Motivation and Emotion*, 1978, *2*, 97–175.

Bornstein, M. H., & Kessen, W. (Eds.). *Psychological development from infancy*. Hillsdale, N.J.: Lawrence Erlbaum, 1979.

Bringuier, J. *Conversations with Jean Piaget*. Chicago: University of Chicago Press, 1980.

Creer, T. L., Renne, E. M., & Christian, W. P. Unpredictable problems in applying social learning principles in a child care facility. *Child Care Quarterly*, 1978, *7*, 142–255.

Damon, W. (Ed.), *Social cognition*. San Francisco: Jossey-Bass, 1978.

Deci, E. E. *Intrinsic motivation*. New York: Plenum Press, 1975.

Eimer, B. N., Mancuso, J. C., & Lehrer, R. *Children's conceptions of parental reprimand: A stage developmental analysis*. Unpublished manuscript, 1980.

Fine, M. J. *Parents vs. children*. Englewood Cliffs, N.J.: Prentice-Hall, 1979.

Forehand, R., & Atkeson, B. M. Generality of treatment effects with parents as therapist. *Behavior Therapy*, 1977, *8*, 575–593.

Forehand, R., Sturgis, E. T., McMahon, R. J., Aguar, D., Green, K., Wells, K. C., & Breiner, J. Parental behavioral training to modify child noncompliance. *Behavior Modification*, 1979, *3*, 3–25.

Francis, R. G. *The rhetoric of science: A methodological discussion of the two by two table*. Minneapolis: University of Minnesota Press, 1961.

Gara, M. A., & Rosenberg, S. The identification of persons as supersets and subsets in free-response personality descriptions. *Journal of Personality and Social Psychology*, 1979, *37*, 2161–2170.

Glueck, S., & Glueck, E. T. *Unravelling juvenile delinquency*. Cambridge: Harvard University Press, 1950.

Goocher, B. E. Behavior applications of an educateur model in child care. *Child Care Quarterly*, 1975, *4*, 84–92.

Greenley, J. R. Alternative views of the psychiatrist's role. In T. Scheff (Ed.), *Labelling madness*. Englewood Cliffs, N. J.: Prentice Hall, 1975.

Grossberg, S. How does a brain build a cognitive code? *Psychological Review*, 1980, *87*, 1–51.

Handin, K. H. & Mancuso, J. C. Perceptions of the function of reprimand. *Journal of Social Psychology*. 1980, *110*, 43–52.

Hoffman, M. L. Empathy, role-taking, guilt, and development of altruistic motive. In T. Lickona (Ed.), *Moral development and behavior*. New York: Holt, Rinehart, Winston, 1976.

Johnston, J. M. Punishment and human behavior. *American Psychologist*, 1972, *27*, 1033–1054.

Kahneman, D. *Attention and effort*. Englewood Cliffs, N.J.: Prentice-Hall, 1973.

Kelly, G. A. *The psychology of personal constructs*. New York: W. W. Norton, 1955.

Kohlberg, L. Stage and sequence: The cognitive developmental approach to socialization. In D. A. Goslin (Ed.), *Handbook of socialization theory and research*. New York: Rand McNally, 1969.

Lindsley, D. B. Psychophysiology and motivation. In M. R. Jones (Ed.), *Nebraska Symposium on Motivation: 1957*. Lincoln: University of Nebraska Press, 1957.

Mancuso, J. C. Current motivational models in the elaboration of personal construct theory. In A. W. Landfield (Ed.), *Nebraska symposium on motivation: Personal construct psychology*. Lincoln: University of Nebraska Press, 1977.

Mancuso, J. C. Reprimand: The construing of the rule violator's construct system. In P. Stringer & D. Bannister (Eds.), *Constructs of sociality and individuality*. New York: Academic Press, 1979.

Mancuso, J. C., & Adams-Webber, J. R. Anticipation as a constructive process: The fundamental postulate. In J. C. Mancuso & J. R. Adams-Webber (Eds.), *The construing person*. New York: Praeger, 1982.

Mancuso, J. C., & Allen, D. A. Children's perceptions of a transgressor's socialization as a function of type of reprimand. *Human Development*, 1976, *19*, 277-290.

Mancuso, J. C., & Ceely, S. G. The self as memory processing. *Cognitive Therapy and Research*, 1980, *4*, 1-25.

Mancuso, J. C., & Handin, K. H. Comparing high and low-rated child care worker's attributions of reprimand effectiveness. *Child Care Quarterly*, 1980, *9*(4), 275-288. (a)

Mancuso, J. C., & Handin, K. H. Training parents to construe the child's construing. In A. W. Landfield & L. M. Leitner (Eds.), *Personal construct psychology*. New York: Wiley, 1980. (b)

Mancuso, J. C., Morrison, J. K., & Aldrich, C. C. Developmental changes in social-moral perception: Some factors affecting children's evaluations and predictions of the behavior of a "transgressor." *Journal of Genetic Psychology*, 1978, *132*, 121-136.

Mancuso, J. C., & Sarbin, T. R. The self-narrative in the enactment of roles. In T. R. Sarbin & K. Scheibe (Eds.), *Studies in social identity*. New York: Praeger, 1983.

Mandler, J. M., & Johnson, N. S. Remembrance of things parsed: Story structure and recall. *Cognitive Psychology*, 1977, *9*, 111-151.

Norton, G. R. *Parenting*. Englewood Cliffs, N.J.: Prentice-Hall, 1977.

Ornstein, P. A. (Ed.). *Memory development in children*. Hillsdale, N.J.: Lawrence Erlbaum, 1978.

Parke, R. D. Rules, roles, and resistance to deviation. In A. W. Pick (Ed.), *Minnesota Symposia on Child Psychology* (Vol. 8). Minneapolis: University of Minnesota Press, 1974.

Patterson, G. R. Interventions for boys with conduct problems: Multiple settings, treatments, and criteria. *Journal of Consulting and Clinical Psychology*, 1974, *42*, 471-481.

Pepper, S. C. *World hypothesis*. Berkeley, Calif.: University of California Press, 1942.

Piaget, J. *The child and reality*. New York: Viking Press, 1974.

Powers, W. T. *Behavior: The control of perception*. Chicago: Aldine, 1973.

Rosch, E. Principles of categorization. In E. Rosch & B. B. Lloyd (Eds.), *Cognition and categorization*. Hillsdale, N.J.: Lawrence Erlbaum, 1978.

Rosenberg, S. New approaches to the analysis of personal constructs in person perception. In A. W. Landfield (Ed.) *Nebraska symposium on motivation: Personal construct psychology*. Lincoln, Neb.: University of Nebraska Press, 1977.

Rychlak, J. E. *Personality and psychotherapy*. Boston: Houghton-Mifflin, 1981.

Sarbin, T. R. Contextualism: A World View for Modern Psychology. In A. W. Landfield (Ed.), *Nebraska Symposium on Motivation*. (Vol. 24). Lincoln, Nebraska: University of Nebraska Press, 1977.

Sarbin, T. R., & Mancuso, J. C. *Schizophrenia: Medical diagnosis or moral judgment*. Elmsford, N. Y.: Pergamon, 1980.

Sattath, S., & Tversky, A. Additive similarity trees, *Psychometrika*, 1977, *42*, 319-345.

Sears, R. R., Maccoby, E. E., & Levin, H. *Patterns of child rearing*. Evanston, Illinois: Row, Peterson, 1957.

Selman, R. L. *The growth of interpersonal understanding*. New York: Academic Press, 1980.

Sigel, I. E. The distancing hypothesis: A causal hypothesis for the aquisition of representational thought. In M. R. Jones (Ed.), *Miami symposium on the prediction of behavior: The effect of early experience*. Coral Gables, Florida: University of Miami Press, 1970.

Sigel, I. E. Constructivism and teacher education. *The Elementary School Journal*, 1978, *78*, 333-338.

Sigel, I. E., & McGillicuddy-DeLisi, A. V. *Parental distancing, beliefs and children's representational competence within the family context*. Princeton, New Jersey: Educational Testing Service, 1980.

Sigel, I. E., McGillicuddy-DeLisi, A. V., & Johnson, J. E. *The effects of spacing and birth order*

on problem-solving competence of pre-school children, Report prepared for Office of
Population Research, National Institute of Health, 1980.

Simpson, R. L. Behavior modification and child management. In M. J. Fine (Ed.), *Handbook
on parent education*. New York: Academic Press, 1980.

Sperlinger, D. Aspects of stability in the repertory grid. *British Journal of Medical
Psychology*, 1976, *49*, 341–347.

Spinetta, J. J., & Rigler, D. The abusing parent. *Psychological Bulletin*, 1972, 77, 296–304.

Thorndyke, P. W. Cognitive structures in comprehension and memory of narrative discourse.
Cognitive Psychology, 1977, *9*, 77–110.

Tversky, A. Features of similarity. *Psychological Review*, 1977, *84*, 327–352.

Uzgiris, I. C., & Weizman, F. (Eds.), *The structuring of experience*. New York: Plenum Press,
1977.

Wasserman, S. The abused parent of the abused child. *Children*, 1967, *14*, 175–179.

White, B. L., Kaban, B., Shapiro, B., & Attanucci, J. Competence and experience. In I. C.
Uzgiris & F. Weizman (Eds.), *The structuring of experience*. New York: Plenum Press,
1977.

Whiting, J. M., & Child, I. L. *Child training and personity: A cross cultural study*. New
Haven: Yale University Press, 1953.

CHAPTER 7

Individual Differences in Participation in a Parent-Child Support Program

DOUGLAS R. POWELL

Most descriptions and evaluations of programs designed to enhance parent-child functioning have given scant attention—or none—to the determinants and nature of individual differences in participants' program experiences. The tendency has been to conceptualize the treament as a unidimensional construct rather than a set of variables. Typically the treatment is viewed as either present or absent. Yet informal knowledge suggests there is considerable variation in program experience at the individual level. Cursory examination of a human service program indicates that workers do not carry out identical tasks in a uniform manner and that participants do not "receive" a program with similar intensity. The essence of a program may be characterized best by exploring these individual differences. Information about the range of experiences within intervention programs might help evaluators explain program effects with greater power and precision and, moreover, might assist program designers in improving the effectiveness of services.

This chapter examines the ways in which parents' life conditions relate to variations in participation in a parent-child support program. The major premise is that parents enter a program with diverse socio-ecological circumstances that may contribute to the quantity and quality of their program experience. An exploratory analysis of differences in parents' participation in a family support project is presented in an effort

DOUGLAS R. POWELL ● Wayne State University, College of Liberal Arts, Department of Family and Consumer Resources, Detroit, Michigan 48202. The parent-child program discussed in this paper is supported by a grant from the W. K. Kellogg Foundation.

to suggest a conceptual framework for examining the nature and correlates of individual variations in program experience. Attention is given to the relation of parents' social networks, participation in social or community events, and everyday stress to different forms and processes of involvement in a parent–child program. Implications for program development and further research are discussed.

Degradation of the Treatment Variable

Concern about the degradation of the treatment variable in evaluation studies is not new (e.g., Sigel, 1975). The problems in identifying and measuring treatment in field studies have been ignored to the extent that in the behavioral and social sciences and in education the treatment labels may be meaningless or misleading, or accurate but imprecise (Boruch & Gomez, 1977). Extensive disregard for the complexity of program experiences in early childhood education, for example, has led Zimiles (1977) to suggest that the primary method of evaluating early childhood programs should be to describe in considerable detail what programs consist of and how they operate, and then hypothesize theoretically how a given program will affect children.

The tendency of evaluation research to reduce intensive human service programs to a set of causal relationships perpetuates the concept of the treatment as a static, categorical variable. Attempts to measure the treatment variable in depth have largely reflected an interest in the fidelity of the program plan and hence a desire to determine whether an intervention effort has been implemented according to program principles and design. Here the interest is in the integrity of the program intention and not the nature and effects of variations in program experience. Rarely have attempts been made to link individual differences in programs with outcome variables.

A thoughtful effort to examine parent program dimensions in relation to outcome variables has been made by Goodson and Hess (1976). In an analysis of the effects of 28 programs designed to train parents to prepare their children for school achievement, they reached the conclusion that five major features of the intervention programs were modestly related to magnitude of program effectiveness. Even though this analysis was based on across-program rather than within-program differences, the findings are informative relative to our discussion of the treatment variable in parent programs. Program effectiveness was found to be positively related to the amount of emphasis placed on parent training (greater parent emphasis yielded greater program effects), one-to-one teacher–parent interaction (compared to group instruction), and the degree of structure in parent–training activities (more structure, greater effects). The study found no relationship between the content of the curriculum used by parents and the magnitude of impact on children. It also found no relationship between the degree of specificity in instructing parents and program effectiveness. Although the analysis found the programs to be successful in terms of achievement score gains, the study concluded tentatively that the five program features did not account for the very large differences among effects of different programs.

What emerges from the Goodson and Hess analysis of parent education programs is that it is easier to produce effects in intervention programs than it is to identify the specific factors which contribute to success. This interpretation is similar to the findings of other analyses of the effects of preschool and infant intervention programs (Levitt & Cohen, 1975; Miller & Dyer, 1975; Weikart, Epstein, Schweinhart, & Bond, 1978). For instance, the curriculum comparison studies conducted by Weikart and his colleagues (1978) suggest that the particular activities employed in any curriculum are not as important as the way a curriculum is implemented by its staff. Weikart *et al.* conclude that the principal issue in early childhood education is not which curriculum to use but how to manage any curriculum to achieve positive results. Perhaps this conclusion may be applied to parent programs as well.

Few attempts have been made to examine variations in individual program experiences in relation to participant characteristics. There is some evidence to indicate that the educational status of parents is related to their level of attendance at parent group discussion meetings (Gabel, Graybill, DeMott, Wood, & Johnston, 1977). Again, informal knowledge would suggest that socio-ecological variables may be related to the quality and type of program experience. No doubt individuals approach a program with differing stresses, resources, and interests. Little is known about the influence of these and other life conditions on parents' experiences in a formal program (Chilman, 1973).

The concept of the treatment as a unidimensional variable is particularly problematic for programs which make relatively few assumptions about the attributes and needs of parents, and do not engage in predetermined prescriptive or restorative approaches to working with parents. Such programs typically do not adhere to the traditional deficit-model paradigm and are more open to the influences of parents on program activities than conventional parent intervention programs. In fact, in programs such as these the notion of "treatment" is a foreign concept. A program is what happens when parents and staff come together, not what staff "do" to or for parents. Hence, in some programs the need to approach participant experiences along multidimensional lines is in part a function of broadly defined goals and methods.

Concept of Life Conditions and Program Experiences

This chapter addresses the general question of how different life conditions are related to variations in participants' experiences in a parent–child support program. Discussed below is the framework utilized to identify and define specific socio-ecological variables and major dimensions of parents' participation in a parent–child program.

Life Conditions

Three major sets of variables pertaining to life conditions were examined: (a) selected attributes of participants' personal social networks; (b) economic hardship and everyday life stress; and (c) participant involvement in community or social activities.

The interest in personal social networks stems from the growing body of research data which suggest that an individual's relationships with kin, friends, neighbors, and acquaintances play a significant role in mediating family stress (see Unger & Powell, 1980) and in influencing parent–child relations (see Powell, 1979). Studies indicate that personal social networks serve as informal family support systems, providing help during crises, aiding in the care of children, and dispensing information and advice. It appears that persons living in crisis conditions rely heavily on primary social network systems for support (e.g., Stack, 1974). Cochran and Brassard (1979) have suggested that members of a parent's social network influence parents and, in turn, children by providing emotional and material assistance, encouraging or discouraging particular patterns of parent–child interaction, and serving as role models. There also is evidence to suggest that social networks influence adjustment to the parenthood role (e.g., Hobbs & Cole, 1976).

More germane to the present analysis is the role of social networks in facilitating access to and use of formal human services. Research has found the nature of parents' interpersonal ties to be related to strategies for locating out-of-home child care (Powell & Eisenstadt, 1982) and relations with child care centers (Powell, 1978). Also, characteristics of personal social networks have been found to be related to the utilization of prenatal medical services (McKinlay, 1973) and Family Service Agency services (Kammeyer & Bolton, 1968).

The potentially significant influence of personal social networks on involvement in a parent education program is suggested in an important study by Kessen and Fein (1975). In examining the effects of three different home-based infant education curricula, the researchers found that social networks may play an important role in determining maternal responsiveness to change agents outside the family milieu. The study found unexpectedly that parents belonging to extensive family networks were more open to change and were more responsive to curriculum interventions than parents with restricted family networks. Kessen and Fein tentatively interpreted the findings as indications that extensive family networks may provide parents with a secure, stable framework which makes it easier to welcome and utilize new information from persons who are outside the family constellation.

The present analysis examined the following specific attributes of parents' social networks: (a) level of involvement in informal helping relationships surrounding such instrumental problems as financial needs, medical concerns, clothing and transportation needs; (b) use of peers in dealing with instrumental problems; (c) perceived level of support from social network members for participation in the parent-child program; and (d) the number of relatives and friends contacted frequently.

The relationship of economic hardship and everyday life stress to program participation seems obvious at a general level but more opaque at a specific level. It appeared plausible to us that economic difficulties and everyday stress might correlate with differences in parents' experiences in the program, but we were unable to locate relevant studies which would provide direction as to possible specific relationships.

With regard to parents' involvement in other organizations, it was thought that the level of participation in social and community events might be related to differences in involvement in the parent-child program.

Program Experiences

We conceptualized the parent-child program as a set of distinct behavior settings which collectively provide participants with opportunities for different roles and types of involvement with others. The quality and quantity of participation within and across these settings served as indicators of program experience.

Program experience may be analyzed according to the *form* and *process* of participation. Form refers to the major behavior settings offered by the program. Three settings within the parent-child program are considered in the present work: regular group sessions, an open evening session, and special events (i.e., trips, family picnics). Note that there is a loose adherence to Barker's concept of the behavior setting. The three settings are major ones; embedded within each is a set of subsettings. For instance, the "regular group session" setting consists of progressive movement through five different settings, beginning and ending with a gathering around a kitchen table. The "special events" setting does not have a constant location, either. The rituals associated with this form are similar across time, however. The study reported herein excludes the informal forms of involvement, or what Joffe (1977) calls the program "underlife." An example from the present program would be a parent-initiated weekend trip by some program staff and parents to a staff member's cottage.

Our concept of program process was influenced by Barker's (1968) notion of the interconnected "circuitry" or relationships within a setting. Process refers to the quality of involvement within and across the major forms of participation. The concept places considerable emphasis on participants' relations with program staff and other participants. The rationale for this focus is that researchers are increasingly pointing to staff–client relations as the core activity in human service programs (Hasenfeld & English, 1974). In the present analysis we broadened this notion to include parent–parent relations as well as parent–staff relations. Specifically, the indicators of program process include participants' (a) use of program staff as information and referral helpers, (b) friendships with other program participants, and (c) perceived level of self-disclosure with fellow participants.

The variables considered in the analysis are listed in Table 1.

Table 1. List of Major Variables

| | Program participation | |
Life-conditions	Forms	Processes
Attributes of participant's social network Involvement in helping relationships Use of peers in everyday coping Number of relatives and friends contacted frequently Perceived support for program participation Everyday stress Hardship Participant involvement in community organizations and social events	Attendance at regular group sessions Attendance at evening session Attendance at special events	Use of staff services Friendships with program participants Self-disclosure among group members

Background of the Study

The aim of the investigation was to examine associations between parents' life circumstances and program participation. Correlational analyses were made of each indicator of life conditions (social networks, involvement in community organizations, stress) in relation to each indicator of program participation (forms and processes). Relations among indices of program participation also were investigated. The sample for this work was small; it consisted of 21 parents who had been involved in the family project for at least 12 months.

It is important to emphasize that the analyses reported here are exploratory in nature and the interpretations are tentative. The data are limited for testing specific hypotheses, but they do provide insight into the dynamic relationship between life circumstances and program participation. The data also serve as a source of ideas for further empirical investigation and for parent program development efforts.

The remainder of this section describes the parent-child program which was used for the analyses, and the characteristics of the parent sample. It also discusses instrumentation.

Program Description

The study reported in this paper utilized evaluation data from an experimental parent-child support program designed to examine the processes and effects of a neighborhood program that seeks to enhance the lives of parents and their very young children. The project, the Child and Family Neighborhood Program, is located in a compact, low-income, working-class neighborhood in a Detroit suburb.[1] The project gives considerable emphasis to the conditions of parenthood (Bronfenbrenner, 1978); parents and staff are actively engaged in seeking ways to better cope with forces external to the parent-child system that influence parents' ability to care for young children. The program also gives attention to parents' contribution to child development by providing parents with information about the care and development of children. Parents begin the program when their child is between 0 and 6 months of age and are encouraged to remain through the child's third year.

Operationally the program is intensive. Parents meet in small groups

---

[1] The project was initiated by The Merrill-Palmer Institute. In 1981 project sponsorship was assumed by the YWCA of Western Wayne County, Michigan.

twice weekly for two hours at a renovated HUD house which serves as the program's headquarters. A community-based paraprofessional staff member facilitates the sessions. The focus of specific discussions or activities is determined largely by parent interests, although staff members play a major role in contributing information and ideas. A content analysis of group discussions indicates that about 39% of formal group time is devoted to conditions of parenthood topics, 33% to child development concerns, and 28% to group functioning. Philosophically the program adheres to a supportive rather than restorative approach to working with families. The project does not have a packaged treatment plan built on assumptions about the needs and characteristics of parents. The parent groups follow a problem-solving model for their work. The flavor of most group sessions is this: "What are the barriers to being the parent I wish to be, and how can this program help me remove these barriers?" Also, the program does not have eligibility criteria which distinguish parents by conventional special needs. There are two criteria: Parents must live in the neighborhood and, at the time of entry, have a child 6 months of age or less.

In addition to the twice-weekly group sessions, there are two other forms of possible participation. One evening per week the house is open to anyone who wishes to attend. The focus of these evening sessions varies greatly in structure and content. Generally it is a time when one or more parents share their skills with other parents. One recent evening, for example, a parent taught macrame. The evening session is distinct from the regular sessions in that there is no effort to form a group; typically, parents who attend the evening session collectively cut across all groups. It also is perceived by staff and parents as an optional activity, not the core of the program. A third form of participation is special events such as family picnics, trips to the zoo, and guest speakers (e.g., City Hall officials). There were 18 such events in the 12-month period used in the analyses discussed in this paper.

From a program perspective, parents have equal access to these three forms of participation. Transportation is always provided and events which might cost participants money are avoided. Also, with the exception of the evening session, child care is provided.

In addition to the paraprofessional staff who facilitate group sessions, there are three other staff members who potentially may have considerable contact with parents concerning specific problems. These include a part-time public health nurse, a part-time community outreach worker, and a full-time site coordinator. One of the functions of these staff members is to provide specialized information and referral when, and only when, parents request assistance. The staff person most often utilized in this regard is the nurse. Her role, however, is to facilitate parents' linkages with existing services and not to provide services (other than educational) directly. Social service issues such as food stamps tend to be handled by the outreach worker. This avenue of participation is considered a process rather than a form of participation because it is not (like forms) a regularly scheduled event which all parents are invited to attend.

Regarding parents' relations with other parents, the opportunities for contact are obvious from the above descriptions of the program operation. What must be made explicit is that program staff intentionally and consistently encourage parents to make use of one another in carrying out child-rearing responsibilities and in dealing with everyday needs.

Sample Characteristics

The sample of 21 cases—almost one-third of the total number of program participants—is fairly homogeneous in terms of many demographic variables. It is entirely white and female (even though there is a handful of male participants, only females were included in the present analysis). About three-fourths of the parents (16 of 21) have 2 or more children. There is variation within the sample regarding income. Eight of the 21 cases have yearly family incomes of under $7,500; 8 reported incomes between $10,000 and $15,000; and 5 indicated yearly incomes over $15,000. Spouse employment tends to be in unskilled or semiskilled labor dependent in a major way on the automobile industry and subject to significant instability. Only about one-fourth of the women (5) were employed at the time of data collection, generally part-time in service jobs (i.e., fast-food restaurants, nursing homes). More than one-half of the sample (13) has finished high school but none has done college work. The vast majority of the families rent their housing units (16), typically without the security of a lease (13).

The pool of program participants, from which this sample was selected, was recruited through various means, including neighborhood canvassing, referrals from hospitals and social service agencies, and local publicity. The 21 cases used in the present analysis represent parents who had been in the program for at least 12 months and for whom we had complete data at the time the exploratory analyses were carried out. Subsequent work will be done with a considerably larger sample, including those parents who terminated their involvement with the program prior to 12 months of participation.

Data Collection

Sources of data include in-depth structured interviews, observations of parent group meetings, and staff records. Most of the life condition variables included in this study were measured at point of program entry. All program experience indicators represent the twelfth month of involvement or a sum of the relevant measure across a 12-month period. Data were collected by three trained M.A.-level research assistants. A brief description of each measures follows.[2]

All life condition variables were measured through use of interview data. In regard to attributes of parents' social networks, two indices of involvement in helping relationships were used. In one measure (instrumental reciprocity index) the level of involvement in informal helping relationships was determined by computing a weighted score based on (a) the number of incidents of instrumental help provided by relatives and friends with whom the parent has frequent contact, and (b) the level of reciprocity in these relationships surrounding instrumental needs. A more simple variant of this measure was also used; it was based on the number of different helping relationships used by the parent in dealing with everyday problems (number of helping relationships).

The use of peers in everyday coping situations was measured by computing the percentage of peers among all persons (unrelated peers, relatives, agencies) who provided instrumental help to the parent. The score pertaining to the number of relatives and friends contacted frequently was derived by summing the number of friends, parents, grandparents, and siblings with whom the parent maintained once a week or more frequent contact.

Parents' perceptions of the level of social network support for participation in the parent–child program were measured on a four-point scale in which parents rated spouses, their mothers, and significant others on their (parents') perceived degree of support for program involvement.

Everyday stress was measured through adapted use of the Ilfeld (1976) Current Social Stressor Scales. Three subscales were used: marital, homemaker, and financial stress. Two measures of economic hardship were utilized. The basic hardship measure was a sum of scores on six items pertaining to home ownership, receipt of government assistance, difficulty in making monthly payments, and adequacy of income for basic expenses, leisure, and household furniture. The discretionary hardship measure

---

[2] A detailed description of each measure and scoring procedure may be obtained by writing to the author.

dealt with the parents' perceived level of hardship and was more of a reflection of aspiration than the basic hardship measure. The measure consisted of a sum of scores on five items having to do with perceptions of whether there were adequate funds for housing, clothing, furniture, medical care, and an automobile. Involvement in social events and community organizations was a simple count of the number of events or organizations in which the parent was a participant.

Relationships among all life condition variables are reported in Table 2.

In regard to program experience measures, attendance at regular group sessions, evening sessions, and special events was expressed as a percentage of sessions attended within each form. Data were obtained from staff records. Perceptions of disclosure of information about self to fellow group members were measured with a four-point disclosure rating scale, the scores of which were weighted and summed. Determination of the number of friendships with other participants was made by scoring the self-disclosure data and other interview data regarding friendship networks. Both members of a friendship dyad needed to indicate a similar level of involvement in the dyad in order for the relationship to be classified as a friendship.

Staff services provided to parents were measured in two ways. First, detailed staff telephone logs were coded to indicate the level and nature of assistance. Second, staff logs regarding home visits and consultations (excluding telephone calls) were coded to reflect the level and frequency of aid provided and the number of different staff members utilized.

Major Findings and Discussion

Major Findings

The first set of analyses examined relations between life condition variables and indicators of program experience. Pearson product-moment correlations for the three forms of program participation are reported in Figure 1 and for the processes of participation in Figure 2.

Attributes of social networks and economic hardship are major correlates of attendance at regular group sessions and at special events. Involvement in helping and reciprocal relationships with persons not involved in the program is negatively related to the frequency of attendance at group sessions and special events; that is, the lower the involvement in reciprocal ties among friends and relatives, the higher the level of

Table 2. Correlation Matrix of Life Condition Variables

	1.	2.	3.	4.	5.	6.	7.	8.	9.
1. Instrumental reciprocity index	—								
2. Number of helping relationships	.14	—							
3. Use of peers, everyday coping	-.31	-.13	—						
4. Number of relatives, friends contacted frequently	$.36^a$	.16	$-.42^a$	—					
5. Perceived support for program involvement	.05	-.06	.34	.10	—				
6. Everyday stress	-.07	-.01	.02	-.11	$-.49^b$	—			
7. Basic hardship	-.03	.21	.27	.01	$-.46^b$	$.47^b$	—		
8. Discretionary hardship	.12	-.32	.26	-.14	$-.35^a$	$.72^c$	$.37^a$	—	
9. Involvement in community organizations	.23	.04	$.44^a$	.02	-.03	$-.42^a$	.31	-.19	—

$^a p < .05.$
$^b p < .01.$
$^c p < .001.$

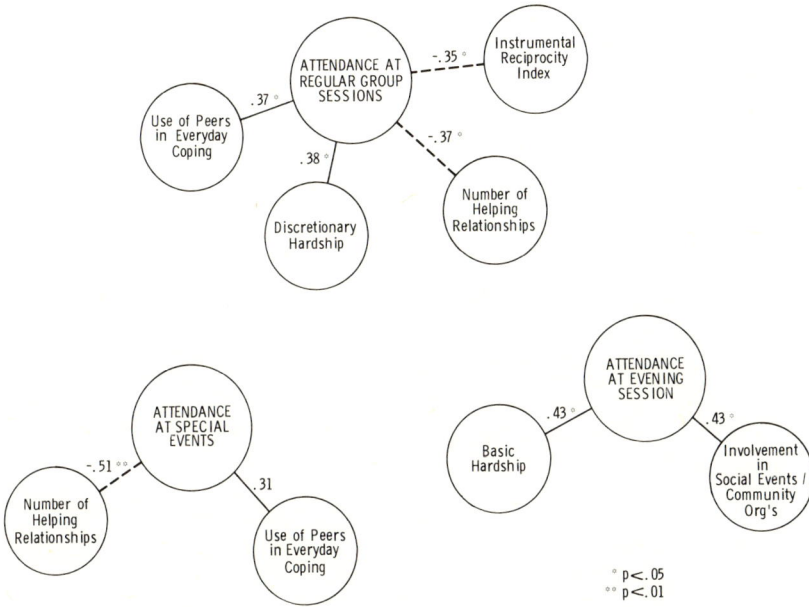

Figure 1. Forms of program participation and their life condition correlates.

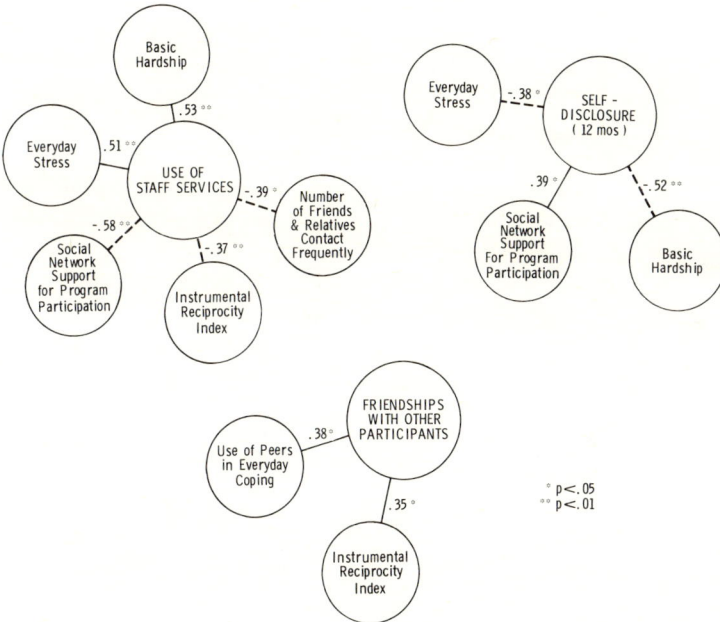

Figure 2. Processes of program participation and their life condition correlates.

attendance. Significant use of peers in coping with everyday problems is also related to attendance at group meetings and special events. It further appears that the level of economic hardship is positively related to the level of attendance at regular group and evening sessions. Involvement in community organizations and social events is positively correlated with participation in the evening session but not with the two other forms of program participation.

The life condition variables relate to the various indicators of program process in ways that distinguish the process dimensions of program participation (see Figure 2). Basic hardship is positively correlated with use of staff services but negatively related to self-disclosure. Similarly, everyday stress is positively related to use of staff services but negatively related to self-disclosure.

The degree to which parents are involved in reciprocal and helping relationships with friends and relatives has a distinctive relationship with several indices of program process. The index of instrumental reciprocal ties is positively correlated with the development of friendships in the parent group but negatively correlated with use of staff services. Also, perceived social network support for participation in the parent–child program has a positive relationship with self-disclosure with fellow group members but a negative relationship with use of staff services. Significant use of nonprogram peers in dealing with everyday problems is positively correlated with the development of friendships within the parent groups, but is not related positively or negatively to any other program process indicator. The number of friends and relatives with whom the parent maintains frequent contact is negatively related to use of staff services.

Relationships among indicators of program form and process were examined. The data are reported in Figure 3. There is a strong positive relationship among the three forms of participation: attendance at regular group sessions, at special events, and at the evening meeting. There is also a positive relationship between attendance at special events and self-disclosure, and between self-disclosure and development of friends within the group. However, there is a negative relationship between self-disclosure and use of staff services.

Discussion

The findings suggest several important facets of participation in a parent–child program and the relationship of life conditions to participation.

Two distinct clusters of participation processes and life condition

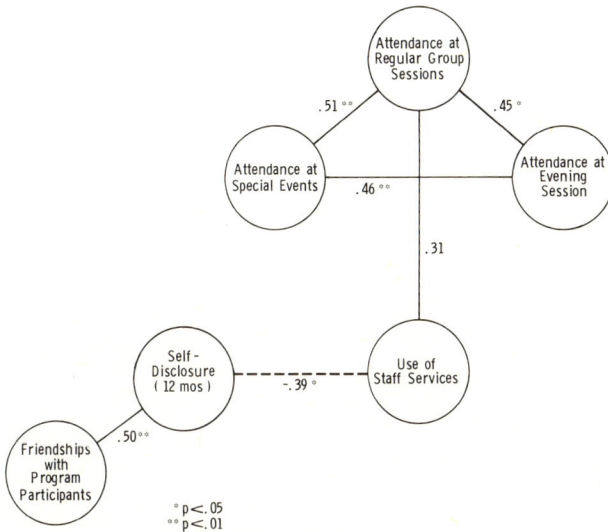

Figure 3. Correlations among forms and processes of program participation.

correlates are suggested by our analyses. The patterns are represented in Figure 4. In terms of program participation, there appear to be a staff orientation and a peer orientation. The staff orientation is characterized by high use of staff services and a low level of interpersonal involvement with program participants (i.e., low self-disclosure among participants and few or no friendships with fellow participants). The peer orientation is the converse of the staff orientation: a high level of interpersonal involvement with program participants (i.e., high number of friendships with fellow participants and high self-disclosure) and minimal or no use of staff for medical and social services. Parents' life conditions are related to these two program participation patterns in distinctive ways. Use of staff services is positively correlated with everyday stress and economic hardship. Use of staff services is negatively correlated with social network support for involvement in the program and with involvement in reciprocal and helping relationships with nonprogram persons. Conversely, self-disclosure among group members is positively related to social network support for involvement in the program and negatively correlated with everyday stress and hardship. The development of friendships with fellow program participants is positively related to involvement in reciprocal, helping relationships with nonprogram persons.

The two patterns of program participation suggest that significantly different perceptions of the program may be held by parents. Parents whose

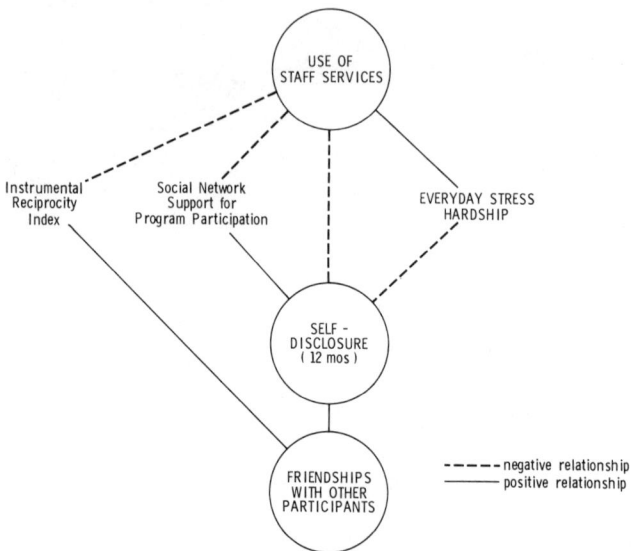

Figure 4. Major patterns of program participation and their life condition correlates.

program involvement is characterized by a peer orientation may approach the program as a voluntary association, like a church or parent–teacher association. The role of staff is to facilitate program activities and not to assist in the direct resolution of problems. The dominant interpersonal ties are with program peers. A view of the program as a social service agency may be prevalent among parents whose involvement is marked by a high use of staff services. Here the program is used primarily as a resource for dealing with life problems associated with hardship and everyday stress. Staff members, not fellow participants, are the source of assistance.

The relationships between the two modal participation patterns and parents' life conditions raise questions about whether the program serves as a supplement to or substitute for parents' existing resources and interpersonal ties. For some parents the program seems to function as a supplement to relationships with relatives and nonprogram friends. The positive relationship of use of peers in everyday coping situations to frequency of attendance at group meetings and to the development of friendships among program participants suggests that the program may supplement or complement existing peer networks. A substitution role may be at play in other situations. For example, the positive association between discretionary hardship and attendance frequency suggests the program is a rich resource for meeting a variety of life needs and hence is attractive to persons living in severe hardship. A substitution role is suggested also in the negative relationship between attendance and involvement in reciprocal and helping ties; perhaps some parents view the program as an opportunity to become involved in intensive interpersonal ties. The important question here is what factors contribute to a "goodness of fit" between a program's structure and resources and a parent's needs and interests. Clearly there is a variety of reasons why parents join child-rearing support programs, and there is a good deal of variance in whether or not parents utilize or attempt to utilize a program to supplement or substitute for existing resources.

Another set of questions raised by our findings about parents' life conditions and program participation pertains to the ways in which parents' past and present life circumstances facilitate involvement in certain aspects of the program. Several findings point to this issue. One is the positive relationship between use of nonprogram peers in everyday coping situations and the development of friendships with program peers. Another is the positive correlation between evening session participation and involvement in nonprogram social events (e.g., bingo) and community organizations (e.g., church). An interpretation of the former finding is that involvement in a peer network prior to program entry is useful in establishing important relationships with peers within the program. An interpretation of the latter finding is that the evening session is a *different* rather than a *new* social experience for parents; it attracts those with previous experiences in negotiating social systems and settings, not those with limited or no experience in social organizations.

The above interpretations lead to the question of whether parents who join the program with certain types of social skills—such as developing and maintaining friends and handling social settings—extend and perhaps broaden these skills to carve out a meaningful personal niche within the program. Previously-learned social skills enable certain types of involvements in the program (i.e., making friends or attending social events). This possibility raises questions about parents who lack such skills in terms of their involvement in specific program forms and processes. Is lack of social skills, for instance, a barrier to forming friendships with other parents and to involvement in settings which require personal sophistication in social relations?

This interpretation also prompts the question of whether a certain level of social skill is required for participation in a program whose delivery system format is small peer groups. We are addressing this question in our evaluation work related to the parent–child program. For this discussion it is important merely to raise the question and to emphasize again that the present analyses include only the "joiners and survivors"— those who joined and have remained with the program for at least 12 months. Life conditions may play an important role in distinguishing parents who stay in the program from those who drop, and parents who join from those who do not join.

Conclusions and Implications

Our effort to uncover the social-psychological texture and detail of participation in a parent–child program leads us to conclude that:

1. Participation in a parent–child program and presumably in a human service program may be described more accurately and precisely when the treatment is conceptualized as a continuum or set of continua rather than a static nominal variable.
2. Examination of the *processes* of participation in a program (e.g., relations with others) may prove to be a more productive characterization of program experience than exclusive focus on the structural *forms* of participation (e.g., attendance).
3. Diverse patterns of program participation are related to the socio-ecological contexts of participants' lives.

The significantly different patterns of participation in the parent–child program analyzed here support the concept of the treatment variable as a multidimensional construct. The diverse range of involvements in the program underscores the serious limitation of lumping all participants into a single treatment category. Clearly the program interacts with family circumstances and individual characteristics; presumably all parents are not equally influenced by the program curriculum or intervention strategy.

The framework and methods of the present study may be useful for evaluations of other parent-oriented interventions and human service programs in general. A fine-grained program analysis from the participants' perspective is likely to enhance our understanding of the ways in which parent characteristics and program properties interact to yield effects in participant functioning. In particular, detailed program process evaluations hold promise of examining what Clarke-Stewart (1978) has called the untested assumptions of the parent program movement. Among these assumptions are the following: (a) that what the program designer intends is what really happens; (b) that the message the parent training intends is what gets through to the mother; (c) that all mothers are equally ready for parent training; (d) that the mother's goals for herself and her child are the same as the program designer's; and (e) that changing the mother's behavior causes the child's improved performance.

An implication of the present work, then, is that it may contribute to the development of a methodology for program evaluations that attempt to link outcome with program process while considering the socio-ecological context of participants' lives. Such approaches and methodologies are not without difficulties. For instance, at a theoretical level there is the problem of how to conceptualize the participant's program experience. What dimensions of the program environment are to be deemed critical? Our approach—describing program experience in terms of structural forms and social-psychological processes—may be a useful framework for other work. For human service programs, in which interpersonal relationships typically make up the substance of the program, an emphasis on the process rather than the form of participation may be the most salient way to describe meaningful variations in participant experiences. How are these dimensions to be measured? The reliability and validity of process measures are especially problematic (see Boruch & Gomez, 1977). If we are to tease out the processes and effects of interventions, researchers will need to invest energies in the development of adequate methodologies.

A key message of the findings is that there is a strong relationship between patterns of program participation and participants' life conditions. In spite of the seemingly homogeneous nature of our population group, different participation processes were found to be associated with economic hardship, everyday stress, and attributes of participants' social networks. The role of the program as a substitute for—versus a supplement to— aspects of participants' lives is variable. Some processes of participation appear to supplement existing life circumstances (e.g., development of friendships), while other processes seem to fill a void (e.g., instrumental aid from staff).

The analyses have several implications for further research. First, relations between specific dimensions of program participation and outcome variables need to be examined. For instance, in what ways, if any, do different types of program experience relate to parent–child interaction? Do parents who display certain behaviors in interacting with peers at a program exhibit a similar set of behaviors in interactions with their child? Are parents who are responsive in interactions with others also responsive in relating to their child? Parent functioning independent of the child also may be related to program involvement. A peer-oriented participation pattern may enhance shills for, and heighten interest in, participation in other community organizations, such as PTA and civic groups. Is a peer-oriented pattern of program involvement predictive of subsequent participation in community affairs and local institutions? What is the result of a staff-oriented pattern? Do parents learn (via staff role models) effective ways to negotiate agencies and institutions?

Second, research is needed to determine the relations between particular life conditions and program experiences. Of use here would be a longitudinal perspective that permits investigation of possible changes in program involvement across time, as well as the correlates of change. An important question is whether the level and type of program participation remains constant over time and, if not, what factors are associated with changes in involvement. Correlates of change in program involvement may be related to program participation (e.g., interpersonal conflicts with participants) or to participant life conditions. As an example of the latter, consider the effects of a cluster of stressors initiated by the onset of marital separation and subsequent divorce. There is likely to be financial stress, perhaps a new job, significant emotional responses, tensions in relations with children, an alteration of one's personal social network, and a change in informal sources of material and emotional support. How does a parent respond vis-à-vis involvement in a parent program? Does the level and nature of involvement change? Do the stressors function as barriers to participation or as motivating forces for increased involvement? If the participation level is increased, in what ways does this occur? Is there "more of the same" type of involvement or is there a shift in the ways the parent participates (i.e., movement from a peer to a staff orientation)?

Third, research is needed on the role of the program in facilitating or hindering participant involvement in various program forms and processes. What influence do staff members have on participants' roles and activities in the program? To what extend do staff members encourage parents to assume certain patterns of involvement (akin to high school curriculum tracking) based on staff perceptions of participant needs and interests? Are leadership roles emphasized among socially skilled parents? Are parents who are perceived as "needy" encouraged to make use of special staff services? More than life conditions may influence the style of participation.

The findings of our exploratory analyses raise questions about the design and operations of intervention programs. Our data suggest that persons respond in different ways to the same program setting; they seem to assimilate selectively from a program environment what is needed and meaningful to them. This interpretation of the data prompts questions about the ways in which programs enable diverse patterns of participation. Policies which mandate such participant behaviors as minimum attendance levels, involvment in specific program activities, and the duration of participation suggest that participants have similar needs (e.g., qualitatively similar support systems external to the program). Such policies also contribute to staff expectations about the ideal form of client participation (e.g., perceptions of low attendance as "poor" and high attendance as "good"). It appears that designers of intervention efforts need to develop and sustain program structures and policies that accommodate an array of participation patterns. Sensitivity is needed in discerning the ways that program activities might cancel out or inhibit certain types of participant involvement. When a specific activity is planned for all participants, what assumptions are made about the needs of participants and the requisite skills for involvement? If parents relate to a program environment in a manner consistent with past and present life circumstances, as our data suggest, then it is imperative that program designers and staff carry out their work in ways that acknowledge the parent, not the staff, as the primary organizer of the intervention setting.

ACKNOWLEDGMENTS

I am grateful to Jeanne Watson Eisenstadt, Donna Solovey, and Julie Kusiak for their assistance in the development of this paper.

References

Barker, R. G. *Ecological psychology: Concepts and methods for studying the environment of human behavior.* Stanford: Stanford University Press, 1968.

Boruch, R. F., & Gomez, H. Sensitivity, bias and theory in impact evaluations. *Professional Psychology,* 1977, *8*(4), 411–434.

Bronfenbrenner, U. Who needs parent education? *Teachers College Record,* 1978, *79*(4), 767–787.

Chilman, C. S. Programs for disadvantaged parents: Some major trends and related research. In B. M. Caldwell & H. N. Ricciuti (Eds.), *Review of child development research: Child development and social policy.* (Vol. 3). Chicago: University of Chicago Press, 1973.

Clarke-Stewart, K. A. Evaluating parental effects on child development. In L. Shulman (Ed.), *Review of research in education* (Vol. 6). Itasca, Ill.: F. E. Peacock, 1978.

Cochran, M., & Brassard, J. A. Personal social networks and child development. *Child Development,* 1979, *50,* 601–616.

Gabel, H., Graybill, D., DeMott, S., Wood, L., & Johnston, L. Correlates of participation in a parent group discussion among parents of learning disabled children. *Journal of Community Psychology,* 1977, *5,* 275–277.

Goodson, B. D., & Hess, R. D. *The effects of parent training programs on child performance and parent behavior.* Unpublished manuscript, School of Education, Stanford University, 1976.

Hasenfeld, Y., & English, R. *Human service organizations.* Ann Arbor: University of Michigan Press, 1974.

Hobbs, D. F., & Cole, S. P. Transition to parenthood: A decade replication. *Journal of Marriage and the Family,* 1976, *38,* 723–731.

Ilfeld, F. Characteristics of current social stressors. *Psychological Reports,* 1976, *39,* 1231–1247.

Joffe, C. E. *Friendly intruders: Childcare professionals and family life.* Berkeley, California: University of California Press, 1977.

Kammeyer, K. C. W., & Bolton, C. D. Community and family factors related to the use of a family service agency. *Journal of Marriage and the Family,* 1968, *30,* 488–498.

Kessen, W., & Fein, G. *Variations in home-based infant education: Language, play and social development.* Final report to the Office of Child Development, Department of HEW, August, 1975.

Levitt, E., & Cohen, S. An analysis of selected parent intervention programs for handicapped and disadvantaged children. *Journal of Special Education*, 1975, *9*(4), 345–365.

McKinlay, J. B. Social networks, lay consultation and help-seeking behavior. *Social Forces*, 1973, *51*(3), 275–292.

Miller, L. B., & Dyer, J. L. Four preschool programs: Their dimensions and effects. *Monographs of the Society for Research in Child Development*, 1975, *40*, whole #162.

Powell, D. R. The interpersonal relationship between parents and caregivers in day care settings. *American Journal of Orthopsychiatry*, 1978, *48*(4), 680–689.

Powell, D. R. Correlates of parent-teacher communication frequency and diversity. *Journal of Educational Research*, 1979, *71*, 333–341.

Powell, D. R., & Eisenstadt, J. W. Parents' searches for child care and the design of information services. *Children and Youth Services Review*, 1982, *4*, 239–253.

Sigel, I. E. The search for validity or the evaluator's nightmare. In R. A. Weinberg & S. G. Moore (Eds.), *Evaluation of educational programs for young children: The Minnesota Round Table on Early Childhood Education II*. Washington, D.C.: The Child Development Associate Consortium, 1975.

Stack, C. B. *All our kin: Strategies for survival in a Black community.* New York: Harper & Row, 1974.

Unger, D., & Powell, D. R. Supporting families under stress: The role of social networks. *Family Relations*, 1980, *29*, 566–574.

Weikart, D. P., Epstein, A. S., Schweinhart, L., & Bond, J. T. *The Ypsilanti preschool curriculum Perry Preschool Project: Preschool years and longitudinal results through 4th grade.* Ypsilanti, Mich.: High/Scope Educational Research Foundation, 1978.

Zimiles, H. A radical and regressive solution to the problem of evaluation. In L. G. Katz (Ed.), *Current topics in early childhood education* (Vol. 1). Norwood, N.J.: Ablex, 1977.

CHAPTER 8

Beyond the Deficit Model

The Empowerment of Parents with Information and Informal Supports

MONCRIEFF COCHRAN and FRANK WOOLEVER

Introduction

Today we acknowledge that the massive alteration of the natural environment made possible by modern technology and industrialization can destroy the physical ecology essential to life itself. We have yet to recognize that this same awesome process now has its analogue in the social realm as well, that the unthinking exercise of massive technological power, and an unquestioning acquiescence to the demands of industrialization can unleash social forces which, if left unbridled, can destroy the human ecology—the social fabric that nurtures and sustains our capacity to live and work together effectively and to raise children to become competent and compassionate members of society. (Bronfenbrenner, 1981)

In an article entitled "Children and Families: 1984?" Urie Bronfenbrenner refers to George Orwell's prophetic prediction of the destruction of free Western society and its basic institutions, including the family, by the year 1984. He goes on to argue that while Orwell may have picked the right year and outcome, he was wrong in attributing that outcome to human efficiency rather than human ineptitude. Bronfenbrenner sees the erosion of the power of the family and the child-rearing system as a product of public indifference, and he feels that we are failing to come to terms with some hard realities. The family intervention program described in this chapter is being carried out in an attempt to confront some of those realities.

The Family Matters project was established in 1976 with support from

MONCRIEFF COCHRAN and FRANK WOOLEVER • Department of Human Development and Family Studies, New York State College of Human Ecology, Cornell University, Ithaca, New York 14853.

a variety of funding sources[1] to study the "capacity (of urban American environments) to serve as support systems to parents and other adults directly involved in the care, upbringing, and education of children" (Bronfenbrenner & Cochran, 1976). To conduct such a study we set out in two complementary directions: one toward a better understanding of existing formal and informal support systems as they are currently affecting families with preschool children, and the other toward supplementing what was already in existence. In this latter endeavor, trained neighborhood workers were made available to families to provide child-, family-, and community-related information through home visits and cluster groupings.

The first direction is primarily descriptive and involves cross-cultural comparisons. Colleagues in Sweden, Israel, Wales, and West Germany have been gathering data from families with preschool children; these data bear upon the relationship between stresses experienced in the parenting and the work roles and the support systems, informal as well as formal, which are utilized in reponse to those stresses. We have been gathering similar data in Syracuse, New York, and expect to be comparing our findings with those of our colleagues overseas in order to understand better the part played by public investment at the community level in recognizing and supporting the parenting role.

The focus of this chapter is, however, on that purely American aspect of our enterprise, the intervention. It is important to understand at the outset that this program for families with young children has been designed as much to illuminate our understanding of the ecologies of family life as to empower parents.

The Family Matters program was designed with some hypotheses in mind about how the worlds containing families are organized, and with some beliefs associated with those understandings. Therefore, before describing what has actually been taking place in our 12 study neighborhoods in Syracuse, we shall provide a brief outline of our social scientific world view and a short list of the beliefs underlying the programmatic activities which have been underway now for several years. This presentation of conceptual framework and underlying beliefs will be followed by a description of program activities and processes and some early anecdotal indications of impact. And in conclusion, we will raise a set of emerging

[1] The project has been supported at one time or another by the Administration for Children, Youth, and Families; the Carnegie Corporation of New York; the Ford Foundation; the Kettering Foundation; the W.K. Kellogg Foundation; the Lilly Endowment; the C.S. Mott Foundation; the National Institute of Education; the National Institute of Mental Health; the Needmor Fund; Mr. and Mrs. George D. O'Neill; and the Spencer Foundation.

and unresolved questions that deserve continued consideration as the research proceeds.

A Conceptual Framework

The premise that is probably most fundamental to the Family Matters project is that in order to understand what is happening in families and how they function as contexts for human development it is not enough simply to examine the internal states of individuals, or even the interaction patterns of family members as they go about their daily activities inside the home. There are other social and structural systems surrounding the family beyond the micro-level which have received relatively little attention from professionals involved with American families but which may well contain the keys to a clear understanding of family dynamics and individual attitudes and behaviors (Bronfenbrenner, 1979a). One such system—into which all families with children are tied—is what has been referred to in the sociological and anthropological literatures as "the informal social network" (Cochran & Brassard, 1979). Made up of relatives, neighbors, co-workers, and other friends, the social network plays a clearly documented part in the provision of information, social norms, goods and services, and crisis assistance to parents and children (Adams, 1968; Furstenburg, 1976; Gottlieb, 1979; Stack, 1974). A second major system encompassing individuals and families is institutional in character. The elements of this system are those work places, schools, formal social services, governing bodies, and other legally established structures in our society which directly affect some family members and indirectly affect others (Bronfenbrenner, 1979a). Finally there is the most all-encompassing system of all—that set of beliefs which distinguishes our culture from others, and in so doing serves as a blueprint for the patterns of institutional structure, network linkage, family interaction, and individual perception characterizing American life (Bronfenbrenner, 1979a). We argue that it is not enough simply to account for the influences on family life of forces at these four different levels of social and societal organization; one must also examine interactions among them. One must consider, for example, how American ideologies are reflected in the organization of the workplace and school (Carnoy & Levin, 1976), how having 15 relatives living close by affects child-rearing practices and parental self-concept, how working overtime might affect relationships with spouse or activities with children.

This view of the ecology of human development as a nested set of social and psychological structures led us, when contemplating the design of an intervention program, to conclude that it is not enough to aim at individuals' perceptions of themselves or others ("self concept"), or at spousal interaction patterns in isolation ("family dynamics"), or at neighboring behavior ("networking"), or at changes in the behavior of schools or employers toward the families they rely upon ("organizational change"). We decided then—and we continue to believe—that it is important to keep all these aspects of family ecology in mind while developing a program, and in the implementation which follows to look constantly for ways in which those systems interact to affect the lives of certain families or individuals. It is precisely this kind of ecological frame that was used in the development of the Family Matters program; through it we are viewing the events and changes that take place in the process of program implementation.

Beliefs Underlying Program Development

It is important to touch briefly on the beliefs which we brought with us to developing the intervention, which are reflected in what the program looks like today. First and foremost is the belief that all families have *some* strengths. This conviction is based on our experience with parents over the years, and it is as fundamental to the success of the program as it is difficult for some people to understand—including, in the beginning, some of our program workers and a number of participating parents. We are consciously and actively engaged in an attempt to counter the deficit perspective (Bronfenbrenner, 1979b) which is one of the basic tenets of service provision in the United States. From this perspective comes the conviction that one need clearly demonstrate inadequacy or incompetence in order to become eligible for community-based, family-focused programs. So it is that with Aid to Families with Dependent Children (AFDC), day care subsidy, or job training programs in this country the client must prove he or she cannot support a family for assistance to become available. This perspective leads, in turn, to the "blame the victim" syndrome (Ryan, 1971), in which the poor or unemployed person is viewed as the instigator of the very circumstances he or she is enduring. To avoid this stigmatizing aspect of intervention in the American mold we have made the Family Matters program available to a cross-section of the young family population Syracuse: Middle- to low-income families, white and black families, two-parent and one-parent families, and mothers working inside as well as outside the home are all included. After open eligibility, the cornerstone of our education program is the concept of family strengths, rather than deficits. Later in this chapter we will elaborate upon this concept.

A second belief central to our programming approach is that the most valid and useful knowledge about the rearing of children is lodged among the people—across generations, in the networks, the historical folkways of ethnic and cultural traditions, rather than in the heads of college professors, trained professionals, or the books written by so-called experts (see Berger & Neuhaus, 1977). We believe that the fundamental body of knowledge needed to raise children is firmly rooted in the collective consciousness of those among us who have already done it or are working at it right now. This does not mean that individuals necessarily know all they need to know in order to raise children successfully. We are convinced, however, that a given parent knows more about his or her child than anyone coming in from outside the family (except perhaps a close relative or friend), and that in this sense parents are experts and should be treated as such. What are increasingly difficult to identify are the naturally occurring vehicles that transmit the expertise from one generation to the next, and that validate the knowledge that young parents have accumulated from various sources. We believe that knowledge housed in the collected experiences of group members can be made explicit and can be shared among individuals by linking people together at the neighborhood or community level and by reinforcing linkages that already exist. At the same time, the Family Matters staff operates with an appreciation of the forces which are pushing in the opposite direction, separating young families from each other and from experienced informants in older generations (Bronfenbrenner, 1974).

The third belief underlying program development is that various different family forms are legitimate and can promote the development of both healthy children and healthy adults. This belief is buttressed by a growing body of evidence (Hoffman, 1974; Kriesberg, 1970) which shows that it is not whether a parent is married or single, working outside or inside the home, black- or white- or red- or yellow-skinned that determines that parent's capacity to rear a child successfully: The determining factor is none of those personal or family characteristics *per se*. We believe that successful child rearing is dependent on the resources that parents marshal and bring to bear on the task. Thus one important goal for this research has been to understand better what really constitutes "resources," and how different types of supports and stresses interact to make parenting either easier or more difficult.

Just as mothers can contribute to the strength of the family unit through work for pay outside the home, so fathers can help by playing an active role in activities with the child and in household tasks. This belief is buttressed by recent research documenting the contribution made by fathers to child development (Lamb, 1976). The Family Matters program contains elements designed expressly with fathers in mind.

The final belief underlying the development of the program is an extension of several already mentioned. Cultural differences are both valid and valuable. If families have strengths, and if the parental knowledge that is the basis for those strengths is rooted in historical and social ties and in the rituals and traditions associated with those ties, then there must be value in the cultural and ethnic heritages which embrace those traditions and rituals. That ethnic and cultural groups distinguish themselves from one another within the urban context need not be perceived of as divisive. This distinguishing behavior might better be thought of as essential to the maintainance of stability in a sea of uncertainty and change.

What Is Empowerment?

According to the dictionary, "to empower" means "to enable." The Family Matters staff is attempting to enable adults to take a more active role in the development and education of their children. We believe that the first step in this empowering process is the creation in parents of a more positive image of the parenting role. The change in self-perception accompanying this more positive image will in turn lead to a desire to engage in the role more actively, through direct involvement with the child, by new or renewed interest in obtaining information about child rearing, or by transactions with other settings affecting the child (day care center, school, neighborhood). Central to the empowering process are the concepts of power and control. Parental action is stimulated by the parents' perception that they have some control over their own lives and the lives of their children. Parental action is circumscribed by any forces—whether external or a part of their internal perceptual field—which prevent parents from behaving in ways which maximize the growth of their children. In order to enable them to take positive action on behalf of their children, those working with the parents must constantly provide them with opportunities to feel powerful and to exercise that power responsibly. The efforts of the Family Matters staff in that regard are described below.

The Family Matters Program

The task of developing an educational program for young families was therefore undertaken with a clearly articulated set of beliefs and a multi-systems view of the forces affecting family life. The goals of the program are ambitious:

1. To reduce isolation;
2. To give recognition to parents as experts;
3. To reinforce and encourage parent–child activities;

4. To share information about children, neighborhood, services and work;
5. To encourage the exchange of resources among neighboring families;
6. To facilitate concerted action by project participants on behalf of their children.

To accomplish those goals we have undertaken a pair of strategies, each aimed at a different level in the overall ecological framework within which we are operating. Before describing the strategies in greater detail, however, we must say a few words about setting and sample.

The Sample

About 150 families in Syracuse are being offered the program, in 12 different urban and suburban neighborhoods. Each of these families contained a child who was three years old at the time of program entry. Families in two of the 12 neighborhoods piloted the program, beginning 9 months ahead of the rest. The remaining 10 program sites were randomly selected from a pool of Syracuse area neighborhoods stratified by income level (low, moderate, middle); geographic location (city, suburban); racial composition (white, mixed, black); and ethnic composition (ethnic, non-ethnic). Selected at the same time and using the same criteria were eight other neighborhoods, which are serving as an untreated contrast group.

Within each neighborhood families with three-year-old children were recruited using a house-to-house survey, local informants (preschools, day care centers, elementary schools, etc.), and birth records. Parents were told that Cornell University was conducting a study of family life, and that some, but not all, of those participating would be eligible for visits from a Family Matters worker interested in being useful to parents with young children. Within each neighborhood participating families were then selected using a stratified random sampling procedure, with special attention paid to race of child, sex of child, and family structure. This process produced an overall sample somewhat skewed in the direction of one-parent and black families, compared with the population of the Syracuse metropolitan area as a whole.

The Intervention

Before learning more about the two-pronged approach that we have been employing for the sharing of information with these families, the reader must understand that we began, not by combining the two strategies, but rather by trying each approach separately in different neighborhoods; parent–child activity home visits were conducted in some neighborhoods and group-building activities in others. With time, evidence accumulated which justified combining the two approaches in a single program for all participating families. That evidence is discussed further, below, after separate presentations of the two information-sharing strategies.

Activity Home Visits

Our home- and family-focused strategy takes the form of home visits with parents and their children. It is designed to give recognition to the parenting role, reinforce and enrich parent–child activities, and share information about child care and community services. Our approach, stimulated by the work of Levenstein (1970) and Karnes (1969), supplements an emphasis on parent–child activities with an explicit focus on information-sharing among parents. Since the starting point is that the parents are experts about their own children, early home visits are dedicated to learning the parents' views of the child and seeking out examples of activities that are carried out with the child, activities defined by the parent as important for the child's development. Some parents, when asked what kinds of things they do in relation to their three-year-old, could be quite concrete and specific. Others, however, did not know what our home visitors were talking about; that is, they found it extremely difficult to think of the child-rearing process as a set of skills or of activities that could be performed more or less systematically. For parents in the latter category, our workers have been able, via participant observations, to identify instances in which a parent has coped successfully with a child-related situation or carried out a useful parent–child activity. By pointing out these accomplishments it has been possible to help the parent begin to view child care as a skills-related and important undertaking. Although the interactions between worker and parent involve both participants in the process of defining success and importance, every effort is made to emphasize the parents' definition.

Once parents begin to sense that we are serious in our belief that they are important, and to figure out what is meant by parent–child activity, they identify for us the things that they do with their children which they think are "special" and which make a difference to both parent and child. Our workers bring such activity examples back to the office, write them up in a standard format, and return them to the parents along with a request that other project workers be permitted to share the activity idea with other families in the program. This process accomplishes two goals: First, it recognizes the parent as important and productive, and second, it is a way of gathering parent–child activity information from parents for parents, rather than relying on the "professional as expert" model which many of our parents had come to expect from outside agents.

The final effect, we suggest, is a change in many parents' perceptions of themselves. Our sense is that they stop viewing themselves as adults trapped by the important but unrewarding job of raising children, and begin to see parenthood as a central part of community life, in which they have a unique contribution to make and for which they deserve special recognition. It is this change in perception of self-as-parent which we will be assessing in our final evaluation of the program, to see, first, whether our impressions can be documented, and second, whether changes were more likely to occur with families in some circumstances than in others (e.g., single vs. married, low vs. middle income, black vs. white).

As time passed and a strong trust relationship was forged between home visitor and family, some parents began to request other kinds of information. These requests were of three general sorts: for information about child development ("Is my child developing normally?"), for suggestions as to where to turn for resources to address needs not directly related to parenting (like landlord difficulties, or marital discord, or trouble getting food stamps), and for a list of the other families in the neighborhood belonging to the Family Matters project and receiving home visits. We have provided basic child development and child-rearing information to families in fact sheet form from the local Cooperative Extension office. For such basic needs as housing, employment, legal assistance, and food we have tried to make referrals to other local agencies and organizations in as personalized a fashion as possible.

Clusters and Groups

The requests for information about other families in the neighborhood by home-visited families were extremely important, because they served as a bridge to the other aspect of the program, the linking component. The goals of this linking strategy have been to reduce feelings of isolation by bringing families together at the neighborhood level, to encourage the sharing of information and resources among families, and, when parents voiced a need for changes in the neighborhood, to facilitate action in pursuit of those changes. In this second approach we have stressed the value of systems of clusters and groups of families, as opposed to the self and parent–child systems. The systems of special interest are those natural helping networks of neighbors, relatives, and friends upon whom many families depend for information and a wide variety of essential services (Cochran & Brassard, 1979; Gourash, 1978).

During the initial home visits in the group-building neighborhoods, the worker and the family got to know each other, and the worker learned from the parents how they felt about the neighborhood as a place to bring up children. After this initial period of familiarization with the individual families, the worker arranged a first group meeting, the purposes of which were to introduce neighboring families to one another in a friendly and supportive atmosphere and to get a sense from the group of what changes in the neighborhood might contribute to making life easier for the families who were living there. Since child care is provided at all Family Matters gatherings, parents were encouraged to bring their children with them. Time was always provided for parents to socialize with each other, while the worker/facilitator looked for ways to encourage participants to utilize each other as resources outside the regular group.

Program Evolution

Our ecological, systems-oriented approach to development would lead one to expect that home visits which focused initially on self-esteem and parent–child activities could be combined with linking and group-building activities at the network and neighborhood levels to produce a program more likely to empower parents than either the home visits or the group-building alone. We had predicted in our original grant proposal (Bronfenbrenner & Cochran, 1976) that the combination would be more attractive to parents than either of its separate parts, and two early findings reinforced that hypothesis. One has already been mentioned: Once some families became comfortable with home visiting they began to express an interest in meeting their neighbors in the program. This pressure to move beyond the ecological limits of the emphasis on the immediate family implied by the home-visiting approach placed workers in the difficult position of having to resist the constructive initiatives of parents in order to prevent confusion with the cluster-building approach. The second sign that parents might need home visits as well as clustering opportunities was negative, and manifested itself in the group-building neighborhoods. Only about half of the invited families in those neighborhoods could be coaxed out of their homes and into group activities.

Based, then, on two sources of pressure—active initiation by some home-visited parents and passive resistance by parents uninterested in neighboring—we decided to merge the two approaches. Working in the group-oriented neighborhoods began to make themselves available as often as every two weeks for home visits focused initially on parent–child activities, and those who had been doing only home visits started to facilitate the formation of neighborhood groups and clusters.

Once all of the families had access to both components of the newly integrated program, overall program participation began to increase. Initially this increase took the form of more parent–child activity home visits, made primarily to families who had previously been offered only the neighborhood-linking alternative. We view this development as an indication that a significant number of families feel so alienated from their neighbors that they must go through a trust-building process within the security of their own homes before they will consider venturing out into neighborhood-oriented cluster group activities. More recently, however, we have observed more families that were willing to get involved in clusters and groups or to participate simultaneously in home-visiting and neighborhood-based group activities.

As the children associated with the program have grown older and approached the age of entry into kindergarten and first grade, we have placed increased emphasis on programming related to the transition from home to school. These activities, prepared for delivery in both home-visiting and cluster-grouping formats, have focused on such topics as the values of home and school, evaluating kindergarten and first grade classrooms, preparing for a parent–teacher conference, understanding the child's report card, and parent–child activities for school readiness. The emphasis in each of the activities is always on the parent as the most important adult in the life of the developing child.

Participation

About 20% of the program families have shown no real interest in any of the participant options offered them. In some of these families the day-to-day crises accompanying extreme poverty prevent parents from accumulating the energy needed to plan and execute participation in the program. A second group of parents has recognized the importance of financial resources in the betterment of their own lives and the lives of their children. In this group both parents work overtime or at extra jobs and simply cannot fit the program into their well-organized and busy schedules. Still other parents feel confident and secure with themselves as parents and with the progress of their children; they foresee no added benefits from participation in the program. One of the strengths of the non-categorical nature of the Family Matters program is that it encourages parents to do their own needs assessment and to choose nonparticipation as available and legitimate option.

Effects of the Program on Families

Although we have not yet compared the changes over time in our program families with the changes of the carefully matched control group (from whom we also collected baseline data on parent–child activities, network helping patterns, and environmental stress), process-oriented monitoring or participating families gives us reason for some optimism. Anecdotal evidence, gathered from program workers and families, indicates that program involvement is affecting families at a number of different levels, starting with changes in perceptions of self and progressing outward through the dynamics of nuclear family life to neighboring patterns and community action.

Self-perceptions

At the most personal level, consider the mother who explained to the home visitor that she was no good at arts and crafts. After a year of involvement with parent–child activities she is now doing the story hour at the local library, drawing the story as she goes. Or consider the mother who, when first approached by a Family Matters worker, was quiet and homebound, uninterested in meeting neighbors. Attracted to a group meeting by interest in a special topic, she suddenly blossomed, and is now a member of a neighborhood committee and a local scout leader.

Also at the individual level, and more directly affecting the child, are lessons learned by some parents from the home visitor, lessons which make it possible for the parents to manage the complexities of family life more successfully (Keniston, 1977). Some of this knowledge has pertained to choice of school for Family Matters children when they became five years old. This choice has been complicated by a busing system instituted to integrate the public schools. One black mother was able to get her five-year-old into the same school as an older sibling because of information about the system provided by the home visitor. In another case a single mother who needed a kindergarten program to fit her work schedule was helped by discussion with a sympathetic Family Matters worker. These examples, although they differ in detail, contain some common elements. In every case the home visitor/neighborhood worker hoped to change the parent's perception of him or herself as a parent by creating a dialogue controlled by the parent and emphasizing the positive activities already being organized by the parent. Out of this dialogue came a trust relationship between parent and worker. The combination of a more positive view of self-as-parent and feelings of trust toward the worker produce a climate in which both parent and worker can take risks—the parent by introducing arenas in which she or he feels inadequate or frustrated, the worker by introducing information from sources outside the immediate situation, with the conviction that the parent will have the strength to reject what is clearly inappropriate.

Interconnections

Once families in the neighborhood have been introduced to each other, those informal helping patterns which are described in the literature as so characteristic of natural networks begin to unfold. Three short vignettes illustrate the phenomenon. First, in one of our racially mixed neighborhoods a black family and a white family met through the program. The white parents felt positive toward and had good connections with the nearby elementary school; the black parents and children were strongly negative toward the same school. However, via the connections of their new friends, the black parents were able to find a way to make the school work for them. At the same time, the black teenagers began to baby-sit for the neighboring Family Matters child.

In the second case, two families in a different neighborhood became friends through the program. When one couple decided to separate, each partner received emotional support from the same sex counterpart in the other couple.

The third example involves a couple who had been advised by a nursery school teacher not to enroll the Family Matters child in kindergarten at the prescribed time, but to wait a year. Eager to have the child start school, but anxious to do the "right" thing, the parents voiced their concerns in the neighborhood cluster to which they belonged. The other parents in the cluster supported the idea of kindergarten enrollment, pointing out that the social experiences would be positive and that the worst possible consequence would be the need to repeat the year of kindergarten. The parents went ahead with confidence and a commitment to work with the school in order that the experience be a positive one for the child.

Information, advice, connections, baby-sitting, emotional support, response to crisis—this is the stuff of informal support and that elusive sense of community. At times our neighborhood groups have become energized enough to undertake changes in the neighborhoods, such as getting the city to fence in a creek bed dangerous to children, pushing the Department of Parks and Recreation to clean up the local park, establishing a neighborhood safety watch, and identifying and improving utilization of rent subsidies available to low-income parents. But more often the changes have been less visible and perhaps more lasting: the informal exchanges of information, advice, goods, and services that characterize a healthy community.

Measuring Program Impact

In our general model we postulate that face-to-face parent–child activities are prerequisites to successful performance by the child outside the home. We go on to propose that the ability of the family to provide such developmental experiences for the child is dependent on the amount of recognition and support provided to the parents by the social and economic world outside the family. Our intervention programs are designed to provide recognition and support to parents at two levels: inside the home and within the social fabric of the neighborhood. Program effects must be therefore looked for in the ways parents relate to key formal institutions (especially the school), in the relationships of parents inside their own social networks (especially with neighboring families), in parental perceptions of support or stress in key domains (neighborhood, school, work), in parents' perceptions of themselves as parents and as partners, in their perceptions of the child as easy or difficult to rear, in the quantity and quality of the activities they engage in with the target children, and in the success with which the child engages in activities (including school) beyond the parent–child dyad. These indicators of program impact are spelled out in greater detail below, and location in our research instruments of data bearing on the indicators is specified. (S & S = Stress and Supports Interview, SN = Social Networks Interview, CCA = Caregiver–Child Activities Interview.)

1. *Parental transactions with key institutions in the exosystem.* Special emphasis on the primary school, as programs aim to empower parents in ways which will be reflected in school-related transactions (S & S).

2. *The expansion of informal network ties, and the increase in exchanges with key members* of the pre-existing network. Changes should be especially apparent in the neighborhood sector (SN).

3. *Parental perceptions of support and stress.* There should be more positive perceptions of the neighborhood, child care arrangements and key agencies and organizations, including the primary school (S & S).

4. *Parental self-perceptions*, as parents and partners. The programs are designed to increase self-esteem and involve the father in child rearing. These changes should be manifested in both mother's and father's perceptions of self as parent and spouse (S & S).

5. *Parental perceptions of the child.* With increased recognition of the parenting role, both by the home visitor and the neighborhood network, should come changes in the perception of the child as blessing or burden (S & S).

6. *Parent–child activities.* A major thrust of the program is encouragement of these activities. Parents should be more aware of the importance of activities and more involved in carrying them out (CCA).

7. *Child Performance*, in first grade and in activities at home when not in interaction with caregivers. Teacher and parent perceptions (S & S, Teacher interview).

Unresolved Issues

Scientific inquiry has a tantalizing way of raising more questions than it answers. The Family Matters project has been no exception in that regard. The issues raised by staff have ranged from the highly theoretical to the very practical, from issues of great moral import to those of the day-to-day pragmatist. Three overarching questions that have been in the front of our minds as the Family Matters program has evolved are presented below and discussed briefly.

Should Emphasis Be on Family Life Stage or on All Neighborhood Residents?

While trumpeting the neighborhood as an ecological niche containing elements crucial for human development, we have focused our program resources on only one segment of those populating the niche: families with three-year-old children. If we are really interested in neighborhood, and in their revitalization as contexts for development, might we not better seek allies from all neighborhood residents rather than limiting our focus to those with three-year-olds?

Our decision to concentrate primarily on families with preschoolers was a pragmatic one. Interested in parent–child activities as well as neighborhood linkages, and committed to home visits as well as voluntary associations, we determined that the task of merely facilitating connections among the families with young children would mean a great stretching of available human resources. An approach less anchored in parent–child activities might well profit from the involvement in shared undertakings of a wider range of neighborhood residents: teenagers, young adults, childless couples, senior citizens. It would be interesting to see whether, with a program focus on building supports and reducing stress, such broadly based neighborhood efforts would naturally translate, in families with young children, into more developmentally enhancing parent–child activities.

How "Standardized" Should a Family-Oriented Program Be?

In the course of developing and carrying out the home visits and grouping activities which constitute the Family Matters program we have become increasingly aware of a tension between our desire to practice sound science by standardizing the "treatment" or "stimulus" and our recognition of ecological and psychological reality. So one can argue persuasively—as some visitors to the project have done—that in order to understand clearly how families in differing life circumstances respond to the program, the input from workers to families should vary as little as possible from one family to the next. In that way we may avoid the claim that differences in the responses of families are attributable to variations in the "treatment" rather than to differences among the families themselves. At the same time, several realities have impelled us to focus as much on the differences among our families as on the standard form of our offerings when delivering the program. First, we found fundamental differences in family circumstances from neighborhood to neighborhood—and even within neighborhoods—in Syracuse; these differences dramatically alter the perceptions parents bring to Family Matters activities. In our sample there is an Irish neighborhood, a middle-income black neighborhood, a white-collar suburb, a blue-collar suburb, and a public housing tract. Within neighborhoods 30% of our parents are not married; some unmarried parents live alone with the child or children, others live with a boyfriend, and still others live with their own parents. In some of our families the three-year-old is the first, or even the only, child; in others there are teenagers, whose needs, from the parents' perspective, far outweigh those of the three-year-old. Employment patterns vary tremendously in our sample: They include two parents, one working full-time; two parents, one working full-and the other working half-time; two parents, both working full-time; two parents, one working $1\frac{1}{2}$ jobs; one parent, working full-time; one parent, working part-time; one parent, unemployed. The temptation to tailor program offerings to accommodate at least some of these differences has been too great to resist. Perhaps that temptation is the curse of the ecological perspective. At the same time, we have taken refuge in the fact that our fundamental, underlying goals have remained the same for all families: to promote in parents a positive self-awareness through recognition for the parenting role, to encourage constructive dyadic activities involving the child and one or more regular caregivers (usually the parent or parents), and to link families together at the neighborhood level by facilitating the formation and maintenance of family clusters and groups.

How Best to Achieve a Balance between the Competing Demands of Program Delivery and Research?

It has become clear to many of us, after almost three years of attempting to deliver the program effectively within the constraints of a carefully designed research paradigm, that the effectiveness of the intervention has been substantially reduced by the associated research. Three examples of this tension between doing and evaluating are instructive. First, in order to insure that families recruited in the experimental and control neighborhoods did not base their choice to participate upon whether or not they were to receive the program, we recruited families before program or control decisions had been made for each neighborhood. This meant that we lost some parents because we could not guaranteee them program participation. Second, in an attempt to evaluate the separate effects of home visiting and neighborhood clustering as support strategies, we delivered one or the other, but not both, to program neighborhoods during the first 9 months of the intervention period. We made this separation even though all of us were convinced that a combination of the approaches would be more powerful than either approach alone. Subsequent events have led us to believe that we lost considerable impetus by making this separation, especially in the "clustering" neighborhoods. Third, it has become increasingly obvious over time that a program of this sort needs the recognition of the larger community if it is to have an impact on the major institutions affecting family life, such as the schools and the major employers. Yet we have had to check a strong desire to take advantage of the highly interested Syracuse media, out of fear that they would have a positive effect on our Family Matters control families, and that this would contaminate the comparison. So we have not been able to use newspapers, television, and radio to the extent that we might have wished, to give recognition to Family Matters families and groups and thus energize them further. In our struggle to carry out a respectable, quantitatively oriented evaluation we may be delaying the very effects that we set out to achieve and to measure. This tension between program delivery and research is real, and cost-effective ways to reduce the tension are not immediately obvious. These constraints, moreover, combine to reduce the impact of the program. Thus, any effects which may be documented through the strategy employed before post-evaluation will be thought of as conservative, compared with the impact to be expected from an intervention that is less fettered by the constraints of scientific inquiry.

Family Matters and the Future

Our neighborhood-based program in Syracuse ended in the summer (1981). However, we are initiating a major national program dissemination effort, which will continue for a two-year period with the support of the Cooperative Extension Service, USDA; the Kellogg Foundation; and the

Office for Families, A.C.Y.F. This undertaking involves development of a set of educational materials for statewide pilot testing and national dissemination. One component consists of a consciousness-raising film and discussion guides. The film, which is currently in production, contrasts the debilitating effects of major stresses in the neighborhood and the world of work, with the enhancing effects of formal and informal supports which build on existing family strengths and rely on parents to define their own needs. The discussion guides are being designed to help viewers clarify their thoughts and reactions to the film, and to become thoroughly grounded in the basic concepts of empowerment.

The other major component in this set of educational materials consists of three action modules. These modules are training packages designed to assist educators, family service workers, and nonprofessionals in validating the efforts of parents through the provision of useful information from a variety of sources. The following subject matter areas are considered for these training modules:

1. *Home activities*: a guide to home-visiting from the empowerment perspective. Useful to audiences like parent aides and public health nurses.
2. *Cluster groupings*: a guide to the formation and maintenance of informal neighborhood groups.
3. *The home-school interface*: designed to improve communication between parents and teachers, and increase the involvement of parents in school decisions affecting their children.
4. *The parent as worker*: ways of helping parents examine the fit (or lack of it) between their roles as parent and worker. Strategies for change.

We plan to pilot test these materials in a variety of upstate New York sites, and in New York City, and then introduce them to colleagues in other states through a series of regional workshops.

Empowerment from Within or Without?

Perhaps the most important question raised by our research is whether strategies for empowering family members are better applied at the individual and network levels or at the levels of the institutions and belief systems which govern so much of daily life. Family Matters has clearly opted for the former strategy. Fortunately we have done so within the framework of a theoretical perspective which is very sensitive to the more encompassing forces affecting development. So although we are firmly committed to the task of energizing parents on behalf of themselves and their children, we are also highly cognizant of the factors that seriously impede the good intentions of parents and of parent groups. Reference was made earlier to anecdotal evidence which indicates that program activities are having some of the positive impacts sought by their designers. Just as important, however, is what we are learning about the circumstances that families face over which they have little control, even when they are organized into groups—circumstances which do much to define the quality of their lives and the future propects for their children. In our sample we encountered the following.

1. Jobs which require parents to work alternate shifts and to see each other only in bed and on weekends.
2. Absentee landlords who raise the rent so often that some of our families have moved four or five times in the two years that we have known them.
3. Young mothers who, unable to find a job or other source of decent income, turn to prostitution.
4. Fathers who, having lost their jobs, will not leave the house, even to visit friends.
5. Men who are working two jobs and going to night school in order to move up out of poverty but feel guilty because they have no time left over to spend with their children.

These—the kinds of situations that we are documenting—are being further exacerbated by the current economic downturn. Stimulating parent–child activities, well-functioning helping networks, and optimal access to existing formal services cannot alter these overriding societal forces; they can only cushion children and parents against their more devastating effects. In Family Matters we have chosen to employ a strategy which asks parents to test the limits of their capacity to change neighborhood helping patterns, parent–child acitivities, and home–school ties in ways which will enhance the development of the child. Perhaps the constraints imposed by these limits leave so little room for negotiation that attempts to intervene at the individual or family level are unrealistic. If so, then the alternative, assuming an unwavering commitment to improving the circumstances within which young families must rear children, is to intervene at a higher ecological level. Within our model that means the exosystem, the world of work, the schools, and the media. There is reason to believe that, of these three institutions, the work place reaches most forcefully into the lives of young families. We are closely examining the work-family interface in our Family Matters sample for indications of work-related practices which, if altered, might make child rearing easier for young parents (Cochran & Bronfenbrenner, 1979). Perhaps most importantly, we recognize that only if we press the family-centered and individual self-help strategy to its limits can we really illuminate the institutional obstacles to its success.

ACKNOWLEDGMENTS

The ideas expressed here have been heavily influenced by colleagues and friends. Urie Bronfenbrenner and William E. Cross, Jr. have both made major contributions. Ingerid Bo helped by forcing us to clarify and sharpen our thinking, as did Ray Rist. Our program and liaison workers in Syracuse deserve the credit for testing early concepts against the crucible of reality. Useful feedback has come also from sources more external to the project: NIE site visitors, colleagues trying similar approaches (David Olds, Peter Dawson, Douglas Powell, Lois Wandersman), and participants at the Educational Testing Service Conference on Changing Families. Finally, and most importantly, participating families have been patient with our false starts and generous with both praise and criticism. We thank them all.

References

Adams, B. N. *Kinship in an urban setting*. Chicago: Markham, 1968.

Berger, P., & Neuhaus, R. *To empower people: The role of mediating structures in public policy*. Washington, D.C.: American Enterprise Institute for Public Policy Research, 1977.

Bronfenbrenner, U. The origins of alienation. *Scientific American*, 1974, *231* 53–61.

Bronfenbrenner, U. *The ecology of human development: Experiments by nature and design*. Cambridge: Harvard University Press, 1979. (a)

Bronfenbrenner, U. Beyond the deficit model in child and family policy. *Teachers and College Record*, 1979, *81*(1), 95–104. (b)

Bronfenbrenner, U. Children and families: 1984? *Social Science and Modern Society*, 1981, *18*(2), 38–41.

Bronfenbrenner, U., & Cochran, M. *The comparative ecology of human development: A research proposal*. Cornell University, 1976.

Carnoy, M., & Levin, H. *The limits of educational reform*. New York: Longman, 1976.

Cochran, M., & Brassard, J. A. Child development and personal social networks. *Child Development*, 1979, *50*, 601–616.

Cochran, M., & Bronfenbrenner, U. Childrearing, parenthood and the world of work. In C. Kerr & J. Rosow (Eds.), *Work in America: The decade ahead*. New York: Van Nostrand Reinhold, 1979.

Furstenberg, F., Jr. *Unplanned parenthood*. New York: Free Press, 1976.

Gottlieb, B. The primary group as a supportive milieu: Applications to community psychology. *American Journal of Community Psychology*, 1979, *7*(5), 469–480.

Gourash, N. Help-seeking: A review of the literature. *American Journal of Community Psychology*, 1978, *6*(5), 413–424.

Hoffman, L. W. Effects of maternal employment on the child: Review of the research. *Development Psychology*, 1974, *2*, 204-228.

Karnes, M. S. *Research and development program on preschool disadvantaged children: Final report*. Washington, D.C.: U.S. Office of Education, 1969.

Keniston, K. *All our children: The American family under pressure*. New York: Harcourt Brace Jovanovich, 1977.

Kriesberg, L. *Mothers in poverty: A study of fatherless families*. Chicago: Aldine, 1970.

Lamb, M. (Ed.). *The role of the father in child development*. New York: Wiley, 1976.

Levenstein, P. Cognitive growth in preschoolers through verbal interaction with mothers. *American Journal of Orthopsychiatry*, 1970, *40*, 440-447.

Ryan, W. *Blaming the victim*. New York: Pantheon Books, 1971.

Stack, C. *All our kin: Strategies for survival in a black community*. New York: Harper & Row, 1974.

CHAPTER 9

Foster Care and Families

RUTH HUBBELL

When parents under stress from poverty, mental or physical illness, alcoholism, or other factors can no longer adequately care for their children, the child welfare system intervenes to remove those children to a surrogate family, group home, or institution. At least 500,000 children (Shyne & Schroeder, 1978) in the United States are currently living in this publicly funded system. Though mandated to help families in times of stress by providing temporary respite for parents and protection for children, foster care in this country has evolved instead into a system that tends to split families too easily and keep them apart too long, often with little hope of reunion.

Until recently, foster care was seen as a haven for vulnerable children who were placed and remained in care because of the problems of their parents (Maas & Engler, 1959). However, recent studies (Emlen, Lahti, Liedtke, Sullivan, Clarkson, Casiciato, & Downs, 1976; Fanshel & Shinn, 1978; Lehman & Smith, 1977) have demonstrated that the foster care system rather than the families is often to blame for the growing numbers of children in care. Bureaucratic policies that have allowed children to be lost in care, that have arbitrarily limited visiting, or that have not focused on permanent planning are some of the contributors to the phenomenon of drift: children living for years in foster care, moving from foster home to foster home with little hope of reunification or adoption.

Despite federal and state laws encouraging rehabilitation and reunification of families (Title IV-A Regulations, Social Security Act, 1975; Ohio Revised Code, 1977; Michigan Statutes Annotated, 1975;

RUTH HUBBELL • Research Associate, CSR Incorporated, 805 15th Street, N.W., Washington, D.C. 20005. This chapter is based on *Foster Care and Families: Conflicting Policies and Values* by Ruth Hubbell, Temple University Press, 1981. The study on which the book is based was funded by grants from the Edna McConnell Clark Foundation and the Foundation for Child Development.

Annotated Laws of Massachusetts, 1975), formal and informal policies and practices at the state and local levels at which families actually encounter the foster care system have been formidable barriers to family reunification.

Family Impact Analysis

In order to examine the impact of foster care on families, we applied a new form of policy analysis—family impact analysis—to the foster care system as it is mandated at the federal level and implemented in one state.

Family impact analysis is a process for examining the ways public policies affect family functioning and how they affect different families differently. The approach used was developed by the Family Impact Seminar, a policy research group which is now part of the National Center for Family Studies, Catholic University. The Seminar was organized as a result of hearings held in 1973 by then Senator Walter F. Mondale on "American Families: Trends and Pressures." Several witnesses, most notably Margaret Mead, called for the development of *family well-being impact statements* on all legislation and policies to determine their effects on families (Subcommittee on Children and Youth, 1973). The Subcommittee on Children and Youth considered this idea but decided that it was premature to mandate the untested approach. The Seminar[1] was then established by Sidney Johnson, who had been the Subcommittee's staff

---

[1] Members of the Family Impact Seminar are Walter Allen, Assistant Professor of Sociology, University of Michigan; Nancy Amidei, Director, Food Research and Action Center, Inc.; Mary Jo Bane, Associate Professor of Government, Harvard University; Terrell Bell, Secretary of Education, U.S. Department of Education; Urie Bronfenbrenner, Professor of Human Development and Family Studies, Cornell University; Wilbur Cohen, Professor of Public Affairs, University of Texas at Austin; Beverly Crabtree, Dean, College of Home Economics, Oklahoma State University; William Daniel, Jr., Professor of Pediatrics, University of Alabama; John Demos, Professor of History, Brandeis University; Patricia Fleming, Administrative Assistant to Congressman Ted Weiss; Robert Hill, Assistant Director, Bureau of Social Science Research; Nicholas Hobbs, Late Professor of Psychology Emeritus, Vanderbilt University; A. Sidney Johnson, III, Director, American Association for Marriage and Family Therapy; Jerome Kagan, Professor of Psychology, Harvard University; Sheila Kamerman, Professor of Social Policy and Planning, Columbia University; Rosabeth Moss Kanter, Professor of Sociology, Yale University; Luis M. Laosa, Senior Research Scientist, Educational Testing Service, Princeton; Robert Leik, Director, Family Study Center, University of Minnesota; Salvador Minuchin, Professor of Child Psychiatry and Pediatrics, University of Pennsylvania; Robert Mnookin, Professor of Law, University of California at Berkeley; Martha Phillips, Assistant Minority Counsel, Ways and Means Committee, U.S. House of Representatives; Chester Pierce, Professor of Psychiatry and Education, Harvard University; Isabel Sawhill, Co-Director, Changing Domestic Priorities, The Urban Institute; Carol Stack, Director, Center for the Study of Family and the State, Duke University.

director, to study the idea. During the first three years of the Seminar's existence an analytic approach to family impact was developed and applied to three public policy areas: flexible work schedules and their impact on families, the impact on families of policies directed toward teenage pregnancy, and the impact on families of foster care policies.

Our approach to family impact analysis relies on several important presumptions: First, there is an ecological perspective which holds that families are most validly viewed within the human and physical contexts in which they live—their kin and friendship relationships, their neighborhoods, communities, and the larger society. Consideration must be given to the external factors that affect families and are in turn affected by them (Bronfenbrenner, 1979; Hobbs, 1975; Minuchin, 1974). Second, public policies are most accurately studied by assessing them at all governmental levels, from federal laws to local practices; the implementation of the laws at the local level is often the most critical in terms of family impact. Implementation is the policy phase most often neglected by the analysts (Hargrove, 1975), although it is too frequently the stage at which humanely designed public policies break down (Pressman & Wildavsky, 1973). Further, in order to assess how public policies affect families, it is crucial to talk with families. Their perspectives are invaluable in determining the convoluted and serendipitous ways that policies and practices actually affect them despite the policies' stated intentions. Finally, values implicit in public policies must be examined. Although written in objective legal terminology, policies contain judgments and beliefs about the people to be affected by them. It is important to delineate these values for an accurate understanding of the policy components. It is also crucial to define the values of the policy analyst, for they also affect the analysis.

Research and Values Relating to Foster Care and Families

In the United States, both our democratic heritage and our social science have upheld the primacy of the family. Interpretations of the United States Constitution have emphasized the integrity of families.

> The rights to conceive and to raise one's children have been deemed "essential," "basic civil rights of man," and rights far more precious than property rights. It is cardinal with us that the custody, care and nurture of the child reside first in the parents, whose primary function and freedom include preparation for obligations the state can neither supply nor hinder. The integrity of the family has found protection in the Due Process of the Fourteenth Amendment, the Equal Protection Clause of the Fourteenth Amendment, and the Ninth Amendment. (New Jersey Superior Court, 1967)

Psychological research has confirmed the validity of these beliefs in the importance of parents to the development of children. The multiple benefits of "mothering" and "attachment" of the infant to the mother for optimal development comprise a strong theme in the child development literature (Ainsworth, 1966, 1978; Bowlby, 1951; Fraiberg, 1977). The detrimental effects of the separation of young children from their mothers in hospitals or child care institutions have been repeatedly demonstrated (Dennis, 1976; Spitz, 1945; Tizard & Hodges, 1978). Although recent research on children separated from their parents for day care has shown no detrimental effects on development or attachment (Kagan, Kearsley, & Zelaza, 1978), the day-care experience is quite different from that of foster care. In foster care, a child is abruptly separated from his or her parents (and often from siblings). He or she is placed in a different home, often for several years; frequently the child is shifted from home to home during those years. The foster homes may differ dramatically from the natural family in child-rearing approaches, socioeconomic class, and neighborhood environment. The child sees the natural parents infrequently, and although he or she has surrogate parents, they may change several times during the child's life in foster care. The average foster child's life is not the ideal one of a safe, stable haven in a loving substitute family.

In the most valuable study of the impact of foster care on children, Fanshel and Shinn (1978) followed 624 children entering foster care in New York City between 1966 and 1971. Using a variety of measures, they found no evidence that children who stayed in foster care suffered more with respect to social and personal adjustment than children who returned home. They even found some evidence of enhanced IQ for those children who remained in care for longer periods of time. However, even these authors are reluctant to champion foster care: "We fear that in the inner recesses of his heart, a child who is not living with his own family or who is not adopted may come to think of himself as being less than first-rate, as an unwanted human being."

Despite the concern about the effects of separation and maternal deprivation, and the legal bases for the sanctity of family life, courts and social service agencies have intervened in family life, removing children to foster care in increasing numbers. The foster care population has risen from 249,000 in 1933 to approximately 500,000 today (Fanshel & Shinn, 1978). The premise for this intervention is that the court must act in the best interests of the child:

> [The judge] acts as *parens patriae* to do what is best for the interest of the child. He is to put himself in the position of a "wise, affectionate, and careful parent". . . . and make provision for the child accordingly. He may act at the intervention of a kinsman. . . . but equally he may act at the instance or on the motion of anyone else. (Cardozo, 1925)

This standard was developed and has been used increasingly to protect the vulnerable child from his parents, and in this it is an important and valuable device for society. It allows intervention to protect children and relieve families in times of danger and severe stress.

However, the "best interests" standard has expanded into an amorphous guideline so undefined that it encourages highly personal, individual interpretations by judges and social workers alike (Mnookin, 1975, 1979; Wald, 1975). The standard strictly applied focuses only on the child, ignoring the rights, interests, or roles of the parents, siblings, or relatives in relation to the child. The standard also judges parental behavior rather than potential or real harm to a child, thus further allowing inconsistent, highly personal, and class-bound judgments of parental morals, housekeeping standards, or child-rearing methods (Goldstein, Freud, & Solnit, 1979; Mnookin, 1979; Wald, 1975).

Finally, the standard is based on indeterminate futures for children (Mnookin, 1979). A judgment to remove a child from a home is based on a comparison between a known biological home and an unknown and often idealized foster home. The supposition is that the foster home will always be better. It fails to recognize the inability of social science to predict with certainty the outcome, for a particular child, of life in one family situation versus another. Resilient children may respond to the adversity of a less than optimal family life and develop strong, normal personalities, and they may be traumatized by separation; on the other hand, they may be harmed by remaining with their parents. But social science cannot yet predict for an individual the outcomes of these situations (McFarlane, 1964). However, predictive accuracy is implied by judicial decisions that remove children to foster care.

The application of the best interests standard can extend into a general paternalism toward the family, for it gives the social service agency immeasurable power over the family. Social workers, with the backing of judges and under the auspices of benevolence, can extend their control to regulate the parents' contact with the child, their life styles, their friendships and employment, and the potential for reunification with their children. The vague standards and lack of external controls on these agencies allow almost unlimited intrusion and power over families; control that would not be allowed a "non-benevolent" agency such as the police (Glasser, 1978).

The argument against the best interests standard does not advocate ending governmental involvement, but rather developing narrow and precise child neglect standards that would reduce intrusion. Such standards would foster the objective and thus more equitable application of justice, relying less on the individual values of the judge. They would also help to focus efforts on assisting the family through a variety of preventive services, maintaining the child in the home rather than removing him precipitously. Such standards would still protect those children who are abused or seriously neglected (only 10% of foster children) while helping to spare children in troubled families the rigors of a life in foster care.

A Case Study of a Foster Care System

Because our review of the literature found little information about the actual working of foster care systems at the state and local levels or about the impact of foster care on biological families, we undertook an in-depth study of foster care in one state and of some of the families it affected.

A national advisory committee of experts in foster care and adoption assisted us in selecting a state for study.[2] The particular state was chosen because it was not undergoing a major administrative upheaval, it had both urban centers and rural communities, it was moderate in size of population, and it had a sizeable black population, allowing us to explore the impact of foster care on black as well as white families. Since the state was implementing some innovative foster care measures it also served as a laboratory for study of several proposed remedies of foster care nationally. The state human resources administration was given the option of remaining anonymous, and its director chose to exercise this option. Therefore the state is given the pseudonym of Big River.

We reviewed the history of foster care in Big River through reports from the state Department of Human Resources (DHR), newspaper accounts, and some preliminary interviews of DHR staff and outside

[2]Members of the Foster Care Advisory Committee were Marylee Allen, Director of Child Welfare and Mental Health, Children's Defense Fund; Nancy Amidei, Director, Food Research and Action Center, Inc.; Gregory Coler, Director, Department of Children and Family Services, Illinois; Elizabeth Cole, Director, North American Center on Adoption; William Daniel, Director, Adolescent Unit, University of Alabama; Peter Forsythe, Vice President, Edna McConnell Clark Foundation; Mary Funnye-Goldson, Professor of Social Work, Columbia University School of Social Work; Ruthann Haussling, Adoptive Parent, Great Falls, Virginia; Richard Higley, Director, Placement Services, Office of Children and Youth Services, Michigan Department of Social Services; Robert Hill, Assistant Director, Bureau of Social Science Research; Nicholas Hobbs, Late Professor of Psychology Emeritus, Vanderbilt University; Jerome Kagan, Professor of Psychology, Harvard University; Luis Laosa, Senior Research Scientist, Educational Testing Service, Princeton; Salvador Minuchin, Professor of Child Psychiatry and Pediatrics, University of Pennsylvania; Robert Mnookin, Professor of Law, University of California; Martha Phillips, Assistant Minority Counsel, Ways and Means Committee, U.S. House of Representatives; and Beverly Stubbee, Foster Care Specialist, Children's Bureau, Administration for Children, Youth and Families, U.S. Department of Health and Human Services.

advocates. We analyzed the state laws governing child neglect and abuse, dependency hearings, and the various service innovations, and we studied the state policy manual which explicated the guidelines for the operation of the foster care system at the local level. The major data collection effort consisted of a series of in-depth personal interviews. We interviewed 43 state officials, supervisors, legislators, judges, and caseworkers who were part of the foster care system. We also interviewed 14 people outside of the system whom we termed "advocates." They were observers of the system, private child-care agency social workers, or staff from Legal Services. In each of two cities in Big River we interviewed five "family networks." These included the biological parents of a current or former foster child, the child, the foster parents and the family's foster care worker. In a small town we interviewed three family networks. The demographic characteristics of these families appear in Table 1.

Our primary focus was on the policies and practices which are barriers to the reunification of biological families. Although we examined the implementation of a number of foster care laws and policies in relation to this focus, we concentrate here on our findings in regard to the development and use of foster care plans, relationships between foster and biological families, parent–child visitation, and foster care review boards.

Most foster children in Big River live in foster homes under the aegis of the state Department of Human Resources (formerly the Welfare Department), which also operates a variety of income support and social service programs. There are a large number of children in private, particularly church-related institutions and foster homes, plus public detention centers and training schools. However, our focus was on the public foster care system operated by DHR.

Table 1. Characteristics of Children of Families Interviewed

Child	Status of child	Age	Sex	Race	Reason for placement
A	In foster care	12	F	W	Unruly child
B	In foster care	10	F	B	Alcoholic parent neglect
C	In foster care	13	M	W	Unfit home
D	Reunited	7	F	B	Hospitalized mother neglect
E	Reunited	10	F	W	Hospitalized mother
F	In foster care	9	M	W	Neglect
G	Reunited	17	F	W	Truant child
H	In foster care	5	M	W	Neglect
I	In foster care	9	F	B	Neglect
J	In foster care	14	M	W	Hospitalized mother/neglect
K	Reunited	15	M	B	Neglect
L	Reunited	15	M	W	Alcoholic parents/neglect
M	In foster care	8	M	W	Neglect/abuse

Entry into Foster Care

Families enter the foster care system in Big River from several sources. They may already be receiving agency services in conjunction with Aid to Families With Dependent Children (AFDC) payments, when a major family crisis precipitates placement. The family may be previously unknown to the agency, but suspected child abuse or neglect brings the child into foster care. Or the family may be facing such severe problems that they themselves seek placement on a voluntary basis.

Ideally, of course, family problems would not precipitate foster care placement. Preventive services could be provided which would preclude the need to move the child out of the home. However, when there is a serious crisis and a need for services to the family, the only alternative is usually placement; preventive services are rarely available in Big River.

Eighty-six percent of the children enter the system through DHR's protective service division because of dependency or suspected neglect or abuse. Reports may come from neighbors, relatives, teachers, physicians, or police. A DHR caseworker investigates, and if the case is deemed severe, a petition for removal of the child from the home is filed. A juvenile court judge must rule on the petition within seven days.

The caseworker develops a foster care plan for the child and parents, outlining the requirements for reunification and informing the parents of the potential for termination of parental rights if the requirements are not met. Such criteria may include obtaining counseling, improving housing, controlling alcoholism, securing stable employment, and so forth. Under a new state law the plans are reviewed annually by an external foster care review board that recommends action to the judge and agency. When requirements are met, the family can be reunited following the judge's order.

Family poverty is an important factor relating to the placement of at least half of Big River's foster children. These children were members of families eligible for AFDC payments. Many other foster children were in families near the poverty level. According to DHR data, the average child in foster care in the three communities we studied was a black, 9½ year-old boy who had been in foster care for 3½ years. During that time he had lived in 1.8 foster homes. Usually he had been placed in care under court order because of suspected neglect, abuse, or mistreatment. The national foster care population is similar (although national data are scanty): The children are the same average age (9.7 years); but more of these foster children are white (72.4%), and they stay in care a shorter time (about 29 months compared to Big River's 40.2 months). About half the children nationally live in more than two foster homes during their time in foster care; they appear to be placed for roughly the same reasons (neglect, dependency, abuse), but over half are classified as being placed for "other reasons" (Shyne & Schroeder, 1978).

Once a family comes under the purview of the court and the DHR in Big River, their rights and leverage are stringently limited. However, there are several key provisions in the foster care laws in Big River that are designed to assist the family in regaining their child's custody. The first of these is the foster care plan or contract.

Foster Care Plans

In 1976, the Big River legislature passed a law requiring a plan for each child in foster care. Such plans had been used successfully in other states to structure the foster care experience and to move children out of the system (Knitzer & Allen, 1978). Foster care plans have long been considered an important aspect of good casework, but they have rarely been legally mandated, subject to outside review, or available to parents. Big River's approach had all of these innovations.

According to the law, a foster care agency must prepare a plan for a child within 30 days after assuming responsibility for the child. The plan must state as a goal one of the following: returning the child to a parent, adoption, further foster care, or placement with relatives. It also details the responsibilities of the agency, the caseworker, and the child's natural parents, and includes the legal definition of an abandoned child and the procedures for terminating parental rights. A parent's failure to comply with the requirements listed in the plan may be grounds for termination of rights. The plan is forwarded to the juvenile court for approval after being signed by both the caseworker and the biological parents. The caseworker and the parents receive copies. The court reviews the plan after six months of foster care; after that, reviews are annual.

The process by which the foster care plan is developed may greatly affect the future relationship between a caseworker and a family; its contents, specificity, and plausibility may strongly influence the potential for family reunification. The plan may be the agency's first rational clarification of a family's perceived failings. The process involved in developing the plan may also be the first attempt at a cooperative venture between the agency and a family (Pike, Downs, Emlen, Downs, & Case, 1977).

The future relationship between parents and caseworker can be shaped by this experience. Whether parents are treated with respect or patronized as incompetent may affect their desires and abilities to fulfill the plan requirements. Further, the extent to which parents are allowed to participate in the development of the plan may correspond to their willingness to work toward the stated goals and perhaps regain full responsibility for their children (Chilman, 1973).

Despite the obvious importance of involving the parents in developing the plan, Big River's law states that it is the sole responsibility of the agency to develop it. The statute makes no reference to the roles or rights of parents, But DHR's policy manual for foster care plan development recognizes the need to involve parents:

> The goals and responsibilities are, in part, established by the parents who are required to commit themselves to carrying out their responsibilities. . . . it is exceedingly important that responsibilities be based on a realistic assessment of individual capacities and resources and that specified goals should logically result from the agreed upon activities.

This statement recognizes—at least minimally—the role of the parents in the process. But there is a convenient loophole in the policy that can easily exclude parents or be used against them if they do not agree with the plan: "If parents or the child's guardian are unavailable for planning or cannot reasonably agree to responsibilities due to temporary impediments, then the document should be written by the caseworker with an explanation of these circumstances and an indication of efforts which may lead to a future plan."

For parental commitment to the goals to be obtained, knowledge of the requirements is not enough. Participation in the process of developing them is crucial.

It would be to everyone's advantage for agencies to involve parents in developing the foster care plans and to ensure that they fully comprehend the plan, yet most of the natural parents we interviewed were ignorant of the details of their plans or had been so at the beginning of the placement. Nine of the 13 families said they either were not informed of the requirements for reunification when their children entered care or were unclear about them. The remaining four families said they knew of the requirements. Two of the 9 said the plan had changed. Several flatly stated there had been no written plan.

By the time of our interview, however, all but one parent could list changes required of them before their children could be (or could have been) returned. In 5 cases there was substantial agreement between the worker and the family about the conditions for reunification. (Three of the 5 were families that had been reunited.) In the remaining eight cases, the workers and families disagreed on the activities needed for reunification. One mother said only that she had to keep men out of her house and cut down on her drinking, although the caseworker said she had to budget her money, control her drinking, keep her house in order, receive homemaker services, and cooperate with the caseworker. With over half of the families and caseworkers disagreeing on criteria for return, there were clearly problems in communication and lack of parental involvement in planning. Although it is possible that some of the parents may not have wanted to admit to such problems as alcoholism, it is not plausible that there would have been so many discrepancies between the caseworker and the parents— and so many on relatively unembarrassing conditions, such as maintaining contact with their caseworkers or visiting their child.

Another disturbing phenomenon was the alteration of initial contracts for court-ordered placements and the imposition of new conditions on families which had voluntarily placed their children in foster care. Although this phenomenon was not widespread, it had occurred with several families we interviewed. One couple recalled,

> We had just moved here and had trouble with the neighbors; there were problems with Mary [their daughter] and the boys. Both of us had to go to work and we couldn't keep an eye on her. The caseworker suggested that for her welfare and ours that she go into foster care. . . . But after she went into care, the caseworker said we had to get a three-bedroom house, visit her regularly, contribute to her support, have a stable home, keep employment, and go to a marriage counselor and psychiatrist. They think we're half nuts! Part of this is fair and part isn't. The three-bedroom house and job are fair, but the marriage counselor and psychiatrist? Digging into our personal life isn't fair at all.

Another mother said, "I was in the hospital when [my children] were made wards of the court. I thought when I got well I could get them back. Now there are four or five things I have to do. . . . the original plan was changed. I don't know why."

These experiences illustrate how an agency extends its authority over a family by making additional demands to remedy other perceived deficiencies. In the first case, the lack of supervision for the teenager was the problem that brought the family to the attention of the agency. Then, with the family under its control, the agency added other requirements, such as improved housing, which were irrelevant to the original problem.

The second situation may illustrate the phenomenon noted by child welfare critics in which the foster family becomes the standard against which the natural family is judged. Although the original problem may be solved, the worker begins to compare the foster and biological families and finds the biological family inferior. Additional requirements are added to try to bring the biological family up to the foster family standard. Then the worker can feel better about returning the child. However, the family may never meet these changing requirements, and the child can remain in care for years.

The existence of a law and policies requiring written foster care plans should support and strengthen biological families. But these policies need to be modified to increase their sensitivity to families and to allow greater parental participation in their development.

Relationships between Foster and Biological Families

Continuity for a foster child is enhanced and separation eased if the family is demographically similar to the biological family, if there is frequent contact between the child and his biological parents, and if a positive relationship exists between the biological and foster families. These conditions can contribute to the maintenance of the nurturant relationship between the child and parents and promote swifter reunification. If these ties weaken, the child is likely to remain in care longer, and the potential for the child's ever returning home drops accordingly (Fanshel & Shinn, 1978).

We found virtually no contact between the two types of families, despite DHR's explicit policy to the contrary. The department's foster care policy manual states that "the foster parents will need help in developing and maintaining an adequate working relationship with the child's own parents, helping them particularly to not become involved in the parents' personal problems and to help the child with the conflict of loyalties between foster parents and their own parents." Although the policy does not allow the foster family to be a source of emotional support to the biological parents, it does encourage contact and cooperation. Yet 9 of the 13 biological families interviewed said that they and their respective foster families did not know each other. One couple said, "We don't know if they know anything about us. We've never met." Another mother confirmed, "Well, I don't know anything about them. I called Jane and Betsy's foster mother and she told me I had the wrong number and hung up."

The only instances discovered of contact between foster and biological parents occurred when the biological parents had managed to locate their children surreptitiously or when they identified the foster parents through friends. Only four families had met with the foster families more than once. One biological mother was very enthusiastic about this contact. After her son was returned to her, she told us that his foster parents had "tried to help me. . . . If I need advice, I'll call them. They are just like relatives to Davey [her son] and me. [The foster father] gives me advice. They bought Davey some nice clothes. They help me. We go to church together. We talk all the time." And Davey's caseworker confirmed that he now "visits back and forth with [his former foster parents]; they don't get paid any longer. They are just like friends."

One foster mother suggested that increased contact would be helpful to her and to the natural parents.

> The foster parent would understand the child better. . . . and when the child leaves there would not be so much readjustment; it would help the child and the real parents. Maybe once a month, I would like to have the mother over for dinner. When the children are taken away, the mother has some mean thoughts and attitudes. This would change if they could be together [more often].

Although close contact between biological and foster families might not be desired or desirable for all families, it is an approach worth testing, according to the president of the Big River Foster Parents Association. "We have to be understanding, it could be any of us [having our children in foster care]." He extended the concept of support of the biological families into a broader form of foster care: families fostering families. "We need to build an extended family-type welfare system. We need to build a social welfare system to keep families together."

Maintaining Contact between Parents and Children

When a child is removed from the home, one of a family's primary functions—its ability to nurture that child—is severely limited. Visitation can help to maintain that function, albeit at a greatly decreased level.

Fanshel and Shinn's study (1978) of foster care demonstrated how important these contacts are. The study affirmed the importance of visitation in preserving parents' ties with a child and facilitating their ultimate reunification. The authors concluded that their data showed "a strong association between the frequency of parental visiting and the discharge of children from foster care. Examining visiting data for the first years, we see that subjects whose parents visited the maximum permitted by the agency or who visited frequently but irregularly were almost twice as likely to be discharged eventually as those not visited at all or only minimally." Although the parents' initiative in visiting is important, an agency's visitation policies and practices can also affect whether or not it occurs.

Big River's foster care policy handbook notes the importance of visitation: "Parent–child relationships and ties are exceedingly important and should be maintained and nurtured through planned visits between the parents and the child." The state supervisor of social services elaborated on this policy:

Visiting is dictated by circumstances and caseloads. The official state policy sets once a month as the minimum visit, though some caseworkers may interpret this as the maximum. There may be a "cooling off" period when no visiting is allowed; or individual mental health professionals may limit visiting. . . .We generally encourage visits. If visits require a caseworker's presence, especially in cases where the parent would "run with the child," the worker has to go on the visit.

The state foster care supervisor concurred, but was more critical of actual visitation practices: "Visits are usually held in county offices. This is hard on the child and the parents. It's an old practice, a carry-over, that just hasn't changed. Sometimes it's more convenient."

Most DHR officials and staff agreed that monthly visits were standard practice, with visiting more frequent as the return home grew closer. From the caseworker's viewpoint, even the once-a-month frequency was difficult, especially for those with a caseload of 30 or more, since they have to be with the children during these visits. Occasionally, they must give up time during their weekends to chaperone the children who are in school the rest of the week or whose parents work. Monthly visits were, indeed, the most common experience for the 13 families we interviewed. Six families said they visited their children monthly; one visited less than once a month; three visited every two weeks; and three visited every week. Two families said that the visits had become more frequent as the child's return home became imminent.

The frequency, duration and location of visits thoroughly annoyed the parents. "Once a month for an hour and only at the office," complained one parent. "Offices are horrible environments to visit with kids." The reasons for requiring visits in these offices were not lost on the parents. "I never visited in the foster home. It's against the rules of DHR because they're afraid the parents will steal their children."

Further adding to visiting difficulties was the refusal of DHR or of foster care institutions to bend their rules for parents. One biological father was angry because "they [DHR] won't arrange visits outside of business hours, so I can't see my sons this month." The antiquated social work practice of a cooling off period infuriated another couple who could not see their son for the first four months he was in foster care. They protested, "Even when someone's in prison, you can at least see them once a month."

The desire of parents to see their children and of children to see their parents was so strong that some workers used it as a motivator even though official policy states that "denial of visits violates the rights of parents and children. Failure to allow visits also creates a situation which prohibits termination of parental rights by abandonment. Only courts may deny the right to visit." Some caseworkers ignored the policy: "She [the mother] didn't want to go to counseling. I told her I wouldn't arrange visits if she didn't go for counseling so she went." Although a powerful tool, denial of visitation is a dangerous practice, akin to denying a patient medication because he won't stay on his diet. Visitation is the strongest force for maintaining nurturant ties; to deny it is to risk the endurance of that tie.

Foster Care Review Boards

Along with the foster care plan legislation, the 1976 reforms in Big River also brought foster care review boards. These are intended to reduce the drifting of foster children. Patterned after a model developed by South Carolina, the boards are appointed by juvenile court judges in each county. Their purpose is to serve as an external control on the department, periodically reviewing the cases of foster children to assure that goal-oriented plans are being made for them and steps being taken to meet those goals. They are an example of the external review cited by Glasser (1978), available to bridle the "benevolent" agency.

According to the legislation, each county board reviews foster care plans after a child's first year in the system, and annually thereafter. It makes recommendations to the judge who, in turn, rules on the case. The board has no legal authority; it can only advise the DHR and the judge. (But a board that has full support of a judge may wield considerable *de facto* power and the diverse expertise of its members may invaluably aid a court.) Unfortunately, the board reviews are not open to parents; they have no opportunity to present their cases to the board that advises the judge. Further, the law excludes from review children in private child care agencies or under the authority of other state agencies (such as Education or Corrections). Thus not all foster children are covered.

By January 1978, 18 months after the bill's passage, only 52 of the state's 95 counties had organized boards; only 36 of these had met at least once. According to some respondents, many judges feel threatened by the boards or feel that they have too few foster care cases in their counties to warrant their creation. This reluctance to form boards was explicitly criticized in a DHR report, but the department took no action against those judges who had failed to act.

Despite the breakdowns in implementation of the law, reactions to the boards, even by DHR officials who had originally opposed the bill, were generally positive. Of 40 officials, caseworkers, and foster care advocates asked to evaluate the work of the boards, 29 were positive and 11 were negative or critical. State officials were the most pleased. Among those positive state officials was the DHR deputy commissioner who said, "They have helped us refocus our purpose. It has added weight and the impetus to move us."

One supervisor gave them guarded support. "It's working," he said. "It's taking up a lot of time for the workers to complete the reports. It helps parents to know that they and what they've done are to be reviewed. It helps the worker to help the parents have a more time-limited plan—and, for sure, no children are going to get lost in foster care." Generally, the caseworkers favored the boards since they promoted contact with the children and encouraged proper planning for them.

The harshest criticism came from the foster care advocates. The most common reaction was exemplified by an advocate who contended that "the board doesn't see the full caseload; there's no teeth in the law [to require] the judges to put it into operation. DHR is protecting DHR." Other advocates differed. "The majority of the boards are functioning effectively," one said. "[But some] do not meet because the judges don't want to hassle with them and are afraid of being second-guessed by knowledgeable citizens on the board." And, said another advocate, "They are fairly effective; many more terminations are occurring."

Despite the optimistic evaluations, our examination of the foster care placement and reunification data in the state from 1967 through 1978 did not reveal an increase in children leaving care.

As Figure 1 shows, foster care placements nearly doubled in Big River between 1967 and 1973. Although tapering, this increase continued through 1978—despite the enactment of the foster care review board bill in July 1976.

The number of children leaving care, the number leaving care for family settings (reunification with parents or relatives or adoption), and the number returned to their biological parents are indicated on the lower part of the graph. Clearly a large number of children remain in care.

Point C on the line signifies the highly publicized death of a child from abuse. An increase in the reporting of child abuse and in protective service caseloads occurred almost simultaneously. Remarkably, the foster care caseloads did not increase proportionately.

It is important that these data be cautiously interpreted. Foster care review had only been in operation for two years when this information was accumulated, and only half the boards were functioning. It can be hoped that social policy analysts have learned the lesson of precipitate evaluations and verdicts. Lengthier and fuller operation of the boards is necessary before rendering a definitive opinion on their efficacy.

Children were entering protective service and foster care caseloads while strong new social forces pressured their families. During these years the cost of living rose rapidly, unemployment was high (Economic Report of the President, 1976), and the number of single-parent female-headed families increased (Characteristics of American Children and Youth, 1976).

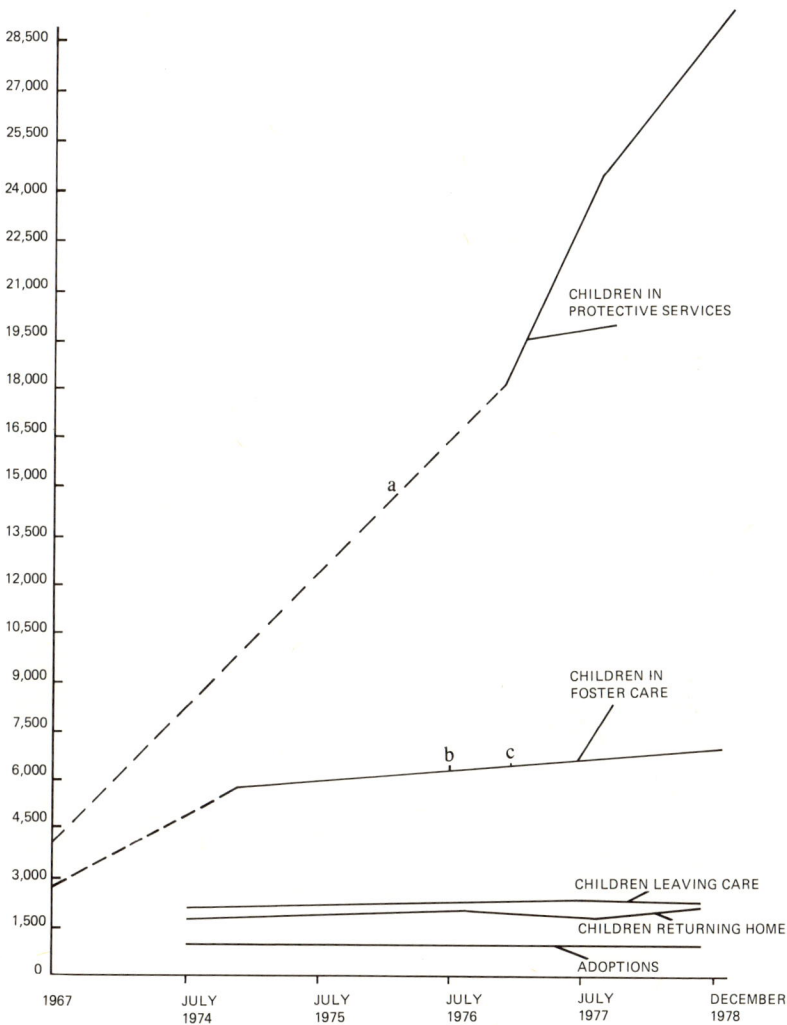

Figure 1. Children in foster care and protective services in Big River, 1967–1978, and children leaving care: (a) no data available for periods indicated by dashed lines; (b) foster care review board bill passes; and (c) child's death from abuse.

Thus, families were beset by the kinds of economic pressure that may lead to foster care placement through an increase in family stress. On the other hand, more women, particularly middle-class women, were entering the labor market. Thus, the primary source of foster families was contracting. The rate of foster care placement may have been rising as slowly as it was partially because of the unavailability of foster homes.

Big River's foster care system may have been holding its own under the considerable economic pressures on families and the pressure of increased protective service referrals, but compared to other states with new foster care review boards, its results were not impressive. For example, in South Carolina the percentage of children leaving foster care swelled between 1976 and 1978; from 5.8% departing within one year after entry to 33% departing after six months in the system (Knitzer & Allen, 1978). This increase occurred only two years after that state's foster care review board system was implemented.

Although other states have demonstrated the value of such reviews, the half-hearted implementation in Big River, hampered further by strong societal forces, had produced little success in reducing placements. The Big River situation is a good example of how well-intentioned laws designed to help families can be subverted at the local level.

Reforms at the Federal Level

In 1980 the Adoption Assistance and Child Welfare Act (PL-96-272) was passed by Congress after nearly five years of frustrating efforts, led by Congressman George Miller, Senator Alan Cranston, and a coalition of child advocacy organizations, with the support of the Carter Administration. This law mandates a number of reforms and safeguards in foster care systems. If fully implemented, the law will require case plan development, external review of cases, the right of appearance of parents at those reviews, and no placement until reasonable efforts are made to prevent them. It can provide funds for services to prevent placement and reunify families, for transportation for home visits, and for assistance to states with adoption subsidies for handicapped and other hard-to-place youngsters. These services and safeguards, however, are predicated on financial triggers which require the appropriation of certain amounts of money by Congress before implementation is required of the states (Adoption Assistance and Child Welfare Act, 1980). Although the passage of the bill went far in re-establishing federal leadership in child welfare services, the current budget-slashing and deregulation by the Reagan Administration threaten the initiation of the hard-won provisions of the law.

Nearly two years after the passage of the law, no regulations had been promulgated to guide its implementation. Fortunately the law itself was quite specific on the steps to be taken, so individual states are implementing them. As of February 1982, 34 states had certified themselves as being in compliance to the degree necessary to obtain additional funds. In the spirit of deregulation, the Administration is hesitant to audit the states' claims of compliance.

Although efforts to block grant the new law have been successfully opposed, the Administration continually reintroduces bills to lump it with other programs. Child welfare advocates feel such efforts will effectively rescind the law's crucial provisions.

These efforts to weaken the law come at a time when state welfare administrators are faced with major and mounting cuts in funds for staff, training, and preventive services, such as day care. These cutbacks only increase pressures on the states as they try to comply with the new law. It now appears that the law must be implemented through the commitment of these administrators (and the vigilance of local advocates), if foster care and child welfare services in this country are to become social welfare systems that are supportive of families.

References

Adoption Assistance and Child Welfare Act of 1980, Approved, June 1980. U.S. Public Law 96-272.

Ainsworth, M. D., Andry, R. G., Harlow, R. G., Lebovici, S., Mead, M., Prugh, D. G., & Wootton, B., *Deprivation of maternal care*. New York: Schocken Books, 1966.

Ainsworth, M., Blehar, M., Waters, E., & Wall, S. *Patterns of attachment*. Hillsdale, N.J.: Lawrence Erlbaum, 1978.

Annotated Laws of Massachusetts, Chapters 113-121. Rochester, New York: Cooperative Publishing Company, 1975.

Bowlby, J., *Maternal care and mental health*. Geneva: World Health Organization, 1951.

Bronfenbrenner, U. *The ecology of human development*. Cambridge, Massachusetts: Harvard University Press, 1979.

Cardozo, B. *Finlay v. Finlay*. 240 N.Y. 429, 433-34, 148 N.E. 624, 1925.

Characteristics of American children and youth. Washington, D.C.: Bureau of the Census, 1976.

Chilman, C. Programs for disadvantaged parents: Some major and related research. In B. Caldwell & H. Riccuiti (Eds.), *Child development and social policy: Review of child development research* (Vol. 3). Chicago: University of Chicago Press, 1973.

Dennis, W. Children of the crèche. In A. Clarke & A. D. B. Clarke (Eds.), *Early experience, myth and evidence*. London: Open Books, 1976.

Emlen, A., Lahti, J., Liedtke, K., Sullivan, M., Clarkson, D., Casiciato, J., & Downs, G. *Barriers to planning for children in foster care*. Portland, Oregon: Portland State University, 1976.

Fanshel, D., & Shinn, E. *Children in foster care: A longitudinal investigation.* New York: Columbia University Press, 1978.

Fraiberg, S. *Every child's birthright: In defense of mothering.* New York: Basic Books, 1977.

Glasser, I. Prisoners of benevolence. In W. Gaylin, I. Glasser, S. Marcus, & D. Rothman, (Eds.), *Doing good: The limits of benevolence.* New York: Pantheon Books, 1978.

Goldstein, J., Freud, A., & Solnit, A. *Before the best interest of the child.* New York: The Free Press, 1979.

Hargrove, E. *The missing link: The study of the implementation of social policy.* Washington, D.C.: The Urban Institute, 1975.

Hobbs, N., *The futures of children.* San Francisco: Jossey-Bass, 1975.

Kagan, J., Kearsley, R., & Zelaza, P. *Infancy: Its place in human development.* Cambridge, Massachusetts: Harvard University Press, 1978.

Knitzer, J., & Allen, M. *Children without homes.* Washington, D.C.: Children's Defense Fund, 1978.

Lehman, E., & Smith, D. *Evaluation of foster care in New Jersey.* New Jersey: Center for Policy Research, 1977.

Maas, H., & Engler, R. *Children in need of parents.* New York: Columbia University Press, 1959.

McFarlane, J. Perspectives on personality consistency and change from the guidance study. *Vita Humana*, 1964, *7*, 115-126.

Michigan Statutes Annotated—1975 Revision of Volume 12: Welfare and Charity—Labor. Chicago, Illinois: Callahan and Co., 1975.

Minuchin, S. *Families and family therapy.* Cambridge, Massachusetts: Harvard University Press, 1974.

Mnookin, R. Child-custody adjudication: Jucicial functions in the face of indeterminancy. In *Law and contemporary problems: Children and the law.* Duke University Law School, 1975, *39*, 226-293.

Mnookin, R. Foster care: In whose best interest? In O. O'Neill & W. Ruddick, (Eds.), *Having children: Philosophical and legal reflections on parenthood.* New York: Oxford University Press, 1979.

J. S. & C. Matter of, 129 N.J. Superior Court, 486, 324 A. 2d. 90 (1974) as cited in Krause, H. *Family law in a nutshell.* St. Paul, Minn.: West Publishing Co., 1982.

Ohio Revised Code Annotated 1977 Supplement. Title 51, Public Welfare. Cincinnati, Ohio: Anderson Publishing Company, 1977.

Pike, V., Downs, S., Emlen, A, Downs, G., & Case, D. *Permanent planning for children in foster care: A handbook for social workers.* Washington, D.C., DHEW, 1977.

Pressman, J., & Wildavsky, A. *Implementation.* Berkeley: University of California Press, 1973.

Shyne, A., & Schroeder, A. *National study of social services to children and their families.* Washington, D.C.: National Center for Child Advocacy, ACYF, DHEW, 1978.

Social Security Act, Section 408, *U.S. Code 42*, Section 608, 1935.

Spitz, R. Hospitalism: An inquiry into the genesis of psychiatric conditions in early childhood. In A. Freud, H. Hartmann, & E. Kris, (Eds.), *The psychoanalytic study of the child* (Vol. 1). New York: International Universities Press, 1945.

Subcommittee on Children and Youth. *American families: Trends and pressures.* Hearings before the U.S. Senate, 1973.

Title IV-A Regulations, Social Security Act, Section 408. *Code of Federal Regulations*, 233.110, 1975.

Tizard, B., & Hodges, J. The effect of early institutional rearing on the development of eight-year-old children. *Journal of Child Psychology and Psychiatry*, 19, 99-118, 1978.

Wald, M. State intervention on behalf of neglected children: A search for realistic standards. *Stanford Law Review*, 1975, *27*, April, 985-1040.

CHAPTER 10

Parents

The Mental Health Professionals' Scapegoat

RICHARD R.J. LEWINE

Introduction

The deinstitutionalization of psychiatric patients during the past two decades has clearly had a major impact on those who care for the chronically mentally ill (APA, 1979; Bassuk & Gerson, 1978; Klerman, 1977). Especially striking is the role that the families of many of these patients have had to assume. With an estimated 54% of discharged psychiatric patients returning home, these families have had to undertake the often burdensome task of primary caretaker (APA, 1979; Carpenter, 1978; Hatfield, 1978; Hilton, 1979). For many patients and ex-patients the family is the only social network available (Mosher & Keith, 1980).

Despite an increasing awareness of the family's importance in the long-term care of chronically mentally ill individuals, families have not received adequate emotional support, resources, or professional services (Bernheim, Lewine, & Beale, 1982; Hatfield, 1978). Much of the mental health professional's interest in the family has focused on the family's role in the cause of disorder or on the use of the family to implement treatment for the individual (Hatfield, 1978). The pioneering efforts of researchers such as Clausen (Clausen, Yarrow, Deasy, & Schwartz, 1955; Clausen, 1975; Freeman, 1961; Schwartz, 1957) have been largely restricted to the assessment of family attitudes toward mental illness. As has been forcefully pointed out (Hatfield, 1979), families who care for the chronically mentally ill have needs in their own right.

This chapter analyzes the professional climate into which parents of the mentally ill must currently venture, presents the results of a survey of

RICHARD R. J. LEWINE • Illinois State Psychiatric Institute, 9-West, 1601 West Taylor Street, Chicago, Illinois 60612.

families' evaluation of mental health professionals, and offers suggestions for future research and training. Most importantly, this chapter acts as a counterpoint to the still predominant view that behind the identified patient stands a sick family.

The Professional's View of Parents[1]

"Our shattered faith in family life needs to find its own gradual rerooting to grow again" (Brodkin, 1980, p. 16). So concluded a review of family therapy. Mental health professionals have traditionally taken a rather critical view of the family. Consider, for example, the following observation of a leading schizophrenia researcher (Alanen, 1980):

> Most professionals who have experience in the psychotherapy of schizophrenic persons and their families soon become convinced of the great significance of intrafamilial psychic processes and interactions for both the genesis and treatment of this disorder. That the atmosphere in these families is almost invariably pathological has been shown by numerous family studies (p. 285)

Mothers, especially, have been the object of considerable attention, having been variously accused of causing epilepsy, colitis, asthma, homosexuality, rheumatoid arthritis, ulcers, anorexia nervosa, manic-depressive illness, juvenile delinquency, and drug addiction in their children (Lester, 1975; Rickels, 1950; Sheehan & Hackett, 1978). The mother–child relationship came under critical scrutiny with Fromm-Reichmann's (1948) coining of the "schizophrenogenic mother," who was thought to cause schizophrenia through her dominance, combination of aloofness and emotional overinvolvement, and the pathological use of her offspring to fulfill frustrated desires—never mind that the same mother may have reared several other offspring with no psychiatric problems. Nor were fathers exonerated from blame. Theirs, however, was sin by omission; they were withdrawn, uninvolved, and passive.

Communications theory hypothesized that parents caused schizophrenia by conveying contradictory messages at different levels of communication to the child (Brodkin, 1980; Sanua, 1980). This "double-bind" situation made it impossible for the child to respond in a way that would please the parents, thereby causing schizophrenia, a natural reaction to communication pathology.

Another popular belief among many professionals is that the

---

[1] I shall be primarily concerned with the parents of schizophrenic individuals because much of the literature is devoted to schizophrenics and my own experience is largely with this group. However, many of the professional attitudes and behaviors to be discussed are probably generalizable to the families of most mentally ill.

identified patient serves to draw off marital conflict (Lidz, Fleck, & Cornelison, 1965; Lidz, 1976b, 1980). The presumed casual relationship between parental behavior and problems in the child is from parent(s) to child: "A great deal of the family life had been markedly disturbed or distorted in each of these families from before the patient was born and persisted through the time the patient was hospitalized in adolescence or early adult life" (Lidz, 1980, p. 47). From this perspective, the identified patient is the scapegoat, who is sacrificed to divert the expression of marital difficulty and to save the marriage.

Myth of the Family in the Etiology of Schizophrenia

It is still commonly believed that parental pathology causes disorder in the offspring (e.g., Alanen, 1980; Lidz, 1980; Wynne & Singer, 1963; Wynne, Toohey, & Doane, 1979). Although concepts such as interaction and transaction (Endler & Magnusson, 1978) are used to describe the relationship between parent and child, family theories often imply that parents are specific causal agents (Meehl, 1973). In other words, pathology in the parents is assumed to predate and cause disorder in the child (Lidz, 1980). However, methodological flaws in the studies suggesting family etiology and empirical findings contradicting family etiology should put to rest any simple, unidirectional cause–effect theories of family pathology.

As Reiss (1980) has pointed out, most family studies are cross-sectional in design. That is, one of the family members is already identified as a patient. Any theories about the development of the disorder are based on data gathered after the onset of illness. When we study an individual with an already existing disorder in the context of some variable (in this case, the family), we have the tendency to assume that the contextual variable is the cause of the disorder (Fontana, 1966). This assumption is often made and stated as if it were proven. Cross-sectional designs also mean that investigators must rely heavily on retrospective accounts of family relations. Aside from the impact of the illness itself on family members' perceptions and behavior (Mednick & McNeil, 1968), there is evidence suggesting that we are poor at recollecting objective events (Liem, 1980; Yarrow, Campbell, & Burton, 1970). For example, Jenkins, Hurst, and Rose (1979) have shown that as little as six months after the occurrence of significant life events, people report them very selectively or not at all. In addition, there are the oft-cited difficulties with sample size (too small), sample bias, and the limits of correlational data (Foley, 1974; Liem, 1980).

We know, furthermore, that the attempt to study etiology in adult psychiatric patients can only be a source of hypothesis generation at best. As catalogued by Mednick and McNeil (1968), the current status of the patient is affected by hospitalization, medication, treatment, social responses, impact on developmental stages, and knowledge of the disorder, among other agents. In short, there are many potential sources of explanation in trying to reconstruct cause in the adult psychiatric patient, and it is highly improbable that the exclusive study of adult patients will ever lead to the discovery of a single etiological agent.

It may appear to some that the family engages in defensive, confusing, or destructive behavior that leads to schizophrenia. However, we cannot know that such behaviors are causes of mental illness in the offspring since they could just as well be responses to mental illness (e.g., Anthony, 1968; Arieti, 1974; Hirsch & Leff, 1975). For example, we know from the study of families with a seriously organically ill member that the effects of such an illness upon other family members and the family as a unit can be devastating (e.g., Kalnins, Churchill, & Terry, 1980; Olshansky, 1962). Therefore when serious family pathology exists, it is just as reasonable to assume that this family pathology is a product of the individual's illness as to assume that it is a cause. To thus confuse response and cause is another source of inferential error.

Liem (1980) notes in a recent review that through 1975 the etiological role of the family had not been established. Since then, less than two dozen empirical family studies have been reported, with the majority based on only five independent samples. At best, there may be some correlational evidence that links certain family communication deviances with schizophrenia. However, samples remain small and multi-method assessments of communication fail to converge. Although family studies have provided a wealth of description of family interaction, there is no evidence that interpersonal or communication style is a specific cause of schizophrenia (Jacob, 1975; Riskin & Faunce, 1972; Schuham, 1967).

Even if we were able to demonstrate a causal effect of family deviance, we would still have to address the specificity issue (Lewis, 1980). That is, to what extent can we isolate family interactions that are specific to the development of schizophrenia? Cross-sectional data suggest that the classical patterns of parental behavior thought to characterize the parents of schizophrenics (such as double-bind communications, marital skew, marital schism, etc.) are not specific to schizophrenics' parents (Foley, 1974; Goldstein & Rodnick, 1975; and Maher, 1966). Kohn and Clausen (1956), for example, noted that "patterns of parent–child relations similar to those we find in schizophrenia have been described for several other types of illnesses: manic-depressive psychosis, ulcers, and anorexia nervosa as well as for juvenile delinquency and drug addiction" (p.312). Maternal overprotection and serious family conflict have been found in parents of children with scoliosis and osteomyelitis (Kammerer, 1940), diabetes (Crain, Sussman, & Weil, 1966), hemophilia (Mattson & Gross, 1966), and infantile paralysis (Rosenbaum, 1943). In addition, there are many more families having a schizophrenic member who do *not* show any of the deviations or communication styles thought specific to "schizophrenic" families than who do show such deviations (Arieti, 1974).

Finally, developmental psychologists are beginning to question the continuity between infancy/early childhood and adulthood (e.g., Goldberg, 1978). It has been commonly thought that early childhood behavior predicts adult behavior and that early experiences have a deterministic effect on later development. Freud's theories, for example, emphasized the impact of infantile conflicts in determining adult neuroses. For parents, the notion of determinism has often meant searching for the critical mistake made in rearing their offspring that led to schizophrenia. In fact, no such critical mistake can be found. Early childhood experiences are not necessarily related in any simple way to adult outcomes. There are many intervening variables (such as school, other family members, friends, and fortuitous circumstances) that affect an individual's development.

A reasonable and scientifically sound view of etiology is the diathesis-stress model of schizophrenia (see Bernheim & Lewine, 1979). Briefly, this model proposes that a genetic predisposition is a necessary but not sufficient factor in the ontogenesis of schizophrenia. In order for people predisposed to schizophrenia to develop the clinical disorder, stress is necessary. This stress can come from many different sources, one of which may be the family. Furthermore, according to this model, no amount or type of stress can lead to schizophrenia in an individual who does not have the genetic predisposition.

In sum, we can say with some confidence that parents have not been demonstrated to be specific etiological agents in the development of their children's schizophrenia. Although parents may add to the general stress of their offspring, such stress is not likely to result in schizophrenia in individuals not genetically predisposed to the disorder. Parental styles such as overprotection and withdrawal, previously thought to be specific to "schizophrenic families," have been observed in parents of children with many other disorders, and are just as likely to be responses to as causes of deviance in the offspring.

Parents Speak Back: A Survey

A search of the literature yields scattered evidence of families' mounting criticism of the mental health system and professional attitudes and behavior (Creer & Wing, 1974; Hatfield, 1979; Kreisman & Joy, 1974;

Lamb & Oliphant, 1978; and Wasow, 1978). However, these early reports have relied on small, selected samples and have often been based solely on interview material. Furthermore, as reflected clearly in journal publications, there continues to be a general lack of professional awareness of and response to the family–caretaker's needs.

With these factors in mind, we decided to conduct a survey of the families of the chronically mentally ill. It was our intent to generate a larger sample of family members than had been done previously and to identify in greater quantitative and qualitative detail the families' satisfaction or dissatisfaction with professional services.

A description and results of the entire survey are presented elsewhere (Holden & Lewine, 1982). Briefly, the survey was designed to assess satisfaction with mental health professionals and the services received, as well as to identify areas of need. The majority of questions were in a forced-choice format, with respondents instructed to choose the one response that best characterized their situation. A number of open-ended questions invited elaboration of problems or concerns surveyed, while a final question asked for comments about areas not covered in the survey.

Of the 500 surveys mailed out to self-help groups composed of families with a chronically ill member (largely schizophrenic), 218 (44%) were returned. Of the 218 respondents, 145 (66%) were mothers with a schizophrenic offspring. Holden and Lewine (1982) reported results from the entire sample of respondents. Specific attention is turned toward the mothers' responses below.

Table 1 lists the demographic features of the respondents. Clearly, these mothers come from the more advantaged segments of our society. They are all white, a majority have had some college education, and a large percentage are employed in higher status jobs. Their children have a mean age of 27.8 years, most (87%, $n = 97$)[2] have a diagnosis of schizophrenia, and most (73%, $n = 145$) are males. Approximately 32% ($n = 133$) live at home, 22% in a state or county facility, 26% in an apartment, and the remainder are in various living facilities.

The general level of satisfaction with professionals was quite low. Fully 45% ($n = 132$) were greatly dissatisfied, with another 25% somewhat dissatisfied. Only 3% were very satisfied, and the remainder (26%) were somewhat satisfied.

Table 2 presents the mothers' global impression after having worked with mental health professionals over the years. It is striking that one-third of them were left frustrated, while only 3% felt they had gained greater

---

[2] The n varies from question to question since there were omissions because responders either failed to answer some questions or gave more than one response.

Table 1. Characteristics of Mothers in Self-Help Groups Responding to Survey

Variable		n^a	Percentage
Race	White	143	100
Marital status	Married	114	79
	Divorced	16	11
	Widowed	15	10
Education	7th–11th grade	9	6
	H.S. graduate	36	26
	1 year of college	29	21
	College graduate	66	47
Employment	Professional	16	13
	Business	6	5
	Semiprofessional	30	25
	Lesser white collar	23	19
	Skilled laborer	5	4
	Semiskilled	1	1
	Homemaker	39	32
Age	Mean = 56.5		

$^a n = 145$, 65% of Total Survey.

understanding through their contacts with professionals. In a separate, two-alternative forced-choice question, 66% ($n = 125$) expressed no confidence in the treatment given by mental health professionals.

In addition to these general evaluations, mothers had more specific complaints. Seventy-five percent ($n = 139$) reported that the explanation of their offspring's diagnosis was inadequate. The reasons for this inadequacy are presented in Table 3. Clearly, professionals are not too technical, as only 4% marked this as a reason. Rather, explanations are avoided entirely or are too vague and not thorough. Despite the fact that 95% ($n = 144$) of the patients received medication for their mental disability, only 54% ($n = 135$) of the mothers were told why medication was needed and only 20% ($n = 127$) were warned about side-effects.

Far more striking than these quantitative results are the mothers'

Table 2. Mothers' Impressions after Having Worked with
Mental Health Professionals

Response	n	Percentage
Confidence	10	9
Guilt	4	4
Powerlessness	14	13
Frustration	36	33
Anger	3	3
Understanding	3	3
Unhelpful	29	26

Table 3. Reasons Given for Inadequacy of Explanation of
Diagnosis/Illness

Reason	n	Percentage
Vague	35	34
Technical	4	4
Not Thorough	34	33
Avoided	23	22
Other	6	6

comments about their treatment by and view of professionals. Some
representative comments (of literally hundreds) are given below:

> We have found that most professionals put the family down and
> give them a guilt trip by placing all the blame on the mothers' shoul-
> ders for the illness of their child.

More specifically:

> Doctors are inclined to blame the mother for "over-protecting"
> the individual. With a few exceptions, mental health professionals
> have given little help or support and shown little concern for the
> family, especially the mother who, until recently, has usually been
> blamed for the problem.

> Professionals go along with and seem to encourage (the) patient
> to vent any and all accusations of mistreatment regardless of whether
> founded in fact or not. Professionals should be educated more in
> cooperating with involved family members.

> While I realize that there is a danger of the ill person being too
> dependent on family, I do believe it would be nice if the doctor would
> make an effort to know family members and if appropriate, consider
> the family an asset rather than a liability.

Regardless of the motivations and qualifications of professionals, mothers
have written:

> Most doctors in this field play God and do not help and in most
> cases find a nice income from someone else's pain. No one has given up
> their time to help the parents and we have suffered greatly.

> Feelings of hopelessness, frustration and anger toward society and
> particularly psychiatrists who appear to be in it solely for the money.
> These do not seem at all willing to help the family and almost
> invariably copped out by using the label "chronic." They are poorly
> equipped to handle these difficult cases.

> Psychiatrists don't keep up to date. My daughter is now doing very
> well on lithium carbonate. Lithium was readily available in this

country in 1972—it was never used on my daughter until 1979. Seven years wasted.

As a conservator, I recently was shown some confidential papers which showed that in two hospitalizations due to crises [our daughter] arrived at the hospital with: toxic dose of lithium and mixed dose (polypharmacy). I believe that surveillance of medication being given patients in the community is rock bottom. I am angry and disgusted with the four private psychiatrists to whom we have paid tens of thousands and received very little emotional support and little or no help for my sick daughter. We are disenchanted with psychotherapy and finally realize that any help that might come for schizophrenia will undoubtedly come from research labs and not beautifully decorated offices.

One [therapist] was sweet and listened for a while, but yawned visibly each visit. One whose interest in settling his bill was greater than his concern for my daughter. . . . This is the same doctor who cut her visit in half because he had no comment to make about her problem that she could not cope with at the time.

Irrespective of the intent and actual behavior of therapists, the mothers of schizophrenic individuals are generally unhappy with the way they have been treated by mental health professionals and perceive many of them as incompetent, hostile, and motivated by money. We might argue that these mothers' perceptions of mental health professionals are unrealistic, colored by the frustrations of living with schizophrenia, or even reflect their own psychological problems. However, the respondents in our survey had a realistic picture of the illness and its prognosis. They did not have naive hopes or expect miracle cures; rather, they repeatedly reported a need for practical guidance. They were seeking information and support, not simply looking for reassurance or easy answers. Nevertheless, the mothers in our survey negatively evaluated many of the professionals with whom they had contact.

Of course, we should be cautious in generalizing our findings to all mothers of schizophrenics. As previously mentioned, these women are better educated, come from higher income homes, and have more resources available to them. They are, therefore, more likely to have higher standards for the delivery of many services.

Despite these factors, support for the realistic nature of parents' perceptions comes from the professional field itself. Manfred Bleuler, son of the famed Swiss psychiatrist who first coined the word "schizophrenia," has spent a lifetime treating, studying, and living with many patients and their families. He has this to say about the treatment of the family at the hands of many of his colleagues (1978):

But in every one of his counseling sessions temptations arise for the
psychotherapist, from the unavoidable tendency to identify with the patient, for
him to find a scapegoat for all the misery. In the psychotherapist's irrational
emotions, the parents often become those scapegoats, even when the therapist's
rational thinking did not dictate that. (p. 135)

Living with Schizophrenia: The Family's View

Many mental health professionals have a restricted view of family life
with schizophrenia (Bernheim, Lewine, & Beale, 1982; Wasow, 1978).
What is it like for the family that must take care of a chronically mentally ill
relative on a daily basis? What effect does chronic mental illness have on the
other family members? Several survey and interview studies have attempted
to answer these questions (Creer & Wing, 1974; Grad & Sainsbury, 1968;
Hatfield, 1978, 1979; Holden & Lewine, 1982; National Schizophrenia
Fellowship, 1974; Yarrow, Schwartz, Murphy, & Deasy, 1955).

A review of the literature (Griffin & Lewine, 1981) reveals considerable
consistency in the schizophrenic's behaviors that families identify as
problems on a day-to-day basis. Table 4 presents a composite summary of
the specific behaviors with which the families of schizophrenic individuals
have difficulty.

Predictability is one aspect of life that reduces strain and conflict.
Schizophrenia frequently is accompanied by unpredictable behavior.
Family members do not know when something they say or do might trigger
off an "episode," such as sullenness or anger. Indeed, sometimes it feels as if
the family members' actions are irrelevant. The schizophrenic person
seems to his family to be wired in a random fashion.

Many families, especially older parents, sometimes live in fear of
physical or verbal assault. This strain only becomes worse as parents age,
becoming weaker and less able to defend themselves. As one parent has put
it, "There are no mental vacations. You worry twenty-four hours a day,
every day."

The ill family member may engage in socially inappropriate behavior,
causing embarrassment to the family. One young schizophrenic girl, for
example, would shout obscene words from her bedroom window to all
passersby. Families may be accused of poisoning food or trying to harm the
individual in other ways. At the other extreme from hostile accusation, the
schizophrenic person may simply withdraw entirely from the family.
Although living physically in the midst of the family, the schizophrenic
guarantees emotional separation by remaining in a different room, sleep-
ing during the day and staying awake at night, not talking, and showing up
only for an occasional meal. Often, this parallel existence of the ill family
member intrudes upon the normal functioning of the family, as when the

Table 4. Summary of Problem Behaviors according to Type

Emotions	Thought
Ups and downs of moods	Thinks people talk about him
Nervous, irritable	Nonsensical talk
Underactivity	Handles money poorly
Overactivity	Forgets to do things
Depression	Poor concentration
Lacking motivation	Fails to consider future
Restless	Irrational beliefs and fears
Suicidal	Hypochondriacal preoccupations
	Expressions of inadequacy and
	hopelessness
	Strange or bizarre thoughts

Interpersonal	Other
Withdrawal	Hears voices
Aggression	Unusual sleeping and eating patterns
Violation of codes of decency	Destruction of property
Uncooperative and contrary	Drinking
Unpleasant speech or behavior	Harmful drugs
Lack of conversation	Poor grooming and personal hygiene
Socially embarrassing behavior	Refuses medication
Threats of violence	Unpredictability
Sexually unusual behavior	Laughing, talking to self
Social inappropriateness	Few leisure interests
Not contributing to household tasks	Slowness
Antisocial behavior	Odd postures and movements
Asocial behavior	Poor mealtime behavior
Steals from the family	Deviations from routines
Argues too much	

schizophrenic plays the stereo at four o'clock in the morning or throws out all the white clothes in the house because "voices" tell him to.

In some instances of serious disorder, ill family members may completely neglect personal hygiene, fail to eat properly, wander about if not watched, and generally place themselves in life-threatening situations (Wasow, 1978). The sexual vulnerability of female schizophrenics, although not life-threatening *per se*, is a constant source of concern for parents. A mother has described lying awake at nights worrying about her daughter's well-being and wondering, each time her daughter went out, if she would ever return.

The constant vigilance and care required for the more seriously disturbed schizophrenic person take their toll on all the family members. If there are other children in the family, they often receive less attention than the ill child. This imbalance may cause jealousy and hostility among the siblings. Once mental illness is diagnosed, the healthy siblings may feel guilt over what they perceive as their part in having caused schizophrenia.

These same siblings may fear mental illness in themselves. Furthermore, the healthier offspring may see their parents suffer and try to ease the burden by sharing the care of the schizophrenic with their parents. Sometimes encouraged by parents who need help, these siblings may become "adult" very quickly, long before it is age-appropriate. They may thus be deprived of important developmental experiences, thereby reducing their psychological resources.

Unlike brothers and sisters of schizophrenic individuals, parents have less freedom to leave the ill family member. Healthy children eventually grow up and leave the home, thus increasing the parents' task. Parents at this time may feel even more abandoned than would be the case normally. At a time in their lives when some peace, contentment, and leisure might ordinarily be enjoyed, the parents of schizophrenic individuals face the dismal realization that once they die, their children will be left alone. This issue was addressed by one father in a recent self-help family group newsletter: "As I've said before, your next door neighbor isn't going to exert himself, and neither are your relatives. Think about it. Where do you want your child to live after you've gone? Well, what are you going to do about it?" (Families Unite for Mental Health Rights, Incorporated Newsletter, August 1980). One parent has described a recurrent nightmare in which both she and her husband die, leaving their son to fend for himself. She wakes up frightened, asking "What now?"

As parents begin to recognize the chronic nature of some schizophrenic disorders, they may experience increasing disappointment with their offspring's failure to fulfill their early hopes and dreams. Guilt often accompanies disappointment as parents believe they should not feel this way about an ill person.

As is true in the case of any chronic disorder, marital conflict often increases as a consequence of constant stress. Sometimes this conflict ends in divorce. For others, physical disorder may result or worsen. Migraine headaches, hypertension, cardiac problems, and a host of other physical ailments have been reported by family members to be associated with the strain of providing constant care for the chronically ill (Holden & Lewine, 1982).

The increased time, effort, and financial costs required to care for a chronically mentally ill relative often mean a restricted social life. How does the schizophrenic's parent go to a movie, dinner, or a friend's house, when that parent is exhausted, trying to cut economic corners, or worried the schizophrenic will wander away? Even if these obstacles are overcome, social stigmas remain. What does the parent say when a friend asks about the ill family member? How often can the parent remain calm in the face of unvoiced accusations that he or she is a "bad" parent? It is far easier to turn down social invitations until they are no longer extended.

The family troubles and conflicts that arise in response to schizophrenia are much like those encountered in any family with a seriously ill member (e.g., Bernheim, Lewine, & Beale, 1982; Olshansky, 1962). There is, however, one critical difference: the families of people with epilepsy, multiple sclerosis, cancer, and other clear-cut organic disorders are generally met with compassion, sympathy, and support for their attempt to cope with the disorder. They are not implicated in the causation of the disease. In the case of schizophrenia, however, families are often perceived as causing the disorder, not as having changed because of the difficulties they have faced. Parents provide for their adult children out of love and because they know that if they did not, no one else would. The heaviest burden of all for families may be to act out of love and concern and yet to receive few rewards from their children and frequent blame from professionals.

Some Speculations on Family Myth

Despite the empirical evidence, many mental health professionals continue to write about and treat the parents as the specific cause of schizophrenia. M. Bleuler (1978) has suggested one explanation for the adversary role into which many families and professionals have fallen: that therapists turn against families in frustration and anger. However, therapists' perceptions have been molded long before they begin to see schizophrenic patients and their families. What, then, may affect mental health professionals' view of the family?

Theoretical and Cultural Beliefs

American psychiatry and psychology emerge from a strong tradition of psychodynamic theory that emphasizes the role of the parents in child development and intentional motives for individual behavior (see Brodkin, 1980; Liem, 1980; Sanua, 1980). Parents, traditionally viewed as the molders of an otherwise unbridled individual, are important agents in the transmission of moral and cultural beliefs. The focus of etiological theory has been unidirectional, from parent to offspring. The work of people such as Thomas and Chess (1977), however, points clearly to the utility of a notion of "fit" between parent and child. For example, a very active child would be praised and rewarded by parents who think a healthy child should be energetic. On the other hand, different parents, placing a high value on quiet artistic endeavors, might punish the same behavior. The characteristics of the parents and of the child are not sufficient by themselves to understand problem behavior. It is necessary to analyze whether the child's style matches the parents' style and expectations to understand conflict or harmony. This view of "fit" differs most from a systems perspective in acknowledging the importance of the individual child's constitutionally given behavior in the development of the parent–child relationship. In the absence of an interactive view of parent and child and a notion of fit, we may be more likely to look only to the parents when something goes wrong in the family.

Whether from the perspective of dynamic role relationships or of communication deviance (Liem, 1980), family therapists tend to view all behavior as meaningful. The therapist's task may be to uncover unhidden conflict or to clarify communication. The problem posed for parents of schizophrenic individuals is that professionals are forever looking for the unconscious motives or hidden meanings underlying the parent's interaction with each other and their children. Even among mental health professionals, sympathetic to the family, we can find evidence of this attitude. It was recently pointed out, for example, that our professional lexicon is filled with words that ascribe intention and blame (Lewine, 1979). Parents "resist," "deny," "refuse," or "sabotage"; they are rarely described as "assertive," "unaware," "unwilling," or "disagreeing" with a professional. Because our theoretical heritage is imbued with the search for hidden meanings, unconscious conflicts, and symbolic interpretations, behavior is rarely taken at face value and parents are frequently distrusted. As stated by Coles (1971):

> Why is it that so many of us, who are concerned about the "true feelings" of others . . . simply cannot accept at face value some of the things we hear? And why is it so hard for us to believe that sometimes people don't say things, or believe things, simply because they don't—and not because they have some "problem" or are "defensive" about this or that?. . . Do we get very far by turning every coin over saying that "really" this is that, and that what seems to be one thing is "secretly" or "deep down" something else? (pp. 377, 385)

Professionals, as well as the general public, may be more likely to provide sympathy and understanding to families of someone who suffers a clear-cut medical disorder. As we have already emphasized, parents are rarely perceived as the cause of cancer, multiple sclerosis, or epilepsy in their offspring. Rather, they are given help, national organizations are formed to raise money, and prominent public figures call on us to lend a hand. When there is no obvious organic cause, as in the case of schizophrenia, we tend to substitute a handy one, often simplifying complex interactions in the process.

There seems to be, furthermore, an unwillingness among significant numbers of those involved with mental health to accept the notion of individual psychopathology. In the extreme, some professionals (e.g.,

Rosenhan, 1973; Sarbin & Mancuso, 1980; Szaz, 1961) write as if schizophrenia and other serious forms of psychopathology were labels reflecting moral judgments, not individual dysfunction; to do away with the labels would do away with many of the current problems associated with "schizophrenia." Such a view has been articulately counter-argued (Spitzer, 1975). In addition, some two decades of cross-cultural (e.g., Murphy, 1976) and diagnostic (e.g., Spitzer & Endicott, 1968; Wing, Cooper, & Sartorius, 1975) research has yielded strong evidence of the existence of common patterns of deviant behavior in and the diagnostic reliability of schizophrenia. However, these "anti-labeling" views continue to be widely disseminated.

Clinical Training and Practice

For the most part, professionals are not trained to treat chronically mentally ill persons. In recognition of this fact, the National Institute of Mental Health has recently requested that training programs in clinical psychology make treatment of the chronically mentally ill one of several priority areas (NIMH, 1979). When trained in emergency rooms or outpatient clinics, trainees' contact is limited and therapists rarely see patients on a long-term basis. As a result, they do not appreciate the post-hospital difficulties encountered by ex-patients and their families.

Two opposing reactions may ensue from training in long-term institutions. One is that discharge itself becomes the primary goal, irrespective of the patients' chances of successfully remaining in the community (Orlando, 1983). It is as if the release of a patient from the hospital were itself a cure. The other attitude is that long-term hospitalization is the "end of the line." Hope is lost and creative innovations are discarded (Lovejoy, 1982; Peterson, 1974). In short, there are insufficient role models in which to train professionals for the care of the chronically mentally disabled.

Furthermore, the models of therapy in which many mental health professionals are trained rely on reflective, interpretive, one-on-one therapy in which talking is the primary source of change, except for medication (Bernheim & Lewine, 1979). Behavior therapy (e.g., Paul & Lentz, 1977) has been focused primarily on the patient, rather than on the family. Teaching social and work skills is only one part of the professional's tasks. The therapist must be active, may have to assume unfamiliar roles (advocate, social worker, employment agent), and must learn to live with considerable ambiguity and unpredictability—as have the families of schizophrenic individuals.

Working with the schizophrenic individual on a long-term basis is not always rewarding: the schizophrenic person often cannot pay for therapy, appointments are missed, and therapists must be far more active than their training has often led them to expect. Often, therapists may be engaged in long-term relationships with only modest change in the patient, thereby depriving therapists of an important source of reward, namely patient improvement.

Finally, therapists may be committing the "clinician's fallacy," that is, the inappropriate generalization of a phenomenon on the limited basis of those people that they see in therapy. On a purely statistical basis, we can expect that 5–15% of the parents of schizophrenic individuals will also be suffering from schizophrenia (M. Bleuler, 1978). If therapists have seen mostly these schizophrenic parents, they may have inappropriately assumed that all parents are similarly disturbed. The fact is that the overwhelming majority of parents are not disturbed in this way.

What Next?

Changing Professionals

Many of the current interactions between families and mental health professionals tend to alienate everyone involved. Ultimately, we are all concerned with the same problem: mental disability. What can we do, therefore, that will lead to alliances rather than adversary relationships?

An important step in changing attitudes begins with the training of professionals. We can begin to redefine professional models by assigning students to work with families, rather than at a specific location (such as a hospital or clinic). Students would, in other words, travel the mental health maze with the families. Ongoing exposure to the families' difficulties and the obstacles they face would go a long way toward generating a more empathic view of the family.

Current, data-based models need to be incorporated into or used to modify mental health professionals' work with families. For example, we might adopt a diathesis–stress view of schizophrenia and explain to families their presumed role in the development of the disorder, as was discussed previously. Another strategy is to use the concept of fit between an individual and his environment in helping families to cope with mental illness. Whatever model and strategy are adopted, the orientation is one which both helps to capture the complexity of the etiology of mental illness and reduces the unrealistic blame placed on families.

As professionals, we must be willing to admit that chronic mental illness exists. Cure is not always possible. Our tradition of insight-oriented psychotherapy has limited applicability to the difficulties and life stresses encountered by schizophrenic individuals and their families. In many cases, supportive counseling is more appropriate than psychotherapy (Bernheim & Lewine, 1979).

Professionals may also need to change their expectations of families. Rather than assuming that the families will present obstacles to therapy, we might begin by giving them the benefit of the doubt. We can learn to listen and cooperate, rather than dismissing family members' input about the patient or interpreting such input as family pathology. A specific task we can initiate is the formalization of strategies for coping with the kinds of daily problems created by mental illness that were outlined above. One such innovative project is currently underway (Leff, 1980). Previous work by this London group found that the family's "Expressed Emotion" (a combination of criticism, over-involvement, and hostility) predicted relapse in schizophrenic patients (Leff, 1976; Vaughn & Leff, 1976). An interesting finding from these original studies was that some families have developed quite effective strategies for handling their schizophrenic member's behavior. Leff and his colleagues, therefore, decided to bring together the families that had developed these strategies with those that had not. According to early, as yet unpublished reports (Leff, 1980), "reductions in EE (Expressed Emotion) levels in a number of relatives, both experimental and control" have been observed. To the extent that Expressed Emotion influences relapse, the chances of relapse should be decreased. By combining families' coping strategies with professionals' expertise in human behavior, perhaps we can begin to devise specific programs that will help other families.

That families have repeatedly requested more information from professionals is reflected in survey studies. These families are in need of information about the latest research, the most effective models of therapy, how to reduce the chances of relapse, how to cope with practical behavior problems caused by mental illness, and what to expect as a family (e.g., chronic depression in response to the presence of the chronically ill person in the home—Bernheim, Lewine, & Beale, 1982). Qualified professionals have a responsibility to communicate both what is known and what is not known about mental illness to families, rather than leaving this task to unqualified persons.

Some Questions for Research

We recognize that any phenomenon is an inextricably interactive event. Nevertheless, it is convenient to talk about specific targets or foci for intervention and change. We concentrate on the mental health professional and the family in asking questions that suggest modes of intervention.

Mental Health Professionals

One set of questions addresses professional attitudes and the differential impact of various professional orientations on the family.

1. Is there any evidence that systems family therapy is more or less effective than a behavioral or supportive family counseling (Bernheim & Lewine, 1979) approach?
2. What are families' perceptions of the various orientations: Are they more willing to submit to change with one than another?
3. Are there therapist variables (personality, training) that distinguish the proponents of various views of the family, and to what extent do those variables, rather than theoretical orientation influence interactions between families and professionals?
4. What do therapists actually think and feel about the families with whom they work? What are the therapists' emotional reactions to these families? How does a therapist's emotional response affect his choice of intervention? How do professionals' attitudes toward mental and physical disability differ?

Another set of questions can be subsumed under the rubric of information processing and attitude information. There often appears to be a serious discrepancy between empirical knowledge and clinical belief (see, for example, the exchange between Gottesman & Shields, 1976, and Lidz, 1976b, regarding behavior genetics).

1. How do professionals form their opinions about families? What role does training have? What role is played by personal experience?
2. What are the parameters that affect professionals' attitudes toward the families of the chronically mentally ill?
3. How do professionals keep abreast of recent research and clinical findings?
4. How do therapists' attitudes and opinions about families change as a function of time and experience?
5. Is there, as it seems a disproportionate impact of clinical case histories (vs. statistical studies) on opinion formation? If so, why? How might we go about correcting such a bias?
6. Why do so many professionals find it difficult to accept the concept of psychopathology? What function does an "anti-labeling" perspective serve the professional?

The Family

To date, we are still largely ignorant of how families have fared at the hands of mental health professionals and of the impact of chronic mental disability. Although there have been a few attempts to assess the family's status, they have been directed at very selected and usually small samples.

1. What are the perceptions and evaluations of minority families of the chronically mentally ill? Do they have the same needs as others?
2. What are the long-term, longitudinal effects of chronic mental illness on the family? How are physical health, psychological health, work functioning, and social relations affected?
3. What do families expect and need at the time of first contact with the mental health system? Over the course of a chronic illness?
4. How do family members feel about themselves and their role in the disorder? How are these feelings affected by mental health professionals? What is the impact of these feelings on the family's relationship with the ill person?
5. How does the family's perceptions of the mental health professionals affect its relationship with the ill person?
6. What is the effect of giving families and patients concrete information about mental illness?
7. Can we devise specific behavioral management programs for families to use in the daily care of their ill relative?

Clearly, the shift in perspective of the family that is suggested in this chapter leads to a great many questions about the nature of the family and its interactions with mental health professionals. The perspective suggests, furthermore, that we attend just as much to the professional as to the family in trying to understand these interactions.

Some Concluding Comments

Chronic mental illness clearly has a major impact on both patients and families (Klerman, 1977). Returning home by thousands, former patients have often found communities unwilling or unable to deal adequately with them. The burden of care, therefore, often falls on the family, as some 54% of discharged psychiatric patients return home to live with their families (Carpenter, 1978). Perhaps as a result of this pressure, families have begun to take a hard, critical look at what they get from mental health professionals.

Unhappy with their treatment, many families have turned to self-help groups, self-education, and political activity (Lewine, 1982). In short, not getting what they need from professionals, families have started to rely on themselves. At the same time, they are asking professionals to account for their attitudes toward and their treatment of families. Thus, I would like to interpret the theme of this volume—Changing Families—in the following way:

Families of the chronically mentally ill are changing. They are becoming more informed, critical, and vocal. As they shed the generations-old cloak of guilt and shame, they perceive more clearly the biased views which have greeted them in therapy. They are asking, sometimes demanding, to be treated with respect and as people who face a difficult task, not as failures, "bad" parents, siblings, or children. The challenge is to change with the families and in so doing lay the groundwork for alliances that are ultimately to the benefit of everyone.

ACKNOWLEDGMENTS

I would like to thank Kayla Bernheim and Caroline Beale for their influence on my thinking; Deborah Holden, Dana Gladden, Sharon Griffin, and Snora Haynes for their enthusiastic research help; Alison Sommers for her invaluable comments on an earlier draft of this paper; and Phyllis Jones, Sharon Medlock, and Cheryl Peterson for their preparation of the manuscript. The family survey was supported by funds from the Psychology Department, University of Denver.

References

Alanen, Y. O. In search of the interactional origin of schizophrenia. In C. K. Hofling & J. M. Lewis (Eds.), *The family: Evaluation and treatment.* New York: Brunner/Mazel, 1980.

American Psychiatric Association's Ad Hoc Committee on the Chronic Mental Patient. Position statement: A call to action for the chronic mental patient. *American Journal of Psychiatry,* 1979, *136,* 748–752.

Anthony, E. J. The developmental precursors of adult schizophrenia. In D. Rosenthal & S. Kety (Eds.), *The transmission of schizophrenia.* Oxford: Pergamon Press, 1968.

Arieti, S. An overview of schizophrenia from a predominantly psychological approach. *American Journal of Psychiatry,* 1974, *131,* 241–249.

Bassuk, E. L., & Gerson, S. Deinstitutionalization and mental health services. *Scientific American,* 1978, *238,* 46–54.

Bernheim, K., & Lewine, R. *Schizophrenia: Symptoms, causes, treatment.* New York: Norton, 1979.

Bernheim, K., Lewine, R., & Beale, C. *The caring family: Living with chronic mental illness.* New York: Random House, 1982.

Bleuler, M. *The schizophrenic disorders: Long-term patient and family studies.* New Haven: Yale University Press, 1978.

Brodkin, A. M. Family therapy: The making of a mental health movement. *American Journal of Orthopsychiatry,* 1980, *50,* 4–17.

Carpenter, M. D. Residential placement for the chronic psychiatric patient: A review and evaluation of the literature. *Schizophrenia Bulletin,* 1978, *4,* 384–398.

Clausen, J. The impact of mental illness: A twenty-year follow-up. In R. D. Wirt, G. Winokur, & M. Roff (Eds.), *Life history research in psychopathology.* Vol. 4. Minneapolis: University of Minnesota Press, 1975.

Clausen, J., Yarrow, M. R., Deasy, L. C., & Schwartz, C. G. The impact of mental illness: Research formulation. *Journal of Social Issues*, 1955, *11*, 6-11.

Coles, R. *The south goes north*. Boston: Atlantic-Little, Brown, 1971.

Crain, A. J., Sussman, M. B., & Weil, W. Jr. Family interactions, diabetes and sibling relationship. *International Journal of Social Psychiatry*, 1966, *12*, 35-43.

Creer, C., & Wing, J. Living with a schizophrenic patient. *British Journal of Hospital Medicine*, 1974, 73-82.

Endler, N., & Magnusson, D. But interactionists do believe in people. Response to Krauskopf. *Psychological Bulletin*, 1978, *85*, 590-592.

Families Unite for Mental Health Rights, Inc. Newsletter, 1980 *3* (3).

Foley, V. *An introduction to family therapy*. New York: Grune & Stratton, 1974.

Fontana, A. F. Familial etiology of schizophrenia: Is it a scientific methodology? *Psychological Bulletin*, 1966, *66*, 214-227.

Freeman, H. E. Attitudes toward mental illness among relatives of former patients. *American Sociological Review*, 1961, *26*, 59-66.

Fromm-Reichmann, F. Notes on the development of treatment of schizophrenia by psychoanalytic psychotherapy. *Psychiatry*, 1948, *11*, 263-273.

Goldberg, S. Early experiences and behavior. *Science*, 1978, *202*, 1177-1178.

Goldstein, M., & Rodnick, E. The family's contribution to the etiology of schizophrenia. *Schizophrenia Bulletin*, 1975, Issue No. 14, 48-63.

Gottesman, I. I., & Shields, J. A critical review of recent adoption, twin, and family studies of schizophrenia: Behavioral genetics perspective. *Schizophrenia Bulletin*, 1976, *2*, 360-401.

Grad, J., & Sainsbury, P. The effects that patients have on their families in a community care and a control psychiatric service—A two year follow-up. *British Journal of Psychiatry*, 1968, *114*, 265-278.

Griffin, S., & Lewine, R. *Living with chronic mental disability: The problems of family-caretakers*. Submitted for publication, 1981.

Hatfield, A. Psychological costs of schizophrenia to the family. *Social Work*, 1978, *23*, 355-359.

Hatfield, A. The family as partner in the treatment of mental illness. *Hospital and Community Psychiatry*, 1979, *30*, 338-340.

Hilton, J. "Home sweet nothing. The plight of sufferers from chronic schizophrenia." Surrey, United Kingdom: National Schizophrenia Fellowship, 1979.

Hirsch, S., & Leff, J. *Abnormalities in Parents of Schizophrenics*. London: Oxford University Press, 1975.

Holden, D., & Lewine, R. Families of schizophrenic individuals: An evaluation of mental health professionals, resources, and the effects of schizophrenia. *Schizophrenia Bulletin*, 1982, *4*, 626-633.

Jacob, T. Family interaction in disturbed and normal families: A methodological and substantive review. *Psychological Bulletin*, 1975, *82*, 33-65.

Jenkins, C. D., Hurst, M. W., & Rose, R. M. Life changes. Do people really remember? *Archives of General Psychiatry*, 1979, *36*, 379-384.

Kalnins, I. V., Churchill, M. P., & Terry, G. E. Concurrent stresses in families with a leukemic child. *Journal of Pediatric Psychology*, 1980, *5*, 81-92.

Kammerer, P. C. An exploratory study of crippled children. *Psychological Record*, 1940, *4*, 47-100.

Klerman, G. Better but not well: Social and ethical issues in the deinstitutionalization of the mentally ill. *Schizophrenia Bulletin*, 1977, *3*, 617-631.

Kohn, M., & Clausen, J. Parental authority behavior and schizophrenia. *American Journal of Orthopsychiatry*, 1956, *26*, 297-313.

Kreisman, D. E., & Joy, V. D. Family response to the mental illness of a relative: A review of the literature. *Schizophrenia Bulletin*, 1974, Issue No. 10, 34-57.

Lamb, H. R., & Oliphant, E. Schizophrenia through the eyes of the families. *Hospital and Community Psychiatry*, 1978, *29*, 803–806.

Leff, J. Schizophrenia and sensitivity to the family environment. *Schizophrenia Bulletin*, 1976, *2*, 566–574.

Leff, J. Personal Communication. April 11, 1980.

Lester, D. *Unusual sexual behavior: The standard deviations*. Springfield, Illinois: Charles C Thomas, 1975.

Lewine, R. Parents of schizophrenic individuals: What we say is what see. *Schizophrenia Bulletin*, 1979, *5*, 433–434.

Lewine, R. A dialogue among patients, families, and professionals—Editor's introduction. *Schizophrenia Bulletin*, 1982, *4*, 603–604.

Lewis, J. M. The family matrix in health and disease. In C. K. Hofling & J. M. Lewis (Eds.), *The family: Evaluation and treatment*. New York: Brunner/Mazel, 1980.

Lidz, T. *The Person*. Revised Edition. New York: Basic Books, 1976. (a)

Lidz, T. Commentary on "A critical review of recent adoption, twin, and family studies of schizophrenia: Behavioral genetics perspective." *Schizophrenia Bulletin*, 1976, *2*, 402–412. (b).

Lidz, T. The family and the development of the individual. In C. K. Hofling & J. M. Lewis (Eds.), *The family: Evaluation and treatment*. New York: Brunner/Mazel, 1980.

Lidz, T., Fleck, S., & Cornelison, A. *Schizophrenia and the family*. New York: International Universities Press, 1965.

Liem, J. H. Family studies of schizophrenia: An update and commentary. *Schizophrenia Bulletin*, 1980, *6*, 429–455.

Lovejoy, M. Expectations and the recovery process. *Schizophrenia Bulletin*, 1982, *4*, 605–609.

Maher, B. *Principles of psychopathology*. New York: McGraw-Hill, 1966.

Mattson, A., & Gross, S. Adaptational and defensive behavior in young hemophiliacs and their parents. *American Journal of Psychiatry*, 1966, *122*, 1349–1356.

Mednick, S., & McNeil, T. Current methodology in research on the etiology of schizophrenia: Serious difficulties which suggest the use of the high-risk group method. *Psychological Bulletin*, 1968, *70*, 681–693.

Meehl, P. E. Specific genetic etiology, psychodynamics, and therapeutic nihilism. In P. E. Meehl (Ed.), *Psychodiagnosis: Selected papers*. New York: Norton, 1973.

Mosher, L., & Keith, S. Psychosocial treatment: Individual, group, family, and community support approaches. *Schizophrenia Bulletin*, 1980, *1*, 10–41.

Murphy, J. M. Psychiatric labeling in cross-cultural perspective. *Science*, 1976, *191*, 1019–1028.

National Institute of Mental Health. Guidelines for Clinical/Services Program. Washington, D. C.: DHEW, July, 1979.

National Schizophrenia Fellowship. Living with schizophrenia—By the relatives. Surrey, United Kingdom: National Schizophrenia Fellowship, 1974.

Olshansky, S. Chronic sorrow. *Social Casework*, 1962, *43*, 191–194.

Orlando, M. J. *The chronic patient as activist: An odyssey in the community mode*. Unpublished manuscript, 1983.

Paul, G., & Lentz, R. *Psychosocial treatment of chronic mental patients: Milieu versus social learning programs*. Cambridge, Mass.: Harvard University Press, 1977.

Peterson, R. *What are the needs of chronic mental patients*. Paper presented at the American Psychiatric Association Conference on the Chronic Mental Patient. Washington, D. C., 11–14 January 1974.

Reiss, D. Pathways to assessing the family: Some choice points and a sample route. In C. K. Hofling & J. M. Lewis (Eds.), *The family: Evaluation and treatment*. New York: Brunner/Mazel, 1980.

Rickels, N. K. *Exhibitionism*. Philadelphia: Lippincott, 1950.

Riskin, J., & Faunce, E. An evaluative review of family interaction research. *Family Process*, 1972, *11*, 365–456.

Rosenbaum, S. Z. Infantile paralysis as a source of emotional problems in children. *Welfare Bulletin*, 1943, *34*, 11–13.

Rosenhan, D. On being sane in insane places. *Science*, 1973, *179*, 250–258.

Sanua, V. D. Familial and sociocultural antecedents of psychopathology. In H. C. Triandis & J. G. Dragons (Eds.), *Handbook of cross-cultural psychology* (Vol. 6). Boston: Allyn & Bacon, 1980.

Sarbin, T., & Mancuso, J. *Schizophrenia: Medical diagnosis or moral verdict?* New York: Pergamon Press, 1980.

Schwartz, C. Perspectives on deviance: Wives' definitions of their husbands' mental illness. *Psychiatry*, 1957, *20*, 275–291.

Schuham, A. I. The double-bind hypothesis a decade later. *Psychological Bulletin*, 1967, *68*, 409–416.

Sheehan, D., & Hackett, T. Psychosomatic disorders. In A. Nicholi (Ed.), *The Harvard guide to modern psychiatry*. Cambridge, Mass.: Belknap Press, 1978.

Spitzer, R. L. On pseudoscience in science, logic in remission, and psychiatric diagnosis: A critique of Rosenhan's "On being sane in insane places." *Journal of Abnormal Psychology*, 1975, *84*, 442–452.

Spitzer, R., & Endicott, J. DIAGNO: A computer program for psychiatric diagnosis utilizing the differential diagnostic procedure. *Archives of General Psychiatry*, 1968, *18*, 746–757.

Szaz, T. *The myth of mental illness*. New York: Dell, 1961.

Thomas, A., & Chess, S. *Temperature and development*. New York: Brunner/Mazel, 1977.

Vaughn, C., & Leff, J. The influence of family and social factors on the course of psychiatric illness. *British Journal of Psychiatry*, 1976, *129*, 125–137.

Wasow, M. For my beloved son David Jonathan: A professional plea. *Health and Social Work*, 1978, *3*, 127–145.

Wynne, L. C., Toohey, M. L., & Doane, J. Family studies. In L. Bellak (Ed.), *Disorders of the schizophrenic syndrome*. New York: Basic Books, 1979.

Wynne, L. C., & Singer, M. T. Thought disorder and family relations of schizophrenics. II. A classification of forms of thinking. *Archives of General Psychiatry*, 1963, *9*, 199–206.

Wing, J., Cooper, J., & Sartorius, N. *The measurement and classification of psychiatric symptoms*. Cambridge: Cambridge University Press, 1975.

Yarrow, M. R., Campbell, J. D., & Burton, R. V. Recollections of childhood: A study of retrospective method. *Monographs of the Society for Research in Child Development*, 1970, *35*, 1–83.

Yarrow, M. R., Schwartz, C. G., Murphy, H. S., & Deasy, L. C. The psychological meaning of mental illness in the family. *Journal of Social Issues*, 1955, *11*, 12–24.

CHAPTER 11

Intervention Research on Families

A Pediatric Perspective

IVAN B. PLESS

This chapter addresses three aspects of the general theme of this volume: The first is the knowledge base from which physicians who care for children operate when intervention is called for; the second is a description of programs of intervention aimed at children with chronic physical disorders; and the third is a brief review of the attempts of others to intervene at a family level within the pediatric context. This discussion is limited to consideration of interventions that are oriented toward the family (or at least toward family members other than the child) and of published studies in which at least some objective data are described. Within these limits one minor but potentially important deviation is allowed: The "pediatric context" is defined as including not only children who are cared for by pediatricians, but also those for whom primary care is provided by family physicians.

In one sense it seems scarcely credible to suggest that *any* physician caring for a child can ignore the family context. Virtually all health care of children is mediated by one or both parents; it is they who present and interpret the child's symptoms to the physician and it is they who execute the therapeutic actions recommended by the physician. Nonetheless, there are amazingly few data that indicate that a family orientation to care is the rule, not the exception. The knowledge most physicians have of a child's family is remarkably limited. The very fact that there are only a handful of systematic studies describing the breadth and depth of that knowledge illustrates how little importance is attached to the family as a diagnostic or therapeutic unit. Outside of medicine there is an extensive literature on family dynamics (e.g., Ackerman, 1958; Foley, 1974; Satir, 1964) which has

IVAN B. PLESS ● McGill-Montreal Children's Hospital Research Institute, 2300 Tupper Street, Montreal, Quebec, Canada H3H 1P3.

been accepted by social workers, psychologists, and others for use in clinical situations in which family therapy seems indicated. In like manner sociologists and anthropologists have repeatedly documented the critical role of key family variables in health and health care (Crawford, 1971). The same is true of much of the work of clinical epidemiologists and others conducting health care investigations (Kaplan & Cassel, 1975). In summary there is no longer any reason to doubt that such factors as maternal and paternal education, social class, marital status of the child's parents, member of siblings, ordinality, religion, ethnicity, work patterns, and the like are each closely related to diagnositc processes or the outcomes of medical care in a wide range of situations (Picken & Ireland, 1969).

Given the large body of apparently useful knowledge about family dynamics that has accumulated over the years, how can it be that so little of it has trickled through into the practice of medicine? It is a paradox that is particularly prominent in the case of pediatrics, where the child is, in most instances, functionally inseparable from the family. The likeliest explanation is a pragmatic one: that in most instances physicians are convinced that they manage well enough without such information, or that only selected parts of the corpus of knowledge about family structure or function are needed. This explanation implies relevant knowledge is used only if and when the physician believes it is warranted. Whether physicians can manage better with this information already at hand in particular instances has yet to be demonstrated.

The Family Knowledge Base

As has been indicated, few reports exist that describe what pediatricians or generalists who care for children know about the families of their patients. Two preliminary studies are summarized which represent a first attempt at documenting this area of knowledge. One study took place in Rochester, N.Y., and the other in Nottingham, England, both in the mid-1970s.

Both studies involved a group of physicians selected from the community. Although the samples were intended to be representative, the need to ensure cooperation makes it likely that some degree of self-selection was present, resulting in a bias toward more cooperative and perhaps more enlightened persons in the sample. In each instance the sample of physicians studied was probably somewhat atypical of their colleagues, in that they were willing to participate in a study of this nature. It seems almost certain that if those studied were different, they were most likely to be more knowledgeable or more enlightened than their peers, rather than the reverse.

Table 1. Family Knowledge Questions (Pediatric Version)

1. Do both parents in this family live at home?
2. What work does the father do?
   If *yes*, does he have work problems?
3. What work does the mother do?
   If *yes*, does she have work problems?
4. If mother works, who takes care of the children?
5. What sort of housing does this family have?
6. Has either parent ever been married before?
7. Are there any other adults living at home?
8. What are the approximate ages of the children in the family?
9. What is the approximate level of education of each parent?
10. Does this family have grandparents, etc., living close by who could help in the care of the family?
11. Does this family have difficulty in coming to your office because of lack of transportation?
12. Does this family now have any stress in problem areas such as marriage, economic, legal, housing, school, etc.?
13. Are there any impediments to medical care such as language, cultural, religious, other?
14. Is there any other piece of information (not asked here) about this family which you feel has been important in your management of this family?

An interviewer met with the physician who was asked to respond, with the help of the patient's record, to a series of questions dealing with the family of the patient selected. These questions are described in Table 1. In general, the questions represent quite elementary and, it is to be hoped, pertinent information which a physician could reasonably be expected to know about all patients seen on a regular basis. They deal with areas of knowledge which are of potential value to the physician, regardless of the specific medical problem presented by the patient. For example, there is good reason for the belief—unproven but based on child development theory—that it is important for a physician to know whether the parents of the child he is treating live together.

In the case of the study in Nottingham, England (Fuchsman & Pless, 1975), the physicians involved had cooperated in a descriptive study of all office visits over a two-month period of the previous year. From this study, patients with problems of a chronic or undifferentiated nature (such as back pain or headache) were selected. This choice was made because in such cases it seems most reasonable to assume that knowledge of the family could be helpful—either by providing clues to the underlying diagnosis or in facilitating compliance with therapy.

With respect to the diagnostic process it is likely, for example, that a physician who has previous knowledge of marital difficulties might readily consider stress as the cause of a complaint of "headache." Similarly, knowing that the head of the household is a manual laborer who frequently complains of back pain should facilitate the diagnosis of a similar symptom in a child as being "imitative" or "attention-seeking." Or, in regard to compliance with treatment, the physician who takes account of the adequacy of day-care arrangement for a preschool child requiring a course of antibiotics would use such information in determining the method of drug administration; for example, an injectable preparation might be used rather than one that has to be given four-hourly for a week or ten days. Thus it was reasonable to hypothesize that a direct relationship could exist between the level of the physician's knowledge of the child care arrangements or family situation and the rapidity with which a satisfactory diagnosis could be made and a satisfactory treatment program instituted.

In the study in Rochester, N.Y. (Vance & Pless, 1975), only pediatricians were involved. The specific nature of the child's health problems were not used as a basis for selection of the families. Instead, all patients seen in the previous week were eligible for inclusion in the study sample regardless of the reason for the child's visit. In other words, the sample was not influenced by the nature of the child's complaint or illness. The questions were the same as those in Nottingham (see Table 1); they could be answered either from memory or by reference to the patient's record. The accuracy of the response was not important. Rather we sought to determine the frequency with which the physician was willing to admit that he simply *did not know* or *could not even guess* at the information being sought.

The results for Nottingham appear in Table 2. It shows the number of questions answered "Don't Know" by each of the 14 doctors studied. The variations in levels of knowledge for each group of patients belonging to a

Table 2. Family Knowledge Profile (Nottingham): Ignorance Scores

Doctor number	Number patients	Mean score	Range
1	5	7.8	0–11
2	9	2.2	0–4
3	8	1.7	0–8
4	8	2.8	0–8
5	9	8.3	1–16
6	6	2.3	0–4
7	11	1.7	0–4
8	9	1.7	0–5
9	10	5.2	0–11
10	7	2.1	0–6
11	10	1.1	0–3
12	12	0.8	0–5
13	9	0.9	0–4
14	6	0.8	0–1

Table 3. Family Knowledge Profile (Nottingham):
Specific Questions by Percentage Not Known and Assessment of Importance[a]

| Question | Importance | | |
	Percentage not known	Mean score	Range
Previous marriages	34	3.5	(2-5)
Husband's occupation	29	3.0	(1-4)
Work problems	29	2.0	(1-4)
Wife's occupation	25	2.5	(1-3)
Work problems	7	3.0	(2-5)
Husband's education	13	2.7	(1-5)
Wife's education	18	2.7	(1-5)
Number of children	24	2.9	(2-4)
Parent's marital status	10	2.4	(1-5)
Other adults in home	14	3.1	(2-5)
Relatives or friends nearby	27	2.2	(1-4)
Care for child	3	2.9	(2-4)
Family under stress	9	1.6	(1-5)
Language and cultural barriers	2	2.3	(1-5)
Transportation difficulties	3	2.9	(1-5)

[a] Importance ratings assigned by 8 lectures in family medicine: 1 = important to 5 = unimportant.

particular physician was as great (if not greater) than the variations between physicians. In other words, the mean "ignorance" score for physician number one is 7.8 (ranging from 0 to 11 for the 5 patients selected), whereas for physicians numbers 12 and 13, the mean scores are 0.8 and 0.9 (ranges 0 to 4 or 5) for 12 and 9 patients respectively. These figures suggest that there are some patients whose families the physician knows extremely well, but the families of others they do not know at all. There are also, however, less striking but potentially important differences among physicians.

The specific items in which the level of ignorance was greatest are highlighted in Table 3. Also shown in this table are the mean and range of "importance scores" assigned to each item by a panel of eight faculty members from the Department of General Practice in Nottingham. These scores reflect the lack of consensus or even reasonable agreement on the part of the faculty panel about the relevance of each of the questions. Thus, although the questions seem well-founded in theory they are not necessarily so viewed by faculty in this clinical discipline, or at least not all are seen as equally important or relevant to the future general practitioner. A value of one is "very important"; five is "very unimportant."

Regarding more than one-quarter of the families, the physicians were ignorant of such background matters as previous marriages, occupation of the parent(s), number of children in the family, or the availability of relatives for child care. However, the total ignorance score was not found to be related significantly to either the number of tests of referrals needed to make a diagnosis, nor the amount of time until the symptoms had reportedly resolved.

As Table 4 shows, the relationship may, paradoxically, be reversed; that is, the more the physician knows about a family the less efficient the process of diagnosis and the slower the recovery time. This result, if confirmed by further data, is an intriguing one. Although it seems unlikely on the face of it that the more knowledge a physician has the less he is able to help the patient, it is conceivable that this is true. For example, it is possible that with more knowledge it is more difficult to make decisions to act on the patient's behalf.

Although these results may suggest that there is little reason to pursue the question of whether such knowledge is relevant or useful clinically, it nevertheless seems premature to draw this conclusion. The literature in family medicine contains little on this subject, and when these findings have been discussed with colleagues in Family Medicine the reaction was one of surprise and bewilderment. Few teachers in this "specialty" seriously doubt these figures. The only conclusion to be drawn is that family physicians either have reservations about the value of this information, or they assume that whenever the occasion warrants it the information will be obtained; that is, they feel that there is little point in seeking it routinely.

Thus it is entirely possible that physicians in practice are aware of the potential value of family information but are simply being cautious about when and how it is obtained. Clearly the issue is one of perceived relevance. However, as has been stated previously and will be elaborated later, there are equally sound reasons for believing that even after the fact—that is, following a point when the information should be highly relevant to patient management—it is not obtained.

Table 4. Relation of Family Knowledge to Diagnosis and Recovery Time

	Ignorance score		
Diagnostic tests	Low (0–1)	Med (2–4)	High (5+)
None	38 (63%)	19 (63%)	16 (84%)
One or more	22 (37%)	11 (37%)	3 (16%)
Total	60 (100%)	30 (100%)	19 (100%)
Time to recovery			
Less than 2 weeks	25 (42%)	13 (46%)	11 (68%)
2 weeks or more	34 (58%)	15 (54%)	5 (32%)
Total[a]	59 (100%)	28 (100%)	16 (100%)

[a] Total is less than 119 since 16 were reported as "not known."

A Family Functioning Index

The discussion so far applies directly to the realm of family "structure" as opposed to "functioning." The latter is an area equally devoid of a solid base of empirical data, although there are numerous theories of potential interest. These theories arise from several disciplines within the social and behavioral sciences and—much less frequently, and much more belatedly—from the small fraternity of academicians within the ranks of family medicine or pediatrics.

The distinction between family functioning and family structure is an important one. *Family structure*, as I view it, includes information pertaining to the fundamental composition of the family unit. It deals with such questions as "Is this a single parent unit or are both parents present?"; "Are there children, and if so, how many and what are their ages?"; "Is the family nuclear or extended?" By *family functioning* I mean how family members relate to one another; how they interact; how they share responsibilities; the quality of their relationships, and so forth. Structure is a static statement, dealing essentially with composition; functioning is a dynamic expression of how the unit operates.

The importance of this distinction arose at a time when we were planning a project, one goal of which was to determine the extent to which family factors were predictive of the risk of maladjustment among a sample of children with a variety of chronic physical disorders. Assessing structural factors define along the above lines appeared to be straight-forward. The assessment of functioning was quite another matter. A careful review of all the measures inventoried by Strauss in 1969—at the time the most comprehensive compendium of family measures available—failed to reveal any that appeared suitable for our purposes. Objections to the measures listed were both practical and conceptual. At a practical level we needed something with reasonable reliability and validity that could be used in a field setting with a representative sample of parent respondents. Conceptually we sought an assessment tool that would tap the same sort of dimensions of functioning which enable a sensitive clinician to decide that one family is more "at risk" than another. Precisely what information physicians actually use to make such judgments (if indeed they do so at all) is, however, entirely unknown. It is likely that they act intuitively, using bits and pieces and clues gleaned subtly during the course of many patient visits. It is possible that under some special circumstances, such as those being addressed in the proposed study of children with chronic physical illness, some physicians may go about trying to obtain some information about the family in a more deliberate or systematic fashion. However, there are no suggestions in the literature that this occurs, or if it does, how often, or what it is that the physician seeks to learn or how the information is used.

There is also no reason to think that physicians in Strauss's time were using any of the measures he listed. Nor should this be in the least surprising, since very few appear to have been intended to serve these clinical objectives. Few, in fact, actually seemed to deal with the construct of family functioning as it has been defined here. Instead, the more than 300 family measurement techniques described are dominated by out-dated examples of attempts to predict marital stability or family harmony. Such measures include, for example, Jansen's Family Solidarity Scales, Adam's Marriage Adjustment Prediction Index, and the Burgess-Cottrell Marital Adjustment form. Perhaps the most potentially relevant of the measures was Anthony and Bene's Family Relations Test, but this deals primarily with the child's feelings toward each member of the family and in any case was not suitable for field settings. At another level several of the measures described by Blood and his colleagues, such as the Division of Labor Index, were also pertinent and ultimately influenced the construction of the new index.

Thus for several reasons it became clear that a void existed in the area of family functioning assessment, and, accordingly, we devised a new measure, the Family Functioning Index (FFI). The FFI comprises 15 questions covering such areas as communication, closeness, and marital satisfaction. Using a simple scoring procedure, we compiled a total index score and took steps to determine its reliability and validity. Test–retest reliability was established on a sub-sample of 30 families studied over a five year period. The Pearson product moment correlation between the original and retest FFI total scores was 0.83 ($p < .001$). The correlation for 8 families who had received therapy over the 5 years was 0.76. The correlation between the husband's FFI score and that of the social worker was significant ($r = 0.48$, $p < 0.01$). Further evidence of validity was obtained by comparing the mean FFI scores for 43 families who had sought and were receiving counselling from these Family Service Association social workers. This mean score, representing a group of families who perceived themselves as functioning sufficiently poorly so that they obtained professional help, was compared with that obtained from the random sample of 356 families who served as healthy controls in the chronic disease study. The values were 19.1 (SD = 6.5) and 24.5 (SD = 4.9) respectively ($t = 7.7$, $p < 0.001$).

The FFI, simple as it is, filled an important void in the area of family research. That void, as stated previously, is for a reliable, valid, inexpensive measure of functioning that conceptually taps the dynamics of family life relationships. In this respect, the term family functioning is used as synonymous with family dynamics, although properly speaking the latter represents a broader, more complex construct. It is important that the measure's limitations be appreciated; if used properly it serves as a useful screening tool, or perhaps as a covariate. It is not likely to be useful as an outcome measure in evaluation studies because it is not sufficiently sensitive to detect changes resulting from an intervention or the occurrence of an untoward event. Nonetheless, it has been popular among investigators who have tried to use it as a dependent variable in evaluation research.

Although the Family Functioning Index is a useful research tool in certain situations, it has not found its way into clinical practice, nor is it likely to do so. This fact may reflect perceived limitations of the measure, but it is consistent with the apparent lack of interest on the part of physicians to attend to family functioning factors.

The latter explanation seems to be the most plausible one, explaining why physicians fail to use formal assessment tools to supplement their intuitions in this area of clinical medicine. Other measures are available which attempt to assess similar family life characteristics; these are not used. Thus, it is unlikely that the lack of interest in family assessment applies only to the FFI. One other measure deals with family disorganization: It is intended for use by social workers based on their critical observations (Geismar, LaSorte, & Ayres, 1962), and it is a crude method for evaluating reasonably intact families. Another approach is directly intended for use by physicians: the Family APGAR (Smilkstein, 1978). However, there is little indication that it has been adopted widely, if at all.

Virtually no other assessment procedures currently in use conceptualize family functioning in ways—such as those discussed previously—and are also reasonably easy to use in clinical settings. All of the measures tend to be biased toward middle-class values and assumptions; they are also time consuming. The former objection may also be applied to the FFI; for example, the scoring is such that it is of limited value when assessing single parent families or those without children.

These statements are made based on a mixture of an idealized and a realistic construction of the physician's role. On the one hand, if that role is seen in a predominantly mechanistic, technical light, then it is certainly reasonable to argue that the physician needs little if any information about the family, or for that matter about the patient as a person, regardless of the type of problem the patient presents. On the other hand, if the role is seen to be even marginally broader—one in which psychosocial issues facilitate the execution of technical acts involving diagnosis and treatment—then family knowledge becomes more pertinent. In the case of the truly comprehensive role, in which the lines between "psyche" and "soma" are indistinguishable, this knowledge, and much more, should always be relevant and useful. Thus, depending on which model one applies most generally—or which model one would like to foster—it can be agreed that in the routine examination of a healthy child the pediatrician needs no knowledge of family dynamics whatsoever (or very little), or that he needs a great deal. As has been stated, it is my contention that in the case of most illnesses, especially those that are chronic, some knowledge of the family is essential. But what, precisely, that knowledge should consist of, and how it can be proven that it is useful, is unknown. Much depends on how the physician sees his role and what assumptions he makes about how family dynamics affect the child's development, care, and well-being.

Family-Focused Interventions by Physicians

This somewhat pessimistic appraisal of the state of knowledge at the clinical level is highly pertinent to the basic theme of this volume. It seems quite unlikely that anything remotely approximating "family intervention," however broadly this may be construed, can be executed effectively without reasonably comprehensive prior knowledge of the family. It can be argued that at least in the case of pediatrics, the care of an essentially healthy child, or a child with an acute episodic illness, may benefit little from such knowledge. However, in the case of children with emotional problems, school difficulties, or a chronic physical disorder, it is inconceivable that the physician can be effective without knowledge of the family, at least at the level described.

There is still a remarkable lack of information from systematic studies of physicians' treatment of children with emotional or school problems. Some studies do suggest, however, that far fewer of these children are seen in office practices than actually exist in the general population. By contrast, in recent years a considerable body of knowledge has emerged dealing with the care of children with chronic physical disorders (Pless & Pinkerton, 1975). Most of the care of these children rests with disease sub-specialists who are almost invariably based in hospitals where support staff, such as social workers, are called on to obtain whatever family information seems pertinent. Regardless of who provides the main body of medical care for these children, there is much evidence suggesting that emotional problems are a frequent consequence of the underlying physical disorder. What was not known prior to 1965, however, was the extent to which the type of disorder or its duration or severity was related to these emotional problems; nor was it known whether the family contributed to their occurrence to any significant extent. Accordingly in 1965 a broad-based series of studies was initiated in Rochester, N.Y., in which one specific theme was the role of the family in the genesis of psychological problems consequent to the under-lying illness (Pless, Roghmann, & Haggerty, 1972). The main study in-volved a random sample of the total population of school-age children in Monroe County. From this sample, 200 children with a variety of chronic disorders were identified, as well as a comparison group of about 100 healthy children. Psychosocial functioning was assessed, using a battery of self measures, peer assessment, teacher ratings, and parent ratings. An overall adjustment index (or, more properly, a "maladjustment" index) was derived from these measures. Although sick children as a group were similar to the healthy controls with respect to all major social and demo-graphic characteristics (including FFI scores), they differed markedly with regard to the frequency of maladjustment. Among the sick children aged 6-11 years, 33% were judged to be maladjusted, compared with only 18% of the healthy controls. However, the results were also related, as hypothesized, to lower levels of family functioning as assessed by the Index constructed for this purpose. Neither the type, duration, nor the severity of the illness were equally related to the child's development (Pless & Satterwhite, 1975).

The design of the study was cross-sectional; that is, it was a prevalence study, not one conducted prospectively. Although the relationship between physical and emotional illness is strong and statistically significant ($p < .05$), it cannot be proven from such a research design that the illness was "caused by" the former, although this is by far the most plausible interpretation. The conclusions were interpreted cautiously. It was felt that further evidence was needed to support the basic hypothesis. In particular, the results prompted a closer look at the role of changes in self-concept, which, influenced by the literature of the time, we believed to be central to the sequence of events leading to maladjustment. To do this a family intervention based on this premise of changing self-concept was successful, it would provide further evidence of the importance of self-concept and the mediating role of the family.

Intervention by Family Counsellors

A group of six nonprofessional women was carefully selected to serve as counsellors to these families. The original cohort of counsellors (the program was repeated for 5 years) was selected following an interview with the project director. At this interview an essay was written by each of the applicants; this essay was used as one basis for selection. The process of selection was intuitive: We sought women who were self-confident, imaginative, aggressive in a positive sense, adventurous, and intelligent. Later, when it became clear that we had chosen wisely, we asked the counsellors to complete the 16 Personality Factor Scale. The results suggested that the group was indeed different from a normative population, with respect to the extent of their display of the following characteristics: intelligence, emotional stability, assertiveness, placidity, venturesomeness, and being more experimenting. So in future years the 16 Personality Factor Scale became a part of the selection procedure.

A counselor was assigned to work for a period of one year with eight families, each with a child with a chronic physical disorder. These families were selected by a random process after stratification into those with high and low family functioning scores. By the same method a comparable group of control families was also selected after stratifying for family functioning. The groups appeared to be similar with respect to the spectrum of the children's illnesses, social status, etc. The experiment proceeded with the counsellors providing intervention aimed at strengthening the child's self-concept through a focus on the child's positive attributes together with deliberate attempts to de-emphasize the illness. This de-emphasis was accomplished by the counsellors' acknowledging the illness as such at the outset and making it clear that they were in the home to help the child deal with the illness. Thereafter, however, unless specific questions or problems that were unavoidably illness-related arose, the counsellor would deliberately avoid such questions as "How are you feeling?" and "What did the doctor say (or do)?" Instead, as stated, the relationship with the child was built around what the child could do well or would like to do well and by the counsellors' helping the child to do so with appropriate reinforcement and praise. With the parents, the illness provided the necessary entree, and in many cases it remained the focus of the relationship with the counsellor. In other cases, however, the illness was quickly supplanted by other issues that affected the illness and the care provided for it by the parent in an indirect manner only.

An important aim of this intervention was to provide support for the mother and the family as a whole. This aim was accomplished through attempts to modify other stressful elements placed on the family which might interfere with their ability to provide the sick child with the emotional support needed. Some excerpts from one of the routinely kept logs illustrates the counsellor's perception of the range of services provided: "Problems for the month include making school arrangements for L. in the Fall; getting parents to keep appointments at the Family Service Agency and dealing with concerns about the oldest sister's delinquent behavior." Among the actions taken were "sending letter of referral to specialist for treatment of mother's arthritis; talking to the new family social worker; encouraging the patient, L., to return to school for a full day after a period of being confined to home."

In a later entry for the same child, who was afflicted with juvenile rheumatoid arthritis, the notes reveal the family counsellor's attempts to deal with the child's emotional withdrawal through a focus on her artistic talents. Arrangements were made to have her art work assessed. At a more practical level the counsellor also facilitated a meeting between parents and surgeon to discuss possible treatment. It becomes clear that the counsellor had begun to serve as a key link between the child, the family doctors, and the school: "L. is talking quite freely to me now, about herself and her concern for her parents' relationship."

The program was evaluated in several ways. Interviews were conducted by someone other than the counsellor with the parents and physicians involved to determine their satisfaction (or disappointment) with the services provided and their desire to continue to receive these services, and to elucidate specific examples of how the counsellor had been helpful. Where the responses were favorable (and in almost all instances they were), parents were asked if they would be willing to pay for the counsellor's help if need be, and if so, how much. This crucial test was quite convincing evidence of the high value placed on the program by most parents.

However, the most pertinent assessment comes from the measurement of psychological functioning, since this measurement provided the *raison d'etre* for the program in the first place. Thus a battery of measures selected from among those used when the population was assessed originally (specifically, the California Test of Personality, the Piers Harris Self-Concept Measure, and the Children's Manifest Anxiety Scale) were all repeated at the end of the study year, administered by interviewers who were blinded as to the child's status in the program; that is, whether they were part of the experimental or the control group. The actual differences in the scores found were as follows:

> Of the 56 children in the counseled group, 33 (60%) showed improvement in psychological status, compared with only 17 (41%) of 42 controls who were not counseled. Conversely, only 33% of the study children showed a worsening in scores, compared with 52% of the controls. These results are statistically significant ($p < .05$). Thus the counselors' efforts appear to have had a measurable effect on the psychological well-being of the children themselves, in spite of the relatively small amount of attention paid to them. (Pless & Satterwhite, 1975, p. 297)

Evaluation also involved systematic interviews with the parents and doctors by persons not associated with the program. The results indicate widespread satisfaction with the services provided. Interestingly, the parents generally judged the services provided for themselves to be more helpful than those provided for the child. Nonetheless the enthusiasm for this form of intervention is indicated by a willingness by parents to pay for such services in the future if this were necessary. Unfortunately the doctors' enthusiasm did not extend this far; few of them indicated that they were prepared to pay counsellors either directly or through adjusted fees.

Equally as important as the scientific evaluation is the conviction by all involved that this program was well conceived and filled a genuine need. Proof of this lies in the fact that the program has continued, in hospital-based specialty clinics, for the 9 years since its initiation. Most specialists who have had experience with these family counsellors have come to depend heavily on them. The counselling apparently makes the care provided by the doctor much more satisfying.

Since the initial report describing this program, a number of similar projects have been developed in other parts of the country. None, however, focuses on children with chronic illnesses, although most emphasize the use of nonprofessional persons working in the home as the most effective method for offering intervention at the level of the family. Two examples in particular are relevant. The first deals with families judged to be at increased risk for child abuse or neglect—a project being conducted in Colorado (Dawson, 1980). The second is one of several which attempt to modify various problems that occur in early childhood (e.g., accidents) by counselling given by public health nurses or nonprofessionals to low-income mothers during and after pregnancy. The results suggest that for those babies whose mothers received the counselling during pregnancy, there was a significant reduction in the number of accidents as well as some improvement in utilization of preventive services. Encouraging as these findings may be, it should be noted that the trends are found only up to the age of 12 months and tend to diminish later. Nonetheless, there is growing evidence that this type of home-based intervention may have an important influence on some aspects of child development, if it is offered at as yet unspecified "critical" periods (Larson, 1980).

Impact on Families

It is generally accepted that in cases of children with chronic illnesses, knowledge of the level of family functioning may be a useful predictor of the probability that the child's psychological adjustment will be adversely affected by the disease. In this paradigm the family is viewed as a causal factor—albeit by no means the only one—in the sequence leading to maladjustment. The other side of the coin provides another example, whereby families may be changed, or may need help because they have been changed, when they have a child with a chronic condition. This example is based on a paradigm which suggests that the child's illness has a significant impact on the family, and that this impact may cause changes in the family's structure or functioning.

Results from the Rochester surveys (Pless & Satterwhite, 1975) provide relatively little evidence that the structure of the family unit (or indeed its functioning, as measured by the scores on the Index described previously) is significantly affected by the severity of the child's disability. That is to say, the effects of the disorder on the family as reported by this sample of parents are by no means as severe (e.g., divorce, acting out, etc.) as many previous reports had suggested (Pless & Pinkerton, 1975, pp. 163–167). The structure of the family unit was not affected, as would be the case if, for example, the disorder had lead to divorce or had influenced a sibling to leave the home. Nor were any more subtle effects reflected in the FFI scores, although it seems certain that in many cases such effects were, in fact, present. This lack may reflect the insensitivity of the measure, or it may be a function of the relative stability of family functioning. More importantly, it may also indicate that the impact on the family is much less than is generally assumed or that such impact is not a direct reflection of severity. There is an extensive literature dealing with the impact on family of chronic childhood disorders of varying kinds (Pless & Pinkerton, 1975).

Unfortunately many of the earlier studies in this regard dealt with severe mental retardation (e.g., Farber, 1959), and many more recent studies either failed to use adequate comparison groups or used measures of impact of doubtful validity. Thus, as has been stated, most earlier studies concluded that the presence of a handicapped child in the family resulted in a wide range of often devastating burdens, involving both structure and functioning of the family unit. Whether further research will prove these findings correct—or, if correct, whether they apply equally across the wide range of handicapping conditions—is debatable. It is probable that they will not confirm earlier impressions, but rather that they will yield a more balanced view. The general conclusion may well be that some families are actually benefited by the presence of a handicapped child while others are, for a time at least, quite decidedly stressed.

The most important inadequacy of most recent research on family impact is the absence of suitable comparison groups. However, even if adequate controls are used, it is extremely difficult to obtain appropriate and unbiased responses to the usual sort of questions asked from both subject and comparison groups. The pertinent areas usually examined in most studies include the emotional effects on parents and siblings, marital stress, finances, and disruption in daily routine. Although the respondents themselves may not do so, investigators tend to attribute all such problems to the child's illness; in the absence of appropriate controls, however, this is a tenuous conclusion.

Results from the Isle of Wight Surveys (Rutter, Tizard, & Whitmore, 1970) suggest that by comparison with matched families in which all children are reportedly healthy, those who have children with a chronic disorder do indeed have more difficulties of various kinds. Particularly noteworthy is the increased frequency of ill health among parents. Nonetheless, because these studies are cross-sectional, it cannot be determined if this ill health reflects the stress generated by the child's illness, if it is merely a coincidence, if it represents a common hereditary predisposition, or even, conceivably, if it is an etiologic factor in the illness itself.

The difficulties in drawing firm conclusions about causal connections attributed to cross-sectional studies should not be interpreted as implying that such studies are of no value. On the contrary, they have been of enormous help in suggesting relationships and their strengths, and in many instances, if proper attention is paid to the critical issue of appropriate controls, reasonable conclusions about the sequence of events can be drawn. This is especially true when logic makes accepting alternative hypotheses about the sequence relationships in time highly improbable. Although again it is difficult to sort out cause and effect, it is also difficult to accept the argument that the major chronic disorders of childhood are of psychosomatic origin. Some of the work in Britain on asthma, most popularly presumed to be a psychosomatic disorder, provides little support for this argument (Graham, Rutter, Yule, & Pless, 1967). It must be appreciated first that the genetic basis of many conditions is well established, and second that many others begin at birth. These facts speak strongly against the alternative hypothesis: that emotional problems lead to physical disorders. Nonetheless, the only ideal way in which the questions about impact on the family can be answered definitively is to enroll large populations, preferably from birth, and follow them longitudinally until such time as a substantial number of children develop the illnesses in question. Some results of this kind may be expected from several of the major longitudinal cohort studies that have been conducted in Britain.

A Rochester study which questioned families of children with nephrosis attempted to correct some shortcomings in design by asking the same questions of families with healthy children (Vance, Fazen, Satterwhite, & Pless, 1980). The problem is that if one asks a question in relation to the illness, the form of the question is likely to be leading; if one does not mention the illness, genuine problems to which the family has adapted may be overlooked. Thus special efforts were made to overcome this difficulty: Identical questions were asked initially, and they were followed by appropriate disease-related probes when indicated. None-theless, the results fail to support popular impressions, because even when the two forms of answers were combined, the differences between the families—those with a sick child and those without—were much smaller than what has usually been reported.

Investigators in New York (Stein & Riessman, 1980), studying a heterogeneous population of children with chronic disorders, have developed an "Impact on Family Scale" which has become highly popular in studies of this type. A factor analysis of responses to the 24 items used suggests the existence of four principal dimensions, termed by the authors "financial," "familial/social," "personal strain," and "mastery."

The development of scales such as this, together with a greater appreciation of the importance of suitable controls, has resulted in some progress in this area. It is clear that there are individual differences in how families cope with chronic illness of a child—some families are much more affected than others. As stated earlier, severity of the illness is not a key determinant of this coping ability.

Discussion

The importance of research of this kind in the context of this volume is clear only if certain assumptions are accepted about the role (passive or active) of medicine in general, and pediatricians in particular, in relation to "changing families." If, for example, it is argued that the presence of a chronic illness often serves to change families by virtue of the way in which it modifies relationships and the daily lives of individual family members, then surely this is of relevance to the practitioner caring for the child or any other member of the family. Under such circumstances the impact on the lives of all who are affected must be lessened, for example, through an intervention such as the family counsellor program. It follows that for practical as well as theoretical reasons it is desirable to find some method to identify families at greatest risk. The results thus far support the view that basic knowledge of the family, together with certain clinical information about the child, provides a reasonable first approximation for the assessment of risk in this regard.

In this chapter I have tried to show that in the case of children with chronic disorders, there is both a need and an opportunity for someone to intervene at the family level. The *need* is based on data which suggest that the child's psychosocial adjustment is often adversely affected by a chronic illness and that the family's equilibrium may likewise be affected. Although neither of these findings is conclusive, those attributed to the Rochester studies are, for the most part, supported by a reasonably extensive body of work which reaches the same basic conclusions: that children with chronic disorders, as a whole, do have an increased risk of emotional problems and that their families likewise are often, although not invariably, affected adversely. Thus, taking both findings together, a strong case can be made for intervention aimed at the child and the family. The experience with the counsellors suggests that such home-based efforts appear to be successful within certain broad limits. The question remains whether the same approach can be equally effective for other difficulties, such as emotional disorders or school problems.

The opportunity arises from an appreciation of the key role played by physicians in the lives of children with a range of difficulties, especially those with physical disorders. The actual problems being addressed may well be those for which the pediatrician is much less qualified than many other professionals, but the reality remains that, rightly or wrongly, the illness places the first line of responsibility squarely with the physician. It is he (or she) to whom parents are most likely to turn with problems that seem in any way related to an underlying medical condition. Whether they are equally likely to do so for non-medical problems such as school difficulties or behavior problems is less clear. It is not that parents are convinced that physicians hold all the answers; it is simply that the access routes to other professionals are less clearly understood. Thus in many such instances the pediatrician serves as a traffic cop, by directing persons needing help to the appropriate services. It should be further appreciated that medical personnel offering primary care to children are inclined to spend less time and energy on therapeutic services than they do on services involving the diagnostic process. This is especially true for time-consuming, poorly remunerated interventions such as counselling.

It is therefore noteworthy that a comparison of the figures shown in Tables 3 and 5 suggest that economic factors *and* training may both play a role in influencing the level of fa.nily knowledge possessed by a physician. The American physicians were, on the whole, more often ignorant of family matters than their English counterparts. Such comparisons are open to criticism, especially in view of the fact that it is not just the presence or absence of comprehensive health insurance that distinguishes between physicians in these countries. Nonetheless, it does seem reasonable to hypothesize that economic factors determine to a considerable extent the amount and quality of information about families which a physician obtains. In view of the time that is required to acquire this information in a form that can be useful in guiding the actions of the physician, this is hardly surprising.

A comparison of the figures for general practitioners (GP) versus pediatricians (Table 5) suggests that the latter are generally more ignorant with respect to a number of key items regarding the family than are the GP's. This in turn may reflect on the respective training programs, or on

Table 5. Family Knowledge Profile (Rochester): Pediatricians & General Practitioners

Question	General practitioner (n = 48)	Pediatrician (n = 77)	Total
Previous marriages	36%[a]	30%	32%
Husband's occupation	23	32	29
Work problems	17	34	29
Wife's occupation	18 [a]	10	13
Work problems	24	21	45
Work pattern	39	40	40
Husband's education	35	33	34
Wife's education	21	26 [a]	24
Other adults in home	17	30 [a]	25
Relatives/friends nearby	33	49 [a]	43
Care for child	55	50	50
Family under stress	2	14 [a]	10
Language or cultural barriers	2	4	3
Transport difficulties	2	5	4
Marital closeness	6	12 [a]	17
Family functioning	18 [a]	11	13

[a] Percentage not known.

the simple reality that whereas 56% of the GP's reported caring for all members of the family, pediatricians treat only children.

It must be remembered that in both studies the respondent physicians were able to guess rather than admit that they "did not know"—hence the differences may also reflect the greater truthfulness of one group as opposed to the other, rather than their actual ignorance. However, it seems much more probable that although the figures obtained underestimate the level of ignorance by a considerable margin, the inaccuracies are not biased systematically. Thus, although one-third of the sample of American physicians confessed ignorance of the educational level of the head of the household (and apparently had no written record of it), it seems very likely that the true figure is much higher. Further, it is likely that those who do claim to have some idea about the level of education, for example, few have accurate information.

In spite of these generally negative findings, it should be emphasized that much lip-service is still paid to a "family orientation" in training programs for both general practice (family medicine) and pediatrics. Almost every basic textbook in these specialties contains a section on or numerous allusions to the need for maintaining an appreciation of the family context of the patient. In pediatrics, there is a large body of scientific literature which dwells on parental influence on child development. Interestingly, there have been few attempts either to build on this solid base or to expand on it, so that the student gains an awareness of the fact that there is more to child development than simple mother–child interactions. There is little evidence of the same rigorous approach being applied at the level of the family as a whole. More importantly still, there is little literature dealing with interventions that are clinically applicable, to either child development or behavioral problems. Even the more numerous publications—theoretical, empirical, but rarely experimental—which offer guidance on the use of intervention to help a physically ill child, are equally limited when it comes to truly practical application.

The emphasis on the term *clinically applicable* warrants further elaboration. What it refers to are those techniques of intervention that can be applied by the busy physician in a real-life office setting. Even in more artificial settings the evidence of success in applying theoretical concepts about family intervention is somewhat limited. For example, Minuchin and his colleagues (Minuchin, Baker, Rosman, Milman, & Todd, 1975) have, for some time now been using family therapy strategies in a specialized setting, the Philadelphia Child Guidance Clinic. Their main focus is on children with so-called psychosomatic conditions, among which they list anorexia nervosa, "brittle" diabetes, and asthma. Although some (perhaps many) would quarrel with the assumption that these conditions share common psychosomatic etiologic mechanisms, the main issue is the effectiveness of their model and its ultimate adaptability to the practice setting.

The orientation of the Philadelphia group is a structural one: an open systems or multiple feed-back model. Early claims to a success rate of "over 80%" in disorders like anorexia nervosa, using a short-term approach in an attempt to change the organization of a family, seemed to be appealing to mechanistically inclined physicians. In a recent description, Minuchin *et al.* (1975) postulate that three factors are necessary for the "development and maintenance of severe psychosomatic problems." These are: physiological vulnerability of the child; families with certain transactional character-istics (enmeshment, overprotectiveness, rigidity, and lack of conflict resolution); and the specific role played by the sick child in conflict avoidance.

The authors emphasize the importance of arriving at an explicit differentiation of "symptom choice, the perpetuating event, and the maintenance of the symptom." Through a focus on the family component in each of these stages, relatively rapid and impressive results are described. For example, of the 13 cases of super-labile diabetes treated in this manner, good results were obtained after 2 to 15 months of therapy involving all family members. Seven of 9 cases of intractable asthma improved markedly after 6–22 months of therapy, and the same general results were found among the 25 anorectic patients who received therapy involving both in-patient treatment of the child and family therapy, over periods ranging from 4-12 months. Impressive as these results may seem, it must be remembered that the effectiveness of this approach has never, to my knowledge, been proven using conventional scientific methods. Equally important, there is nothing to indicate that the approach described has proven feasible in a practice setting.

A more recent contribution with a similar orientation is a text by Allmond, Buckman, and Gofman, *The Family is the Patient* (1979). The authors' orientation is a synthesis of the structural views of Minuchin *et al.* (1975), the problem-solving approach of Haley (1976), the communication model of Satir (1964), along with Gestalt therapy. Each of these is carefully described at both theoretical and applied levels and is well elaborated with case illustrations. In short, the book is designed to clarify the "hows" of family therapy—"how to gather. . . diagnostic family information, how to use it, and how to facilitate a change in a family's behavior" (Allmond *et al.*, 1979, p. 20).

The book's subtitle is *An Approach to Behavioral Pediatrics for the Clinician.* Hence it is reasonable to seek in it a realistic appreciation of the physician's main dilemma: time versus money. Only one section—a very brief one—addresses this issue squarely. The authors acknowledge that their ideas cannot be compressed into a brief visit. They argue for setting aside "well-protected" blocks of time—usually an hour—for such sessions, and that these be paid for appropriately. "The physician is entitled, and indeed has a responsibility to himself and his staff, to charge for his time, which may mean the equivalent of a bill for four 15-minute appointments." Full marks are due the authors for clearly confronting this most real of all barriers to the implementation of family therapy.

The book's keynote is sounded in the *Foreword* by Haggerty: "Clearly family therapy is not for every pediatrician." This text will help those who are on the fence decide whether they want to obtain the training to do it well. Doing it well requires not only training under supervision but also considerable experience and skill. We still do not have carefully controlled studies which demonstrate which patients are most likely to be helped or how the long-term effects of such therapy compare with other methods of treatment. However, there is so much validity to the cases presented that most readers will be convinced that the methods and results ring true. For pediatricians who recognize that the family is the patient, this book will be a guide to an exciting new diagnostic and therapeutic skill.

The absence of quantitative data about effectiveness, even at the superficial level offered by Minuchin *et al.*, is indeed disappointing. But I agree with Haggerty—the book does ring true, and it provides a clear path to follow for those who wish to. It remains to be seen how many physicians will choose to move in this direction.

A broader, more unusual viewpoint relating the family to the health of children is offered by Pratt (1976), who suggests that the "energized family" is the structural form which is most effective in determining the family's use of health services, their health care practices, and the general health of family members. Pratt's approach derives from sociologic theories about social systems and accordingly places heavy emphasis on interaction both within the family and beyond it.

Of particular interest is Pratt's idea that if physicians were able to identify "non-energized families" (i.e., those who lack the tendency to provide freedom to support or respond to rather than to restrict or block their members efforts to cope and function fully"), the doctor would have an early warning system predictive of certain health problems. This proposition is supported by empirical data from a relatively small sample of families, and it applies, in the case of children, only to measures of "freedom" and "responsiveness of family organization." Significant correlations with health are found with "aversive control of child by parents," "obstructive conflict between husband and wife," "support of child by parents," and "child's autonomy." The highest correlations reported were between the mother's health and that of her child (see Pratt, pp. 136–140).

Pratt acknowledges that the causal direction may be reversed, that is, the findings might represent the influence of health on family structure. The argument that the originally hypothesized direction is the more likely one is based on the time order of the variables. Analyses controlling for parent's level of health indicate the importance of the relationship between "punishment" and the child's level of health.

The sociologist author advocates changing families in relation to the medical care system by augmenting "family power," for example, through consumer control of health services, participation in voluntary associations, collaboration with the consumer movement, or simply by assertiveness in client–professional relationships. Although few would quarrel with the desirability of many of these changes, they have limited relevance for the practicing physician, at least in so far as active intervention is concerned.

Pratt's contribution is singled out primarily because it offers a somewhat distinctive perspective on the family. It must be made clear, however, that it is but one in a still growing literature ranging from books to research reports, some of which offer even more pertinent insights for the physician. As was stated earlier, several major non-medical disciplines, principally sociology and psychology, are represented in this literature. There is also increasing evidence of a growing awareness of the family dimension in the medical literature, in that of family medicine in particular. Notwithstanding all the theoretically important information available to the doctor, it nevertheless remains true—as suggested by the data presented earlier—that little of what it appears logical for the pediatrician to know is, in fact, known.

One explanation for this shortcoming may be the way physicians actually function in day-to-day clinical situations. For many of them the approach to a routine patient encounter is highly mechanistic. There is a set form to follow, a critical path that involves obtaining as rapidly as possible the minimum amount of information needed to make a diagnosis and to prescribe treatment. Time is an important factor in these encounters, since time means money. Hence the appeal of quick (if not dirty) methods for obtaining all the relevant information is great. If it is assumed that this includes information about the family, the available data gathering procedures which can be considered in the office setting are few indeed.

The Family Functioning Index described previously is quite widely used among investigators, but it has never been popular among practicing physicians. If they were to use any such measure they would probably prefer the Family APGAR, a test designed to assess five areas of family function: Adaptability, Partnership, Growth, Affection, and Resolve. The author (Smilkstein, 1978) describes the APGAR as "a brief screening questionnaire designed to elicit a data base that will reflect a patient's view of the functional state of his or her family." However, Smilkstein confesses that "in most instances the physician needs minimal or no family data to handle a complaint." In his view it is only in some selected situations that "knowledge of the structure and function of the patient's family may be required to resolve the health problem."

Several of the components in the APGAR parallel items in the Family Functioning Index. Unlike the FFI, however, the APGAR is based in part on the use of open-ended questions. A simpler form consisting of five closed questions with scaled responses ranging from "almost always" to "hardly ever" is also available. A comparison of the results from the APGAR with the FFI show high correlations, as might be expected ($r = 0.80$). In the author's advice to physicians about situations in which family information may be useful he includes the following occasions: when the family will be involved in the patient's care, at the time when a new patient is introduced into the practice, and when the physician is helping a family in trouble. Furthermore, it is recommended that the responses serve as cues for the "therapeutic measures" to be taken.

Two points bear comment. The first is the apparent ambiguity between "selected" use of this information and the recommendation that it be obtained routinely when new patients are introduced into the practice. This compromise may reflect a recognition of the realistic problems involved in getting such a "data base" for all patients, including those who have been in the practice for many years. On theoretical grounds a case can be made either way; it is not clear whether Smilkstein is advocating a comprehensive approach or a more restricted one.

It is also unclear what kind of "therapeutic measures" he has in mind. Assuming that it is intervention at the psychotherapeutic level, there is no reason to believe that the issue of time will not again seriously interfere with any reasonable chance of obtaining effective results. That is to say, no matter how helpful either the FFI or APGAR may be in providing insights into the family, it is still very difficult to see how most clinicians can find the time or basic skills needed to use those insights to help families or individuals who require help.

Beyond the APGAR or the many measures described by Strauss (1969) there are, of course, still other attempts at systematic assessment of family activities. Most of the remaining measures are, however, designed for research purposes. Douglas, Lawson, Cooper, and Cooper (1968) assess family interactions by direct observation, which is followed by attempts to obtain systematic recall of a 24-hour period; Roghmann and Haggerty (1972) describe the use of diaries kept over four weeks in which special emphasis is placed on perceived stress; and Rutter and Brown (1966) have used very detailed, reasonably structured interviews.

Thus the issue is not so much *how* family life, structure, or function can be measured, but *whether* it can or should be so assessed in clinical settings. It seems apparent that under certain circumstances this knowledge may yet prove to be an essential element in the diagnostic process or in influencing the effectiveness of therapy, both medical and psychosocial. What is less apparent is the case for obtaining this information *routinely*, that is, without a specific application in mind. Also unclear is the question of whether it is better to do so formally, that is, objectively, rather than through a more casual approach. It should also be acknowledged that in instances in which the physician cares for all members of a family, particularly when he has done so for a long while, the knowledge required may be obtained simply by accretion. The question of ultimate usefulness depends heavily on how the information obtained is interpreted. McWhinney (1972) offers a thoughtful approach which focuses on "the problem-solving strategies" of family physicians. In relation to this diagnostic process, he views knowledge about the family as being useful in providing "cues" to "hypotheses" about the nature of the underlying problem. Cues, in turn, are defined as "items of meaningful information." McWhinney notes that "there has been little study of the contribution of personal knowledge to decision making in family practice, but experience suggests that it may be the most important distinguishing feature." In a related study by Stewart and Buck (1977), five family physicians were interviewed to establish the extent of their knowledge about their patient's problems and how they, the doctors, responded to these problems. Perfect scores (based on 299 patients) were obtained in only 46% to 62% of the cases, and only in such areas as complaints, discomfort, worry, etc. By comparison the average figure for knowledge of social problems was 23%. The doctor's responses to these problems were equally disproportionate, with perfect scores being lower for worry, disturbance of daily living, and social problems as opposed to complaints of discomfort.

Another paper, by Smith and McWhinney (1975), compares the diagnostic methods of family physicians with those of internists. Using three clinical problems and a "programmed patient," the authors made an analysis of tape-recorded interviews which showed that family physicians asked fewer history questions, requested fewer items of data about physical examination, and ordered fewer laboratory examinations than did their internist colleagues. However, the family doctors asked more questions about mental status and life situations. If, for the purpose of this paper, one considers life situations to include matters relating to the family, the proportion of history questions in this category ranged from 7% to 34%, depending on the type of patient involved. Interestingly, the internists were more consistent among themselves in the range of questions asked. There were, however, no significant differences in the final diagnoses reached by the two groups.

Although it would be unreasonable to conclude from these results that family information is of no consequence in reaching a diagnosis (usually of a medical problem, if such a distinction can reasonably be made), it is regrettably the case that no other results are available with which one can either support or refute this conclusion. This lack of data in itself says much about the value placed on this type of inquiry by the doctors for whom it would appear to be the most relevant.

Conclusion

In the final analysis one is forced to conclude that, in the absence of any evidence to the contrary, family intervention in the psychotherapeutic sense is rarely seen in clinical practice. There seems to be a major discrepancy between rhetoric and reality. This discrepancy is equally evident in family medicine and in pediatrics. Considering the nature of most pediatric training today it is perhaps not surprising that so little in the way of family intervention exists. But to find that the same situation appears to exist in family medicine is truly surprising. Family practice residents in one study ranked family dynamics and family therapy as second in importance to the need for greater counselling skills in a critique of their training program (Shienvold, Asken, & Cincotta, 1979). And patients seem to share this value system. In a study by Hill (1968), patients attending doctors who characterized themselves as family physicians stated that most important to them was "a doctor who knows you and your family situation fairly intimately." It seems reasonable therefore to assume that the groundwork has been laid for future developments, including the systematic acquisition of information about the family by those who profess to specialize in this area and the ultimate application of this information through appropriate interventions.

Unfortunately at this point in the development of family intervention by physicians that there is still no agreement about what information is actually needed. Nor is it clear how it would be decided what information should be obtained routinely and what can be deferred until situations arise in which it is essential to dig deeper. Finally, no criteria have been determined for helping physicians select the information that might prove to be pertinent. Only theoretical arguments and suggestions abound; and to date even these appear to have been almost universally ignored.

References

Ackerman, N. *Psychodynamics of family life.* New York: Basic Books, 1958.

Allmond, B. W., Buckman, W., & Gofman, H. F. *The family is the patient—An approach to behavioral pediatrics for the clinician.* St. Louis: C. V. Mosby, 1979.

Crawford, C. O. *Health and the family: A medical-sociological analysis.* New York: Macmillan, 1971.

Chamberlin, R. W. (Ed.), Conference exploring the use of home visitors to improve the delivery of preventive services to mothers with young children: Sponsored by the American Academy of Pediatrics, Washington, D.C., June 15–17, 1980.

Dawson, P. *The parent infant project* In R. W. Chamberlin (Ed.), Conference exploring the use of home visitors to improve the delivery of preventive services to mothers with young children. Sponsored by the American Academy of Pediatrics, Sessions II & III. Washington, D.C., June 15–17, 1980.

Douglas, J. W. B., Lawson, A., Cooper, J. E., & Cooper, E. Family interaction and the activities of young children—Method of assessment. *Journal of Child Psychology and Psychiatry,* 1968, *9,* 157–171.

Farber, B. Effects of a severely mentally retarded child on family integration. *Monographs of the Society for Research in Child Development,* 1959, *24* (2, Serial No. 71).

Foley, V. *An introduction to family therapy.* New York: Grune and Stratton, 1974.

Fuchsman, D., & Pless, I. unpublished data, 1975.

Geismar, L. L., LaSorte, M. A., & Ayres, B. Measuring family disorganization. *Marriage and Family Living,* 1962, *24,* 51–56.

Good, M. J., Smilkstein, G., Good, B. J., Shaffer, T., & Arons, T. The Family APGAR Index: A study of construct validity. *Journal of Family Practice,* 1979, *8,* 577–582.

Graham, P., Rutter, M., Yule, W., & Pless, I. B. Childhood asthma: A psychosomatic disorder? Some epidemiologic considerations. *British Journal of Preventive and Social Medicine,* 1967, *21,* 78–85.

Haley, J. *Problem-solving therapy: New strategies for effective family therapy.* San Francisco: Jossey-Bass, 1976.

Hill, M., McAuley, R. G., Spaulding, W. B. Validity of the term "Family Doctor": A limited study in Hamilton, Ontario. *Canadian Medical Association Journal*, 1968, *98*, 734-738.

Kaplan, B. H., & Cassel, J. C. (Eds.), *Family and health: An epidemiological approach.* Chapel Hill, North Carolina: Institute for Research in Social Science, 1975.

Larson, C. P. Efficacy of prenatal and postpartum home visits on child health and development. *Pediatrics*, 1980, *66*, 191-197.

McWhinney, I. R. Problem-solving and decision-making in primary medical practice. *Proceedings of the Royal Society of Medicine*, 1972, *65*, 934-938.

Minuchin, S., Baker, L., Rosman, B. L., Liebman, R., Milman, L., & Todd, T.C. A conceptual model of psychosomatic illness in children: Family organization and family therapy. *Archives of General Psychiatry*, 1975, *32*, 1031-1038.

Picken, B., & Ireland, G. Family patterns of medical care utilization: Possible influences of family size, role and social class on illness behavior. *Journal of Chronic Diseases*, 1969, *22*, 181-191.

Pless, I. B., & Pinkerton, P. *Chronic childhood disorder—Promoting patterns of adjustment.* London, England: Henry Kimpton, 1975.

Pless, I. B., & Satterwhite, B. A measure of family functioning and its application. *Social Science and Medicine*, 1973, *7*, 613.

Pless, I. B., & Satterwhite, B. B. The family counselor. In R. J. Haggerty, K. R. Roghmann, & I. B. Pless (Eds.), *Child health and the community*, New York: Wiley, 1975.

Pless, I. B., & Satterwhite, B. Chronic illness. In R. J. Haggerty, K. R. Roghmann, & I. B. Pless (Eds.), *Child health and the community*. New York: Wiley, 1975.

Pless, I. B., Roghmann, K. R., & Haggerty, R. J. Chronic illness, family functioning and psychological adjustment: A model for the allocation of preventive mental health services. *International Journal of Epidemiology*, 1972, *1*, 271-277.

Pratt, L. *Family structure and effective health behavior—The energized family.* Boston: Houghton Mifflin, 1976.

Ritchie, O. W., & Koller, M. R. *Sociology of childhood.* New York: Appleton-Century-Crofts, 1964.

Roghmann, K. J., & Haggerty, R. J. The diary as a research instrument in the study of health and illness behavior: Experiences with a random sample of young families. *Medical Care*, 1972, *10*, 143-163.

Rutter, M., & Brown, G. W. The reliability and validity of measures of family life and relationships in families containing a psychiatric patient. *Social Psychiatry*, 1966, *1*, 38-53.

Rutter, M., Tizard, J., & Whitmore, K. *Education, health and behavior: Psychological and medical study of childhood development.* New York: Wiley, 1970.

Satir, V. *Conjoint family therapy: A guide to theory and technique.* Palo Alto, Calif.: Science and Behavior Books, 1964.

Satterwhite, B. B., Zweig, S. R., Iker, H. P., & Pless, I. B. The family functioning index—Five year test-retest reliability and implications for use. *Journal of Comparative Family Studies*, 1976, *7*, 111-116.

Shienvold, A., Asken, M., & Cincotta, J. Family practice residents' perceptions of behavioral science training, relevance, and needs. *Journal of Family Practice*, 1979, *8*, 97-101.

Siegel, E., Bauman, K. E., Schaefer, E. S., Saunders, M. M., & Ingram, D. D. Hospital and home support during infancy: Impact of maternal attachment, child abuse and neglect, and health care utilization. *Pediatrics*, 1980, *66*, 183-190.

Smilkstein, G. The family APGAR: A proposal for a family function test and its use by physicians. *Journal of Family Practice*, 1978, *6*, 1231.

Smith, D. H., & McWhinney, I. R. Comparison of the diagnostic methods of family physicians and internists. *Journal of Medical Education*, 1975, *50*, 264-270.

Stein, R. E. K., & Riessman, C. K. The development of an impact-on-family scale: Pre-
   liminary findings. *Medical Care*, 1980, *18*, 465–472.
Stewart, M. A., & Buck, C. W. Physician's knowledge of and response to patient's problems.
   Medical Care, 1977, *15*, 578–585.
Strauss, M. A. *Family measurement techniques: Abstracts of published instruments,
   1935–1965*. Minneapolis: University of Minnesota Press, 1969.
Vance, J. C., & Pless, I. B. *Family knowledge and patient care: A preliminary study*.
   Unpublished data, 1975.
Vance, J. C., Fazen, L. E., Satterwhite, B., & Pless, I. B. Effects of nephrotic syndrome on the
   family: A controlled study. *Pediatrics*, 1980, *65*, 948–955.

Author Index

Subject Index

94